There is not a single inch of the whole terrain of our human existence over which Christ . . . does not proclaim, "Mine!"

Abraham Kuyper

The Reformation made all secular life into a vocation of God. It was like a baptism of the secular world. It refused any longer to regard the specially religious calling of priest or monk as higher in moral scale than the calling of cobbler or prince. Christian energy was turned away from the still and the contemplative towards action. The man who would leave the world turned into the man who would change it.

Owen Chadwick

CREATING A CHRISTIAN WORLDVIEW

Abraham Kuyper's Lectures on Calvinism

PETER S. HESLAM

William B. Eerdmans Publishing Company
Grand Rapids, Michigan / Cambridge, U.K.

The Paternoster Press
Carlisle

To my former mentors at Oxford and Cambridge

Oliver O'Donovan, Alister McGrath,
Tom Wright, Graham Cray, and Jeremy Begbie

breathers of the Kuyperian spirit

255 Jefferson Ave. S.E., Grand Rapids, Michigan 49503 /
P.O. Box 163, Cambridge CB3 9PU U.K.

First published 1998 jointly
in the United States by
Wm. B. Eerdmans Publishing Company
and in the U.K. by
The Paternoster Press,
P.O. Box 300, Carlisle, Cumbria CA3 0QS

Printed in the United States of America

03 02 01 00 99 98   7 6 5 4 3 2 1

Library of Congress Cataloging-in-Publication Data

Heslam, Peter Somers.
Creating a Christian worldview : Abraham Kuyper's Lectures on Calvinism / Peter Somers Heslam.
p. cm.
Includes bibliographical references and index.
ISBN 0-8028-4326-3 (pbk. : alk. paper)
1. Kuyper, Abraham, 1837-1920. Lectures on Calvinism.
2. Calvinism. I. Kuyper, Abraham, 1837-1920. II. Title.
BX9422.5.K883H47 1998
284'.2'092 — dc21   97-38526
CIP

Paternoster ISBN 0-85364-889-1

Contents

Preface

This book is about the origins of a Christian worldview. Worldview belongs to the vocabulary of modernity, and the current collapse of that system has brought with it a deep suspicion of worldviews because of the totalizing tendencies they so often embody. Nevertheless, the ultimate questions of reality that worldviews have always sought to address are now being asked with increasing intensity. Postmodernity's rejection of ultimate answers is accompanied by a fresh and uninhibited interest in questions of meaning, purpose, and identity. This presents an enormous challenge not only to professional Christian thinkers but to the whole of the Western church as it seeks to live and work with integrity in a postmodern world. An understanding of its own history and a willingness to reflect upon it in a spirit of openness, gratitude, and humility will be integral to meeting the challenge. It is with this in mind that I offer this book to Christian readers. At the same time I wish to acknowledge the interest already shown in this book by scholars and general readers from a variety of persuasions and walks of life. A century ago, when Kuyper gave his Lectures on Calvinism at Princeton, the intellectual world was ready to embrace the notion of worldview. It was not, however, as prepared as it is now to accept the kind of fundamental criticisms of modernity that Kuyper had to offer. Although at odds with Kuyper on his Christian assertions, postmodern people of today find much to agree with in Kuyper's critique of modernity, especially of its core beliefs in human progress and autonomy.

Ideas of writing a book on Kuyper began to form a decade ago when I was an exchange student from Hull at the Free University *(Vrije Universiteit)* of Amsterdam. There I carried out research on Kuyper at the Historical Documentation Center for Dutch Protestantism *(Historisch Documentatiecentrum voor het Nederlands Protestantisme, 1880-heden).* I am grateful to the director of the Center, Professor Jan de Bruijn, as well as to his colleagues Dr. George Puchinger, Dr. George Harinck, and Hans Seijlhouwer, for the encouragement I received to further my research at doctoral level and for their assistance at the Center during my frequent visits from Oxford to gather material. I am also indebted to Father Constance Dölle and the members of the Carmelite order in Amstelveen for their hospitality during 1992-1993 whilst I was completing my research. For the investigations carried out in America I appreciate the help provided by the staff at the archives of Princeton Theological Seminary and of Calvin College, Grand Rapids. The entire project was enabled by scholarships from the British Academy, the Institute for Historical Research (London University), the Squire and Mariott Bursary (Oxford University), and the Society *(Vereniging)* of the Free University, for which I am very grateful. I have received advice and inspiration for this book from a number of people, but I should particularly like to record my thanks to my former supervisors Professor Oliver O'Donovan and Dr. Geoffrey Rowell, as well as to Dr. John Platt, Dr. Michael Wintle, Dr. Jonathan Chaplin, Professor Gerard Schutte, Professor Henk Woldring, Professor Stephen Sykes, Professor David Alton, Dr. Lawrence Osborn, and Dr. James Bratt. I am also much obliged to those who made it possible for me to finish the writing of this book at the Stellenbosch Theological Seminary in South Africa, and to Pamela King, Debbie Tye, and Katy Coutts for their assistance in preparing the typescript for publication. At Eerdmans, Jon Pott and Jennifer Hoffman have been models of patience and good humor. My warmest gratitude and affection go to my family, and especially to Judith, my wife.

Cambridge PETER SOMERS HESLAM
Epiphany 1998

Introduction

Abraham Kuyper (1837-1920) dominated the religious and political life of the Netherlands for nearly half a century, and his ideas continue to inspire an international school of thought. This book discusses these ideas within the context in which they were formed, by providing an historical commentary on the book in which he gave them their most significant expression, the *Lectures on Calvinism.* This is the published version of a series of six lectures Kuyper gave at Princeton Theological Seminary in 1898. Central to the analysis will be a discussion of the motivation of Kuyper's thought: why did he maintain the standpoints he did, and what did he hope to achieve by doing so? In order to answer these questions, Kuyper's position will be explained relative to others of his time and in connection with the events of his own career.

Although Kuyper is well known in Europe, America, and South Africa, he may be less familiar to readers elsewhere. This introductory chapter will therefore review Kuyper's significance and explain why the *Lectures on Calvinism* are of special interest. This is followed by an outline of the historical context in which the *Lectures* were given, and the scholarly context within which the present study falls.

1. Kuyper's Significance

One reason why Kuyper stands out as a figure of exceptional interest is that he achieved positions of eminence in a number of different fields. As a scholar he established himself early in his career as an academic theologian and later provided the chief impetus towards the founding of the Free University at Amsterdam, where he was both Professor of Theology and Rector Magnificus (Chancellor). As a journalist he founded *De Standaard (The Standard)*, one of the first popular daily newspapers in the Netherlands, and remained its chief editor for almost fifty years. As a politician he organized the first modern Dutch political party, the *Anti-Revolutionaire Partij* (Anti-Revolutionary Party), and remained its leader for some forty years, during which time he served a four-year term as Prime Minister. As a writer of devotional and religious literature he launched *De Heraut (The Herald)*, a weekly religious journal, and published scores of meditations and works of applied and pastoral theology. As a church reformer he led a major secession from the *Nederlandse Hervormde Kerk* (Dutch Reformed Church) and established a new confederation of *Gereformeerde Kerken* (Reformed Churches).

This thumbnail sketch of Kuyper's achievements is sufficient to indicate not only that he enjoyed a distinguished and multifaceted career — which makes him of great biographical interest — but that his personal achievements were significant landmarks in modern Dutch history. In virtually every area of his activity he sparked off new developments. His establishment, for instance, of the Anti-Revolutionary Party (ARP) in 1879 along modern, democratic lines signalled the end of liberal domination in Dutch politics and helped to make way for the rise of a more democratic and representative form of government based on modern party organization. Together with the founding of the Free University the following year, the establishment of the ARP stimulated the foundation of a great number of social, educational, and political institutions, based on a constitutional expression of Reformed principles. This in turn encouraged the development of a pattern of social organization which has come to be called, somewhat ironically, *verzuiling* ("pillarization"). This pattern, which found its most complete expression between about 1920 and 1960, was a mode of social organization whereby the principal differences in society were vertical (ideological) rather than horizontal (socioeconomic). Each ideological group in Dutch society, such as Catholic, Protestant, Liberal, and Socialist, organized and developed its own social and political institutions with minimal government interference and in accordance with its own ideological persuasions. Society was thus divided into vertical *zuilen* (pillars), based on common ideologies rather than on class loyalties, with only the élites in each pillar in consultation with each other, the ordinary members of each having little or no mutual contact. As this model characterizes the social structure of the Netherlands for the greater part of the twentieth century, Kuyper, as a principal force in its shaping, was one of the most important founders of modern Dutch society. In recent decades the system of *verzuiling* as a politico-sociological phenomenon has attracted international attention from a large number of social and political scientists.[1] Opinion among them concerning the exact nature and causes of this system varies considerably, and there is little indication that a consensus is likely. In general, however, they agree that the process which led to *verzuiling* cannot be explained adequately without reference to Kuyper and his anti-revolutionary movement, thus ensuring that the question of Kuyper's place in the development of Dutch society stands at the center of a lively current debate.[2]

The growing interest in *verzuiling* has been complemented recently by a heightened awareness amongst historians and political analysts of the

1. See, for example, A. Lijphart, *The Politics of Accommodation: Pluralism and Democracy in the Netherlands,* 2nd edition (Berkeley: University of California Press, 1975); H. Daalder, "Consociationalism, Center and Periphery in the Netherlands," in *Mobilization, Center-Periphery Structures and Nation-Building,* ed. by P. Torsvik (Bergen: Universitetsforlaget, 1981), pp. 181-240; Siep Stuurman, *Verzuiling, kapitalisme en patriarchaat: aspecten van de ontwikkeling van de moderne staat in Nederland* (Nijmegen: Socialistische Uitgeverij, 1983); *Consociationalism, Pillarization and Conflict-Management in the Low Countries,* ed. by M. P. C. M. van Schendelen (published as a special-theme edition of *Acta Politica* [1984/I]); Michael Wintle, *Pillars of Piety: Religion in the Netherlands in the Nineteenth Century, 1813-1901* (Hull: Hull University Press, 1987); Peter van Rooden, *Religieuze regimes: Over godsdienst en maatschappij in Nederland, 1950-1990* (Amsterdam: Bert Bakker, 1996).

2. Peter van Rooden's study, the latest contribution to the debate, stresses Kuyper's importance for an understanding of *verzuiling.* He admits, however, that serious historical research into the origins of *verzuiling* is still in its infancy. See van Rooden, *Religieuze regimes,* pp. 34-7 (including footnote 38), 161-68, 185, 191-96. Most recent studies concentrate on specific geographical areas. See *Broeders sluit u aan: Aspecten van verzuiling in zeven Hollandse gemeenten,* ed. by J. C. H. Blom and C. J. Missert (Amsterdam: De Bataafsche Leeuw, 1985), and a review article of this and other such studies by van Rooden, 'Studies naar lokale verzuiling als toegang tot de geschiedenis van de constructie van religieuze verschillen in Nederland', *Theoretische Geschiedenis* 20 (1993): 439-54.

phenomenon of Christian Democracy in Europe and the role of Christianity in the politics of non-European states. A number of developments have contributed to this, including the acceleration of European economic and political cooperation, and the new democratic freedoms experienced in Eastern Europe at the end of the 1980s and in South Africa in the early 1990s. These developments have occurred at the same time as Christian Democratic parties have been in government in a number of European states and constitute the second largest group in the European Parliament. There is now a growing sense that in the past historians have paid disproportionate attention to secular political ideologies, such as Communism and Fascism, which have proved less durable than political philosophies based on some form of Christian foundation. Commentators of all ideological persuasions are therefore taking a fresh interest in the relationship between Christianity and democracy.[3] As a result, Kuyper, as founding father of the Anti-Revolutionary Party, which in 1980 merged with two other Dutch confessional parties to form a new Christian Democratic party, *Christen-Democratisch Appèl,* once again occupies an important place in contemporary political discourse.

Kuyper's historical importance also lies in the fact that he represents an unusual blend of theological orthodoxy and cultural progressiveness. Although he sought a revival of traditional Calvinistic religion, he did not advocate a return to pre-Enlightenment conditions in the hope that this would help the cause of Christian civilization. Indeed he was keen to distance himself from many of his conservative and Catholic contemporaries whom he considered to be *contra*-revolutionary. His party, in contrast, was *anti*-revolutionary, in that it aimed to offer an alternative program for cultural and political renewal to that offered by the Enlightenment ideals of the French Revolution, which it believed was having a damaging effect on Dutch society at every level. With his persistent agitation for greater educational, social, and political freedoms for minority groups in society, Kuyper aimed to be a progressive and innovative leader. He was not content to confine himself to sideline issues of public morality but sought to shape the future of the entire

3. See, for example, David Alton, *Faith in Britain* (London: Hodder & Stoughton, 1991); Michael Fogarty, *Phoenix or Cheshire Cat? Christian Democracy Past, Present . . . and Future?* (Ware: Christian Democrat Press, 1995); *Religion, the Missing Dimension of Statecraft,* ed. by D. M. Johnston and C. Sampson (New York: Oxford University Press, 1994).

sociopolitical order. This in itself challenges the validity of the stigma often borne by Calvinism, that it represents an otherworldly, backward-looking way of life of little relevance to the pressing issues of contemporary society. It also challenges the currently prevailing bias in historical studies — a bias that has roots in the Weber thesis — that social differentiation and political modernization go hand-in-hand with the decline of religion; in other words, that modernization is always accompanied by secularization. Kuyper's anti-revolutionary movement is a potent demonstration that, although modernization and secularization may accompany each other, they may also move in opposite directions.[4]

Kuyper was also remarkably successful in realizing his political objectives. Michael Fogarty, the British Catholic historian of Christian Democracy, wrote in 1957 that "Dutch Protestants have built up over the last century one of the most successful, and in many ways the most instructive political, economic, and social movements to be found anywhere in the Christian world."[5] When Kuyper began his public career in the early 1870s he became the leader of a marginalized minority group. Less than ten years later, however, due in large part to his tireless activities, this same group was in possession of powerful journalistic organs, a sociopolitical program, a political party, and a university. Ten years after that it found itself in the seat of power, taking part with Catholics in the first confessional cabinet in the Netherlands (1888-1891). Over the century that has passed since that cabinet took office, Kuyper's ideas have continued to influence Dutch politics at a profound level. This influence is partly due to the fact that between 1901 and 1939 there were only two periods, one of two years and the other of five years, when the Netherlands was not governed by coalition cabinets which included Anti-Revolutionaries and Catholics.

Kuyper is also the founder, finally, of a school of thought (often called "Kuyperian," or "neo-Calvinistic") which exercises considerable influence today, not only in the Netherlands but also in the United States,

4. James W. Skillen and Stanley W. Carlson-Thies, "Religion and Political Development in Nineteenth-Century Holland," *Publius: The Journal of Federalism* 12 (1982): 43-64 (pp. 43, 64); James W. Skillen, "From Covenant of Grace to Equitable Public Pluralism: The Dutch Calvinist Contribution," *Calvin Theological Journal* 31 (1996): 67-96.

5. Michael P. Fogarty, *Christian Democracy in Western Europe, 1820-1953* (London: Routledge and Kegan Paul, 1957), p. xv.

Canada, Britain, South Africa, Australia, and South Korea.[6] The Movement for Christian Democracy in Britain, the Center for Public Justice in the United States, and the Citizens for Public Justice in Canada, for instance, draw guidance from the Dutch experience of Christian Democracy for their own political visions. Groups concerned with Christian education in Britain, North America and other parts of the English-speaking world espouse the Kuyperian notion of sphere-sovereignty as justification for the establishment of Christian schools, colleges, and research institutions.[7] Artistic and intellectual groups in Britain such as the Arts Centre Group in London, the Christian Studies Unit in Bath, the L'Abri Fellowship centres in Ealing and Greatham, the Greenbelt Festival; the Institute for Contemporary Christianity in London, the West Yorkshire School of Christian Studies, the Centre for Technology and Social Studies in Salford, and *Third Way* magazine owe much of their founding vision and continuing inspiration to the Kuyperian concept of a Christian worldview that encompasses the whole of life, including scholarship and the arts.[8] The same is true for a host of higher education institutions in the United States and Canada, including the Institute of Christian Studies (ICS) in Toronto.[9] This institute, along with the philosophy departments of Calvin College in Grand Rapids (Michigan) and the Free University, has been at the forefront of critical

6. This school has both formal and "diffuse" aspects. Those connected to it do not always have a first-hand knowledge of Kuyper's thought, nor do they necessarily identify themselves as "Kuyperian." See George M. Marsden, *Understanding Fundamentalism and Evangelicalism* (Grand Rapids: Eerdmans, 1991), p. 151.

7. See Chapter Six for a discussion of this doctrine.

8. Several British scholars have noted that the current revival of evangelical social ethics in the U.K. is closely linked to a growth of interest in Kuyperian theology. See, for instance, Ronald H. Preston, *Church and Society in the Late Twentieth Century: The Economic and Political Task* (London: SCM Press, 1983), p. 81; Peter Sedgwick, "Theology and Society," in *The Modern Theologians: An Introduction to Christian Theology in the Twentieth Century*, ed. by David F. Ford, 2nd ed. (Oxford: Blackwell, 1997), pp. 286-305 (p. 295); articles by A. B. Cramp on "Economic Ethics" and by R. A. Russell on "Herman Dooyeweerd" in the *New Dictionary of Christian Ethics and Pastoral Theology*, ed. by David J. Atkinson and David H. Field (Leicester: IVP, 1995), pp. 115-21 and 317 respectively.

9. Recent publications from the ICS include *An Ethos of Compassion and the Integrity of Creation*, ed. by Hendrik Hart and Brian J. Walsh (Lanham, Maryland: University Press of America, 1995); J. Richard Middleton and Brian J. Walsh, *Truth Is Stranger Than It Used to Be: Biblical Faith in a Postmodern Age* (London: SPCK, 1995).

engagement with contemporary philosophical thought from the background of the Kuyperian tradition. The ongoing vitality of this tradition is heavily indebted to two of its most outstanding spokesmen in the areas of law and philosophy, Herman Dooyeweerd (1894-1977) and D. H. T. Vollenhoven (1892-1978).[10] These men held chairs at the Free University from 1926 to 1965 and from 1926 to 1963 respectively, and influenced the thinking of several generations of students both in the Netherlands and abroad.[11] Many of those they have influenced now hold academic posts in universities and colleges, and include such capable scholars and

10. For English-language introductions, see L. Kalsbeek, *Contours of a Christian Philosophy: An Introduction to Herman Dooyeweerd's Thought,* ed. by Bernard and Josina Zijlstra (Amsterdam: Buijten en Schipperheijn, 1975); Jonathan Chaplin and Brian Walsh, "Dooyeweerd's Contribution to a Christian Philosophical Paradigm," *Crux* 19 (1983): 8-22. More detailed treatments can be found in *The Legacy of Herman Dooyeweerd* (Lanham, Maryland: University Press of America, 1985), ed. by C. T. McIntire; J. Stellingwerff, *D. H.Th. Vollenhoven (1892-1978): Reformator der wijsbegeerte* (Baarn: Ten Have, 1992); *Herman Dooyeweerd 1894-1977: Breedte en actualiteit van zijn filosofie,* ed. by H. G. Geertsema and others (Kampen: Kok, 1994); *Dooyeweerd herdacht: Referaten gehouden op het Dooyeweerd-symposium op 18 november aan de Vrije Universiteit,* ed. by J. de Bruijn (Amsterdam: Free University Press, 1995); Calvin Seerveld, "Dooyeweerd's Idea of 'Historical Development': Christian Respect for Cultural Diversity," *The Westminster Theological Journal* 58 (1996): 41-61. Major new translations and republications of Dooyeweerd's work are soon to appear from the Edwin Mellen Press (Lewiston, New York).

11. The impact of the Kuyperian school on evangelical thought in America has been particularly pronounced. George Marsden speaks of "The triumph — or nearly so — of what may be loosely called Kuyperian presuppositionalism in the evangelical community." See his "The State of Evangelical Christian Scholarship," *The Reformed Journal* 37 (1987): 12-16 (p. 14); Mark A. Noll, *The Scandal of the Evangelical Mind* (Grand Rapids: Eerdmans/Leicester: IVP, 1994), pp. 216-17, 224-25. Noll concedes that Kuyperian evangelicalism is largely exempt from the scandal he describes. See the review by Peter Somers Heslam in *Anvil* 14 (1997): 67-69. One of the most influential exponents of Kuyperian presuppositionalism in the United States is Cornelius van Til (1895-1987). See Alister E. McGrath, *Bridge-building: Effective Christian Apologetics* (Leicester: IVP, 1992), pp. 36-41; John M. Frane, *Cornelius van Til: An Analysis of His Thought* (Phillipsburg, N.J.: Presbyterian and Reformed Publishing Company, 1995); and the various articles on Van Til's philosophical theology in *The Westminster Theological Journal* 57 (1995). For further examples of Kuyperian influence in American philosophy and theology, see *Life is Religion: Essays in Honour of H. Evan Runner,* ed. by Henry van der Goot (St. Catharines, Ontario: Paideia Press, 1981), and Richard Mouw, "Dutch Calvinist Philosophical Influences in North America," *Calvin Theological Journal* 24 (1989): 101-13.

spokespersons as Nicholas Wolterstorff (Yale), Alvin Plantinga (Notre Dame), Richard Mouw (Fuller), Roy Clouser (Notre Dame), Sander Griffioen, Johan van der Hoeven, and Bob Goudzwaard (Free University), Elaine and Alan Storkey (London), and Philip Sampson (Portsmouth).[12] Others who have more informal associations with the tradition but have benefited from its insights include the British writers Tom Wright (Lichfield), Oliver O'Donovan (Oxford), Alister McGrath (Oxford), Lesslie Newbigin (London), Graham Cray (Cambridge), and Jeremy Begbie (Cambridge).[13] Kuyper's significance is thus partly due to the fact that he is the originator of an international and influential school of thought.

12. See, for instance, Nicholas Wolterstorff, *Until Justice and Peace Embrace: The Kuyper Lectures for 1981 Delivered at the Free University of Amsterdam* (Grand Rapids: Eerdmans, 1983), and "The Grace that Shaped My Life," in *Philosophers Who Believe: The Spiritual Journeys of Eleven Leading Thinkers,* ed. by Kelly James Clark (Downers Grove, Illinois: IVP, 1993), pp. 259-75; Alvin Plantinga, "A Christian Life Partly Lived," in Kelly James Clark, pp. 45-82; Richard Mouw, *Called to Holy Worldliness* (Minneapolis: Fortress, 1980); Roy Clouser, *The Myth of Religious Neutrality: An Essay on the Hidden Role of Religious Beliefs in Theories* (Notre Dame: University of Notre Dame Press, 1991); *What Right Does Ethics Have? Public Philosophy in a Pluralistic Culture,* ed. by Sander Griffioen (Amsterdam: Free University Press, 1990); Bob Goudzwaard, *Capitalism and Progress: A Diagnosis of Western Society* (Grand Rapids: Eerdmans, 1979), and *Idols of Our Time* (Downers Grove, Illinois: IVP, 1984); Elaine Storkey, "Dooyeweerd's Anthropology: The Male-Female Dimension," in *Christian Philosophy at the Close of the Twentieth Century,* ed. by Sander Griffioen and Bert M. Balk (Kok: Kampen, 1995), pp. 85-92; Alan Storkey, *Transforming Economics* (London: SPCK, 1986), and *Foundational Epistemologies in Consumption Theories* (Amsterdam: Free University of Amsterdam Press, 1993); *Faith and Modernity,* ed. by Philip Sampson, Vinay Samuel, and Chris Sugden (Oxford: Regnum/Paternoster, 1996).

13. See N. T. Wright, *The New Testament and the People of God* (London: SPCK, 1992) — see especially Part 2; Oliver O'Donovan, *Resurrection and Moral Order: An Outline for Evangelical Ethics* (Leicester: IVP/Grand Rapids: Eerdmans, 1986); Alister E. McGrath, *A Passion for Truth: The Intellectual Coherence of Evangelicalism* (Leicester: Apollos, 1996); Lesslie Newbigin, *Foolishness to the Greeks: The Gospel and Western Culture* (London: SPCK/Grand Rapids: Eerdmans, 1986), and *Proper Confidence: Faith, Doubt and Certainty in Christian Discipleship* (London: SPCK, 1995); Graham Cray, "A Gospel for Our Culture," in *To Proclaim Afresh: Evangelical Agenda for the Church,* ed. by Gordon Kuhrt (London: SPCK, 1995), pp. 119-32; Jeremy S. Begbie, "Creation, Christ and Culture in Dutch Neo-Calvinism," in *Christ in Our Place: The Humanity of God in Christ for the Reconciliation of the World. Essays presented to James Torrance,* ed. by Trevor Hart and Daniel Thimell (Exeter: Paternoster, 1989), pp. 113-32, and *Voicing Creation's Praise: Towards a Theology of the Arts* (Edinburgh: T & T Clark, 1991).

2. Why the *Lectures on Calvinism?*

Kuyper's wide-ranging activities, numerous publications, extensive correspondence and continuing influence require that any historical study of his thought is restrictive in focus. This is a chief reason for the selection of the *Lectures on Calvinism,* a comparatively short work of only 200 pages, out of Kuyper's voluminous repertoire. It appeared in several editions in English during Kuyper's lifetime, each one receiving his authorization. There are only minor differences between these texts, and such changes as were made were ones of style rather than content. The edition published by Eerdmans Publishing Company in 1931 has been selected for the purposes of this study, its text being identical to that of the version Kuyper published in 1899.[14] The page numbers referred to in this book that are prefixed by "LC" *(Lectures on Calvinism)* correspond to this version.

There are a number of other factors that commend the *Lectures* as the subject of this book. It represents, in the first place, a summary of Kuyper's thought.[15] Each lecture deals with major areas of his thinking about which he had published extensively. Despite its modest size, therefore, it is a work with a broad scope, and a close engagement with it will allow an investigation of the central themes in his thought. Secondly, the Stone Lectures occurred at the high point of Kuyper's career, when he had reached the peak of his intellectual and organizational powers. In 1898, the year in which they were delivered, he was Professor of Theology, Member of Parliament, leader of the Anti-Revolutionary Party, and Chief Editor of *De Standaard.* It was only three years later, in 1901, that he became Prime Minister of the Netherlands.[16] The Kuyper of the *Lectures on Calvinism,* therefore, is Kuyper

14. A. Kuyper, *Lectures on Calvinism: Six Lectures Delivered at Princeton University Under Auspices of the L. P. Stone Foundation* (Grand Rapids: Eerdmans, 1931); A. Kuyper, *Calvinism: Six Stone-lectures* (Amsterdam: Höveker & Wormser, 1899). The advantage of referring to the 1931 version rather than to that of 1899 is that the later one has been more widely distributed, and is more readily available, having been reprinted in 1972, 1978, 1983, 1987, and 1994.

15. Hendrikus Berkhof, *Two Hundred Years of Theology: Report of a Personal Journey* (Grand Rapids: Eerdmans, 1989), p. 109 (note 8).

16. J. C. Rullmann identifies the seven years between 1894 and 1901 as the zenith of Kuyper's career. See J. C. Rullmann, *Abraham Kuyper: een levensschets* (Kampen: Kok, 1928), pp. 178-79. In W. J. van Welderen Rengers's parliamentary history, the period 1897-1901 is taken to represent Kuyper's four great political years. See *Schets eener parlementaire geschiedenis van Nederland sedert 1848,* 4th edition, 4 vols. ('s-Gravenhage, 1950-1955), II (1950), p. 154.

in his prime. Thirdly, Kuyper presented the *Lectures* to a foreign, English-speaking audience to whom his ideas were largely unfamiliar. Whereas in most of his other works he was able to assume that his audience was familiar with the Dutch Calvinist tradition, in the *Lectures* he was faced with presenting his thought in a way that could be grasped by an audience with a different language, culture, and history. Although several of Kuyper's works have been translated into other languages, the *Lectures* is the only substantial work that was originally intended for a foreign audience; it is therefore of singular value in the attempt made in this book to interpret Kuyper's ideas in a context wider than that of the Netherlands alone. A fourth, related reason is that, out of all Kuyper's works, including those that have been translated, the *Lectures* has had the greatest international influence. Their leading idea — that Christianity, particularly in its Calvinistic form, is able to provide a consistent, unified, and all-embracing worldview — has been central to the transmission of Kuyper's influence abroad. Although a number of other eminent Dutch theologians have given the Stone Lectures since Levi P. Stone, a director and trustee of Princeton Seminary, created the foundation of the lectureship in 1871, none of the publications based on these lectures has been as widely circulated or as profoundly influential as Kuyper's *Lectures*.[17] It is nothing short of remarkable that, a century after they were given, this book is still being reprinted and distributed in many parts of the world.[18] Perhaps Herman Dooyeweerd, who was not an uncritical admirer of Kuyper, provides the best clue to the *Lectures'* lasting appeal:

> Where he could be completely himself and could develop his great concept of a Calvinistic life- and world-view, he builds on fundamental reformational principles and produces work of unsurpassed principial clarity and sharpness, work *"aus einem Gusz."* The famous Stone Lectures on Calvinism are perhaps the best example of this.[19]

17. Herman Bavinck (in 1908-9), Valentine Hepp (in 1929-30), and W. A. Visser 't Hooft (in 1946-47) are among those granted the lectureship. See "The L. P. Stone Lectureship. Princeton Theological Seminary, Princeton New Jersey," compiled by Kenneth J. Ross (1988), in the Princeton Theological Seminary archives.

18. The first English-language Indian edition appeared in 1994: A. Kuyper, *The Crown of Christian Heritage: Six Lectures Delivered at Princeton University Under Auspices of the L. P. Stone Foundation.* With an Introduction by Vishal Mangalwadi (Landour, Mussoorie: Nivedit Good Books, 1994).

19. Herman Dooyeweerd, 'Kuyper's wetenschapsleer,' *Philosophia reformata: orgaan van de vereeniging voor calvinistische wijsbegeerte* 4 (1939): 193-232 (p. 197).

To conclude, the *Lectures on Calvinism* may be regarded as a manifesto of Kuyperian Calvinism.[20] Kuyper had laid the groundwork for this manifesto over the two and a half decades of his public career that preceded his visit to the United States. He had accomplished this in the main through his daily and weekly newspaper articles, which were generally written in response to specific issues in the political and religious life of the Netherlands. Because of this, many of the concepts he presented at Princeton he had dealt with previously, and in most cases prolifically, in his journalism. At the apex of his career he made a bold and spirited attempt to bring together the main strands of his thought in a concise, comprehensive, and systematic way, and to emphasize in his presentation of them their dynamic potential. The result is the most complete, cogent, and visionary expression of Kuyperian thought. The extent to which this expression represented a new departure in his thought will become clear later in this book.

3. Historical Context

3.1. Princeton

The immediate context of the *Lectures on Calvinism* was Princeton Theological Seminary in the autumn of 1898. Kuyper was an invited guest who had come to receive an honorary doctorate in law from Princeton University and to deliver the annual Stone Lectures at the adjoining seminary. This seminary, affiliated not only with the University but also with the Presbyterian Church of America, had become renowned for its conservative Calvinistic stance on theological issues, articulated by the four men who in succession held the principal chair of theology from the founding of the seminary in 1812 up to 1921. These four — Archibald Alexander (1772-1851), Charles Hodge (1797-1878), Archibald Alexander Hodge (1823-1886), and Benjamin Breckinridge Warfield (1851-1921) — held a remarkable amount in common in terms of theological position, which was grounded in the Scottish philosophy of commonsense and the doctrines of the Westminster Confession. They are re-

20. Ernst Troeltsch called the *Lectures* the *'Manifest des modernen Calvinismus'*. See his *Die Soziallehren der christlichen Kirchen und Gruppen,* 16 vols (Tübingen: Mohr, 1922), I, p. 732.

ferred to collectively as the Princeton Theologians, their work constituting what is known as the Princeton Theology.[21]

At the time of Kuyper's visit to Princeton, it was B. B. Warfield who held the chair in Didactic and Polemic Theology previously occupied by his three illustrious predecessors. He was instrumental in Kuyper's invitation to deliver the Stone Lectures, and was familiar with his work, cooperating in its translation, publication, and distribution in the United States. In his introduction to Kuyper's *Encyclopedia* of 1898 he expressed his admiration for his Dutch colleague in characteristically swelling terms:

> As a force in Church and State in whose arm those who share his fundamental principles trust with a well-founded hope of victory, Dr. Kuyper is probably today the most considerable figure in both political and ecclesiastical Holland.[22]

With a view to Kuyper's imminent visit and the need to introduce him more widely in the United States, Warfield published a translation of a biographical sketch of Kuyper's career. Again Warfield's introduction is full of eulogy (and not a little exaggeration):

> In the conflict with unbelief and indifferentism, with materialism and pessimism, in brief with all the elements that are undermining the health of the individual or of the people, he [Kuyper] has . . . remained the leader whose forceful words strengthen the hearts of the Christians in Holland, no matter to what ecclesiastical tendency they may adhere.[23]

21. M. A. Noll lists the grand motifs of the Princeton Theology as: devotion to scripture, concern for religious experience, sensitivity to American circumstances, and the full employment of Presbyterian confessions, seventeenth-century Reformed systematicians, and the Scottish Common Sense philosophy. *The Princeton Theology 1812-1921: Scripture, Science, and Theological Method from Archibald Alexander to Benjamin Breckinridge Warfield,* ed. by M. A. Noll (Grand Rapids: Baker, 1983), p. 13. For a detailed history of the seminary, see David B. Calhoun, *Princeton Seminary,* 2 vols. (Edinburgh/Pennsylvania: Banner of Truth, 1996).

22. A. Kuyper, *Encyclopedia of Sacred Theology: Its Principles,* trans. by J. Hendrik De Vries. With an Introduction by Benjamin B. Warfield (New York: Charles Scribner; London: Hodder and Stoughton, 1898), pp. xii, xv-xvi. This work has been republished under the title *Principles of Sacred Theology* (Grand Rapids: Baker, 1980). See also Warfield's introduction to Kuyper's *The Work of the Holy Spirit,* trans. by Hendrik De Vries. With an Introduction by B. B. Warfield (New York: Funk and Wagnalls, 1900). Republished by Eerdmans (Grand Rapids) in 1975.

23. The author of the sketch, which was published in booklet form, had been

A decade later he referred to Kuyper simply as "a theologian of genius."[24]

Warfield was also without question the most eminent theologian amongst Kuyper's Princeton audience,[25] and one who, like Kuyper, was a hard-nosed polemicist, not afraid to throw punches, even in the direction of Kuyper himself when he felt it necessary.[26] He also shared with Kuyper a passion for publishing his views. Scores of scholarly and popular publications flowed from his pen, most articles among them appearing in the *Princeton Theological Review,* which he co-founded, and dominated in a way not unlike Kuyper's domination of *De Standaard* and *De Heraut.*[27] Many of his publications, like Kuyper's, dealt explicitly with the subject of Calvinism,[28] and he shared with Kuyper the conviction that classic orthodoxy had to be articulated further in order to address contemporary questions. It was no doubt because of such affinities that Warfield was known to Amer-

one of Kuyper's students at the Free University and later became president of the Dutch Supreme Court. Witsius H. de Savornin Lohman, *Dr. Abraham Kuyper* (Haarlem: Tjeenk Willink, 1889). English translation: "Dr. Abraham Kuyper," *The Presbyterian and Reformed Review* 36 (1898): 561-609 (562). Warfield rushed a copy of this edition of the *Review* to Kuyper during his stay at Princeton, together with a letter which indicates that Kuyper had provided comments on an earlier draft of the translated Lohman article. *Het Kuyper-archief* (The Kuyper Archive — hereafter KA); *Brieven,* no. 6271 (19 October 1898).

24. B. B. Warfield, "Calvinism," in *The New Schaff-Herzog Encyclopedia of Religious Knowledge,* ed. by Samuel Macauley Johnson (New York: Funk and Wagnalls, 1908), II, pp. 359-64. Republished in B. B. Warfield, *Calvin and Calvinism* (New York: Oxford University Press, 1931), pp. 353-69 (p. 366).

25. Jeremy Begbie refers to Warfield as "that colossus of the Princeton school." Jeremy Begbie, "Who Is this God?: Biblical Inspiration Revisited," *Tyndale Bulletin* 43 (1992): 259-82 (p. 261). Warfield's scholarly acumen was recognized abroad. In 1913 he was awarded his fifth honorary doctorate, from the University of Utrecht. Kuyper congratulated him in a letter written on 2 December of that year. KA; *Brieven,* no. 8051.

26. Warfield and Kuyper did, however, remain on friendly terms. In a letter sent almost exactly a year before Kuyper died on 8 November 1920, Warfield spoke in respectful and intimate terms of the bond of friendship between them — "a bond begun in a devotion to the theology which you have taught with so much distinction through so many years; strengthened through a happy acquaintance with you when you were good enough to visit us in Princeton." KA; *Brieven,* no. 8620 (7 November 1919).

27. Warfield's publications are listed in John E. Meeter and Roger Nicole, *A Bibliography of Benjamin Breckinridge Warfield 1851-1921* (Phillipsburg, N.J.: Presbyterian and Reformed Publishing Company, 1974).

28. See Chapter Ten. Martyn Lloyd-Jones (1899-1981), the popular Bible expositor and pastor of Westminster Chapel, London, declared that Warfield was "the greatest exponent, expounder and defender of the classic Reformed faith in the

ican students as the "American Kuyper,"[29] and that a daughter of Kuyper, named Catharina, translated two of Warfield's papers into Dutch during her father's lifetime.[30] Warfield also struggled, as did Kuyper, against the rising tide of liberalism, although Warfield restricted his opposition largely to the field of theology, and within that to the doctrine of scripture. It was his approach to this doctrine, and to the related issues of apologetics and science, that differed most sharply from Kuyper's, and therefore it is on these matters that their views are compared.[31] Although comparisons between Kuyper and Warfield have until recently escaped detailed scholarly attention, their relevance to current discussions of the same issues is highlighted by George Marsden's comment that "the evidentialist [Warfieldian] and the Kuyperian traditions are two of the strongest influences on American evangelical thought on faith and reason."[32]

---

twentieth century." Cited in Calhoun, II, 320. Both Kuyper and Warfield were responsible for new publications of Calvin's *Institutes.* See *John Calvin, Institutes of the Christian Religion.* Translated from the Latin and collated with the author's last edition in French by John Allen. 7th American edition revised and corrected. With an Introduction by B. B. Warfield (Philadelphia: Presbyterian Board of Education [1913?]); *Institutie, ofte onderwijsinghe in de Christelicke religie. In vier boeken beschreven door Johannes Calvinus. Nu van nieuws uyt het Latijn en François getrouwelick over-geset door Wilhelmus Corsmannus. Herdruk van de uitgave van Paulus Aertz van Ravesteyn 1650 te Amsterdam,* ed. by A. Kuyper (Doesburg: Van Schenk Brill, 1889).

29. 'In memoriam Prof. B. B. Warfield', *De Heraut,* 27 March 1921.

30. B. B. Warfield, *Calvijn als theoloog en de stand van het Calvinisme in onzen tijd.* Trans. by C. M. E. Kuyper, with a Preface by H. Bavinck (Kampen: Kok, 1919); B. B. Warfield, *Het godsdienstige leven van den theologischen student.* Trans. by C. M. E. Kuyper (Kampen: Kok, 1920), first published in *De Heraut,* 4-25 May 1913. Original English version: "The Religious Life of Theological Students," *Union Seminary Magazine* 24 (1912/1913): 208-22. In 1917 Warfield acted as host to Catharina Kuyper on a visit she made to Princeton. The most striking difference between Warfield and Kuyper's careers is that whereas Kuyper enjoyed an active public life, Warfield spent most of his time on the Princeton campus, where he lived with his invalid wife.

31. See Chapter Five and Chapter Seven. Chapter Ten notes the influence of Kuyper's Stone Lectures on Warfield's understanding of Calvinism.

32. George Marsden, "The Collapse of American Evangelical Academia," in *Faith and Rationality,* ed. by Alvin Plantinga and Nicholas Wolterstorff (Notre Dame: University of Notre Dame Press, 1983), pp. 219-64 (p. 247). See also Marsden's *Understanding,* p. 151. Detailed comparisons between Kuyper and Warfield were first made in Peter Somers Heslam, "Abraham Kuyper's *Lectures on Calvinism:* An Historical Study" (unpublished D.Phil. dissertation, Oxford University, 1993), the work on which this book is based.

The way Kuyper introduced his ideas in the Stone Lectures was not soley determined by his audience at Princeton, most of whom were theologians. The worldview he presented in them was one that he deemed to have universal proportions and was therefore relevant to the whole of society. This, he believed, was particularly true of American society, in which Calvinism had reached its highest development. Primarily in his role as editor of *De Standaard,* Kuyper demonstrated a sustained and active interest in American affairs and developed over several decades an image of American history and culture which was inextricably linked to his perception of Calvinism. This book explores, therefore, the way in which America and Calvinism were related in Kuyper's thought; and because this was a relationship that came to the fore during Kuyper's four-month visit to the United States, attention will be paid to the nature and circumstances of this visit (see Chapter Three).

3.2. The Netherlands and Europe

Although Kuyper's ideas in the Stone Lectures were conveyed to an American audience, they were formed within the social, intellectual, and religious context of the Netherlands and Europe in the latter half of the nineteenth century. It is only against this background that his ideas can be understood, let alone evaluated. The Dutch context is of particular importance, given the fact that he did not form his ideas in an ivory tower but "on the ground," where he was engaged in the practical and pressing issues of religious, social, and political life, and where he sought to bring about concrete change. That is why this book discusses Kuyper's ideas in relation to the events of his own career. The basis for this discussion is laid in Chapter Two, which provides an outline of Kuyper's multifaceted career up to his visit to Princeton. Although only an outline, it serves to introduce the man behind the Stone Lectures — his religious and intellectual background, his personality, and the nature of his work. Special attention is paid to those aspects and events that are pertinent to the leading ideas of the *Lectures.* Although Kuyper's career after 1898 was impressive, and he provided much elaboration and application of his ideas in numerous publications, he introduced no more new ideas, and undertook no more major organizational projects.

He did not, however, form his ideas solely in relation to those issues and events that dominated his immediate circumstances. He took an active interest in movements and events outside his own country, helped by the fact that he mastered several European languages, traveled widely abroad, and read both voraciously and eclectically. This is reflected, more than in any other of his works, in his *Lectures,* the contents of which transcend the particular circumstances of the Netherlands and draw attention to ideas and movements on a broader scale. This partly accounts for the fact that the *Lectures* were published in four European languages during Kuyper's lifetime and are largely responsible for creating the international Kuyperian school of thought.[33] The attempt this book makes to contextualize Kuyper's thought involves, therefore, making comparisons with the ideas of contemporary European thinkers, particularly where it can be shown that Kuyper was influenced by them, or was reacting directly against them. This has not yet been undertaken seriously; most historical studies of Kuyper's thought confine their analysis to Kuyper's place in Dutch political history. The task is complicated, however, by the fact that, although Kuyper often displayed an awareness of intellectual trends and of the work of contemporary thinkers, he rarely referred to these thinkers and their works by name. In most of his publications, footnotes and bibliographies are scarce. This is not surprising when it is considered that most of his work, even in the field of theology, his own academic discipline, was written in a popular journalistic style and published for a general audience in his two newspapers. An important exception is his *Encylopaedie der heilige godgeleerdheid,* which is a very scholarly work.[34] However, the discussion of contemporary thinkers contained in this work focuses on technical questions regarding the scope and method of theology (its "encyclopedia"), rather than on the broader themes and issues in theology and culture that he addressed in most of his work. As a journalist and politician with certain strategic ends in view, he tended to portray the thought of his intellectual opponents in a highly impressionistic and polemical way. He was more concerned with the general lines of their theories than with their detail and nuance. He formulated his ideas not so much to contribute to reasoned academic debate as to stimulate activity and to produce practical results. That is why this book takes account of his practical motives in the interpretation of his world of thought. This is not to challenge the sincerity of Kuyper's convictions, but to ground these

33. The *Lectures* appeared in English, Dutch, German, and Hungarian. In 1987 they were published in Korean.

34. A. Kuyper, *Encyclopaedie der heilige godgeleerdheid,* 3 vols. (Amsterdam: Wormser, 1894).

convictions in historical reality. Although traditional religious historiography has tended to avoid such an approach, especially when practiced by theologians rather than historians, it has great value for an accurate and thoroughgoing conceptual analysis.[35] It also makes it possible to judge where Kuyper's insights were distinctive and where they were shared by his contemporaries. Treatments of his ideas that pay scant attention to their historical context often conclude that they may be taken either as timeless guides to the truth or as flagrant illustrations of folly. Returning them to their historical context allows them to be evaluated in relation to the vibrant intellectual and social worlds of the nineteenth century. This is of fundamental importance to any discussion of how they might be relevant today; such discussion must begin with an understanding of how they were relevant to the situation in which they were formed.

Kuyper's ideas are also placed in relation to those of John Calvin at those points where Kuyper makes explicit reference to him in his *Lectures.* The aim here is not to determine the extent to which he was a reliable exponent of Calvin, but to consider the way in which his appeal to Calvin was tied to the realization of his own objectives. As will become clear in the chapters that follow, Kuyper had his own specific usage of the term "Calvinism," which was both far broader and less exact than the sum total of Calvin's thought or that of Calvin's most reliable exponents. Although he once claimed to be nothing but "a copyist of Calvin," he admitted in the introduction to his *Encyclopaedie,* that the aim of his work was "to bring Calvinism into line with the kind of human consciousness that has developed at the end of the nineteenth century."[36] This statement provides the starting point for much of the discussion of this book: how did Kuyper's ideas, which he claimed to derive from

35. The distinguished historian Theodore Dwight Bozeman pointed out over twenty years ago the potential of such an approach for the history of ideas. See his *Protestants in an Age of Science: The Baconian Ideal and Antebellum American Religious Thought* (Chapel Hill: University of North Carolina Press, 1977), pp. xiv-xv. It is an approach not to be confused with the "methodological atheism" of much modern historiography, even though it tries to avoid religious bias. For well-informed historiographical discussions from an evangelical perspective, see Colin Brown, *History and Faith: A Personal Exploration* (Leicester: IVP, 1988), and David Bebbington, *Patterns in History: A Christian Perspective on Historical Thought* (Leicester: Apollos, 1990).

36. A. Kuyper, *Bedoeld noch gezegd: schrijven aan Dr. J. H. Gunning* (Amsterdam: Kruyt, 1885), pp. 12, 17-19; Kuyper, *Encyclopaedie,* 2nd edition, I, vi.

Calvin, stand in relation to the western intellectual milieu (the "kind of human consciousness") at the end of the nineteenth century?

4. Secondary Literature

The controversy that followed Kuyper during his lifetime did not end with his death in 1920. Over the seventy-odd years that have since elapsed, his name has continued to evoke a wide range of emotions, and judgments on his legacy have varied widely. Partly as a result of this, the literature on Kuyper is as diverse as it is vast. It would thus be impossible to provide a comprehensive survey of it in this book; but it will be useful, particularly for readers unfamiliar with the secondary literature, to outline some of its salient features, especially those that help clarify the position occupied by the present study within the field of Kuyper scholarship.[37]

4.1. Works in English

Most English-language works on Kuyper have been produced by North Americans, and it is in the United States and Canada that evaluations of Kuyper's legacy have been the most sharply divided. In this debate, which has tended to concentrate on Kuyper the theologian rather than Kuyper the politician, the main line of division is the prominence given and importance attached to his doctrine of common grace, as opposed to that of the antithesis. Both these doctrines will be dealt with later in this book; here it is enough to note that those writers who stress Kuyper's doctrine of common grace are generally keen to encourage Christian

37. The archives consulted for the primary sources on which this book is based are located at the *Documentatiecentrum voor het Nederlands Protestantisme (1800-heden)* at the Free University, Amsterdam; at the Speer Library, Princeton Theological Seminary, Princeton, New Jersey; and at Heritage Hall, Calvin College, Grand Rapids, Michigan. Kuyper's vast correspondence remains largely unpublished, the two main exceptions being his correspondence with Guillaume Groen van Prinsterer (1801-1876), Kuyper's predecessor as political leader of the anti-revolutionaries, and with A. W. F. Idenberg (1861-1935), Kuyper's close friend and political colleague during the first two decades of the twentieth century. See *Briefwisseling van Mr. G. Groen van Prinsterer met Dr. A. Kuyper 1864-1876,* ed. by A. Goslinga (Kampen: Kok, 1937); *Briefwisseling Kuyper-Idenberg,* ed. by J. de Bruijn and G. Puchinger (Franeker: Wever, 1985).

participation in or engagement with modern "secular" social institutions and doctrines, whereas those of the "antithetical" school tend to seek the embodiment of their religious principles in independent, distinctively Christian institutions.[38]

The most notable works outside the theological literature in English are a number of popular biographies, in the form of books and articles, written mainly by followers or admirers of Kuyper.[39] Scholarly appraisals can be found in three doctoral dissertations, two written in the 1970s and one in 1995.[40] James Skillen's thesis concentrates on the work of Herman Dooyeweerd, but he seeks to evaluate it within the tradition of Dutch Calvinistic political thought, and therefore Kuyper receives considerable attention. By placing him intellectually between Groen van Prinsterer and Dooyeweerd, Skillen is able to show Kuyper not only as providing the foundation for Dooyeweerd's thought but also as carrying forward with power the political and intellectual movement inaugurated by Groen van Prinsterer. In doing so, Skillen lays stress on the fact that Kuyper's thought

38. James D. Bratt describes this debate in some detail in his *Dutch Calvinism in Modern America: A History of a Conservative Subculture* (Grand Rapids: Eerdmans, 1984). Influential among theological treatments of these two doctrines in North America have been Cornelius van Til, *Common Grace* (Philadelphia: Presbyterian and Reformed Publishing Company, 1947); Henry R. van Til, *The Calvinistic Concept of Culture* (Grand Rapids: Baker, 1959); S. U. Zuidema, "Common Grace and Christian Action in Abraham Kuyper," in S. U. Zuidema, *Communication and Confrontation* (Assen: Van Gorcum; Kampen: Kok, 1972), pp. 52-105.

39. These include the following: J. van Lonkhuyzen, "Abraham Kuyper — a Modern Calvinist," *Princeton Theological Review* 19 (1921): 131-47; J. M. van der Kroef, "Abraham Kuyper and the Rise of Neo-Calvinism in the Netherlands," *Church History* 17 (1948): 316-34; Frank van den Berg, *Abraham Kuyper* (Grand Rapids: Eerdmans, 1960); McKendree R. Langley, *The Practice of Political Spirituality: Episodes from the Public Career of Abraham Kuyper, 1879-1918* (Jordan Station, Ontario: Paideia Press, 1984); L. Praamsma, *Let Christ Be King: Reflections on the Life and Times of Abraham Kuyper* (Jordan Station: Paideia Press, 1985); R. E. L. Rodgers, *The Incarnation of the Antithesis: An Introduction to the Educational Thought and Practice of Abraham Kuyper*, with a foreword by Viscount Tonypandy (Durham, U.K.: Pentland Press, 1992).

40. James W. Skillen, "The Development of Calvinistic Political Theory in the Netherlands, with Special Reference to the Thought of Herman Dooyeweerd" (unpublished Ph.D. thesis, Duke University, 1973); Steven E. Meyer, "Calvinism and the Rise of the Protestant Political Movement in the Netherlands" (unpublished Ph.D. thesis, Georgetown University, 1976); Wayne Allen Kobes, "Sphere Sovereignty and the University: Theological Foundations of Abraham Kuyper's View of the University and Its Role in Society" (unpublished Ph.D. thesis, Florida State University, 1995).

emerged out of the *Réveil,* the early nineteenth-century religious revival that began in Switzerland, in which Groen van Prinsterer was a leading figure in the Netherlands. It is, in fact, the religious foundation and motivation of Kuyper's thought that is accentuated throughout Skillen's analysis, together with Kuyper's approach to the social and cultural issues of the period. The emphasis is deliberate and is designed to counter the tendency among some contemporary political theorists to regard religious subcultures as remnants or "outcroppings" of older cultures, of little relevance to contemporary society as a whole.[41] The second doctoral thesis, by Steven Meyer, is also written from the perspective of a political scientist, despite his employment of a historical framework, and interprets Kuyper's legacy largely in terms of the development of *verzuiling*.[42] Wayne Kobes's dissertation concentrates on the theological foundations of Kuyper's doctrine of "sphere-sovereignty" and his understanding of the role and function of the university. Much space is devoted to Kuyper's theology of creation, the fall, common and particular grace, and the kingship of Christ. The result is a valuable and solid introduction to Kuyper's theological framework. However, had Kobes paid adequate attention to the historical context in which this framework was formed he might have avoided proposing (as his central argument) that Kuyper developed and applied a theologically consistent understanding of confessional pluralism and sphere-sovereignty.[43] While the present study does not focus on the theological consistency (or otherwise) of Kuyper's thought, it does point out that the way in which Kuyper expounded his doctrine of sphere-sovereignty was an area of particular inconsistency.[44]

Literature on Kuyper published in the U.K. is far from prolific, but Michael Fogarty's masterly study of the Christian Democratic tradition in Western Europe provides perceptive passages on Kuyper's anti-revolution-

41. Skillen, pp. 225-26. An evaluation of Kuyper (by a Dutch scholar) which places a similar stress on the religious background and motivation of Kuyper's thought and work is G. J. Schutte, 'De ere Gods en de moderne staat: het antwoord van de Anti-Revolutionaire Partij op de secularisatie en democratisering van Nederland: antithese, soevereiniteit in eigen kring en gemene gratie', *Radix* 9 (1983): 73-104.

42. Meyer, pp. 1-38, 268-74.

43. Kobes, p. 2. The assertion with which Kobes begins his study is that "Kuyper's thought forms a coherent whole, a congruous system of thought which he consciously and intentionally attempted to construct on the basis of fundamental biblical principles" (p. 5).

44. See Chapter Six.

ary movement.[45] These are particularly helpful in reviewing the political development of Kuyper's movement alongside that of Protestant and Catholic movements in other European countries. Despite the number of detailed studies that have been carried out on specific movements in various countries since the book first appeared in 1957, Fogarty's book still maintains its value as a first attempt to provide, in English, a general survey of the development of European Christian Democracy. Another survey of similar caliber is that of E. H. Kossmann.[46] Concerned only with the Netherlands and Belgium, this book deals more extensively with Kuyper's place in Dutch history and includes discussion of his influence on social and cultural as well as political developments. Kossmann's evaluation of Kuyper bears striking dissimilarities to that of Skillen, particularly in his typification of Kuyper as politically "conservative" (despite odd references to his originality and progressiveness). Kossmann also claims that Kuyper adopted Groen van Prinsterer's belief in "the unbridgeable gap between Christian truth and modern life," and that Kuyper's intention was not "to reform or dominate modern civilization but to break it,"[47] an interpretation that differs sharply from Skillen's emphasis on the close affinity between Kuyper's religious convictions and his modern approach to contemporary issues.

4.2. Works in Dutch

Doctoral dissertations and scholarly monographs on Kuyper have been in no short supply in the Netherlands. Most were written by theologians just before or soon after the Second World War, and concentrate on specific aspects of Kuyper's theology.[48] An exception is P. Kasteel's pub-

45. Fogarty, *Christian Democracy,* pp. 171-72, 301-3, 317.

46. E. H. Kossmann, *The Low Countries, 1790-1940* (Oxford: Oxford University Press, 1978).

47. Kossmann, pp. 303-4.

48. Such works include: P. Kasteel, *Abraham Kuyper* (Kampen: Kok, 1938); A. A. van Ruler, *Kuyper's idee eener christelijke cultuur* (Nijkerk: Callenbach, 1938); P. A. van Leeuwen, *Het kerkbegrip in de theologie van Abraham Kuyper* (Franeker: Wever, 1946); Simon Jan Ridderbos, *De theologische cultuurbeschouwing van Abraham Kuyper* (Kampen: Kok, 1947); Harm Jan Langman, *Kuyper en de volkskerk: een dogmatisch-ecclesiologische studie* (Kampen: Kok, 1950). Two doctoral dissertations not concerned exclusively with Kuyper but nonetheless providing a thorough analysis of his political and social thought are Isaäc Arend Diepenhorst, *Historisch-critisch bijdrage tot den leer van den christelijke staat* (Amster-

lished doctoral dissertation, which is a full-length biography.[49] It is also exceptional in that the author is a Roman Catholic (most writers on Kuyper belong to the Reformed tradition), and in that it makes use of an impressive variety of historical source material, including large amounts of correspondence. It remains the only scholarly biography to cover the entire span of Kuyper's career. Its main drawback, apart from its somewhat dated style, is that the discussion is limited to Kuyper's ecclesiastical and political activities, leaving his journalism and his influence in the area of society and culture virtually untouched. Nevertheless, together with J. C. Rullmann's three-volume bibliography,[50] which contains commentary on over two hundred of Kuyper's works, it is one of the most important reference works on Kuyper's life and work.

Since the flurry of academic treatments around the 1940s, remarkably little serious research has been carried out on Kuyper. Most literature has tended to be of a semi-popular nature, written by and for Kuyper's anti-revolutionary followers, the intention being to commemorate the heroic achievements of the party's founder and to boost morale.[51] Where criticism is expressed this is generally enveloped in heady expressions of awe and appreciation. It is not surprising that there is an abundance of such literature when it is borne in mind that the Anti-Revolutionary Party remained a powerful and influential force in Dutch politics long after Kuyper's death and was amalgamated into the *Christen-Democratisch Appèl* only as recently as 1980.[52] Consequently,

---

dam: Noord-Hollandsche Uitgevers Maatschappij, 1943), and J. D. Dengerink, *Critisch-historisch onderzoek naar de sociologische ontwikkeling van het beginsel der 'Souvereiniteit in Eigen Kring' in de negentiende en twintigste eeuw* (Kampen: Kok, 1948).

49. P. Kasteel (see footnote above). A number of popular biographies by followers or admirers of Kuyper predate Kasteel's work. These include: W. F. A. Winckel, *Leven en arbeid van Dr. A. Kuyper* (Amsterdam: Ten Have, 1919); Rullmann, *Abraham Kuyper;* P. A. Diepenhorst, *Dr. A. Kuyper* (Haarlem: De Erven Bohn, 1931).

50. J. C. Rullmann, *Kuyper-bibliografie,* 3 vols. (Kampen: Kok, 1923-1940).

51. See, for example, the commemoration volumes *Schrift en historie: gedenkboek bij het vijftig-jarig bestaan der georganiseerde Antirevolutionaire Partij* 1878-1928 (Kampen: Kok, 1928) and *Dr. A. Kuyper: gedenkboek uitgegeven bij gelegenheid van de herdenking op 29 oktober 1937 van het feit, dat Dr. A. Kuyper honderd jaar geleden te Maassluis geboren werd,* ed. by L. W. G. Scholten, C. Smeenk, and J. Waterink (Kampen: Kok, 1937).

52. For recent treatments of the development and ideology of this party see H. E. S. Woldring, *De Christen Democratie: Een critisch onderzoek naar haar politieke philosofie* (Utrecht: Het Spectrum, 1996); R. S. Zwart, *'Gods wil in Nederland': Christelijke ideologieën en de vorming van het CDA (1880-1990)* (Kampen: Kok, 1996).

much of the literature reflects the need for a sense of identity and historical continuity within a dynamic political party. It is also written, in the main, by individuals who had a sense of personal debt to Kuyper. They were often actively involved in the circles of the Free University and the ARP, and were ready to acknowledge that the world they inhabited was largely a product of Kuyper's creative genius. It is only natural, therefore, that such people, living in an age that was fond of commemorating its worthy forebears, should wish to pay tribute to the man they regarded as their God-given leader.

Most of the literature on Kuyper that appeared in 1987, the 150th anniversary of his birth, sounds a very different tone and indicates the extent to which his latter-day Dutch protégés wish to distance themselves from his legacy.[53] Many of the insights that are given into the darker sides of Kuyper's character are valuable in reaching a more rounded assessment of his personality, although the general tone in which they are related occasionally becomes vindictive and threatens to undermine the credibility of the argument at least as much as the heroic tone of the earlier literature. This is particularly true of J. Stellingwerff's book on Kuyper and the Free University, in which the author's frequently disapproving and sometimes virulent treatment of Kuyper detracts from the value of an otherwise informative and interesting study. Not all the commemoration literature shares this approach. In his biography of the young Kuyper, for instance, G. Puchinger combines a personal appreciation and admiration for Kuyper with recognition of his shortcomings.[54] He gives special attention to Kuyper's religious make-up, claiming that he can be understood only if consideration is given to what he became at the start of his career and remained throughout: a religious convert.[55] Puchinger's biography is based on a substantial amount of hitherto unexamined archive material, and although it is only the first part of a proposed six-volume work, it forms a significant contribution to the biographical literature on Kuyper.

53. See, for instance, *Abraham Kuyper: zijn volksdeel, zijn invloed,* ed. by C. Augustijn, J. H. Prins, and H. E. S. Woldring (Delft: Meinema, 1987); J. Stellingwerff, *Dr. Abraham Kuyper en de Vrije Universiteit* (Kampen: Kok, 1987).

54. G. Puchinger, *Abraham Kuyper: De jonge Kuyper (1837-1867)* (Franeker: Wever, 1987).

55. Puchinger, *Abraham Kuyper,* pp. 205-43; G. Puchinger, *Kuyper-herdenking 1987 (De religieuze Kuyper): vijf opstellen en lezingen van de herdenking van de honderdvijftigste geboortedag van Abraham Kuyper, 29 oktober 1987* (Kampen: Kok, 1987).

The two most important historical studies of Kuyper's views on foreign policy were both published in 1992 in doctoral dissertations by Roel Kuiper and Chris van Koppen.[56] Both authors include detailed descriptions of anti-revolutionary policy, particularly towards South Africa and the great powers of Europe, during a period in which the Netherlands followed a policy of neutrality within the international community. Both also accentuate the presence of nationalism in Kuyper's vision of the role of the Netherlands in international affairs, and the place of Calvinism within that vision, though they differ in their evaluations of it (see Chapter Nine of this book). In contrast to the present study, however, neither work attempts to discuss the religious and theological foundations of Kuyper's political thought or to situate his ideas within an intellectual context.

4.3. Literature on Verzuiling

One important theme in the literature on Kuyper, which emerged earlier in this survey, is that of his influence on the development of *verzuiling.* This question is not dealt with in detail in this book, for two main reasons. First, although it is generally agreed that the conditions which allowed for the development of *verzuiling* were laid during the nineteenth century, the *verzuiling* pattern, as mentioned above, is most applicable to the period 1920-1960, that is, after Kuyper's death. This book does not discuss the influence of Kuyper's ideas on a later period but the contemporary realities of the period in which he lived, which shaped his thought. However, while the *verzuiling* debate is not vital to an understanding of the background and context of his ideas, it is relevant to the question whether or not Kuyper's ideas were motivated by a desire to see the development of a pillarized society, and whether his ideas provide a basis on which such a society could have been built. These issues, which are addressed in the chapters on Kuyper's third, fourth, and sixth Stone Lectures, have not received detailed attention in studies of *verzuiling.* It is often simply assumed that because Kuyper's social impact can be explained in terms of *verzuiling,* it was a mode of

56. R. Kuiper, *Zelfbeeld en wereldbeeld: antirevolutionairen en het buitenland, 1848-1905* (Kampen: Kok, 1992); Chris A. J. van Koppen, *De Geuzen van de negentiende eeuw: Abraham Kuyper en Zuid-Afrika* (Wormer: Immerc, 1992).

social organization that he himself advocated; it is taken for granted, in other words, that the origin of *verzuiling* can be found in Kuyper's thought, without discussion of the evidence.[57] Given the far-reaching consequences of *verzuiling* on the development of modern Dutch society, and the level of interest in Kuyperian pluralism in North America,[58] the question of a link between his ideas and the development of *verzuiling* is worthy of thorough investigation. In doing so, however, care would need to be taken to avoid the tendency towards "finalism," which has sometimes characterized treatments of historical developments provided by writers on *verzuiling*. That is to say, some such writers have not always avoided the error of reading back their knowledge of later developments into the particular period under review, thus falling prone to antedating and anachronism.[59] This problem pertains in particular to those authors who seek to interpret *verzuiling* as a means by which ideological groups — such as the orthodox Protestants — were able to undergo a process of emancipation.[60] The hazard does not detract from the feasibility and value of the enquiry, however, and this book aims to offer suggestions as to where the origin of *verzuiling* in Kuyper's thought may be found.

57. E. H. Kossmann, for example, claims that Kuyper was the originator of *verzuiling*, claiming: "The origin of what in later years was disparagingly called *verzuiling* . . . can be found in Kuyper's love of diversity." *The Low Countries*, p. 304.

58. See, for instance, Stanley Carlson-Thies, "The Meaning of Dutch Segmentation for Modern America," in *Sharing the Reformed Tradition: The Dutch-North American Exchange, 1846-1996*, ed. by George Harinck and Hans Krabbendam (Amsterdam: VU Uitgeverij, 1996), pp. 159-75; *Welfare in America: Christian Perspectives on a Policy in Crisis*, ed. by Stanley Carlson-Thies and James Skillen (Grand Rapids: Eerdmans, 1996); James Skillen, *Recharging the American Experiment: Principled Pluralism for Genuine Civic Community* (Grand Rapids: Baker, 1994).

59. Stuurman, pp. 76-77; H. Daalder, 'Politicologen, sociologen, historic en de verzuiling', *Bijdragen en mededelingen betreffende de geschiedenis der Nederlanden* 100 (1985): 52-64 (p. 54).

60. Such as J. Hendriks, *De emancipatie van de gereformeerden: sociologische bijdrage tot de verklaring van enige kenmerken van het gereformeerde volksdeel* (Alphen aan den Rijn: Samson, 1971); D. T. Kuiper, *De voormannen: een sociaal-wetenschappelijke studie over ideologie, conflict en kerngroepvorming binnen de Gereformeerde wereld in Nederland tussen 1820 en 1930* (Kampen: Kok, 1972).

Conclusion

The breadth and influence of Kuyper's thought and works marks him out as a figure of exceptional interest to a wide variety of disciplines. This book takes an historical approach to the core of his intellectual legacy, expressed in the *Lectures on Calvinism,* the primary aim being to assess the motivation and significance of Kuyper's ideas within their historical context. Although a considerable amount of work has been carried out on Kuyper, no treatment of this kind has yet been undertaken, despite its value to the vigorous multidisciplinary debate that surrounds him a century after the *Lectures* were given. As other means of analysis could have been chosen, the evaluation offered in this book makes no claim to be definitive; but it does allow for an assessment of the essential Kuyper.

The Kuyper of the Stone Lectures

Kuyper was born in the Dutch town of Maassluis, near Rotterdam, on 29 October 1837, the eldest son of a Dutch Reformed minister and an ex-schoolmistress.[1] His father, who belonged to the mildly orthodox, supranaturalistic stream in the *Nederlandse Hervormde Kerk* (Dutch Reformed Church), had translated tracts for the Dutch Religious Tract Society at the request of A. S. Thelwall (1795-1863), an English Methodist preacher stationed in Amsterdam.[2] This activity paid unexpected dividends: the secretary of the Society, recognizing the young man's potential, made the necessary financial arrangements for him to study theology at Leiden University. After completing his studies he took up two appointments as minister in the Dutch Reformed Church before arriving in Maassluis in 1834. In 1841 he moved again, with his family, to Middelburg and again in 1849 to Leiden, where he stayed until his retirement in 1868.

1. Although the story of Kuyper's life has been told many times, the account given in this chapter, while making some use of secondary material, is based on primary sources, in order to present as accurate and lively an account as possible.

2. On the supranaturalistic stream in the *Hervormde Kerk,* see Herman Bavinck, "Recent Dogmatic Thought in the Netherlands," *The Presbyterian and Reformed Review* 10 (1892): 209-28 (210-12).

1. Childhood

Apart from a few recollections from later years, little is known of Kuyper's childhood.[3] He received his primary education from his parents before attending grammar school in his hometowns of Middelburg and Leiden from the age of twelve. One archive document in particular, the oldest from Kuyper's own hand, sheds light on his early religious development and dates from 1848, when he was only ten years old:

> A. Kuyper, son of J. F. Kuyper: A remembrance that is holy. To God in Heaven. To the King of kings from a humble heart. It was the 10th October at 10.30 that I went to bed but could not sleep for anxiety about the evil I had committed. Then at 11.15 I was converted and decided to flee from evil and to strive for good. I, Abraham Kuyper, Middelburg, 1848.[4]

In describing his conversion experience in later years in his *Confidentie,* an open letter, which bears striking similarities in both form and purpose to J. H. Newman's *Apologia Pro Vita Sua* of 1864, Kuyper made no reference to this statement of conversion. It is likely, therefore, that he came to regard it as juvenile and conventional. Nevertheless, the young Kuyper's words may bear some relation to the origin of his concept of regeneration, or "palingenesis" as he generally called it, which was central to his later thought.[5]

At school in Leiden, Kuyper proved himself a gifted pupil. On a number of occasions he was granted the honor, as the best pupil of the class, of addressing a vote of thanks *(Gratias)* to the teaching staff at the end of the school year. He was also an avid reader of newspapers, and,

3. Some memoirs are recorded in *De Standaard,* 30 July 1906; J. J. Rammelman Elsevier-Kuyper, *Herinneringen uit de kinder- en jongelingsjaren van Dr. A. Kuyper. Bijeenvergaderd door zijn eenig overgebleven zuster* (Kampen: Kok, 1921); H. S. S. Kuyper en J. H. Kuyper, *Herinneringen van de oude garde* (Amsterdam: Ten Have, 1922).

4. Cited in J. de Bruijn, *Abraham Kuyper: leven en werk in beeld: een beeldbiografie* (Amsterdam: Historisch Documentatiecentrum voor het Nederlands Protestantisme [1800-heden], 1987), p. 12.

5. A. Kuyper, *Confidentie: schrijven aan den weled. heer J. H. van der Linden* (Amsterdam: Höveker, 1873). In his *Encyclopaedie,* his theological *magnum opus,* Kuyper employed the concept of regeneration as the starting point for his theology. See Chapter Seven of this book. The reliability and integrity of Kuyper's *Confidentie* is subject to debate — see, for instance, Stellingwerff, *Dr. Abraham Kuyper,* pp. 23-25; van Rooden, *Religieuze regimes,* pp. 188-89.

according to his own testimony, it was during his school days that he first developed an interest in journalism and politics. In 1897, on the twenty-fifth anniversary of his editorship of his daily newspaper *De Standaard*, Kuyper told how his childhood infatuation with the press was so great that his father banned him from reading newspapers.[6]

2. Student

Having passed his final school exams with flying colors, Kuyper enrolled as a student of theology at Leiden University in the summer of 1855. From the start he devoted himself to his studies, displaying in them the same single-mindedness, energy, and enthusiasm that were to characterize his later work. His efforts did not go unrewarded: within seven years he had received his degree, won a prize essay competition, and completed his doctoral dissertation. Having written both his prize-winning essay and his dissertation on a comparison of the doctrine of the church in the theology of John Calvin and the Polish reformer John à Lasco (1499-1560), Kuyper had laid the groundwork for a career as a church historian.

Two aspects of Kuyper's time as a student are of particular importance to the shape of his later thought. First was his introduction to modernistic theology,[7] which had been growing in force in the Netherlands since the second quarter of the nineteenth century, when it had received a powerful impetus from the *Groninger Richting* (Groninger School). This school, headed by theologians at Groningen University, advocated a move away from the doctrinal rigidity characteristic of much contemporary Reformed theology in favor of a religion of the heart, an emphasis they shared with and appreciated in F. D. E. Schleiermacher (1768-1834).[8] After losing its initial momentum in Groningen, the center

6. *Gedenkboek, opgedragen door het feestcomité aan Prof. Dr. A. Kuyper, bij zijn vijf en twintigjarig jubileum als hoofdredacteur van 'De Standaard' 1872-1897,* ed. by T. Heemskerk (Amsterdam: Herdes, 1897), p. 67.

7. "Modernistic theology" is used here in its broadest sense to mean the trend in nineteenth-century Protestant theology which employed as an explicit principle the idea that the proper response to Enlightenment rationalism ("modern" thought) was to make radical alterations to traditional Christian doctrine.

8. Although the Groningen Theologians were critical of many points of Schleiermacher's theology, they felt a strong affinity towards him, and were re-

of modernistic theology moved to Leiden, where J. H. Scholten (1811-1885) emerged as the dynamic and inspiring exponent of a more liberal and deterministic kind of theology than had hitherto been taught at Dutch universities. Together with his colleagues A. Kuenen (1828-1885) and L. W. E. Rauwenhoff (1828-1889), Scholten laid the foundations of what became known as the Leiden School, which drew much of its inspiration from the discovery of textual criticism as an important component in theological method. Its plea for the renewal of theology along modern, critical lines had great influence, particularly among prospective ministers of the *Hervormde Kerk.* Once these ideas had made their way from the universities to the pulpits they formed a powerful current that swept aside much of the orthodoxy of the churches, which at the time was too weak and uninspiring to resist.[9]

Kuyper, whose period as a student at Leiden (1855-1863) coincided with the high point of the Leiden School's influence, was one of those swept along by the current. The lectures he attended, particularly those of Scholten, made a deep impression on him. At the end of one of them in which Scholten had denied the bodily resurrection of Christ, Kuyper rose with his fellow students to give the lecturer a standing ovation. Later he recounted this incident with regret. "I shall not say that I fell into positivism or atheism," he wrote, "but I preserved nothing of the old treasure of faith."[10] To the American readers of the English translation of the second volume of his *Encyclopaedie,* published in New York soon before his visit to Princeton, he admitted: "He [Kuyper] broke with faith in every form when a student at Leiden, and then cast himself into the arms of the barest radicalism."[11] Four years later, as Prime Minister, he confessed before a sitting of the First Chamber that at Leiden he had been captivated by the "illusion" of modernistic theology, and had remained under its spell for years.[12] According to his own admission,

---

sponsible for introducing his ideas into Dutch theology. See Jasper Vree, *De Groninger Godgeleerden: de oorsprongen en de eerste periode van hum optreden (1820-1843)* (Kampen: Kok, 1984), pp. 153-64.

9. Simon J. de Vries, *Bible and Theology in the Netherlands,* 2nd edition (New York: Peter Lang, 1989), pp. 28-38.

10. Kuyper, *Confidentie,* p. 35.

11. A. Kuyper, *Encyclopedia of Sacred Theology: Its Principles,* trans. by J. Hendrik De Vries. With an introduction by Benjamin B. Warfield (New York: Charles Scribner; London: Hodder and Stoughton, 1898), p. viii.

12. A. Kuyper, *Parlementaire redevoeringen,* 4 vols. (Amsterdam: Van Holkema

therefore, Kuyper had lost the faith he had professed as a child,and had become intellectually and emotionally enthralled with the theology of the Leiden School.

The second important influence on Kuyper during his student period was his reading of *The Heir of Redclyffe,* a novel published in 1853 by Charlotte M. Yonge (1823-1901), a member of the Oxford Movement and a friend of John Keble.[13] Although this was the author's first serious novel, it was a huge success. Its religious and emotional sentiment found wide appeal and even had the effect of reducing some to tears.[14] Among those so affected was the newly-graduated doctor of theology Abraham Kuyper. He received the book as a gift from his fiancée, Johanna Hendrika Schaay, to whom he was married in 1863. Although the young couple read and exchanged comments on a number of books throughout their five-year engagement, it was this book, he wrote, "which for me, I say not in value but in significance for my life, stands next to the Bible."[15] He claimed that in reading it he had come to realize that despite the strength of his will and his aptitude for study he remained a weak and sinful person in need of God's grace: "That masterpiece was for me a means towards the breaking of my self-satisfied, contentious heart."[16] He wrote to Johanna after finishing the book:

> *The Heir of Redclyffe* has done me good. . . . I cried as a child, and knelt to pray — out of remorse. . . . Things were not good with me. I had been too self-satisfied, too desirous of honour, too egoistic, not noble enough, not enough a child of God. For years I had deceived myself, and convinced myself that I was doing good, my conscience, my

---

& Warendorf, 1908-1910), IV, part III, 790 (speech of July 1902). Two years later, still as Prime Minister, Kuyper noted: "I arrived at the Academy as a believing young man, but after being there for one and a half years my convictions were transformed into those of the most absolute form of rationalism." *Parlementaire redevoeringen,* III, part II, 24.

13. In 1836 John Keble had become parish priest in the Hampshire village of Hursley, where Charlotte lived.

14. Margaret Mare and Alicia C. Percival, *Victorian Best-seller: The World of Charlotte Yonge* (London: Harrap, 1948), p. 35. Yonge's very first novel was *Abbey Church,* published in 1844 when she was only twenty years old. *The Heir of Redclyffe* reached its seventeenth edition in 1868.

15. Kuyper, *Confidentie,* p. 41.

16. Kuyper, *Confidentie,* p. 40.

> childlike heart lulled to sleep. I did not know what sin was any more and I knew no contrition. . . . I was alone in my room, and I went upstairs and fell on my knees and prayed, long and fervently. I had not prayed like this for years.[17]

3. Beesd

Thus Kuyper arrived, "inclining towards the gospel" as he later put it, in the village of Beesd, his first parish, in 1863.[18] He came, he wrote, "less in order to give from what was mine, than with the secret prayer that my empty heart might be refreshed and fed by the members of the congregation."[19] At first, however, he was deeply disappointed with what he found:

> In the circles in which I moved, there dominated, not wanting to negate what was good, a strict conservatism, with an orthodox tint, but without real glow, devoid of spiritual energy. . . . People were happy with the way things were. They wanted to receive from me, but they gave me nothing in return.[20]

Kuyper soon heard, moreover, that there were "malcontents" among his parishioners who, out of protest against modernism in the church, refused to attend his services. He was warned by members of the congregation, he wrote in his *Confidentie,* that these people were the sort that caused a nuisance to every minister, and that he would do well to stay out of their way. But he was intrigued, he wrote, and so "with a trembling heart . . . in the course of my house-visitation I knocked on the doors of the 'fine,' enthusiastic members." His reception was apparently far from congenial, and on one occasion he was refused a handshake by a young woman, Pietje Baltus, the daughter of a poor laborer. Despite their awkwardness

17. Letter from Kuyper to Johanna Schaay, 2 March 1863, quoted in G. Puchinger, *Abraham Kuyper,* pp. 186-87. Kuyper related the same incident in his *Confidentie,* p. 42.

18. See Kuyper's leaving address at Beesd, on 3 Nov. 1867. Published in A. Kuyper, *Predicatiën in de jaren 1867 tot 1873, tijdens zijn predikantschap in het Nederlands Hervormde Kerkgenootschap, gehouden te Beesd, te Utrecht en te Amsterdam* (Kampen: Kok, 1913), p. 242.

19. Kuyper, *Confidentie,* pp. 43-44.

20. Kuyper, *Confidentie,* p. 44.

and hostility, however, Kuyper felt a strong attraction to the malcontents, and made a point of paying them regular visits:

> Here spoke a conviction. Here the people had richer resources for conversation than about "beautiful weather" and that "so-and-so was ill" and that "such-and-such had sent away his servant." Here there was interest in the spiritual dimension. Most of all, here was knowledge.[21]

Whereas in Leiden Kuyper had been praised by his professors for his exemplary diligence and outstanding results, in Beesd he found himself sharply reproved by ordinary village people for his ignorance of the most basic truths of Christianity. "With my poor knowledge of the Bible, which I had acquired at the university," he admitted, "I could not measure myself against these humble folk."[22] It was among these people that he claimed to have discovered a living expression of what he had previously only studied for academic reasons:

> I had got to know Calvin and I had got to know à Lasco but in reading them it never occurred to me that this was truth. I opposed them in my heart. I read and studied them for the sake of an historical issue, a formal question. I simply severed their understanding of the Church from its life-root.[23]

He reckoned amongst the most attractive characteristics of the malcontents their coherency of worldview, which for him bore all the hallmarks of Calvin's theology:

> There was not only knowledge of the Bible but also knowledge of a well-ordered world-view, though of old-Reformed style. It was sometimes as though I was sitting on the lecture-room benches hearing my talented mentor Scholten lecturing on the "doctrine of the Reformed Church," but with inverted sympathy. And what, for me at least, was the most attractive, was that here spoke a heart that not only *possessed* but also *understood* a history and experience of life. . . . Those ordinary working people, hidden away in a corner, told me in their rough regional dialect the same thing Calvin had given me to read in beau-

21. Kuyper, *Confidentie,* p. 44.
22. Kuyper, *Confidentie,* p. 44.
23. Kuyper, *Confidentie,* p. 46.

> tiful Latin. Calvin could be found, however misformed, among those simple country-folk, who had hardly heard of his name. He had taught in such a way that he could be *understood*, even centuries after his death, in a foreign country, in a forgotten village, in a room floored with tiles, with the mind of an ordinary labourer.[24]

In Beesd, Kuyper believed he had discovered that Calvinism was more than an historical and ecclesiastical phenomenon: it was a world of thought and a way of life accepted and understood by ordinary people. Having made this discovery, he underwent a second conversion, this time emerging as the orthodox Calvinist he would remain for the rest of his life. His future career would now be dominated by the attempt to expound and apply the principles of Calvinism to the society and culture of his day, an attempt most clearly reflected in the Stone Lectures of 1898.

During his time at Beesd Kuyper continued his work on à Lasco by collecting and publishing his letters and works.[25] This was the result of research Kuyper had carried out at archive collections in various European cities, particularly in London, where for many years à Lasco had been pastor of a congregation of Polish refugees. This work had occasioned Kuyper's first contact with Groen van Prinsterer, who as well as being leader of the anti-revolutionary movement was archivist to the Dutch king. In 1864 Kuyper wrote to Groen asking for his help in gaining access to consult an archive document from a private royal collection. Thus began a relationship of vital importance to Kuyper's thought and career.

The publication of à Lasco's works marked the end of Kuyper's academic work as a church historian. His plans to write a biography of à Lasco and a history of the Congregations under the Cross, the group of churches to which the reformer belonged, were left unfulfilled as his attention was increasingly taken up with contemporary ecclesiastical and political affairs. His decisive entrance into public debate came in 1867 with his publication of a pamphlet on the right of church members to vote on matters arising within the *Hervormde Kerk*.[26] This pamphlet, in

24. Kuyper, *Confidentie*, p. 47.

25. A. Kuyper, *Johannes à Lasco: opera tam edita quam inedita recensuit vitam auctoris enarravit*, 2 vols. (Amsterdam: Muller, 1866)

26. A. Kuyper, *Wat moeten wij doen: het stemrecht aan ons zelven houden of den kerkeraad machtigen?* (Culemborg: Blom, 1867).

which Kuyper placed himself firmly within the orthodox party, brought him into closer contact with Groen van Prinsterer, who praised him for the stand he had taken.

4. Utrecht

Kuyper's conversion in Beesd resulted in a commitment both to the orthodox party in the church and to the anti-revolutionary movement in politics. Later, in his Amsterdam career, it became obvious what these commitments would mean in practice, as he became responsible for important changes in both church and politics. But in Utrecht Kuyper found the space he needed to consolidate his position.

Kuyper's appointment to the *Domkerk* in Utrecht (1867) was accompanied by high expectations on both sides. Utrecht, which had been a bastion of Reformed orthodoxy since the great days of the Dutch Republic, for Kuyper represented a "Zion of God." The expectations of the congregation were centered on Kuyper as a church historian and as author of the pamphlet on the right to vote, which had won their sympathy. Whenever he preached, large numbers of people turned out to hear him. Kuyper's popularity was accompanied by sharp criticism, however, for in Utrecht he became fully engaged in the ecclesiastical conflict, in which he argued forcefully for the maintenance of the traditional creeds of the *Hervormde Kerk.*[27] These were under threat, he claimed, from the forces of liberalism in the church, which were gaining strength under a leadership that allowed too much doctrinal freedom. A stream of pamphlets and sermons ensued which, although they enjoyed a wide and enthusiastic response, also met with fierce opposition, particularly from theologians belonging to the so-called Ethical wing of the *Hervormde Kerk,* such as N. Beets (1814-1903), J. H. Gunning (1829-1905), D. Chantepie de la Saussaye (1818-1874), and J. J. van Toorenenbergen (1821-1903). Despite their orthodox sympathies, the Ethicals embraced the critical appraisal of scripture, and were strongly influenced by Schleiermacher and modern German philosophy. The name "Ethical" signified their rejection of the cerebral intellectualism of rationalism, which they

27. These creeds were known as the Three Formulae of Unity *(De Drie Formulieren van Enigheid):* the Belgic Confession (1561), the Heidelberg Catechism (1563), and the Articles of the Synod of Dordt (1618).

considered characteristic of modernistic theology, in favor of intense personal religious experience. It also symbolized their commitment to the ethical rather than the dogmatic aspects of Reformed religion, and their concern for the promotion of social responsibility.[28] In contrast to Kuyper's confrontational style, they pursued an irenic approach in theological and ecclesiastical controversy.

Along with his involvement in this controversy, Kuyper became thoroughly embroiled in the issue of education. Here again it was members of the Ethical Movement who opposed him. In May 1869 Groen and Kuyper both appeared in Utrecht at the meeting of the Dutch Society for Christian Education, where Kuyper delivered the opening speech.[29] A fierce debate ensued between Kuyper and N. Beets over the question of what the Christian attitude should be towards state education. Both Groen and Kuyper hoped that by denouncing the so-called "neutrality" of state education as in fact the product of certain ideological presuppositions, they would make room to present their case for the expansion of private schools based on a clearly defined Christian confession. Beets argued that state schools were bound by law to educate pupils in Christian virtues and advocated the maintenance and strengthening of the Christian character of state schools, rather than the proliferation of autonomous Christian schools. Groen and Kuyper won the day, causing Beets, Chantepie de la Saussaye, and Van Toorenenbergen to resign as members of the society.

When Kuyper received a call to Amsterdam in February 1870 it did not take him long to accept it. He had been disappointed by the lack of cooperation from orthodox ministers in Utrecht and decided that Amsterdam would be a better center from which to strive towards the reformation of the church. His experience in Utrecht had taught him that church reform could only proceed successfully if public opinion had first been aroused and informed, and this would be carried out more effectively from the country's capital city.

28. A. J. Rasker, *De Nederlandse Hervormde Kerk vanaf 1795: haar geschiedenis en theologie in de negentiende en twintigste eeuw* (Kampen: Kok, 1974), pp. 131-36; Wintle, pp. 50-52.

29. Following this early meeting of Groen van Prinsterer and Kuyper, Groen wrote in his periodical *Nederlandsche Gedachten* of 1 September 1869 that he expected Kuyper to become the future leader of the anti-revolutionary movement. For a summary of Kuyper's speech, see van Rooden, *Religieuze regimes,* pp. 162-65.

5. Amsterdam

Kuyper's reputation as a challenging and talented speaker spread rapidly through Amsterdam, and once again he began to address large and enthusiastic audiences. Characteristic of the polemical style his addresses had assumed was a speech delivered in 1871 entitled "Modernism: A Fata Morgana in the Realm of Christianity."[30] In bold and bombastic tone he argued that, like the Fata Morgana, the extraordinary mirage-like phenomenon sighted most often in the Strait of Messina, liberal theology appeared as a majestic, entrancingly beautiful phenomenon but one that was devoid of reality. Kuyper's rhetoric betrays the extent to which he himself had been captivated by modernistic theology at Leiden.[31]

Kuyper's audience widened considerably when he founded and became chief editor of the daily newspaper *De Standaard* in 1872. Together with the weekly religious newspaper *De Heraut,* of which he had been chief editor since 1871, and which in 1872 became a Sunday supplement to *De Standaard,* the paper gave Kuyper a powerful and effective medium for propagating, expounding, and defending anti-revolutionary principles to a mass audience. "Anti-revolutionary principles" was a term Kuyper adopted from Groen van Prinsterer to denote principles that were opposed to the ones that had inspired the French Revolution and were in accordance with Reformed doctrine as expressed in the Three Formulae of Unity. It was largely due to Kuyper's journalistic capabilities, deployed in these two newspapers, that there began to develop, across the country, a broad basis of support for anti-revolutionary principles, laying the groundwork for political organization on a mass scale. This had been Kuyper's intention from the start, as is indicated by his writing to Groen at the launch of *De Standaard:* "If that paper runs well, in five years time we will be master of the position *intra muros.*"[32] By means of *De Standaard* Kuyper not only mobilized and organized a sector of the population, but placed the issues that faced that group on the

30. A. Kuyper, *Het modernisme: een Fata Morgana op christelijk gebied* (Amsterdam: De Hoogh, 1871).

31. In the preface to his *Encyclopedia of Theology* he also conveyed the extent of his infatuation with modernistic theology. There he wrote that after embracing radicalism he "felt attracted first to the Determinism of Professor Scholten, and then to the warmth of the *Vermittelungs-theologie*" (p. viii).

32. Letter from Kuyper to Groen, 15 December 1871. *Briefwisseling van Mr. G. Groen van Prinsterer,* p. 171.

agenda of national politics. His establishment and editorship of the newspaper also signaled the start of his rise as the publicly recognized leader of the anti-revolutionaries, in the place of the aging Groen van Prinsterer, who had begun to withdraw from the front line of parliamentary politics. On 10 January 1871 Groen wrote to Kuyper: "My parliamentary role is over with. I am no longer equal to such a task." Three months later he acknowledged in a letter to Kuyper that he now considered him to be the journalistic leader of the anti-revolutionaries:

> Both of us have our own vantage point. You as participant in the conflict, as the journalistic leader on the battle-field, as man of action and of practice. . . . I, in contrast, the leader (in so far as this may still be coveted) merely in the area of principles.[33]

Kuyper was to remain the journalistic leader of the anti-revolutionaries until just before his death in 1920, a period of nearly fifty years in which he wrote thousands of articles on a wide range of political, cultural, and educational issues. Daily he added to the reporting of news his own leader columns, which were read avidly and regarded as authoritative statements by his followers across the country. He acted almost like a military commander, keen to summon up the courage of his followers and point out to them the way ahead; but ruthless and merciless towards his opponents. In contrast to the aristocratic courteousness that characterized Groen's writings, Kuyper's columns often taunted his political opponents, seizing every opportunity to expose their weaknesses, both in their positions and in their personalities. He praised other political leaders only if they praised him, and turned on them with all the fierceness of his pen if they ever criticized him in public. He would often place them in the context of a moral conflict and so try to expose them in a damaging light that would generate suspicion. By means of his assertive and ambitious character, sharp intellect, and organizational abilities, *De Standaard* and *De Heraut* became powerful weapons with which he dominated the political and religious debate in the Netherlands for almost half a century — regarded as a menace by some and as a hero by others.[34] It was almost in the middle of this fifty-year period that

33. Letter from Groen to Kuyper, 10 April 1871. *Briefwisseling,* pp. 123-24.

34. G. Puchinger, *Ontmoetingen met anti-revolutionairen* (Zutphen: Terra, [1981]), pp. 24-40. Peter van Rooden believes that Kuyper's greatest talent lay in his ability to create religious contradistinctions. *Religieuze regimes,* pp. 36-37.

Kuyper presented his *Lectures on Calvinism,* which display not only his learning but his journalistic and polemical talent.

In a parliamentary by-election in the district of Gouda on 21 January 1874, Kuyper presented himself as a candidate. The result was a decisive victory, with Kuyper winning a comfortable majority of the votes cast. He now had no choice but to resign from clerical orders, as clerics were constitutionally barred from parliamentary membership.

6. Member of Parliament

On 20 March 1874, at thirty-six years of age, Kuyper took the required oaths and assumed his seat in the Second Chamber in The Hague as the second youngest member of parliament. Contrary to the misgivings of some of his parishioners, he did not consider his change of career to be a forsaking of spiritual and religious concerns. He saw it, rather, as a means by which he could work, together with his anti-revolutionary colleagues, towards the reformation of society according to Christian principles, in areas beyond the range of his influence as an ordained minister. He was also determined not to neglect issues faced by the church — by means of his religious journalism, his position as elder of the church in Amsterdam, and his still frequent addresses to church congregations, he intended to carry on working for the reformation of the church along orthodox Protestant lines.

When Kuyper entered the Second Chamber in 1874 the anti-revolutionaries were small in number and fiercely opposed by both liberals and conservatives, the two main parliamentary factions. The anti-revolutionaries also lacked unity in their political objectives. Except for the "Schools Question" *(Schoolkwestie),* each anti-revolutionary member of parliament followed more or less his own course. Kuyper's efforts to weld this small and fragmented group into an effective working body met with only partial success. But by expounding and defending a clear and decisive position on the leading issues of the day, he did succeed in developing a distinctive political stance around which other anti-revolutionaries could gather.

On 7 December 1874 Kuyper delivered his first full-length parliamentary speech on the Schools Question, now one of the major issues faced by the government. In a similar vein to his speech in Utrecht five years earlier, he argued that education should be entirely autonomous, managed by a system of independent provincial and national education boards, rather than government agencies. Although the state had the right to legislate on general standards of education, it also had the duty to ensure the right of all parents to send their children to schools of their own choice. The following day, the liberal leader J. Kappeyne van de Coppello (1822-1895) entered into the debate, criticizing the anti-revolutionaries' argument that without free (autonomous) schools a minority group in society would be oppressed. He argued that no parents could claim to be acting responsibly if they withheld state education from their children, seeing that this education was provided free of charge. If parents decided to act irresponsibly in this way, then the minority group deserved to be oppressed, and to be treated as "the fly that ruins the ointment," because it would have forfeited the right to exist in Dutch society. Kuyper replied with a scathing attack on "state absolutism" and "liberalistic despotism," and followed up his arguments in a series of articles in *De Standaard*.[35]

7. Brighton and Breakdown

In the early summer of 1875 Kuyper visited England. The American evangelists Dwight L. Moody, Ira D. Sankey, and Robert Pearsall Smith were conducting evangelistic revival meetings at various venues in Britain and had invited Protestants from the European continent to attend a mass rally to be held at Brighton.[36] Kuyper, together with forty delegates from the Netherlands, including several Reformed ministers, accepted the invitation, and gave a report of his experiences in the Sunday supplement of *De Standaard*.[37] Some 8,000 delegates, half of them from

35. *Handelingen der Staten Generaal,* 7 and 8 December 1874. Kuyper's articles on the Schools Question were republished as six pamphlets before the 1875 elections and were later included as supplements in *Ons program.*

36. This invitation was sent personally to several prominent church leaders, including Kuyper, by P. J. Elout van Soeterwoude, a leader of the Dutch *Réveil* movement. Elout had encountered Pearsall Smith in 1874 and 1875 at conferences in Oxford arranged by Moody and Sankey and had entertained him at his home in the Netherlands in the company of members of the Dutch royal family, including Queen Sophie (1818-1877). See H. Krabbendam, 'Zielenverbrijzelaars en zondelozen: Reacties in de Nederlandse Pers op Moody, Sankey en Pearsall Smith, 1874-1878', *Documentatieblad voor de Nederlandse kerkgeschiedenis na 1800* 34 (1991): 39-58 (49-50).

37. *Zondagsblad van De Standaard,* 6 and 7 June 1875.

European countries outside the United Kingdom, attended addresses given by Pearsall Smith and Bible studies led by his wife, and took part in prayer meetings and revival services. Kuyper was impressed with what he saw and heard, describing the conference as a Bethel experience:

> Guilt and sin were never so deeply felt as there in the wonderful presence of the Lord. . . . Hardly a single harsh word could be heard during those days amongst all those thousands of people. Differences melted away. There was love for one another. God's power revealed itself not only around about us, but *in* and *through* the soul.[38]

When members of the Dutch delegation were asked to express their reaction to the conference in a sentence from scripture, before leaving for home, Kuyper replied: "My cup runneth over."[39] As the Dutch delegation formed 10 percent of the total number of foreign visitors, Kuyper entertained high hopes for the influence of this conference in the Netherlands.[40] Once back in the Netherlands he wrote a series of articles in the Sunday supplement of *De Standaard* on themes reminiscent of the Brighton conference, such as "The Sealing of the Elect," "Reformed Fasting," and "The Christian's Vows."

The last of these series ran for only a few weeks before it was suddenly terminated, due to a nervous breakdown Kuyper suffered in February 1876. It is likely that overwork was a main cause. Ever since his appointment to the church in Amsterdam he had worked incessantly on his sermons, newspaper articles, pamphlets, and parliamentary speeches. The relentless and often personal attacks from the powerful conservative and liberal factions, both in parliament and in the press, were added sources of stress, even though they were often a result of his own tactless and abrasive manner. His comparative youth, his clerical background, and his unfamiliarity with parliamentary culture only added to the severity of the opposition he faced. On his doctor's advice, he left the Netherlands to recuperate abroad. From Marseilles he wrote to his

38. *Zondagsblad van De Standaard,* 6 and 7 June 1875.

39. Recorded in Frank van den Berg, *Abraham Kuyper* (Grand Rapids: Eerdmans, 1960).

40. *Zondagsblad van De Standaard,* 6 and 7 June 1875. Later the same summer (5-6 August 1875), Kuyper held a reunion of Dutch delegates to the Brighton conference at his home in order to determine the course the so-called Brighton Movement should follow in the Netherlands. See Krabbendam, p. 52.

wife about the attacks from his parliamentary opponents: "Oh, Jo, God only knows what I have suffered in Holland. Every time I think about how they literally killed me, I burst out in tears."[41] Kuyper had obviously fallen very ill.

It is also likely that Kuyper's Brighton experience was one of the causes of his breakdown.[42] Rumors began to circulate early in 1876 that the reason Pearsall Smith had recently had to return to the United States and abandon his public ministry was that it had become known that he had been involved in an adulterous relationship while conducting his rallies in Britain. This would certainly have come as a blow to Kuyper, not only because it is clear from his articles that he reserved great admiration for Pearsall Smith, but also because following the conference he had entered into personal correspondence with him. In a lengthy response to an encouraging letter from Kuyper the evangelist wrote, soon after he arrived back in the States, about his concern for those Christians involved in "the carnal life" and about "the success of Satan in transforming himself into an angel of light before those more devoted souls who have escaped the grosser allurements of the world."[43]

At the end of a series of articles in *De Heraut* on "Perfectionism" in 1878, Kuyper distanced himself from the Brighton Movement, claiming it was a mixture of true and false elements, and that its influence in the Netherlands had run into dangerous Arminian waters. He acknowledged that his mistake in supporting and advocating the Movement had led to his breakdown.[44] Throughout the rest of his career he spent a great deal of energy confronting the pietistic and subjective tendencies of "Methodism," no less so when he set foot in Pearsall Smith's native America.[45]

41. Letter from Kuyper to Johanna, 20 February 1876. Cited in J. de Bruijn, *Abraham Kuyper,* p. 117.

42. The connection between Kuyper's breakdown and sudden departure and demise of Pearsall Smith as a result of the scandal was first suggested in 1876 in a letter to Groen from the *Réveil* leader G. H. de Marez Oyens. *Briefwisseling van Mr. G. Groen van Prinsterer IV (1866-1876),* ed. by A. Goslinga and J. L. van Essen ('s-Gravenhage: Zuid-Hollandsche Boek-en Handelsdrukkerij, 1967), p. 891.

43. KA; *Brieven,* no. 901 (13 September 1875).

44. The series appeared in *De Heraut* between 17 March and 4 August 1878, and was republished in Kuyper's *Uit het Woord,* 3 vols. (Amsterdam: Kruyt, 1873-1879), III, pp. 61-163.

45. His criticism of "Methodism" is prominent in his *The Work of the Holy Spirit,* which was translated into English soon after his visit to the United States. In

8. Organization of Forces

When Kuyper returned to the Netherlands in May 1877 it was almost a year since Groen van Prinsterer's death, which had left Kuyper as his only obvious successor as leader of the anti-revolutionaries. Having had time to reflect on the situation in the Netherlands while abroad, he pursued his strategy with renewed vision and vigor. He decided it was time to organize and consolidate the forces he had begun to unleash with the founding of *De Standaard* in 1872. In order to concentrate on this objective, he resigned his seat in parliament and resumed his editorship of *De Standaard,* which had been temporarily taken over by the anti-revolutionary politician A. F. de Savornin Lohman (1837-1924).[46] He also re-established *De Heraut* as a religious weekly newspaper, to replace the religious Sunday supplement to *De Standaard,* and became its chief editor. In the first issue of the newly formed *De Heraut,* which appeared on 7 December 1877, he indicated that he was still in a state of convalescence: "Pray, still have some patience with the sick man, now by God's grace recovering. But, with the past experience in mind, let no one expect that I should attempt to do more than I am able." His illness had obviously made clear to Kuyper where the limits of his endurance lay, and he resolved never again to take on more work than he could manage. From now on he would employ a rigid schedule in his work, in order to utilize his energies to their full potential. He did not suffer another breakdown.

Not long after his return to the Netherlands, the conflict over the Schools Question broke out once again. In March 1878, Kappeyne van de Coppello, who was leader of the liberal cabinet between 1877 and 1879, introduced a bill proposing wide-ranging educational reforms. Though the reforms in government-run schools would be financed by the state treasury, independent, or "special" schools would have to finance these themselves. The patrons of non-state schools would continue

---

a Preface written in 1899 specially for this translation he was careful to explain that when he used this term in the book he did not mean to refer to the church organization that bore that name (p. 6).

46. Kuyper's contact with Lohman in connection with the editorship of *De Standaard* was important as the start of a relationship of great significance for Kuyper's career. Although initially on friendly terms with Kuyper, Lohman was among several of Kuyper's anti-revolutionary colleagues who found it hard to accept that Kuyper should continue his struggle for anti-revolutionary principles in *De Standaard* rather than in parliament.

to pay for the entire cost of running their own schools, as well as helping to finance the state school system by the payment of taxes. Despite strong pleas from anti-revolutionaries and Catholics, on the basis that the financial burden on independent schools would become so unbearable that many would be forced into liquidation, the bill was approved by both chambers in the summer of 1878. Only the King's signature was required to make it law. At Kuyper's initiative, it had already been decided among the anti-revolutionary leadership that should the bill be passed by parliament, a petition would be organized, requesting King Willem III (1817-1890) not to sign the bill. A delegation would then present the petition to the King in person. In the three months that elapsed before the presentation of the petition, Kuyper's exceptional organizational and journalistic talents were displayed to the full. Daily in *De Standaard* he attacked the opponents of independent confessional schools, and he employed every other means available to him to do damage to his opponents and to awaken the consciences of the Reformed population to the plight of their children's education. Within five days of launching the petition, 305,000 signatures had been collected. A similar petition, drawn up by Roman Catholics, managed to obtain 164,000 signatures. These numbers are particularly impressive when set against the fact that at this time only 122,000 people had the right to vote for seats in the Second Chamber.[47]

The presentation of the petition to the King took place on 3 August 1878, at the royal palace *Het Loo*. Kuyper was not present among the delegation, the King having made it clear that he was not prepared to receive him. A fortnight later the royal signature was added to the bill, thus making it law. Although the petitions had thereby failed in their immediate purpose, they had demonstrated three things that would be particularly important for the future: the existence of a broad basis of support for non-state education, increasing cooperation between Catholics and Protestants, and the high level of support Kuyper and his fellow anti-revolutionary leaders could expect if the franchise were to be extended. They also, ironically, gave a powerful impulse to the founding of Christian schools, as well as encouraging the growth and development of the anti-revolutionary movement. In January the following year a society called *School met de Bijbel* (School with the Bible) was founded by

47. Figures taken from J. de Bruijn, *Abraham Kuyper*, p. 123.

anti-revolutionaries in order to preserve the enthusiasm aroused by the petition. Although not a political organization, it did exert considerable influence in political debate, and was a powerful and effective body in the extension of Christian education. It also helped to establish the organizational framework of the Anti-Revolutionary Party, which was founded a few months later on 3 April 1879. For a variety of reasons, therefore, the organization of the petition on education may be considered one of the most notable episodes in the history both of the ARP and of Dutch politics in general.[48]

The foundation of the Anti-Revolutionary Party as the first modern, organized, popular political party in the Netherlands was chiefly the work of Kuyper. Before 1879 political parties were no more than loosely associated groups of individuals holding certain political ideas and objectives in common. Groen van Prinsterer had been the leader of the anti-revolutionary "movement," or "faction," rather than of an organized party. Although he did not deny the need for organization, Groen had made no attempt to unite the members of this movement into a party on the basis of a common program. That task fell to Kuyper after Groen's death in 1876. Two years earlier, however, shortly before he became a member of parliament, Kuyper had drawn up a draft program of principles, and the contents of this document had received Groen's general approval. Following further elaborations and revisions, it was published in *De Standaard* on 3 January 1878 and was subsequently accepted by the anti-revolutionary voting societies *(kiesverenigingen)* in twenty-one cities. Kuyper proposed that the party leadership be entrusted to a single national committee and that all shades of anti-revolutionary opinion be welded into a unified and dynamic party formation. He also suggested the establishment of an effective network at local, regional, and national levels, a headquarters, a treasury, and various journalistic organs.

At the first national convention of the ARP on 3 April 1879, at which Kuyper presided, the assembled representatives adopted the proposed constitution and the Declaration of Principles, the party manifesto. The voting societies were amalgamated into a national federation and a

48. Kossmann, *The Low Countries,* p. 305; E. H. Kossmann, 'De groei van de anti-revolutionaire partij', in *Algemene Geschiedenis der Nederlanden,* 12 vols., ed. by J. A. van Houtte and others (Utrecht: De Haan, 1948-1958), XI, pp. 1-22; J. de Bruijn, *Een land nog niet in kaart gebracht: aspecten van het protestants-christelijk leven in Nederland in de jaren 1880-1940* (Amsterdam: Historisch Documentatiecentrum, 1987), pp. 35-36.

Central Committee was elected with Kuyper as chairman. Kuyper thereby became the acknowledged leader of the ARP, a position he held until his death in 1920, except for a break in 1905-1907, when he took leave abroad. The journalistic leader of the anti-revolutionaries had become the officially recognized political leader. In terms of Dutch political history, an important stage had once again been reached. From now on, the ARP would exert a powerful influence in political life, and with its sophisticated organizational structure, its clearly defined principles, and its comprehensive manifesto it would be a force to be reckoned with in the life of the nation. It also set the pattern for all future party political organization at a time when no other party possessed an organizational apparatus or a clearly defined political program. As the result of Kuyper's initiative, party politics would now no longer be the concern of parliamentarians only but of all members of the public, whether or not they had the right to vote.[49]

Kuyper continued with the exposition of the anti-revolutionary manifesto he had begun in 1878 in a series of articles in *De Standaard,* published in 1879 in book form under the title *Ons program,* originally containing around 1,250 pages but reduced the following year to around 400. He made it clear that his exposition of the manifesto was not to be considered the only orthodox or authoritative one, and that party unity was based on the manifesto itself rather than on any exposition of it. Nevertheless, *Ons program,* written in a self-assured, authoritative style, had considerable influence for many years, both inside and outside anti-revolutionary circles.

9. University Founder

It was not only Kuyper's political achievements but his activities as founder of a university and as a professor of theology that attracted the attention of the theologians at Princeton when they came to select a Stone Lecturer. When Kuyper founded the ARP in 1879 there were three universities in the Netherlands, situated in Leiden, Utrecht, and Groningen, all three controlled by the state. Discontent had been growing for a number of years

49. Van Rooden typifies Kuyper as a pioneer of mass politics in the Netherlands. *Religieuze regimes,* pp. 34-37. See also my "The Politics of Abraham Kuyper in Historical Perspective," *Christianity and History* 8 (1991): 9-12.

among Catholics and orthodox Protestants about the predominance of theologians belonging to the Groningen and modernistic schools within the theology faculties of these universities. This discontent gave birth in the early 1870s to plans, in which Kuyper was involved, to establish a Christian college of higher education, based on broadly defined Protestant principles. The task looked a daunting one and the plans were eventually scrapped. But in 1876 parliament passed a bill on higher education, introduced by J. Heemskerk, a conservative member of parliament and leader of the Dutch cabinet from 1874 to 1877, which would make it easier for institutions of higher education to be established. It reaffirmed the principle of the freedom of education, stipulated in the constitution of 1848, and prescribed how and on what conditions non-state universities could be established. It did not, however, accord the legal status of *effectus civilis* to the degrees and diplomas awarded by such institutions, meaning that their graduates would have to pass examinations at the state universities in order to validate their degrees.

The Heemskerk law had been passed while Kuyper was convalescing abroad after his nervous breakdown, during which time he had given much serious thought to the issue of higher education in the Netherlands. On his return to the Netherlands he no longer entertained the idea of a college founded on a broad basis of Protestant principles. He now resolved to push for the establishment of a university that would be based squarely on Reformed principles and entirely free of state control.

On 5 December 1878 the Society for Higher Education on the basis of Reformed Principles *(Vereniging voor Hooger Onderwijs op Gereformeerden Grondslag)* was founded, calling in its manifesto for all Reformed Christians in the country to support the establishment of a new university. This university would be "free" from state control, hence the name Free University *(Vrije Universiteit);* it would be Calvinistic in its underlying principles and national in character. It had been Calvinists, the Society's manifesto declared, who had secured the liberation of the Netherlands from Spanish tyranny in the sixteenth century and had been responsible for the formation of Dutch national character. The Free University was to possess and reflect this same Calvinistic character and develop Calvinism's glorious heritage. By June 1879 the Society had elected the directors and trustees of the new university, and on 6 September they appointed Kuyper and F. L. Rutgers (1836-1917) to the chairs of theology.

It did not take long for fierce opposition to break out against the plans to establish the Free University, particularly from the Ethical theologians, whom Kuyper had originally hoped would cooperate. A pamphlet war ensued between Kuyper and two of their representatives, A. W. Bronsveld and J. J. van Toorenenbergen, who argued against the founding of an exclusively Reformed university. They advocated instead the establishment of "special" orthodox Protestant chairs at the state universities — an option made available in the 1876 law — in order to counterbalance the liberal, modernistic theological education provided by these universities. Disappointed by the antagonism of the Ethicals, but determined to see his plans succeed, Kuyper pressed ahead with preparations for the launch of the new university. He made visits to several Dutch cities in order to address meetings, answer objections, confer with anti-revolutionary colleagues, and encourage financial and moral support for the project from all who called themselves Reformed. Eventually, on 20 October 1880, the Free University was officially opened in the *Nieuwe Kerk* in Amsterdam, accompanied by all due pomp and ceremony. As its first Rector Magnificus, Kuyper delivered the inaugural address, introducing in it the leading idea of his sociopolitical thought, which has characterized neo-Calvinist political theory ever since.[50]

The opening of the Free University represents one of the high points in Kuyper's career. In the two years since planning for the university had first begun, he had succeeded in persuading the orthodox Protestant sector of the population, not noted for its academic interests, social standing, or financial resources (he often referred to its members as the *kleine luyden,* the "little people"), that the founding and financing of an independent university was a worthwhile enterprise. Given the university's charitable status, slender budget, meager resources, and fierce opposition from many sides, it was an enterprise not without considerable risks to Kuyper's credibility and reputation, even in the eyes of his most devoted followers. Similar to the effect of the founding of the ARP in the political realm, Kuyper's founding of the Free University radically altered the shape of higher education in the Netherlands, which came to be organized on religious and ideological lines.

50. A. Kuyper, *Souvereiniteit in eigen kring. Rede ter inwijding van de Vrije Universiteit, den 20sten October 1880 gehouden in het Koor der Nieuwe Kerk te Amsterdam door Dr. A. Kuyper* (Amsterdam: Kruyt, 1880). An almost complete translation of this speech can be found in the Appendix to Kobes's "Sphere Sovereignty and the University." See Chapter Six for a discussion of the "souvereiniteit in eigen kring" (sphere-sovereignty) idea.

10. 1880-1898

During the 1880s and 1890s Kuyper reached the peak of his intellectual powers, and it was during this period, prior to his visit to Princeton, that he published his most significant works. Four of these were the special lectures he gave as Rector Magnificus of the Free University in 1881, 1888, 1892, and 1899. Like the *Lectures on Calvinism,* these addresses were aimed at an academic audience, they were of a learned yet polemical and programmatic style, and they sought to address wide intellectual and cultural issues. In order, they dealt with the rise of biblical criticism in the study of theology; symbolism in the area of art; pantheism in religion; and evolutionism in science and philosophy.[51] This period also saw the production of a large number of theological works under Kuyper's name. These usually appeared first in weekly instalments in *De Heraut* before being collected and published in book form. They were intended for the non-specialist, and represent a form of well-informed but popular theology. They included lengthy treatments of the doctrine of the Holy Spirit, the Heidelberg Catechism, the doctrine of common grace, and Reformed liturgy.[52] The only formal academic treatise during

51. A. Kuyper, *De hedendaagse Schriftcritiek in hare bedenkelijke strekking voor de Gemeente des levenden Gods: rede, bij het overdragen van het rectoraat der Vrije Universiteit, gehouden den 20sten october 1881* (Amsterdam: Kruyt, 1881) [English translation "The Biblical Criticism of the Present Day," *Bibliotheca Sacra* 61 (1904): 409-42, 666-88]; A. Kuyper, *Het calvinisme en de kunst: rede bij de overdracht van het rectoraat der Vrije Universiteit op 20 october 1888* (Amsterdam: Wormser, 1888) [Translated extract "Calvinism and Art," *Christian Thought* 9 (1892); A. Kuyper, *De verflauwing der grenzen: rede bij de overdracht van het rectoraat aan de Vrije Universiteit, oktober 1892* (Amsterdam: Wormser, 1892) [English translation *Pantheism's Destruction of Boundaries* (n.p., n.pub., 1893), reprinted from an article with the same title in *Methodist Review* 75 (1893): 520-37, 762-78; A. Kuyper, *Evolutie: rede bij de overdracht van het rectoraat aan de Vrije Universiteit op 20 October 1899 gehouden* (Amsterdam: Höveker & Wormser, 1899) [English translation "Evolution," translation coordinated by Clarence Menninga, *Calvin Theological Journal* 31 (1996): 11-50].

52. The titles of these works, together with the years in which they appeared in *De Heraut,* are as follows: *Het werk van den Heiligen Geest* (Kampen: Kok, 1888-1889) [English translation *The Work of the Holy Spirit.* With an introduction by B. B. Warfield (New York: Funk and Wagnalls, 1900. Reprinted by Eerdmans in 1975)], in *De Heraut* 1883-1886; *E Voto Dordraceno: toelichting op den Heidelbergschen Catechismus,* 4 vols. (Amsterdam: Wormser, 1892-1895), in *De Heraut* 1892-1895; *De gemeene gratie,* 3 vols. (Amsterdam: Höveker & Wormser, 1902-1905), in *De Heraut* 1895-1901; *Onze eeredienst* (Kampen: Kok, 1911), in *De Heraut* 1897-1901.

this period, apart from the five-volume collection of notes made by students of Kuyper on his lectures on dogmatics, published in 1907, was his *Encyclopaedie,* his three-volume *magnum opus.*[53] It is a remarkable fact that, given Kuyper's significance for the development of Reformed theology, this was his only work of systematic theology, and indeed his only strictly academic work besides his doctoral dissertation and his publication of à Lasco's works. His plans to produce a major systematic treatment of dogmatics were never realized.

During this period Kuyper also published a great number of meditative and devotional works, which also first appeared as series in *De Heraut.* Bearing such expressive titles as "Honey from the Rock" and "Days of Glad Tidings," these works were designed to edify rather than instruct the faithful, and ensured that Kuyper was regarded by his followers not only as their leader in the area of church and politics but also as their spiritual counselor and guide.[54] Many of these works appeared in several editions, and were particularly popular among Kuyper's followers in the immigrant Dutch communities in the United States, where a number of them were translated and published in English after his death.[55] The renowned Dutch Reformed theologian K. H. Miskotte (1894-1976), who was by no means a follower of Kuyper, once wrote that seldom had anyone meditated so fervently as Kuyper.[56] As a rather irregular attender of church, Kuyper often wrote his meditations in the quietness of his own home on a Sunday morning.

Despite his irregular church attendance, this period in Kuyper's career is marked by his efforts toward ecclesiastical reform. He argued persistently for the maintenance of the traditional creeds, the abolition of synodical government, and the admittance of theology graduates from the Free University into the ordained ministry of the *Hervormde Kerk.* When these demands were blocked by the church authorities, he wrote

53. Rasker has called this work "the high point of the Calvinistic revival" of the nineteenth century. Rasker, p. 198.

54. *Honig uit den rotssteen,* 2 vols. (Amsterdam: Wormser, 1880-1883); *Dagen van goede boodschap,* 4 vols. (Amsterdam: Wormser, 1887-1888).

55. These translations include: *To Be Near to God* (Grand Rapids: Eerdmans & Sevensma, 1918); *Keep Thy Solemn Feasts* (Grand Rapids: Eerdmans, 1928); *When Thou Sittest in Thy House* (Grand Rapids: Eerdmans, 1929); *Women of the Old Testament* (Grand Rapids: Zondervan, 1979. 25th reprint); *Women of the New Testament.* 6th edition (Grand Rapids: Zondervan, 1979, 28th reprint).

56. J. de Bruijn, *Abraham Kuyper,* p. 159.

a strongly worded pamphlet in which he defended the right of church reform.[57] The publication of this pamphlet in 1883, timed to coincide with the four hundredth anniversary of Luther's birth, marked the start of an involved and turbulent three-year episode that resulted in a schism from the *Hervormde Kerk* in 1886. Out of this schism, known as the *Doleantie* ("Lament" or "Protest"), which took place under Kuyper's leadership, emerged a new confederation of churches known as the *Nederduitsche Gereformeerde Kerken.* Events came to a climax the same year that Kuyper, Rutgers, and seventy-eight other members of the synod of Amsterdam were officially suspended from the *Hervormde Kerk.* Although many congregations were in sympathy with the *Doleerenden* of Amsterdam, they had reservations about leaving the mother church, and Kuyper met with grave disappointment when few congregations responded to his suspension by joining the *Doleantie.* He nevertheless managed to bring things to a head by inviting delegates from among his potential supporters who still remained within the *Hervormde Kerk* to a conference in Amsterdam in January 1887, where on entry they were asked to sign a declaration rejecting the "yoke" of the synodical government of the *Hervormde Kerk.* Such an act of defiance afforded the opponents of the *Doleerenden* the opportunity to take action nationwide and to suspend the offenders, eventually driving them out of the church and into the waiting arms of the other *Doleerende* churches. The scope of the *Doleantie* is difficult to judge precisely, but the spread was rapid, so that by 1889 two hundred congregations, numbering 180,000 members, and around seventy-six ministers had joined the *Nederduitsche Gereformeerde Kerken.*[58] Kuyper did not succeed, however, in uniting all the orthodox within the church under his leadership. He did manage to unite most of the congregations that had left the *Hervormde Kerk* in 1834 as part of an earlier secession known as the *Afscheiding* (Secession) with his own *Doleerende* congregations in 1892 to form the *Gereformeerde Kerken in Nederland.* But many of the so-called "ultra-orthodox" congregations refused to join, some pre-

57. A. Kuyper, *Tractaat van de reformatie der kerken, aan de zonen der reformatie hier te lande op Luther's vierde eeuwfeest aangeboden* (Amsterdam: Höveker, 1883).

58. Wintle, p. 56; J. van Putten, *Zoveel kerken zoveel zinnen: een sociaal-wetenschappelijke studie van verschillen in behoudendheid tussen Gereformeerden en Christelijke Gereformeerden* (Kampen: Kok, 1968), pp. 204-5; G. J. Schutte, 'Over '86 en '92 en daarna: Kuypers gereformeerde wereld herdacht', *Bijdragen en mededelingen betreffende de geschiedenis der Nederland* 110 (1995): 515-47.

ferring to remain within the *Hervormde Kerk.* Kuyper's colleague at the Free University from 1880 to 1887, the theologian P. J. Hoedemaker (1839-1910), upon whose support Kuyper relied, refused to leave the mother church or to support the *Doleantie,* as a result of which many even among the orthodox of Amsterdam determined to be loyal to the *Hervormde Kerk.*[59]

Kuyper's political involvement as leader of the ARP continued simultaneously with his professorship at the Free University and his efforts towards church reform. An important new development during this period was the increasing desire amongst Kuyper and his anti-revolutionary colleagues to cooperate with Roman Catholics in politics, who were led by Herman Schaepman (1844-1903), a Catholic priest and member of parliament from 1880.[60] Such cooperation did not come naturally to Kuyper and his followers, given the considerable anti-papism that circulated in orthodox Protestant circles. But on social, political, and educational issues they shared a good deal of common ground with Catholics, and neither the anti-revolutionaries nor the Catholic party could expect to gain a majority in the Second Chamber unless they cooperated with each other. Kuyper had already argued in a series of articles between 1873 and 1875 that although anti-revolutionary and Catholic politicians were to retain their own organizational structures, they must agree to cooperate on specific political issues.[61] This argument was adopted as official ARP policy in 1887 at the party's annual convention, and in the general election of 1888, anti-revolutionaries and Catholics won a majority of the seats, allowing them to form the first anti-revolutionary/Catholic coalition cabinet, which took office the same year under the Prime Ministership of anti-revolutionary member of parliament Aeneas baron Mackay (1839-1909).[62] As minister of internal

59. Rasker, p. 256; Wintle, p. 57.

60. Kuyper's admiration of contemporary Roman Catholicism is discussed in Chapter Nine.

61. These articles were first published in *De Standaard* and later in Kuyper's brochure *Rome and Dordt* (Amsterdam: De Hoogh, 1879).

62. In 1888 the Second Chamber of 100 seats had 27 anti-revolutionary and 26 Roman Catholic members. In 1896 Schaepman united Catholics in politics in the *Rooms-Katholieke Staatspartij,* whose program was based on the papal encyclical *Rerum novarum* of 1891. For a collection of articles on the Mackay cabinet, see *Het Kabinet-Mackay: Opstellen over de eerste Christelijke coalitie (1888-1891),* ed. by T. B. F. H. Brinkel, J. de Bruijn, and A. Postma (Baarn: Arbor, 1990).

affairs, Mackay introduced a bill on primary education that made possible the partial subsidy of private education, thus making a modest start towards the resolution of the Schools Question. A second important law to be passed during the Mackay government, introduced by the Catholic Minister of Justice Ruijs van Beerenbroek, outlawed excessive labor by women and children. Despite these two important political achievements, Kuyper was not impressed with cabinet policy, which he thought adhered too loosely to anti-revolutionary principles. He applied the same criticism to the anti-revolutionary parliamentary group under the leadership of De Savornin Lohman, expressing his reservations openly in *De Standaard.* This created tension and estrangement between the two leaders; Lohman felt he ought to be able to count on Kuyper's support. The seriousness of this tension, which mounted with time, became manifest in 1894 when Lohman led a split away from the ARP. Differences in personality and style played an important role, and it was in this division that the dark sides of Kuyper's personality were most clearly revealed. Kuyper's domineering attitude towards his followers contrasted sharply with Lohman's insistence on freedom in the formation of anti-revolutionary opinion and an aversion to party discipline. Whereas Lohman had the aptitude and patience for protracted and careful debate, no doubt a part of his background as a lawyer, Kuyper remained essentially the Reformed minister, who as a proclaimer of the Word, tolerated little contradiction. He insisted on acceptance of the authority and discipline of the party.[63] Lohman was not inclined to accept strict allegiance to programs and dogmas, and he had a natural dislike of tactics and strategic planning. He adopted an open-minded attitude to political issues, in contrast to Kuyper's calculated and tactical approach, which was aimed at the realization of preconceived objectives and was often opportunistic, with the end justifying the means.[64] The judicial, empirical background and personality of Lohman, who tended to adopt a pragmatic approach to the realities of politics, grated with Kuyper's romantic approach, by which he aimed to form reality according to his own will, whatever the cost to party unity.

63. Lohman expressed his preference for principle above party loyalty in his brochure *Partij of beginsel?,* published in 1892.

64. In a letter to Kuyper, Lohman wrote: "I am an enemy of tactics and scheming," and he once called Kuyper, because of his tactical approach, "the greatest actor I have met in the field of politics." Quoted in J. de Bruijn, *Een land,* p. 41.

The direct cause of the split was a difference in opinion between Kuyper and Lohman on the franchise reforms proposed in a parliamentary bill of 1892. While Kuyper claimed that this bill, introduced by a liberal member of parliament and proposing universal male suffrage, came close to the anti-revolutionary ideal of household suffrage, Lohman and nine other anti-revolutionary members of parliament were fiercely opposed to it. Kuyper's position was, however, adopted by the ARP as official policy, forcing Lohman and his supporters out of the party. Following the elections of 1894, they formed a new parliamentary faction of "free anti-revolutionaries," which eventually became part of the *Christelijk-Historische Unie* (Christian Historical Union), a new political party in competition with the ARP. Representatives of this faction were generally members of the *Hervormde Kerk* (even though Lohman himself remained *Gereformeerd*), and were often influenced by the ideas of Hoedemaker, Kuyper's opponent in the *Doleantie,* a fact which indicates that the political break of 1894 was related to the ecclesiastical break of 1886. Many anti-revolutionaries who had remained loyal to the *Hervormde Kerk* in 1886 took the opportunity in 1894 once again to distance themselves from Kuyper, the man who, in their eyes, had done so much harm, and who now had to pay the political price.[65]

The twenty-fifth anniversary celebrations of the founding of *De Standaard,* on 1 April 1897, present a picture of the kind of man Kuyper had become by the time he made his visit to the United States. At these celebrations, attended by a total of five thousand people, Kuyper gave a speech that ended with the singing of a poem he had written about the aim of his life. Although he was not given to verse, it does provide an insight into the motives Kuyper himself considered to dominate his career at this point:

> For me, one desire rules my life
> One urge drives soul and will. . . .
> It is to re-establish God's holy ordinances
> In church and home, in state and school,
> Regardless of the world's protestations,
> For the benefit of the nation.
> It is to engrave those divine ordinances,

65. J. de Bruijn, *Een land,* p. 46.

To which Word and Creation witness,
So clearly on the nation
That once again it bows its knee to God.[66]

In the memorial book that was published to mark the occasion *(Gedenkboek),* extracts from articles in other newspapers marking the occasion were reproduced. Many tributes were paid to Kuyper's journalistic capacities, including one from Schaepman who wrote: "As a journalist Dr. Kuyper is the opponent of the great principles which I am privileged to serve. In a world in which one does not live without opponents I am grateful for such an opponent."[67] Lohman wrote that although he was unable to agree with the opinions Kuyper expressed in *De Standaard,* "this need not and must not hinder us in honouring the extraordinary talents which have allowed the editor of that newspaper to take up a place of honour, or rather *the* place of honour among our journalists."[68] The admiration shown by Kuyper's opponents for his journalistic and literary skills made an obvious impression on Warfield, who wrote in his journal:

> If one desires to know how Dr. Kuyper is really esteemed in Holland today, he should consult the *Gedenkboek,* published last year, commemorating his quarter-centennial of his editorship of *De Standaard.* On this occasion men of all parties united to do him the honour they all felt he had most richly earned.[69]

From the many extracts, articles, and comments recorded in the memorial book, a picture emerges of a man with a powerful and dominant personality, a broad and encyclopedic knowledge, a lively and engaging style, a pedagogic and polemical talent, an inexhaustible reserve of vitality and energy, an aptitude for inspiring, mobilizing, and organizing large numbers of people with constructive capacity and tactical ingenuity. By such characteristics Kuyper had formed and led the orthodox Dutch Protestants, who acknowledged and honored him as a prophetic leader who had led them "out of the house of

66. *Gedenkboek,* pp. 67-68.

67. *Gedenkboek,* p. 109.

68. *Gedenkboek,* pp. 89-90.

69. From Warfield's introduction to W. H. de Savornin Lohman's "Dr. Abraham Kuyper" in *The Presbyterian and Reformed Review* (p. 562).

bondage."[70] By 1898, therefore, when he ascended the rostrum in Princeton to deliver the Stone Lectures, Kuyper the theologian had become a formidable and accomplished communicator, journalist, and politician with few equals among his contemporaries.

70. This was the title of a speech Kuyper gave in 1912: *Uit het diensthuis geleid* (Kampen: Kok, 1912).

Kuyper's Visit to the United States of America

Kuyper was in a pensive mood when he arrived by ship in New York harbor. Six weeks later, on 10 October, he opened his Stone Lectures at Princeton with the words:

> A traveller from the old European Continent, disembarking on the shore of this New World, feels as the Psalmist says, that "His thoughts crowd upon him like a multitude." Compared with the eddying waters of your new stream of life, the old stream in which he was moving seems almost frostbound and dull; and here, on American ground, for the first time, he realises how so many divine potencies . . . are now beginning to disclose their inward splendour, thus developing a still richer store of surprises for the future. (LC, p. 9)

Whereas the previous chapter presented a picture of Kuyper's career in the Netherlands, part of the "old stream" as he called it, this chapter will seek to portray him in the "new stream"—the America in which he gave the Stone Lectures. A picture will be constructed, using extant contemporary documents, of Kuyper's image or "vision" of America, a vision which dominated the speeches and interviews he gave during his four months there, and which is crucial in interpreting the *Lectures on Calvinism.* Placed in its broader historical and intellectual context, this picture will help to explain the background and motivation of some of the leading ideas presented in the *Lectures.* First, however, in order to add to an understanding of the nature and purpose of the *Lectures,* it will be useful to take a brief look at the events that led to Kuyper's trip across the Atlantic.[1]

1. Preparations for Princeton

As editor of *De Standaard* and *De Heraut,* both of which had regular sections on foreign news, Kuyper kept abreast of political and ecclesiastical developments in the United States. Conversely, Dutch immigrants were able to remain informed about developments in their mother country, as both newspapers were distributed in the Dutch-American communities. Chiefly as a result of this exchange of views and information, Kuyper received a large number of letters from American followers and admirers, the majority of which were concerned with immigration problems and with theological and educational issues.[2] B. B. Warfield was among Kuyper's correspondents, together with his younger colleague at Princeton, Geerhardus Vos (1862-1947), whose admiration of Kuyper equalled Warfield's. He wrote to Kuyper from Princeton: "Your work for the Lord and for Reformed theology and the Reformed churches is highly esteemed here, and we thankfully enjoy the fruits that accrue to our use, the latest being your beautiful Encyclopedia *[Encyclopaedie].*"[3]

1. Accounts of Kuyper's visit to the United States can be found in: C. A. Admiraal, 'De Amerikaanse reis van Abraham Kuyper: een verwaarloosd aspect uit de geschiedschrijving over Kuyper' in *Historicus in het spanningsveld van theorie en praktijk: opstellen aangeboden aan Dr. H. Klompmaker ter gelegenheid van zijn veertigjarig studieleiderschap bij de opleiding M. O.-Geschiedenis,* ed. by C. A. Admiraal, P. B. M. Blaas, and J. van der Zande (Leiderdorp: Leidse Onderwijsinstellingen, 1985), pp. 111-64; J. Stellingwerff, *Dr. Abraham Kuyper en de Vrije Universiteit* (Kampen: Kok, 1987), pp. 253-81. The title of Admiraal's article indicates the lack of attention given to this subject. It may be translated thus: "Abraham Kuyper's Trip to America: A Neglected Aspect in the Historiography on Kuyper." See also C. A. Admiraal, 'Abraham Kuyper en de Amerikaanse Revolutie', *Spiegel Historiael* 11 (1976): 426-33; Marianne L. Mooijweer, 'Een voorlijke erfgenaam van Nederland: Abraham en Henriette Kuyper over Amerika', *Spiegel Historiael* 24 (1989): 310-15; Dirk Jellema, "Kuyper's visit to America in 1898," *Michigan History* 42 (1958): 227-36; George Harinck, 'Drie Nederlandse theologen zien Amerika', *Transparant* 6 (1995): 34-42.

2. Kuyper's archive contains over a hundred letters from American correspondents before his visit to the States in 1898.

3. Letter from Vos to Kuyper, 30 April 1896. Vos's letters to Kuyper contain many expressions of appreciation. When Vos was only twenty-four he wrote to

Such admiration and esteem lay behind the invitation to Kuyper to receive an honorary doctorate in divinity at Princeton in 1896. As the invitation explained, the degree would be bestowed at the University's inauguration ceremonies, the occasion being the 150th anniversary of the founding of the College of New Jersey, from which the new university had sprung, on 22 October of that year. In an accompanying letter, Francis J. Patton, the appointed president of the new university, explained that the doctorate could be in law instead of theology and requested that Kuyper should give a guest lecture to the university.[4] To the great disappointment of Warfield and Vos, however, Kuyper declined the invitation on the grounds that matters concerning the *Gereformeerde* churches demanded his full attention.[5] They responded by inviting him to come the following year, but because he planned to put himself forward as a candidate in the 1897 Dutch general election, he asked to be able to come in 1898. At the same time he accepted an invitation from the seminary faculty to present the Stone Lectures—on a theological subject of his own choice—for the academic year 1898-1899, and an invitation from the university to receive an honorary doctorate in law.[6]

Kuyper began work on his Stone Lectures in the New Year of 1898, choosing "Calvinism" as the general theme. After completing the text in Dutch he translated it into English and then sent it to America to be corrected by N. M. Steffens, a lecturer at Dubuque, Iowa. When Steffens sent back the corrected version he pointed out the difficulty of his task, due to Kuyper's style of expression: "You are so terribly original, so strongly individualistic."[7] Kuyper added the final touches to the English text with

---

Kuyper: "both directly and indirectly your labors have exerted a moulding influence on me." Letter from Vos to Kuyper, 28 May 1886. Warfield's admiration of Kuyper was noted in Chapter One. For a discussion of Vos and Warfield's respective approaches to theological method, see Richard Lints, "Two Theologies or One? Warfield and Vos on the Nature of Theology," *Westminster Theological Journal* 54 (1992): 235-53. Vos was America's foremost evangelical spokesperson for and advocate of biblical theology as a theological discipline. The closeness of the relationship between Vos and Warfield is reflected in their reputedly year-long habit of taking midday walks together along a street close to the seminary (Lints, p. 243 [note 33]).

4. See KA; *Brieven,* nos. 5794 and 5862.

5. Letter from Vos to Kuyper, 11 July 1896.

6. Letter from Vos to Kuyper, 9 October 1896.

7. KA; *Brieven,* no. 6258 (30 January 1898).

the help of Miss Ethel Ashton, a resident governess who taught English to Kuyper's daughters, and who recorded the activity in her memoirs:

> Dr Kuyper was a formidable worker. His energy and motivation had such an effect on me that I often sat proof-reading until four o'clock in the morning in order to have them ready by nine o'clock. He was so inspiring, he had such vitality, and he always knew *exactly* what he wanted to say, and this had to be understood to the finest *nuance.* I had to find the one and only correct word, and no other. Sometimes I proposed up to ten or twelve versions of a sentence before I had found the exact words he needed. But once the right words had been found, how he revelled in them! . . . In their final form, which had cost so much effort to establish, the lectures satisfied him completely. For me this was the best kind of reward. But he gave me — and as his present it still belongs to my most precious possessions — a big red book, one of the ten specially bound copies of the lectures. Inside he had written with his own hand: "To Miss Ashton, presented by the author, in thankful remembrance of her linguistic guidance." The following day he left for America — and, oh, the emptiness of the days that followed![8]

On 20 August 1898, after a short visit to London, Kuyper embarked for New York from Liverpool aboard the luxury passenger liner the *RMS Lucania.* On board the ship, which had a library, he consulted works on the history of the United States, including those by the American historians George Bancroft and Henry Cabot Lodge, both of whom emphasized the influence of Calvinism in the history of the United States.[9] The fact that the final text of Kuyper's Stone Lectures includes references to these works indicates that his reading of them on the boat was

8. Cited in H. S. S. Kuyper and J. H. Kuyper, *Herinneringen van de oude garde* (Amsterdam: Ten Have, 1922), pp. 173-79.

9. KA; *Amerika,* no. 52. From notes Kuyper made on the *Lucania's* letterheaded paper it is clear that he consulted George Bancroft's *History of the United States of America* (New York: Appleton, 1891), II; and Henry Cabot Lodge, *Alexander Hamilton* (Boston: Houghton Mifflin, 1892). This was not Kuyper's first acquaintance with Bancroft's work, as evident from his "Calvinism: The Origin and Safeguard of Our Constitutional Liberties," trans. by J. H. de Vries, *Bibliotheca Sacra* (July and October, 1895): 385-410, 645-74 (p. 386) [Original Dutch version: *Het calvinisme: oorsprong en waarborg onzer constitutioneele vrijheden: een Nederlandsche gedachte* (Amsterdam: Van der Land, 1874)]; and from his *Het calvinisme en de kunst: rede bij de overdracht van het rectoraat der Vrije Universiteit op 20 october 1888* (Amsterdam: Wormser, 1888), p. 78 (note 86).

in preparation for his visit to Princeton.[10] The significance of these and other writers for Kuyper's understanding of America will be discussed later on in this chapter.

The *Lucania* arrived in New York harbor on 27 August 1898. Before heading off for a vacation in the Adirondacks, a mountain range north of Albany, Kuyper stayed in New York City, at the Fifth Avenue Hotel in Madison Square. During his stay he contacted the publishers of his *Encyclopedia,* which had just appeared, in order to interest them in the publication of the text of his Stone Lectures, of which he gave them a sample copy. When they returned the copy to him two weeks later at Princeton, they included a disappointing reply, and one which indicates that they had misjudged the potential popularity of the *Lectures:* "We have not read the Lectures in full but from such examination as we could give them [we] have reluctantly come to the conclusion that their sale in book form is too uncertain to justify us in undertaking an American edition." They were prepared, however, to reconsider their decision should Kuyper's *Encyclopedia* prove to sell well.[11] Undeterred, Kuyper succeeded before leaving the United States in securing the agreement of another company in New York, Fleming H. Revell, to publish an English edition.[12] He also visited the Public Library in the center of Manhattan, where he consulted a copy of F. B. Hough's *American Constitutions,* and he worked the notes he made into the text of his lectures for Princeton.[13] Having now made several changes to the text of his lectures, he sent the emended manuscripts to Warfield at Princeton with the request that they should be speedily translated into English. Because of the changes he had made, and despite the laborious efforts of Ethel Ashton, he now required that the entire text of his lectures should be translated once more.

Time was very short indeed, and a handwritten inscription by Warfield in the copy of the Stone Lectures kept in the archives of Princeton Seminary informs the reader how the text came into existence.

10. LC, pp. 15, 78, 87.

11. KA; *Amerika,* no. 14.

12. KA; *Amerika,* no. 46. This edition appeared in 1899, and has exactly the same text (albeit a different subtitle) as the English edition published jointly the same year by Revell (New York), Höveker and Wormser (Amsterdam), T. & T. Clark (Edinburgh), and Simpkin, Marshall, Hamilton, and Kent (London). See bibliography.

13. F. B. Hough, *American Constitutions* (Albany: Weed Parsons, 1872); KA; *Amerika,* no. 58; Portfolio 9, nos. 12, 14, 48, and loose notes; LC, p. 86.

It is an interesting scenario, shedding light not only on the background to the actual text of the *Lectures* and on the differences between the various versions, but on the self-assured way in which Kuyper worked; it is therefore quoted at length:

> The "Stone Lectures" in Princeton Theological Seminary were delivered in the autumn of 1898 by Dr. A Kuyper, of the Free University of Amsterdam. About ten days before the lectures were to begin Dr. Kuyper sent his Dutch ms. and asked that it might be translated for his use. In the short time remaining it seemed necessary to engage more than one hand at the task and the following gentlemen kindly undertook to render the several lectures into English: the Rev. J. H. de Vries, pastor of the Second Presbyterian Church, Princeton, who translated Lectures I and V; the Rev. A. H. Huizinga, P. D. of Fishkirk, N.Y., who translated Lecture II; the Revd. Professor Henry E. Dosker D.D. of Holland, Michigan, who translated lecture III; the Revd. Professor N. M. Steffens of Dubuque, Iowa, who translated Lecture IV; and the Rev. D. G. Vos of Princeton, who translated Lecture VI. The translated text was then set on type at Princeton and the printed sheets provided to Dr. Kuyper for use in the rostrum.
>
> Only a dozen copies were taken off the types — of which the following is one. Before the Lectures were issued to the public in English (New York: Fleming H. Revell Co., 1899), the text was much altered by Dr. Kuyper himself with a view to bettering the English, but with the effect of waning it sadly. . . .
>
> These sheets are worthy of presentation . . . as a souvenir of an interesting occasion, and as a means of communicating the labor of love of the gentlemen who permitted themselves to be hurried through the task of translating these lectures for the use of the lecturer on the rostrum.

It is a tribute to the skill of the translators that, despite the hybrid origins of the English text and the speed with which it was made ready, its expression and style are accurate and consistent throughout. There are no stylistic differences between the lectures themselves that can be attributed to their several translators.

Having sent off his Dutch manuscript to Princeton, Kuyper set off for his break in the mountains. Although little is known about this vacation, Kuyper did record some of his impressions in his *Varia Americana,* a collection of essays on various aspects of American life as he had observed and encountered them on his American tour.[14] He was obviously struck by the prosperity and technical advancement of American life, and he noted the high standards of luxury and efficiency maintained on the steamboats and in the hotels.[15] Kuyper's firsthand encounter with American prosperity served to reinforce his idea that America's material greatness was a product of the Calvinism on which the country had been founded.

2. Visit to Princeton

After some anxiety at Princeton as to whether Kuyper would arrive on time — an anxiety he tried to allay by sending a telegram of reassurance — Kuyper gave his first Stone Lecture in the white Miller Chapel of Princeton Theological Seminary on 10 October 1898. He began his lecture, after opening with the words quoted at the start of this chapter, by introducing the theme and structure of the lectures that were to follow:

> When I was invited most honourably by your faculty to give the Stone Lectures here this year, I could not hesitate a moment as to my choice of subject. Calvinism, as the only decisive, lawful and consistent defence for Protestant nations against encroaching, and overwhelming Modernism, — this of itself was bound to be my theme. (LC, pp. 11, 12)

He then explained that he would expound and defend his theme in each of the following lectures:

1. Calvinism in History
2. Calvinism and Religion
3. Calvinism and Politics
4. Calvinism and Science
5. Calvinism and Art
6. Calvinism and the Future

In all six lectures, he explained, his aim would be to present Calvinism as an all-embracing "life-system" or worldview *(Weltanschauung),* stressing its relationship to God, humankind, and the world. His intention would thereby be to dispel the idea that Calvinism represented merely

14. A. Kuyper, *Varia Americana* (Amsterdam: Höveker & Wormser, 1899).
15. A. Kuyper, *Varia Americana,* p. 37.

a particular type of ecclesiastical structure or doctrinal code. A syllabus of the lectures, giving an overview of the proposed contents, had been published and distributed to Kuyper's audience in advance.[16]

The day following the final lecture, 22 October, marked what for Kuyper must have been the high point of his visit to America, the day he received his honorary doctorate from Princeton University. In the conferment ceremony, Kuyper walked in the procession with Albert Venn Dicey (1835-1922), Vinerian Professor of English Law at Oxford University and Fellow of All Souls College (1882-1909), who was also to receive an honorary degree in law. From Kuyper's word of thanks it is clear there were two reasons why he felt particularly honored to be receiving this degree. Twenty years before, he explained, C. W. Opzoomer, Professor of Theology at Utrecht and, according to Kuyper, "not at all a Calvinist," had put his name forward to the Senate of Utrecht University as a candidate for the same degree in recognition of *Ons program,* Kuyper's exposition of the Anti-Revolutionary Party's manifesto. But the theologians in the Senate, being "strong anti-Calvinists," had opposed the motion so vehemently that Opzoomer had had to withdraw his proposal. Thus, Kuyper admitted, "to receive the same degree twenty years later from a foreign university, is, I don't conceal it, a little revenge on my antagonists." The second reason he gave was less personal and more fundamental to Kuyper's message for America:

> Calvinism is not limited to theology, but unfurled its banner on the whole field of human life, more especially on politics, and in your country as well as mine the political liberties we are so freely enjoying are due to the valiant spirit instilled by Calvin in the heart of our *beggars* and of your *pilgrim fathers.* In your recent war with Spain this after-effect of Calvin's political influence brought our Calvinists onto your side. . . . To have the Degree of Doctor of Laws joined to the Doctor of Divinity is, in my opinion, not in the least a heterogeneous combination, but a well balanced harmony.[17]

Kuyper was obviously eager to take the opportunity afforded him in his word of thanks to add credibility to the thesis he had come to Princeton to defend. To him a true Calvinist would find nothing odd about a

16. Copies are held in the Stone Lectures Collection in Princeton Theological Seminary Archives and in KA; Portfolio 9, no. 53.

17. KA; *Amerika,* nos. 49, 50.

theologian receiving a degree in a non-theological subject, as Calvinism was not just a matter of theology.

Albert Dicey recorded the degree ceremony in a letter to his wife, from which it is obvious that his encounter with Kuyper had made a deep impression on him:

> On the platform were the President and other University officers. Distinguished visitors, such as the ex-president of Cleveland, and the recipients of degrees, viz. Dr. Kuyper and myself. It was a bright, gay scene, but in some ways oddly unlike the giving of degrees at Oxford. . . . We were each asked to say a few words. This led to the most remarkable speech I have heard for a long time. Kuyper . . . looked like a Dutchman of the seventeenth century. He spoke slowly and solemnly. His English was impressive, with here and there a Dutch idiom. He told us he was a Calvinist; that he had been persecuted by anti-Calvinists — this itself sounded like the language of another age. All the good in America had its root in Calvinism, which was as much a legal and an ethical as a religious creed. The Continental States had sympathised with Spain. Not so the Dutch Calvinists. "We have not forgotten our contest with Spanish tyranny; we fought it for a hundred years. In six weeks you have given Spanish power its *coup de grace*; but neither England nor the United States would have been free but for Dutch heroism. Spain has in all countries and in all ages been a curse to the world. . . ." This was the tone of the whole speech. There was not a word of flattery to America. One felt as if the seventeenth century had visibly risen upon us to give the last curse to Spain. After that I spoke, said nothing very remarkable, but dwelt on our ideas of law and justice being the true bond between England and the United States. . . . Then luncheon and a sort of levée — infinite handshakings and introductions. My head whirled over it. . . . This is the outline of our jaunt to Princeton. I brought away an additional LL.D., a gorgeous hood, very pleasant recollections.[18]

In the conferment of an honorary degree Kuyper had received three important things besides the degree itself: recognition by an academic

17. KA; *Amerika*, no. 50.

18. Letter from A. V. Dicey to Elinor May Dicey, cited in R. S. Rait, *Memorials of Albert Venn Dicey. Being Chiefly Letters and Diaries* (London: Macmillan, 1925), pp. 153-55. Kuyper's reference to America's struggle with Spain in the quotation refers to the Spanish American War of 1898.

institution for his work in the Netherlands, something that had been denied him in his own country; praise from a country he greatly admired; and the opportunity to bolster his case for the comprehensiveness of Calvinism.[19]

3. American Tour

Kuyper was deluged with invitations from American universities, colleges, and societies to give lectures and speeches during his visit to the United States.[20] Henry Dosker, whose services Warfield had employed in the translation of Kuyper's Stone Lecture on "Calvinism and Politics," had written to Kuyper before he left the Netherlands inviting him to address audiences in Grand Rapids and Holland in the state of Michigan. At the same time he offered him a guided tour of a number of Dutch immigrant settlements, and invited him to attend a banquet in his honor.[21] Giving priority to Dosker's invitation, Kuyper arrived by train in Grand Rapids on 25 October. Again he was obviously impressed with American public transport. A local Dutch-language newspaper reported his arrival with the words: "The doctor came from New York, showed no signs of tiredness, praised highly our railway carriages, calling them 'rooms on wheels'."[22]

Kuyper's first public address in Michigan, given on 26 October to an enthusiastic gathering of some two thousand people, and reported in the local press, reveals several important elements in his concept of America. Having urged his mainly Dutch immigrant audience to love and defend their adopted country with the same devotion with which their ancestors had defended their liberty and religion in the Netherlands, he again made a comparison between the Dutch Revolt and the recent American-Spanish war:

> As Hollanders a few centuries ago, we freed ourselves from Spanish oppression . . . after 80 years of hard fighting. What it took us 80 years to do you accomplished in 80 days; and we on the other side rejoice with you and admire your greatness.

19. Kuyper had expressed his admiration for America as early as 1874 in his pamphlet *Het calvinisme: oorsprong en waarborg*; C. Admiraal, 'De Amerikaanse reis', p. 113.

20. See, for instance, KA; *Amerika,* nos. 7, 10, 11, 15, 24.

21. Letter from Henry E. Dosker to Kuyper, in KA; *Amerika,* no. 2.

22. *De Wachter,* 2 November 1898.

Before ending his speech Kuyper issued a spirited appeal to his listeners: to become worthy American citizens who would make a positive and valuable contribution to the social and cultural life of the United States, which was bound to become a great nation:

> America is destined to become in the providence of God the most glorious and noble nation the world has ever seen. . . . Some day its renown will eclipse the renown and splendour of Rome, Greece and the old races.[23]

A chief reason for Kuyper's optimism seems to have been his idea that a nation becomes strong through the intermarriage of races, a phenomenon particularly characteristic of the United States. History had proven, he explained, that the "commingling of blood," as he called it, always had a positive effect on the development of a nation.[24] Despite, therefore, the nationalistic sentiment that characterized much of Kuyper's vision of America, as will become clear later on, his ideas on race —his advocacy of the intermingling rather than of the segregation of races—though tainted with racism, were the inverse of what is usually associated with racial prejudice. When, therefore, it was suggested at the end of Kuyper's speech that the choir should sing the nationalistic hymn "Let him in whom true Dutch blood flows untainted, pure and free" he objected strongly, and Luther's well-known hymn *"Ein fester Burg ist unser Gott"* was sung instead. The reporter of the *Grand Rapids Herald* tried to explain the reason for Kuyper's objection: "The professor has Swiss and German blood himself and believes that a nation becomes stronger by intermarriage with other nations."[25]

23. *Grand Rapids Herald,* 29 October 1898.

24. He had expressed the same idea in his Stone Lectures at Princeton (LC, pp. 35-36), and repeated it again in 1907 in his *Om de oude wereldzee,* 2 vols. (Amsterdam: Van Holkema & Warendorf, [1907-1908]), I, pp. 116-17. From the latter it is clear that Kuyper formulated this view in conscious reaction to the ideas of de Gobineau, who held that nations become stronger as they keep themselves racially pure. See Arthur de Gobineau, *Essai sur l'inégalité des races humaines* (Paris, 1853), translated as *The Inequality of Human Races.* With an introduction by Dr. Oscar Levy, editor of the authorized English version of Nietzsche's works (London: Heinemann, 1915). For a discussion of Kuyper's idea from the perspective of a Jewish liberal, see Charles Bloomberg, *Christian-Nationalism and the Rise of the Afrikaaner Broederbond in South Africa, 1918-1948* (Bloomington: Indiana University Press, 1989), pp. 8-9.

25. *Grand Rapids Herald,* 27 and 29 October 1898.

His speech ended with two other important elements in his idea of America: that the American constitution was founded on Calvinistic principles, and that it was the Calvinistic Dutch Republic of the seventeenth century which served as a model for the American state, more so than any British models. He obviously took pleasure in noting that the leaders of both political parties, Theodore Roosevelt (Republican) and Augustus van Wijk (Democratic), were men of Dutch descent.

Commentators on Kuyper's speech in the local press tried to locate Kuyper's political allegiances in terms of American party politics. Apparently Kuyper had declared in his address that he was a "Christian Democrat" and as such was in agreement with a number of points in the 1896 Platform of the Democratic Party, including the one that declared allegiance to "those great principles of justice and liberty upon which our institutions are founded and which the Democratic party has advocated from Jefferson's time to our own." In keeping with its name, the *Grand Rapids Democrat* was delighted with such an apparent display of sympathy for the Democratic cause, and carried a report on Kuyper's address under the bold headline: "He is a Democrat."[26] Kuyper responded by sending an article to the newspaper in which he attempted to clarify what he had said in his speech. He pointed out that, although he had mentioned Thomas Jefferson's name, this was the American president who had openly declared his agreement with the principles of the French Revolution. It was Alexander Hamilton, Jefferson's Republican opponent, he explained, who had declared at the time of the American Revolution that "the American revolution was as little akin to the principles of 1789, as a Puritan matron of New England was like the infidel heroine of a French novel."[27] No true Calvinist, Kuyper concluded, could support a political party that openly declared its sympathy with Jefferson's principles. And although no political party should be supported without question, his own sympathies lay with those among the Dutch immigrants who chose to support the Republican party. He found it a shame, however, that "the Republican platform of 1896 did not as openly reaffirm Hamilton's Calvinistic principles as their op-

26. *Grand Rapids Democrat,* 27 October 1898.

27. Kuyper had cited these words of Hamilton in his Stone Lectures, where he added a quote from Hamilton's correspondence, cited in the book on Alexander Hamilton by Henry Cabot Lodge, which he had consulted *en route* across the Atlantic: "There is no real resemblance between what was the cause of America and the cause of France" (LC, p. 87). Lodge, p. 256.

ponents publicly uphold Jefferson's." Kuyper ended his article by explaining that, although he was happy to be known as a "Christian Democrat" this was not to be interpreted as a sign of affinity with the Democratic Party in the United States. On the contrary, he explained:

> We Christian, or if you please, Calvinistic democrats in the Netherlands, were always considering the principles of the French Revolution, which Jefferson advocated, as the very target of our Calvinistic bullets.[28]

The editor of the *Grand Rapids Democrat* added an apology for having unwittingly misrepresented Kuyper, but insisted that "if he could study American politics for six months he would be the hottest kind of Democrat."[29] This small exchange with the press in Grand Rapids serves to highlight Kuyper's notion that America was a Calvinistic country by virtue of the principles enshrined in its constitution, principles he believed were traditionally represented by the Republican Party.

The following day Kuyper delivered a lecture on "Calvinism and the Future" at the Third Reformed Church in Holland, Michigan. As this was the same lecture he had given at Princeton, the contents will be discussed in Chapter Nine of this book. It is important to note here that Kuyper's optimism regarding the future of America was inextricably linked to his idea of the future of Calvinism:

> America looks forward toward a great future but it needs the principles of Calvinism to strengthen its backbone. . . . The future of the development of Calvinistic principles is no longer in Europe but in America.[30]

Local newspapers carried glowing reviews of the lecture, and from them it is clear that Kuyper's message had come across: the Calvinistic worldview offered America the guarantee of a brighter future.[31]

Following a speaking appointment at Hope College in Holland, and the banquet held in his honor promised by Dosker, Kuyper traveled via Chicago to the Dutch immigrant communities of Iowa.[32] After

28. *Grand Rapids Democrat,* 29 October 1898.

29. *Grand Rapids Democrat,* 29 October 1898.

30. *Holland Daily Sentinel,* 28 October 1898.

31. *Holland Daily Sentinel,* 28 October 1898; *De Hollandse Amerikaan,* 31 October 1898; *De Hope,* 31 October 1898.

32. KA; *Amerika,* no. 59; A. Kuyper, *Varia Americana,* p. 14. The banquet was timed to coincide with Kuyper's sixty-second birthday, on 29 October.

spending four days paying visits and giving speeches, he returned to Chicago, where he received guests at his hotel, prepared his speeches, and dealt with his correspondence. Due to the fullness of his itinerary he declined invitations to give addresses at the University of Chicago and at Johns Hopkins University in Baltimore.[33] He did agree to speak to a large audience in Englewood, a suburb of Chicago, on "The Vocation of Hollanders in America," and gave a series of three lectures at McCormick Theological Seminary.[34] At a second banquet given in his honor, this time by the Holland Society of Chicago, Kuyper gave another speech on what was becoming a familiar subject: the influence of the Netherlands in the foundation of the United States. A newspaper reported:

> Dr. Kuyper said he had never been so proud of the Dutch stock as when he came to America and saw the respect in which the descendants from it were held. In New York he had seen the people eagerly contending which of two men of Dutch blood [Roosevelt and Van Wijk] they should make Governor of their state. He claimed that American institutions were of Dutch warp, although of English woof. It was after the old Dutch republic that they were patterned.[35]

For Kuyper, America was clearly more a product of the Netherlands than of England.

Of all Kuyper's appearances in the United States, his visit to Cleveland, Ohio, was the most well-publicized and reported on, and it gives a clear indication of the enthusiasm with which he was received by his American admirers, and the esteem in which they held him. Lavish programs — 1,500 copies in all — were printed and distributed, bearing a photograph of Kuyper with the words printed in large, bold print: "Cleveland's welcome to Holland's foremost citizen. Professor Abraham Kuyper, D.D., L.L.D., Statesman, Theologian, Literator."[36] The following page contained a racy biographical sketch of Kuyper's career and ended with a comparison with the British statesman W. E. Gladstone, who had died six months earlier:

33. *De Hope,* n.d.

34. *Chicago Tribune,* 6 November 1898.

35. *The Daily Inter-Ocean,* 11 November 1898.

36. KA; *Amerika,* no. 33; *De Heraut,* 11 December 1898.

> He resembles Gladstone in many ways. If Gladstone excelled in statesmanship and was also an accomplished theologian, Dr Kuyper is easily first in theology, and a close second in statesmanship.

It was a comparison that would have satisfied Kuyper, who at Princeton had referred to Gladstone as "the Christian statesman, politically a Calvinist to the very core" (LC, p. 198). The program also gave a list of those involved in organizing the meeting; it is clear from this list that Kuyper's visit had drawn the attention of a number of American university and college presidents, theologians, and clergy.[37]

The speech Kuyper delivered, titled "The Political Principles of Calvinism," contained many of the same ideas he had presented in previous speeches on his American tour. It appears, though, that he set out in a fuller and more systematic way than in Grand Rapids or in Holland (Michigan) the influence of Calvinistic principles in the areas of the state, society, and the church.[38] He thereby echoed themes that had found broader expansion in his *Lectures*. A notable new element was his concern about the destructive potential of atheism in American society, particularly on the life of the masses:

> Some of your cleverest young men now go to the German universities to complete their education. While there they become contaminated with the German spirit of unbelief. The worst of it is that those are the very men who afterwards get to the head of your institutions of learning. Now this spirit of unbelief and doubt, which is a result of the German method of scientific research, may be all right in educated and cultured circles, but let it spread among the masses and loose morals will be the result. . . . The German influence is not only gaining ground in this country, but in England, and I look upon it with much regret. Unbelief is bad for the masses, which can be seen in Germany at the present time, where socialism and many other political heresies are gaining ground.[39]

Many members of the audience came forward to greet Kuyper personally after the formal proceedings were over, and the enthusiastic reports indicate that Cleveland was proud to be honored with so distinguished

37. *De Heraut*, 11 December 1898. KA; Portfolio 9, nos. 3a, 3b, 33, 59.
38. *Cleveland Plain Dealer*, 16 November 1898.
39. *Cleveland Leader*, 15 November 1898.

a guest, even though one newspaper reported that the speech had taken an hour and a half, thus "testing the patience of the audience."[40]

Kuyper arrived back at the Fifth Avenue Hotel in New York just before the elections for the new state governor.[41] The Dutch origins of the two candidates, Theodore Roosevelt and Augustus van Wijk, gave added stimulus to Kuyper's interest in the election campaign, which he followed closely. He was particularly well placed to do so, as Roosevelt was leading his campaign from Kuyper's hotel and the Democrats' headquarters were close by.[42] Roosevelt, the supporter of expansion and annexation and the hero of Cuba, won the election and went on to become President of the United States in 1901, the same year that Kuyper became Prime Minister of the Netherlands. Kuyper's pride in the Dutch influence on the shaping of the United States was strengthened through his encounters with Americans of Dutch descent, who were taking a leading role in contemporary American society.

Kuyper's visit to the United States would not have been complete without a meeting with the then President William McKinley (1843-1901), who was Roosevelt's immediate predecessor. Little is known, however, about the nature and content of Kuyper's talks with McKinley, which took place at the White House on 30 November. Press reports containing only scanty details indicate that Kuyper and McKinley discussed European and American affairs, including peace negotiations and the Transvaal.[43] Unfortunately for Kuyper, his visit came at a time when, as we now know, McKinley was suffering from a nervous disorder, a state reflected in a comment Kuyper made in a press interview immediately after his meeting: "President McKinley looked badly, I thought, and seemed to be suffering from mental exertion and worry. . . . No doubt the strain upon him has been very severe."[44] Kuyper was obviously disappointed with the president, who turned out not to hold the anti-imperialist and pro-Boer position Kuyper had expected of him. No doubt the idealism of Kuyper's view of the United States, which had kept him

40. *De Heraut,* 11 December 1898.

41. *De Heraut,* 11 December 1898. KA; Portfolio 9, nos. 3a, 3b, 33, 59. The *Cleveland Plain Dealer* of 16 November carried a favorable review of Kuyper's speech in Cleveland.

42. Kuyper, *Varia Americana,* pp. 40-41.

43. *De Heraut,* 1 December 1898.

44. *De Heraut,* 1 December 1898.

from reckoning with the real world of American politics, had been unsettled by McKinley's pragmatism.[45]

Kuyper gave two more noteworthy speeches during his visit to America. The first of these was to the Presbyterian Historical Society of Philadelphia on 6 December, bearing the title "The Antithesis Between Symbolism and Revelation." The speech received wide distribution, following the publication of an abstract in *The Christian Intelligencier* of 7 December 1898, and its wholesale publication in booklet form.[46] Kuyper's aim in giving this lecture was to point out the threat to traditional Christianity posed by the rise of the symbolical movement, which he associated with the German pantheistic school of thought, and which he saw expressed in the ritualistic trend in the liturgical developments in the Church of England. His perception of symbolism was closely related to his understanding of the relationship between art and religion, which will be discussed in Chapter Eight. His message was enthusiastically received, and the Revd. W. H. Roberts, representing an international Alliance of Reformed Churches, replied to Kuyper's speech with an ingratiating word of thanks.[47]

Having lectured at Hartford Theological Seminary on 7 December on "Calvinism: A Political Scheme" Kuyper presented his final American lecture at the Collegiate Church in New York City the following day.[48] The title was "A New Development of Calvinism Needed," and the speech ended with an impassioned plea that the significance of Calvinism for the future of the United States should be fully recognized. Along with his final Stone Lecture on "Calvinism and the Future," and his speech on the same subject in Holland, Michigan, it reveals Kuyper's belief that, although the footprints of Calvinism's glorious past could be found in Europe, its future course was undoubtedly located in America. This in part explains why Kuyper should have spoken so much on Calvinism during his visit to America. The destiny of Calvinism, along with the destiny of world civilization, lay in the United States.

After many expressions of thanks from those of Kuyper's hosts who

45. Admiraal, 'De Amerikaanse reis', p. 133.

46. A. Kuyper, *The Antithesis Between Symbolism and Revelation* (Amsterdam and Pretoria: Höveker and Wormser; Edinburgh: T. & T. Clark, 1899).

47. Roberts referred to Kuyper as "one of the strongest thinkers and most influential ministers of the Reformed churches on the continent." *De Heraut,* 25 December 1898.

48. The only record of Kuyper's speech at the Collegiate Church is a few key words jotted down on notepaper in Kuyper's archive: KA; *Amerika,* no. 47.

came to bid him farewell at New York harbor, Kuyper boarded ship for Boulogne, arriving home in Amsterdam on New Year's Eve, 1898.[49]

4. Kuyper's Vision of America

From the account of Kuyper's movements in the United States, the outline of his vision of America emerges: America, he believed, was a Calvinistic invention, primarily of Dutch origin; the future of both Calvinism and world civilization lay in America; the struggle in America was the same as the struggle in Europe — that between the principles of the French Revolution and Calvinism, a struggle represented by the Democratic and Republican parties. Each of these aspects will be discussed in turn within their intellectual context in order to discover not only the origins of Kuyper's America-vision but its motivation and aims.

4.1. The Product of Dutch Calvinism

Although Kuyper made no reference to it during his visit to America, it is clear that his idea of America was strongly influenced by Douglas Campbell's *The Puritan in Holland, England, and America.*[50] Soon after the book was published, Kuyper praised it highly in *De Heraut,* declaring that its author had provided sound evidence that America's development and prosperity was attributable to Dutch mentality, morals, law, science, and most importantly, Calvinism.[51] He was obviously delighted to be able to appeal to the work of an erudite American historian, to bolster his claim that Dutch, rather than English, Calvinism had been the principal factor in the foundation of the United States. Campbell's work clearly refutes the opinion commonly held among American historians at that time that the origin of America's constitutional system lay in England, and emphasizes instead the influence of the Dutch Republic.[52] Camp-

49. It is clear from a report of Kuyper's farewell that his visit had deeply affected his hosts. *The Banner of Truth* 33 (1899), pp. 106-7.

50. Douglas Campbell, *The Puritan in Holland, England, and America: An Introduction to American History,* 2 vols. (London: Osgood McIlvaine, 1892).

51. *De Heraut,* 20 August 1892.

52. Campbell, I, pp. xxiii-xxx. Campbell held that the Dutch *Plakkaat van*

bell's well-documented study impressed many, not least Gladstone, who wrote a letter to Campbell in which he praised the book highly.[53] Following his trip to the United States, Kuyper proudly declared in his *Varia Americana* that "Campbell has made it clear that it was not England but Holland which served as a model for the American Republic."[54]

Together with the work of George Bancroft, one of the authors Kuyper consulted on board the *Lucania,* the writings of the American Darwinist historian and philosopher John Fiske (1842-1901) were also of importance in the formation of Kuyper's America-vision. Fiske's *The Dutch and Quaker Colonies in America,* which would have provided strong support for Kuyper's argument for the role of the Dutch in the founding of the United States, was published too late for him to have consulted it before his American visit.[55] A favorable review of the book did appear in *De Heraut* in 1900, however, pointing out that Fiske's study corresponded with Campbell's arguments for the influence of the Dutch on the political institutions of England and America.[56] Although Kuyper made no reference to it, it is possible that prior to the Stone Lectures he had consulted an earlier work by Fiske on the influence of the Puritans on the establishment of civil and religious freedom in the United States. Fiske had argued in this book that without the Puritans political liberty would probably have disappeared from the world.[57]

Verlatinge, issued by States General of the United Provinces in 1581, provided the model for both the 1689 Declaration of Rights and the American Declaration of Independence (I, p. 234).

53. Letter from Gladstone to Campbell, 17 October 1892, reproduced in the fourth edition of Campbell's work, published in 1916 in one volume by Harper (New York and London).

54. Kuyper, *Varia Americana,* p. 119.

55. John Fiske, *The Dutch and Quaker Colonies in America,* 2 vols. (London: Macmillan, 1899).

56. *De Heraut,* 7 January 1900.

57. John Fiske, *The Beginnings of New England, or the Puritan Theocracy in Its Relations to Civil and Religious Liberty* (Boston: Houghton Mifflin, 1897), p. 37. The issue of the impact of European Calvinism on the foundation of the United States has remained a widely discussed and controversial one up to the present day. Notable treatments can be found in Charles W. Akers, "Calvinism and the American Revolution," in *The Heritage of John Calvin: Heritage Hall Lectures 1960-1970,* ed. by John H. Bratt (Grand Rapids: Eerdmans, 1973), pp. 158-76; R. T. Kendall, *The Influence of Calvin and Calvinism Upon the American Heritage* (London: Evangelical Library, 1976); Stephen E. Lucas, "The Plakkaat van Vertalinge: A Neglected Model for the American Declaration of Inde-

Kuyper had not always laid such stress on the particular influence of the Dutch Republic in the founding of America. In his speech of 1874 on "Calvinism: The Origin and Safeguard of Our Constitutional Liberties," he had emphasized the role of both English and Dutch Calvinism in the origins of America's civil liberties.[58] It is likely that Kuyper's shift to stressing only the place of the Netherlands in the foundation of the United States had to do with his acquaintance with the work of certain contemporary historians, particularly Campbell. But two other reasons may also be suggested.

First, despite Kuyper's long-standing admiration for England, during the 1890s he became increasingly disappointed by its imperialistic policies. He had hoped that Gladstone would have a correcting effect on British politics, not least through his influence on the Whig tradition, which Kuyper regarded as part of the political heritage of William III (1650-1702), the Dutch king of Great Britain and Ireland from 1689 to 1702. But the confrontations with the Boers in South Africa destroyed all such hope, and he saw England giving itself over to an unhindered imperialism, particularly after Gladstone's death in 1898.[59] This sense of disappointment with England, which was strengthened by a sense that its imperialistic policies were a violation and denial of its Calvinistic heritage, may well have undergirded Kuyper's growing tendency to downplay the role of English Calvinism in international affairs, and to stress the role of the Calvinistic Netherlands instead.

A second, more important, reason was Kuyper's nationalistic sen-

---

pendence," in *Connection Cultures: The Netherlands in Five Centuries of Transatlantic Exchange,* ed. by Rosemarijn Hoefte and Johanna C. Kardux (Amsterdam: Free University Press, 1994), pp. 187-207. See also Alister E. McGrath, *A Life of John Calvin: A Study in the Shaping of Western Culture* (Oxford: Basil Blackwell, 1990), pp. 258-60. At least two treatments of the issue are directly indebted to Kuyper's vision: William Elliot Griffis, *The Story of New Netherland: The Dutch in America* (Boston: Houghton Mifflin, 1909); John Clover Monsma, *What Calvinism Has Done for America* (Chicago: [n.p.], 1919).

58. Kuyper, "Calvinism: The Origin and Safeguard," p. 386.

59. Chris A. J. van Koppen, *De Geuzen van de negentiende eeuw: Abraham Kuyper en Zuid-Afrika* (Wormer: Immerc, 1992), pp. 239-40; R. Kuiper, *Zelfbeeld en wereldbeeld: antirevolutionairen en het buitenland, 1848-1905* (Kampen: Kok, 1992), p. 149; J. P. Feddema, 'De houding van Dr. A. Kuyper ten aanzien van de Eerste Wereldoorlog', *Anti-revolutionaire staatkunde: maandelijks orgaan van de Dr. Abraham Kuyperstichting ter bevordering van de studie der anti-revolutionaire beginselen* 32 (1962): 163-64; Admiraal, 'De Amerikaanse reis', p. 123.

timent, alluded to earlier, which centered on the role of the Netherlands in the international context. In contrast to Germany, England, and France in the late nineteenth and early twentieth centuries, the Netherlands did not manifest an aggressive and ideologically inspired, expansionist form of nationalism, but pursued a policy of neutrality in international affairs.[60] Kuyper was forthright in his rejection of all expansionist forms of European nationalism, and insisted that the Netherlands had a vocation to bring the principles of Calvinism to bear within the international community, which in turn would flourish as a result of them.[61] Such an optimistic ideal was grounded in Kuyper's idea of Dutch national character, of which he believed Calvinism to be an integral part.[62] It was an idea reflected in the subtitle to the original Dutch version of Kuyper's speech on "Calvinism: The Origin and Safeguard of Our Constitutional Liberties," which read "A Dutch Idea" *(Een Nederlandsche gedachte)*. His intention was partly to associate the argument of his speech with the ideas of Groen van Prinsterer, who edited a journal of like-sounding name *(Nederlandsche Gedachten)* at that time. But it was also aimed at emphasizing the existence of a link between Calvinism and the Netherlands: Calvinism lay at the heart of Dutch national consciousness.[63] The welfare and development both of Dutch society and of world civilization could best be served by the application of Calvinistic principles to national and international life. Calvinism, as the most highly developed form of religion, and the Netherlands, as a correspondingly highly civilized country, had the moral responsibility to shed their benefits abroad on a world scale. This could be achieved by several means, such as a

60. Cornelius Huisman, *Nederlands Israel: het natiebesef der traditioneel-gereformeerden in de achttiende eeuw* (Dordrecht: Van den Tol, 1983), p. 48.

61. A. Kuyper, *Tweeërlei Vaderland: ter inleiding van de zevende jaarvergadering der Vrije Universiteit* (Amsterdam: Wormser, 1887; A. Kuyper, *Plancius-rede* (Amsterdam: Kruyt, 1884); A. Kuyper, *Antirevolutionaire staatkunde: met nadere toelichting op 'Ons program'*, 2 vols. (Kampen: Kok, 1916), I, pp. 156-59. E. H. Kossmann is quite wrong in his characterization of Kuyper as a nationalist with both militaristic and imperialistic tendencies. Kossmann, *The Low Countries*, pp. 304, 357, 405.

62. A. Kuyper, *Het beroep op het volksgeweten: rede ter opening van de algemeene vergadering der 'Vereeniging voor Christelijk Nationaal-Schoolonderwijs, gehouden te Utrecht, den 18 mei 1869* (Amsterdam: Blankenberg, 1869), pp. 14-18.

63. The same idea was reflected in the first article of the manifesto of the ARP, which declared that Calvinism was the "key-note" *(grondtoon)* of Dutch national character. *Ons program*, 2nd edition (Amsterdam: Kruyt, 1879), pp. 16-21. See also *De Standaard*, 9 December 1892.

colonial policy of "guardianship" which aimed at raising the level of indigenous cultures by means of contact with the principles of Christianity,[64] particularly of Calvinism, and by means of emigration, particularly to the United States and South Africa.[65] In the argument that the Dutch Republic had served as the historical model for the founding of the United States Kuyper found support for his claim that the Netherlands, and Dutch Calvinists in particular, had a moral vocation to further the development of civilization through the application of Calvinistic principles to every sphere of life. He also found that in recommending Calvinism to his American audience he could employ national sentiment to great effect. He spoke of the Calvinism that had secured the glory of the Old World, from which his listeners had originated, and had then gone on to found the United States and given it an even greater glory, admired by the rest of the world. For Kuyper, therefore, America was great because America was founded on Calvinism, the implication being that to be a true American was to be a committed Calvinist. It would be hard to mistake Kuyper's appeal to national sentiment among his American audience in his plea for a rediscovery of Calvinism.

4.2. The Hope of the Future

Kuyper's comments during his American tour that America could expect a bright future due to the Calvinistic principles upon which it was founded cannot be attributed merely to flattery or to wistful optimism. They were derived from his idea that the historical development of civilization had followed a westward path from its origins in the Middle East through Europe to America, where it had crossed from the eastern to the western states, and had now come to a temporary standstill on the shores of the Pacific Ocean, before its likely continuance through China and Japan (LC, pp. 32-33).[66] This was Kuyper's expression of a myth

64. See Peter Heslam, "The Christianization of the East Indies: The Ideas of Abraham Kuyper on Dutch Colonial Policy," *Reflection: An International Reformed Review of Missiology* 2 (1989): 13-17.

65. Van Koppen, pp. 232-33; R. Kuiper, pp. 154-56. Mainly as a result of British policy towards South Africa, Kuyper began to show a distinct preference for emigration to the United States rather than to the Transvaal (van Koppen, pp. 144-45).

66. Kuyper maintained his optimism in America's future prospects after his return from the United States. See *De Standaard,* 7 January 1899 and 22 August 1902.

with a long history, according to which humanity was seen to be following a course of development from east to west, passing from its origins in the river deltas of Asia through Greece and Rome to Western Europe and on to America, from where it would return to Asia, thus completing the circle. The history of this myth of "heliotropic" development can be traced in the works of a host of distinguished writers and thinkers, including the Church Fathers, Richard Sibbs, George Herbert, and William Shakespeare; and, at the time of Kuyper, Walt Whitman, John Fiske, and Josiah Strong.[67] Kuyper is likely to have come across it himself in the writings of the Dutch clergymen and immigrant leaders A. C. van Raalte and H. P. Scholte, who in the 1840s led a group of seceders *(Afgescheidenen)* from the Netherlands to found the communities in Michigan and Iowa that Kuyper visited.[68] He may also have encountered it in the works of these men's spiritual mentor Isaac da Costa, the great poet of the *Réveil,* for whom Kuyper reserved great admiration.[69] Whatever its direct origin in Kuyper's thought, it was an idea that formed the basis of his entire concept of America, and one that he combined with his idea of Calvinism. Accordingly, it was Calvinism that formed the stream of development in the most recent stages of the heliotropic process, which, since the Reformation, had flowed from Switzerland to California (LC, p. 33).[70]

67. Jan Willem Schulte Nordholt, *The Myth of the West: America as the Last Empire,* trans. by Herbert H. Rowen (Grand Rapids: Eerdmans, 1995) [A translation of Jan Willem Schulte Nordholt, *De mythe van het Westen: Amerika als het laatste wereldrijk* (Amsterdam: Meulenhoff, 1992)].

68. Nordholt, *The Myth,* p. 90. In his speech in the Third Reformed Church in Holland, Michigan, Kuyper paid tribute to Van Raalte, the founder of the town. See the *Holland Daily Sentinel,* 28 October 1898. The most recent treatment of Van Raalte is Elton J. Bruins, "'An American Moses': Albertus C. Van Raalte as Immigrant Leader," in *Sharing the Reformed Tradition,* pp. 19-34.

69. See, for instance, Kuyper's *Het calvinisme en de Kunst,* pp. 30-39, and his *Bilderdijk in zijn nationale betekenis: rede gehouden te Amsterdam op 1 oktober 1906* (Amsterdam: Höveker & Wormser, 1906).

70. Kuyper's daughter Henriette echoed her father's heliotropic ideas when she wrote in a book about her six-month stay in the United States: "Human life follows the same course as the light, just as the sunflower follows the path of the sun through the sky." H. S. S. Kuyper, *Een halfjaar in Amerika* (Rotterdam: Daamen, 1907), pp. 441-42.

4.3. The Struggle in America

The contrast Kuyper made between the Republican Party represented by Hamilton and the Democratic Party represented by Jefferson was part of a wider contrast he drew between Washington and Paris and between Calvin and Rousseau.[71] Kuyper's concept of the French Revolution will be discussed in greater detail in the next chapter. The point to note here is that this contrast was one that underlay much of his critique of modern culture. He often posed it as a fundamental dilemma, and he had a tendency to caricature it, as he did in the *Lectures* with his quote (noted above) from Hamilton on the French Revolution being as unlike the American Revolution as a promiscuous woman in a French novel was unlike a Puritan matron in America. For Kuyper the American Revolution and the French Revolution were poles apart; in the Thirteen Colonies there had been a recognition of God's sovereignty, while in Paris there had been an outright rejection of it. Characteristically for Kuyper, it was differences in religious motivation, rather than in practical results, that determined his judgment of historical events. He brought his idea of a contrast in religious motivation to bear on the party struggle (mentioned earlier) between Jefferson and Hamilton in 1793-1794. In this struggle, he claimed, Jefferson had defended the anti-religious ideals of the French Revolution whereas Hamilton had represented the same Calvinistic principles as the English Whigs and the Stadhouder-King William III. It was for this reason that Kuyper took it for granted that Calvinists would support the Republicans rather than the Democrats in American politics. He considered the Republican platform to be based on anti-revolutionary principles.[72]

It is worth noting that whereas Hamilton and Jefferson were certainly antipoles, their differences were not primarily religious ones. Hamilton defended the interests of industry, had a mainly northern constituency, and advocated a powerful centralized government. Jefferson, on the other hand, defended the interests of the agricultural sector, had most of his followers in the West and South, and favored a decen-

71. See for instance Kuyper's *Antirevolutionaire staatkunde,* I, pp. 712-14.

72. Kuyper, *Varia Americana,* pp. 30-31, 120-21; J. W. Sap, *Wegbereiders der revolutie: calvinisme en de strijd om de democratische rechtsstaat* (Groningen: Wolters-Noordhoff, 1993), p. 339; P. Hoekstra, 'The American Party System', *Anti-revolutionaire staatkunde: driemaandelijksch orgaan* 7 (1933): 61-82 (61, 64-65).

tralized authority located in the states themselves.[73] Followers of both parties saw the French Revolution as a triumph of American values, and it was only the excesses in France that divided their judgment of it. George Washington was not opposed to the Enlightenment philosophers *per se,* and he was a deist rather than a Calvinist. In the case of Hamilton, it is not at all clear that religion was the basis of his motivation, and there is even evidence to suggest that Jefferson allowed religion to determine his thought to a greater extent than did Hamilton.[74]

Kuyper's attempt to judge American party politics along the lines of "anti-revolutionary principles" led to the kind of confusion that emerged in the press coverage of Kuyper's appearance in Grand Rapids. It was a confusion derived from the fact that in America the antithesis Kuyper was prone to draw between the Calvinistic principles of the Republican Party and the Enlightenment principles of the Democratic Party did not square with reality; American Calvinists were active in both parties. Kuyper's vision of America was founded on a conflict between Christian and Enlightenment principles, which in actual fact usually formed a synthesis.[75]

His aim in drawing this antithesis was clearly to make his American admirers aware of their task and calling to live and work as "anti-revolutionaries" in a society that served as battleground for the same struggle at work in Europe, the struggle between Christianity and modernism. In drawing the battle lines where he did, he was applying ideas he had developed in the Dutch context, which were not directly applicable to the situation in the United States, resulting in mistakes and overgeneralizations. He succeeded, nevertheless, in alerting his followers to the idea that Christianity's true struggle was not confined to the field of the church and doctrine but encompassed every sphere of life, including the field of politics. It was thus designed as a stimulus to fight in these fields against the forces of unbelief that had received such a powerful impulse in the French Revolution. It must also be seen as part of Kuyper's attempt to inspire confidence among American Calvinists that the principles they

73. Sap, p. 340.

74. Sap, p. 340; Hoekstra, p. 70; D. Adair, *Fame and the Founding Fathers: Essays by Douglas Adair,* ed. by Trevor Colbourn (New York: Norton, 1974), pp. 94-96; J. W. Schulte Nordholt, *Triomf en tragiek van de vrijheid. De geschiedenis van de Verenigde Staten van Amerika* (Amsterdam: Meulenhoff, 1985), p. 56.

75. Sap, p. 341; Hoekstra, p. 71; Schulte Nordholt, *The Myth,* pp. 97-98.

held had provided the very foundations of their country and as such had a glorious history.

Kuyper's ideas were typical of the concept of a "Christian America" which was prevalent during the nineteenth century in both America and Europe.[76] Recent research into this concept demonstrates that the United States leadership, which was predominantly Protestant, tended to assume uncritically that Christian beliefs lay at the heart of American civilization.[77] T. D. Bozeman, for instance, writes: "it became, in fact, often difficult to discern any salient notes of discontinuity between gospel and [American] culture."[78] The notion of a Christian America was not, however, without some justification. Outwardly, in terms of such things as church attendance, foreign missions, social projects, Christian education, and the involvement of Christians in politics, Christianity in nineteenth-century America was a model of success, due largely to vigorous evangelical enterprise. G. Marsden writes of this situation that, in contrast to the wide-scale secularization of Europe, "the United States had not drifted religiously during the nineteenth century. It had been guided, even driven, by resourceful evangelical leaders."[79] Movements towards secularization had certainly begun, most noticeably in the academic world, as will become clear in Chapter Seven; but such changes were at a level most Americans were not aware of, and the outward prosperity of American religion continued to grow.[80] Kuyper cannot be accused of being blind to the early signs of secularization — his awareness of them determined much of the earnestness with which he typified the struggle in modern American society in his Stone Lectures. But the courage he had in characterizing America as a Christian country in terms both of

76. Mark A. Noll, *A History of Christianity in the United States and Canada* (Grand Rapids: Eerdmans, 1992), pp. 220-44 (p. 221); George M. Marsden, *Understanding Fundamentalism and Evangelicalism* (Grand Rapids: Eerdmans, 1991), p. 10.

77. See Theodore Dwight Bozeman, *Protestants in an Age of Science: The Baconian Ideal and Antebellum American Religious Thought* (Chapel Hill: University of North Carolina Press, 1977); Robert T. A. Handy, *A Christian America: Protestant Hopes and Historical Realities* (New York: Oxford University Press, 1971); Martin E. Marty, *Righteous Empire: The Protestant Experience in America* (New York: Dial Press, 1970).

78. Bozeman, p. 173.

79. Marsden, *Understanding*, pp. 11-12.

80. The double-sided phenomenon of religious prosperity on the surface concealing creeping secularization contributed to Mark Twain's famous characterization of the nineteenth century in America as the "Gilded Age."

its heritage and its potential was undoubtedly influenced by the generally accepted idea, even among most European thinkers, that America was essentially a Christian nation.

Conclusion

Kuyper's visit to the United States was a public recognition and appreciation of his life's work from a foreign country. This was expressed both formally, in the honorary doctorate he received from Princeton University, and informally in the spontaneous and enthusiastic reception he received on his tour of Dutch immigrant settlements. All who met him honored him as a great leader in many fields and as a champion of the Calvinistic cause. F. L. Rutgers, a contemporary of Kuyper who also held a chair in theology at the Free University, astutely characterized Kuyper's American visit as a "campaign of conquest" *(veroveringstocht)* for Calvinistic principles[81] — the fighter for Calvinism received a hero's welcome in the Calvinistic camp of a foreign country. As any good hero, Kuyper was not about to disappoint his admirers by failing to grant them a lap of honor.

Kuyper's visit was also, by his own admission, an "investigation." At long last he had received the chance to visit the country he so admired and about which he had spoken so often, ever since his speech in 1874 on Calvinism as the guarantee of constitutional liberties. America represented for Kuyper a test case on a vast scale of what happens when Calvinism engages with culture. In America, he took the opportunity to observe the outcome. In his own mind, at least, his observations confirmed his theory that America's greatness was due in large part to its origins in Dutch Calvinism, and that the positive changes afoot in American society were an outworking of the same struggle that had engaged him in the Netherlands. In opposition to the claim of Kuyper's liberal and conservative political colleagues that Calvinism was irrelevant to modern life, he embraced the commonly accepted concept of a Christian America in order to demonstrate Calvinism's importance and relevance.

Kuyper's American experience may also be seen, finally, in the light of his encounter with the Brighton movement. At the start of his

81. *Jaarverslag van de Vereniging voor Hooger Onderwijs op Gereformeerde Grondslag,* vol. 19, p. xxiv. Cited in Admiraal, p. 151.

career Kuyper had come under the influence of the great nineteenth-century American revivalists, only later to distance himself from the whole experience after suffering a nervous breakdown he believed to be related in some way to the kind of religious experience they encouraged. Twenty-three years later, at the height of his career, he was invited to pay a visit to the country from which these evangelists had come, and in terms of the excitement and triumphalism he helped to arouse, his public appearances bore similarities to theirs. In conscious contrast to the "Arminianism" or "Methodism" of American revivalism, however, Kuyper seized the opportunity to proclaim the benefits of Calvinism as the most perfect and advanced form of Christianity. In doing so he reflected widespread intellectual trends, particularly those associated with nationalism and with the myths of heliotropic development and of a Christian America.

First Lecture: Calvinism a Life-System

Kuyper introduced the theme of his lectures on a note of alarm. Christianity, he declared, was imperiled by great and serious dangers, owing to the onslaught of modernism (LC, p. 11). Two world-views, that of Christianity and modernism, were at war with one another over the further development of history: "This is *the* struggle in Europe, this is *the* struggle in America, and this also, is the struggle for principles in which my own country is engaged" (LC, p. 11). There was only one hope of success for Christianity in this struggle — that it took its stand in "a life-system of equally comprehensive and far-reaching power" to that of modernism (LC, p. 11). Such a life-system or "worldview" was to be found in Calvinism, "the only decisive, lawful and consistent defense for Protestant nations against encroaching, and overwhelming Modernism." Calvinism as an all-embracing worldview was therefore to be the subject of the following lectures (LC, p. 12). But what did Kuyper mean by Calvinism, worldview, and modernism? Once again, attention will be given to the context within which he formed these concepts, in order to evaluate their principal motivations.

1. Calvinism

The Stone Lectures as a whole are Kuyper's exposition of the term "Calvinism"; this chapter will only discuss Kuyper's definition of it in his first lecture. He began by pointing out three uses of the term from which he wished to distance himself. The first of these was the "sectarian" usage, which occurred most commonly in Roman Catholic countries, when derisory reference was made to members of Protestant churches. Second, the "confessional" sense, was that by which a Calvinist was regarded merely as a firm believer in the doctrine of predestination, and for that reason a victim of dogmatic narrowness.[1] The third sense was "denominational," used by groups of Baptists and Methodists, such as the English "Calvinistic Baptists" and the Welsh "Calvinistic Methodists," for the purposes of self-definition. In contrast to these three was Kuyper's "scientific" sense, which included its historical, philosophical, and political aspects. In terms of history, he explained, Calvinism referred to the channel in which the Reformation had moved in so far as it was not Lutheran, Anabaptist, or Socinian. Philosophically it was a "system of conceptions" which, under Calvin's influence, had come to dominate the various spheres of life. Politically it was the movement in the sphere of politics which had secured national and constitutional liberties, first in the Netherlands, then in England and the United States. Kuyper was confident that this was the sense in which Calvinism was generally understood by contemporary scholars (LC, pp. 14-15).[2]

Though Kuyper's Calvinism was thus rooted in a specific type of religious consciousness, it was principally a broad tendency in Western culture. This was clearly designed to counter the idea that Calvinism was merely a particular type of theology, and one that had little relevance to practical life in the modern world. For the same reason he often made a distinction between "Calvinistic" and "Reformed" *(Gereformeerd)*. Whereas the latter was chiefly relevant to matters of church and doctrine, the former applied to the whole range of social spheres. Thus he referred to his political program, for example, as "Calvinistic," insisting that "Calvinistic is not a theological but a politi-

1. It was because of this misunderstanding, Kuyper explained, that theologians such as Princeton's own Charles Hodge preferred to speak of "Augustinianism" rather than of Calvinism (LC, p. 13).

2. Kuyper quoted Bancroft as an example: "Calvinism . . . has a theory of ontology, of ethics, of social happiness, and of human liberty, all derived from God." From George Bancroft, *History of the United States of America* (New York: Appleton, 1882-1884), II, p. 405. This is one of the quotes Kuyper had noted from his reading aboard the *Lucania.*

cal name."[3] This distinction would have been familiar to those in Kuyper's audience who were acquainted with the thought of Herman Bavinck (1854-1921), an orthodox Protestant professor of theology at the theological seminary in Kampen, who made much use of it in his writings. In an article published in 1894 in *The Presbyterian and Reformed Review,* a journal closely connected with Princeton Theological Seminary under Warfield's editorship, Bavinck put forward a characteristically eloquent argument that Calvinism was a particular type of Protestantism, not equivalent in meaning to Reformed:[4]

> The words Reformed and Calvinistic . . . though cognate in meaning, are by no means equivalent, the former being more limited and less comprehensive than the latter. Reformed expresses merely a religious and ecclesiastical distinction; it is a purely theological conception. . . . Calvinist is the name of a Reformed Christian in so far as he reveals a specific character and a distinct physiognomy, not merely in his church and theology, but also in social and political life, in science and art.[5]

Kuyper's definition of Calvinism went further, however, than the idea of Reformed Protestantism in its most comprehensive manifestations. It was also the most consistent form of Christianity, and indeed Christianity's highest expression (LC, p. 190). Later in this chapter this idea will be seen in the light of Kuyper's vision of historical development. He was not, however, entirely happy with the word Calvinism, and in order to avoid too close an association between his ideas and those of Calvin and traditional Calvinism he sometimes preferred the term "neo-Calvinism."[6] His aim in doing so was also to emphasize that Calvin's fundamental ideas had to be understood in relation to the prevailing circumstances of modern times, to which they had to be applied with the same consistency as they were originally expressed.[7] As noted in

3. Kuyper, *Antirevolutionaire staatkunde: met nadere toelichting op 'Ons program'* (Kampen: Kok, 1916), I, p. 624.

4. Herman Bavinck, "The Future of Calvinism," *The Presbyterian and Reformed Review* 17 (1894): 1-37.

5. Bavinck, p. 3.

6. Kuyper, *Antirevolutionaire staatkunde,* I, pp. 626-28. This term was first used by Kuyper's critics (see Chapter Nine), and may well have been influenced by the designation "neo-Catholicism" to refer to the nineteenth-century school of liberal Catholicism emanating from the work of Lamennais, Lacordaire, and Montalembert.

7. Kuyper, *Antirevolutionaire staatkunde,* I, p. 624.

Chapter One, Kuyper considered it an important priority to bring Calvinism up-to-date, in line with changed circumstances. He aimed to awake Reformed theology from its slumbers and to open up to it new vistas hitherto unconsidered. For this reason, his total body of thought, expressed most succinctly in his *Lectures,* may legitimately be referred to as "neo-Calvinism," along with the tradition that emanates from it.

2. Worldview

Kuyper's term "life-system" was intended as an equivalent to the German *Weltanschauung,* usually translated "worldview" in English. Although, he explained, "world-and-life-view" was a more accurate term, and preferable to James Orr's "view of the world," he had chosen "life-system" in the title of his lecture because of its conciseness and because he had understood from his American colleagues that this term was generally used in the United States in the same way as *Weltanschauung* was used in Germany (LC, p. 11, note 1).[8] It is worth clarifying, however, that the evidence is strongly against Kuyper's claim to have used "life-system" in the title of his first lecture. The version of the Stone Lectures he used to deliver his lectures at Princeton, the syllabus of the lectures distributed to each member of his audience, and the press reports of Kuyper's Stone Lectures, all testify to the original title having been "Calvinism in History."[9] Kuyper changed the title of the first lecture to "Calvinism a Life-system" for the published version of the lectures in English, most probably in order to draw attention to the fundamental thesis of the lectures as a whole — that Calvinism was an all-embracing life-system, rather than a narrowly defined set of doctrines or a particular ecclesiology.

In making this the basis of his entire argument, Kuyper demonstrates the extent to which he was influenced by current intellectual trends. The term *Weltanschauung,* coined by Kant in his *Kritik der Urteilskraft* (1790),

8. James Orr, *The Christian View of God and the World as Centring in the Incarnation.* Being the Kerr Lectures for 1890-1891, 4th edition (Edinburgh: Andrew Elliot, 1897), p. 3. (Citations are from this edition.) For a recent reprint of this work see James Orr, *A Christian View of God and the World.* With a foreword by Vernon Grounds (Grand Rapids: Kregel, 1989).

9. A. Kuyper, *Calvinism* [Copy of Stone Lectures held in Princeton Theological Seminary Archives]; *Syllabus of the Lectures on the L. P. Stone Foundation for 1898-99, by the Reverend A. Kuyper, D.D.,* in KA; Portfolio 9, no. 53; *The Daily Princetonian,* 10 October 1898.

became a key word in the thought-world of German Idealism and Romanticism, and was used to denote a set of beliefs that underlie and shape all human thought and action. As such it was akin to philosophy but without philosophy's rational pretensions.[10] Both James Orr in 1891 and Herman Bavinck in 1904 noted the great popularity of the term among contemporary philosophers.[11] The term "worldview" did not find its way into common English usage, however, until well into the twentieth century, at the high point of neo-Kantianism, which partly explains Kuyper's difficulty in finding a suitable English equivalent to the German.[12] As English-speaking philosophers now generally use the term worldview to mean the same as *Weltanschauung* in German, it is this term that is used in this book, except in the case of direct quotations, when other equivalents, such as "life-system" or "world-and-life-view," may be used.

Kuyper's concept of worldview is of particular interest and importance given the influence it has had on the development of neo-Calvinistic thought and activity, especially in the field of education and philosophy.[13] His insistence that worldviews have a determinative effect

10. James H. Olthuis, "On Worldviews," in Paul A. Marshall, Sander Griffioen, and Richard J. Mouw, eds., *Stained Glass: Worldviews and Social Science* (Lanham, Maryland: University Press of America, 1989), pp. 26-40 (p. 39 [note 4]); Albert M. Wolters, "On the Idea of Worldview and Its Relation to Philosophy," in *Stained Glass,* pp. 14-25 (p. 15). Wolters notes that the term was transmitted via Fichte to several well-known nineteenth-century German philosophers including Schelling, Schleiermacher, Hegel, and Goethe.

11. Orr, *The Christian View of God,* p. 365; Herman Bavinck, *Christelijke wereldbeschouwing,* 3rd edition (Kampen: Kok, 1929), p. 8. Bavinck wrote in his introduction to this work that in philosophical circles the search for a unified *("einheitliche")* worldview had become an obsession, due to the disharmony and division of modern life (p. 8). Elsewhere he noted that the notion of worldview became so popular that from 1902 to 1908 no fewer than twelve German books appeared with the word *Weltanschauung* in their titles. Recorded in Albert M. Wolters, "*Weltanschauung* in the History of Ideas: Preliminary Notes." Unpublished paper.

12. In 1917 B. B. Warfield referred to it as a word newly in fashion. Noted in Albert Wolters, "Dutch Neo-Calvinism: Worldview, Philosophy and Rationality," in Hendrik Hart et al., *Rationality in the Calvinian Tradition* (Lanham, Maryland: University Press of America, 1983), p. 114.

13. The editors of a recent book on the subject of worldview note that the histories of the Free University, of Calvin College in Grand Rapids (established by Dutch immigrants in 1876), and the Institute for Christian Studies in Toronto (founded in 1967) would be incomprehensible apart from the conviction that Calvinism was a comprehensive worldview. See Marshall, *Stained Glass,* p. 8.

on the results of scholarship has stimulated the development of a philosophical trend, represented in its early stages by Dooyeweerd, Vollenhoven, and Cornelius Van Til, which has made it a priority to demonstrate the untenability of the idea of the autonomy of theoretical thought. As yet, however, no attempt has been made to investigate the nature, background, and motivation of Kuyper's concept. It is often assumed that it was a concept that dominated Kuyper's thought throughout his career since his conversion in Beesd and provided the initiative for his activities outside the church, particularly the establishment of specifically Christian institutions.[14] Kuyper himself is partly responsible for creating this assumption, chiefly as a result of his reference to the "worldview" of the malcontents in Beesd, recorded in his *Confidentie* of 1873 and reiterated in the preface to his *Encyclopedia,* where he wrote that he had found among "the descendants of the ancient Calvinists"

> a stability of thought, a unity of comprehensive insight, in fact a world-view based on principles which needed but a scientific treatment and interpretation to give them a place of equal significance over against the dominant views of the age. To put forth an effort in this direction has from that moment on been his [Kuyper's] determined purpose.[15]

In his *Lectures on Calvinism,* Kuyper also claimed that the struggle between the Calvinistic and modernistic worldviews was one in which he had been spending all his energy for nearly forty years (LC, p. 11). Such instances create the impression that Kuyper propounded the concept of worldview in the philosophical sense of *Weltanschauung* from the time of his conversion, and that it subsequently provided the motivation for his various activities throughout his career. His use of the word "worldview" early in his career was, however, loose and undefined, and occurred in a way that was more incidental than purposeful.

This is not to deny that elements of Kuyper's worldview concept featured in his thinking before the Stone Lectures of 1898. In his sharply polemical speech of 1871 attacking modernism in theology, for instance (published two years before his *Confidentie*), there is an indication that

14. See, for instance, *New Dictionary of Theology,* ed. by Sinclair B. Ferguson and David F. Wright (Leicester: InterVarsity Press, 1988), p. 347.

15. Kuyper, *Encyclopedia,* p. viii; *Confidentie,* p. 47. See in addition *Predicatiën,* p. 238.

he had begun to think seriously about the influence worldview could have on the results of scholarship. In this pamphlet he remarked on the change in theology of his former mentor at Leiden J. H. Scholten, describing how in 1858, despite his modernist sympathies, Scholten had been committed to defending Johannine authorship of the Gospel of John.[16] Six years later, however, Scholten had published a book in which his entire position had changed to one in which "not a word from the hand of John was contained in the entire gospel."[17] Although Kuyper found it perfectly acceptable that a scholar should change a considered position and maintain his integrity, he was struck by Scholten's admission that the chief reason for his change of position was the transition he had made in recent years from a Platonic to a more Aristotelian worldview.[18] Scholten confessed, in fact, that he had changed his views on John's Gospel when he came to see that "the worldview of the writer of the fourth Gospel . . . no longer fits into the framework of our contemporary worldview, which is based on empirical foundations."[19] In making such admissions, Kuyper declared, "Scholten accepts an idea *a priori* as the guiding star of his criticism."[20] For Kuyper it marked the end of his sympathy for radical biblical criticism: "the reading of this book, supplemented by the memory of his enthusiastic delivery in his lectures, made such an impression on me, that from that time onwards the authority of modern criticism was for me entirely undermined."[21] These remarks coincide with a major element in the worldview concept he presented at Princeton: that scholarship is thoroughly influenced by the worldview held by the scholar, which serves as a starting point or set of presuppositions. He did not, however, develop this idea in his pamphlet of 1871, and he made no suggestion there that Christianity, or Calvinism, possessed a worldview of its own which could serve as an alternative starting point for scholarship. The comment, though important to the structure of his later thought, remained isolated in the speech and was not of any great significance to his argument.

16. Kuyper, *Het modernisme,* p. 14. See R. D. Henderson, "How Abraham Kuyper Became a Kuyperian," in *Christian Scholar's Review* 22 (1992): 22-35 (33-34).

17. Kuyper, *Het modernisme,* p. 14. The book to which Kuyper was referring was Scholten's *Het evangelie naar Johannes: kritisch historisch onderzoek* (Leiden: Engels, 1864).

18. Kuyper, *Het modernisme,* p. 73 (note 52); Scholten, p. iv.

19. Scholten, p. iv.

20. Kuyper, *Het modernism,* p. 73 (note 52).

21. Kuyper, *Het modernism,* p. 73 (note 52).

Three other elements in Kuyper's developed concept of worldview that are evident in his work prior to 1898 are the need for unity and coherency in thought; the need for all thought to proceed from a single principle, a "fixed point of departure"; and the need for a Calvinistic worldview that would oppose the worldview of Paganism. The first two elements were expressed in his address on the subject of pantheism given as Rector Magnificus of the Free University in 1892.[22] In contrast to the Stone Lectures, however, Kuyper made no use here of the term "worldview" with respect to pantheism, speaking rather of such terms as "spirit of the age," "tendency," and "process."[23] The third element occurs in his speech to the general synod of the *Gereformeerde* churches in 1896.[24] While his argument here is clearly echoed in the Stone Lectures, it lacks any attempt to define the contours of a Calvinistic worldview, settling instead for bemoaning the fact that one did not exist. The view, therefore, that the whole of Kuyper's career can be interpreted in the light of the attempt to articulate, both in word and deed, a Calvinistic worldview, needs modification. Despite the existence of certain elements of this concept in his earlier work, it was not until the Stone Lectures that he employed it in a deliberate and specific way, defining it in terms of *Weltanschauung* and using it to give shape to his entire body of thought.

This change was largely due to his encounter with the work of the Scottish theologian James Orr (1844-1913), to which he had referred at the start of his *Lectures* when explaining the difficulty in finding an English equivalent to the term *Weltanschauung*. Orr was the leading United Presbyterian theologian at the end of the nineteenth century, and, like Kuyper, he came to exercise a significant influence in North America, not least through his election as Stone Lecturer for the academic year 1903-4.[25] There is no

22. Kuyper, *Pantheism's Destruction*, pp. 9, 26-27.

23. Elsewhere Kuyper used a number of other terms as well (such as "foundational principle") in a similar way to his use of "worldview" in the general sense. But these should not be confused with or equated to his later concept.

24. A. Kuyper, *De zegen des Heeren over onze kerken: rede ter inleiding op het gebed voor het samenkomen der gereformeerde kerken in generale synode. gehouden in de Noorderkerk te Middelburg, op 10 augustus 1896* (Amsterdam: Wormser, 1896), p. 22.

25. Orr's Stone Lectures were published as *God's Image in Man, and Its Defacement, in the Light of Modern Denials* (London: Hodder and Stoughton, 1905). Orr was also a contributor to the influential series *The Fundamentals*. He was, to use Marsden's words, "the leading British theological critic of liberalism round the turn of the [nineteenth] century." George Marsden, "Fundamentalism as an American Phenom-

evidence that Kuyper and Orr had any direct personal contact with each other, and Kuyper's reference to Orr in the *Lectures* was a fleeting one, dismissed in a footnote. It appears, however, that the *Lectures* were influenced significantly by Kuyper's reading of Orr's Kerr Lectures for 1890-91, which were published under the title *The Christian View of God and the World*.[26] The similarities between Kuyper's argument and Orr's are worth highlighting here, as the question of Orr's influence on Kuyper has so far escaped consideration in studies of Kuyper's thought.

Orr argued that Christianity had an independent, unified, and coherent worldview derived from a central belief or principle, an argument which is virtually identical to that of Kuyper on behalf of Calvinism.[27] Kuyper also resembles Orr in his argument that modern worldviews are expressed in a unified system of thought,[28] that they are derived from a single principle and are embodied in certain forms of life and activity,[29] and that they are antithetical to Christianity.[30] Kuyper's claim, likewise, that Calvinism's only defense against modernism was in the

---

enon: A Comparison with English Evangelicalism," *Church History* 46 (1977): 215-32 (219). Orr's name was well known at Princeton before Kuyper's visit; the year before he had contributed an introduction to Warfield's *The Right of Systematic Theology* (Edinburgh: T & T Clark, 1897).

26. This work, generally regarded as Orr's *magnum opus*, was highly acclaimed following publication in 1893, and launched him on a prolific academic career. Kuyper consulted the fourth edition, which appeared just as he was beginning to turn his mind to the Stone Lectures (see footnote 8 for details).

27. Orr wrote: "though Christianity is neither a scientific system, nor a philosophy, it has yet a world-view of its own, to which it stands committed" (*The Christian View of God*, p. 9; see also pp. 3, 16, 33, 35).

28. Orr, *The Christian View of God*, p. 8: "Everywhere the minds of men are opening to the conception that, whatever else the universe is, it is one — one set of laws holds the whole together — one order reigns through all. Everywhere, accordingly, we see a straining after a universal point of view — a grouping and grasping of things together in their unity."

29. Orr, *The Christian View of God*, p. 6: "knowledge and action are knit up together, and organised into a single view of life."

30. Orr, *The Christian View of God*, p. 9: "It need not further be denied that between this view of the world involved in Christianity, and what is sometimes termed 'the modern view of the world', there exists a deep and radical antagonism." Orr also spoke of a current "clash of systems" (p. 13), a turn of phrase remarkably similar to that of Kuyper (see also pp. 32, 370-72). The same concept of struggle and conflict can incidentally be found in Wilhelm Dilthey's characterization of the plight of modernity as a "Streit der Weltanschauungen" (see Marshall, *Stained Glass*, p. 11).

development of an equally comprehensive worldview, in which principle would be arrayed against principle — is almost indistinguishable from Orr's argument regarding Christianity. Orr wrote:

> No one, I think, whose eyes are open to the signs of the times, can fail to perceive that if Christianity is to be effectually defended from the attacks made upon it, it is the comprehensive method that is rapidly becoming the more urgent. The opposition which Christianity has to encounter is no longer confined to special doctrines . . . but extends to the whole manner of conceiving the world. . . . It is no longer an opposition of detail, but of principle. The circumstance necessitates an equal extension of the line of defence. It is the Christian view of things in general which is attacked, and it is by an exposition and vindication of the Christian view of things as a whole that the attack can most successfully be met.[31]

The conviction that this worldview had bearing not only on the religious sphere but on the whole of theoretical thought was also vigorously defended by Orr, against what he saw as a current trend to revive the idea that there were two types of truth — one religious, the other philosophical — so that it was unnecessary that where the two overlapped they should be in agreement with each other.[32] By this token, Christianity's worldview was valid in terms of religion, but not in terms of philosophy.

Other similarities are also striking. Orr's insistence, for instance, that all true religion possesses, or needs to possess in order to survive, a worldview of its own bears resemblance to Kuyper's claim that the strength of Paganism, Islam, Roman Catholicism, and modernism (in contrast to the weakness of Protestantism) lay in their possession of an independent worldview (LC, p. 19). With an appeal to the pessimistic philosopher Eduard von Hartmann (1842-1906), to whom Kuyper appealed in his Stone Lectures when dealing with symbolism and art (LC, pp. 67, 148, 159), Orr claimed that no religion had ever been found without at least the rudiments of a worldview: "Religion cannot exist without a religious *Weltanschauung*."[33] Perhaps the most striking similar-

31. Orr, *The Christian View of God,* p. 4.

32. Orr (*The Christian View of God,* pp. 26-27) criticized Albrecht Ritschl, who argued in his *Theologie und Metaphysik* (Bonn: Marcus, 1887) that religious knowledge moves only in the sphere of worth- or value-judgments.

33. Orr, *The Christian View of God,* pp. 17-18. The quote is Orr's own translation from E. von Hartmann's *Religionsphilosophie,* II, p. 32.

ity of all is Orr's intention in giving the Kerr Lectures. Orr declared his main objective to be to show

> that there is a definite Christian view of things, which has a character, coherence, and unity of its own, and stands in sharp contrast with counter theories and speculations, and that this world-view has the stamp of reason and reality upon itself, and can amply justify itself at the bar both of history and of experience. I shall endeavour to show that the Christian view of things forms a logical whole which cannot be infringed on, or accepted or rejected piecemeal, but stands or falls in its integrity, and can only suffer from attempts at amalgamation or compromise with theories which rest on totally distinct bases. I hope thus to make clear at least the true nature of the issues involved in a comparison of the Christian and "modern" views, and I shall be glad if I can in any way contribute to the elucidation of the former.[34]

The only significant difference between Orr's intention and that of Kuyper in presenting Calvinism as an independent and coherent worldview resistant to modernism, was that Orr pleaded the merits of a Christian worldview while Kuyper pleaded a specifically Calvinistic one—albeit Calvinistic in the broadest possible sense.

Although such similarities suggest that the emphasis Kuyper gave to the idea of Calvinism as an independent worldview *(Weltanschauung)* among a plethora of antagonistic worldviews was inspired by James Orr's book, it does not challenge the point already made that certain important elements of Kuyper's worldview concept were present earlier in his career, along with uses of "worldview" or other similar terms in a general sense. Neither does it question the fact that Kuyper's use of this concept reflects a trend among nineteenth-century German philosophers to employ the concept of *Weltanschauung* in their work.[35] It is clear, however, that when Kuyper was faced with presenting the fundamentals of his own thought in a cogent and up-to-date form to a foreign audience, he seized on the concept of worldview in the specific "pre-philosophical" (or "pre-scientific") sense of *Wel-*

34. Orr, *The Christian View of God,* p. 16.

35. An example of the kind of German philosophical work that is likely to have influenced Kuyper's idea of worldview is Moriz Carrière, *Die philosophische Weltanschauung der Reformationszeit in ihren Beziehungen zur Gegenwart* (Leipzig: Brockhaus, 1887). Kuyper referred to Carrière in his address on "Calvinism and Art" as Rector Magnificus in 1888. See *Het calvinisme en de kunst,* p. 78 (note 87).

tanschauung, casting his entire thought-world within its conceptual framework. This decision, which marks the beginning of his thoroughgoing use of the worldview concept throughout the rest of his career, cannot be explained without reference to James Orr's Kerr Lectures, which he consulted in preparation for his lectures at Princeton.

3. Modernism

The concept of modernism is vital to the argument in Kuyper's *Lectures,* as the worldview towards which Christianity was diametrically opposed (LC, pp. 11, 190). It was a concept of considerable scope in his body of thought, consisting as it did of three major elements: the principles of the French Revolution; pantheism; and evolutionism. This may be illustrated by the following passage, in which modernism serves as a generic term for these three elements:

> among Protestant nations *Pantheism,* born from the new German philosophy and owing its concrete *evolution*-form to Darwin, claims for itself more and more the supremacy in every sphere of human life. . . . The leading thoughts that had their rise in the *French Revolution* at the close of the last, and in German philosophy in the course of the present century, form together a life-system which is diametrically opposed to that of our fathers. . . . And why did we, Christians, stand so weak in the face of this *Modernism?* (LC, pp. 18-19, my emphasis)

To understand Kuyper's concept of modernism it is thus necessary to understand each of its three constituent parts. Although he held that these were governed by the same essential principle — that of unbelief — he nevertheless regarded them as having an identity of their own: "Although the French Revolution and Hegel's Pantheism and Darwin's Evolution-doctrine spring from the one root of unbelief, they are still distinguishable as sprouts from that one root."[36]

First, however, it is important to note that Kuyper's use of the term modernism changed during the course of his career. In his early writings it was limited to the field of theology. His speech on modernism in 1871, for instance, was an attack on modernistic theology (a "fata Morgana")

36. *De Standaard,* 9 December 1892.

rather than on modernism as a comprehensive worldview that influenced all areas of culture.[37] This reflects not only the fact that the speech was given well before Kuyper's encounter with the work of James Orr, but that he gave it while functioning as an ordained minister, when theological and ecclesiastical issues, rather than wider social and political ones, were his principal concern. By the time of the Stone Lectures, however, he had ceased to regard modernism as a harmless and illusory fata Morgana, likening it instead to a raging storm sweeping through the whole of human life (LC, p. 10). Kuyper's involvement in various aspects of public life between 1871 and 1898 had served to expand his horizons in terms of modernism's potential influence, and made him susceptible to the idea that it was a dynamic, all-embracing, and antagonistic worldview.

Fundamental to Kuyper's objection to the modernistic worldview was that it started out from humanity rather than from God; it aimed to explain all human existence on the basis of natural data rather than divine revelation (LC, pp. 11, 23-24). This, Kuyper claimed, was a direct consequence of the revolutionary principles that culminated in the French Revolution of 1789.

3.1. The French Revolution

Throughout his journalistic and political career, Kuyper made more frequent reference to the French Revolution than to any other historical event, including the Reformation. This was in large part due to the intellectual legacy of Groen van Prinsterer, who emphasized the antithesis between Christian faith and the unbelief *(ongeloof)* of the French Revolution.[38] It was not the historical event itself that Kuyper was at variance with, but the principles behind it—he was willing to concede that God may well have used the Revolution to destroy the tyranny of the Bourbons, even though the principle that lay behind it was

37. P. Kasteel considers this speech to be Kuyper's "public declaration of war on liberal theology." See P. Kasteel, *Abraham Kuyper* (Kampen: Kok, 1938), p. 27.

38. See Harry van Dijk's *Groen van Prinsterer's Lectures on Unbelief and Revolution* (Jordan Station, Ontario: Wedge, 1989), which includes an English translation of Groen's lectures *Ongeloof en Revolutie* (Unbelief and Revolution), delivered in 1847.

"thoroughly anti-Christian" (LC, pp. 10-11).[39] This principle, expressing itself in the revolutionaries' slogan *ni Dieu ni maître,* sought a complete break with all religion, eliminating God not only from the church, but from the state, society, and science (LC, pp. 10, 23, 25, 87).[40] Thus the way was paved for the birth of modernism, "the daughter of the French Revolution" (LC, p. 33), because once the Revolution had rid its worldview of God it retained nothing but isolated and self-seeking individuals standing up for their own independence.[41] Despite the obvious benefits brought about by the Revolution (benefits ultimately derived from Calvinism),[42] the "liberty" proclaimed in 1789 had resulted in egoism and self-interest, often leading to the exploitation of the poor — the declaration of "equality" had led to sharp divisions in terms of private wealth; and the idea of "fraternity" had simply strengthened social demarcations.[43]

The parallels between this critique of the French Revolution and that of Karl Marx are striking. On the basis, obviously, of a radically different view of man and society to that of Kuyper, Marx criticized the right of ownership, which the revolutionaries had declared inviolable.[44] He stigmatized "liberty" in Revolutionary France as being little more than the freedom of individuals to enjoy their possessions without hindrance from others, and to pursue their egocentric interests. "Equality,"

39. See also A. Kuyper, *Het sociale vraagstuk en de christelijke religie* (Amsterdam: Wormser, 1891), p. 12. This is the published version of the speech Kuyper gave at the first Christian Social Congress in the Netherlands organized in 1891 following the publication of *Rerum Novarum.* For an English translation, see the centenary edition, A. Kuyper, *The Problem of Poverty,* ed. with an Introduction by James W. Skillen (Washington/Grand Rapids: The Center for Public Justice/Baker, 1991). This is a thoroughly revised version of an earlier translation: A. Kuyper, *Christianity and the Class Struggle,* trans. with a Preface by Dirk Jellema (Grand Rapids: Piet Hein, 1950).

40. See also *De Standaard,* 4 May 1889; Kuyper, *Het sociale vraagstuk,* p. 13.

41. Kuyper, *Het sociale vraagstuk,* p. 13.

42. Kuyper, "Calvinism: The Origin and Safeguard of Our Constitutional Liberties," trans. by J. H. de Vries, *Bibliotheca Sacra* (July and October, 1895): 405, 409-10; LC, p. 176.

43. A. Kuyper, *Niet de vrijheidsboom maar het kruis: toespraak ter opening van de tiende Deputatenvergadering in het eeuwjaar der Fransche Revolutie* (Amsterdam: Wormser, [1889], pp. 5, 8).

44. Karl Marx, *Die Frühschriften,* ed. by S. Landshut (Stuttgart: Kröner, 1971), pp. 525-60.

therefore, was simply the validation of egoistic values for all citizens. Thus the human person was deprived of its true vocation, which was to be a social and moral being *(Gemeinwesen, Gattungswesen)*. As a result, Marx claimed, the entire political and legal system was aimed at guaranteeing and protecting the rights of property and the unequal distribution of wealth; no so-called human rights could curb the egoistical interests of human beings. Although there is no direct evidence that Kuyper's criticism of French individualism was indebted to Marx, it is clear that his opposition to socialism, or rather to social democracy, was mixed with great respect for Marx's teachings, based on a first-hand acquaintance with his work. In the published version of his speech on the social question in 1891, Kuyper referred to Marx as a man of "outstanding learning and scholarly insight" as evidenced in his *Das Kapital*;[45] in 1895 he spoke of his scholarly constructed system of thought;[46] and in 1897 he declared how Marx stood out among economists in terms of knowledge and power of thought.[47] Kuyper's rejection of Marx's political philosophy does not exclude the possibility that he was influenced by certain aspects of his teaching, especially regarding ideas to which they were both opposed.

Kuyper's frequent acknowledgment of the practical benefits of the French Revolution in modern society reflects two important elements in his background. First, the Netherlands had benefited from several changes during the period of French domination from 1795 to 1813. These included the granting of religious freedoms, a more democratic form of government, and, for the first time, an efficient, centralized bureaucracy. The improvements brought about during the French period in Dutch history were, in fact, more far-reaching than those brought about by the restoration of the House of Orange in 1813. It was not until 1848, with the inauguration of the new constitution, drawn up by the liberal statesman J. R. Thorbecke (1798-1872), that Enlightenment ideals

45. Kuyper, *Het sociale vraagstuk*, p. 64 (note 57). Kuyper's first reference to Marx dates from 1874, about seven years after the publication of the early editions of *Das Kapital*. See *Briefwisseling van Mr. G. Groen van Prinsterer met Dr. A. Kuyper*, p. 290. Marx visited the conference of the First International of 1872, held in The Hague.

46. *De Standaard*, 20 February 1895.

47. See Kuyper's speech to ARP representatives, published in *Geen vergeefs woord: Verzamelde deputaten-redevoeringen* (Kampen: Kok, 1951), pp. 82-90 (p. 84). For Kuyper's criticism of social democracy, see Chapter Six (section 1.2.2).

gained formal and constitutional recognition in Dutch public life. Second, Kuyper's acknowledgment reflects the desire on the part of many anti-revolutionaries (himself included) to distance themselves from the contra-revolutionary tendencies typical of Dutch Catholics and conservatives. Contra-revolutionaries, he explained in 1874, "are bent upon the violent destruction of that which exists by virtue of history."[48] For Kuyper, therefore, both revolutionaries and contra-revolutionaries were guilty of the same error of advocating a radical break in history by means of a reordering and restructuring of the natural processes of history for the sake of a utopian ideal. Not so the anti-revolutionaries, he insisted, who recognized that "the *perspectives du paradis* cannot be realized on earth."[49] While they were not opposed to all forms of revolution (Kuyper admired and approved of the Dutch Revolt, the Glorious Revolution in England, and the American Revolution[50]), anti-revolutionaries were opposed to the specific philosophy behind the French Revolution, not to any recognition of its place in history. It was a position that bore close similarities to that of John Henry Newman (1801-1890), whose formative years coincided with a wave of antipathy against the French Revolution. The joint notions of continuity and development that were at the heart of his thought allowed him to accept social change as inevitable, so long as that change grew out of and preserved what was good in the past.[51] This had also been the teaching of Edmund Burke (1729-1797), whom Kuyper greatly admired, and who in his *Reflections on the Revolution in France* (1790) had urged the necessity of continuity in political change and opposed all violent and radical extremes.

For Kuyper, the French Revolution represented more than the dramatic social, political, and scientific changes of the late eighteenth century in France, which had been of some advantage to Western civilization as a whole. It symbolized primarily a dramatic shift in worldview from one in which God was sovereign to one in which humanity would occupy the highest place, a shift that had given rise to modernism as a new form of religion. Thus he tended to characterize the French Revolution in religious terms. Although he portrayed the Revolutionaries as

48. Kuyper, "Calvinism: The Origin and Safeguard," p. 664.

49. Kuyper, "Calvinism: The Origin and Safeguard," p. 673.

50. See previous chapter.

51. This position was closely allied to his understanding of theological development, famously expressed in his *Essay on the Development of Christian Doctrine* of 1845.

violently anti-Christian, he tried to show, by stressing their belief in the autonomy of the individual, that this did not mean that they were anti-religious. He thereby aimed to strengthen his claim that modernism, the progeny of the Revolution, was not a neutral form of rationalism, to which all enlightened people should subscribe, but a religious form of worldview utterly opposed to Christianity. In doing so he was consciously rejecting the liberal teaching he had imbibed at Leiden. There Scholten's insistence that modernism was the consequence and fulfillment of Calvinism had spurred Kuyper's early fascination with Calvinism, which remained with him for the rest of his life.[52] Following his conversion to Calvinism, Kuyper would argue that the true parentage of modernism was not Calvinism but the French Revolution.

3.2. Pantheism

After receiving its initial impulse in France the modernistic flood spread to Germany, where it was manifested in the form of pantheism (LC, p. 23). Although Kuyper made no attempt in his *Lectures* to define what he meant by "pantheism," the claims he made about it provide some indication as to his meaning: it found its concrete expression in Darwin's theory of evolution; it was intent on exchanging Christianity for a form of modern Buddhism; it maintained the same principle as the French Revolution as regards the expulsion of God from practical and theoretical life; it represented a trend towards a modern form of Paganism. These gleanings do not, however, present a clear picture, and would not have brought Kuyper's audience any closer to understanding what it was that he was so strongly opposing. He thereby reflected a tendency amongst nineteenth-century Protestant theologians, pointed out by Paul Tillich, to discuss pantheism at length without defining what they meant by the term.[53]

52. In 1889 Kuyper edited a Dutch translation of Calvin's *Institutes,* and provided an introduction: *Institutie, ofte onderwijsinghe in de Christelicke religie. In vier boeken beschreven door Johannes Calvinus. Nu van nieuws uyt het Latijn en François getrouwelick overgeset door Wilhelmus Corsmannus. Herdruk van de uitgave van Paulus Aertz van Ravesteyn 1650 te Amsterdam,* ed. by A. Kuyper (Doesburg: Van Schenk Brill, 1889).

53. See Paul Tillich, *Perspectives on 19th and 20th Century Protestant Theology,* ed. by Carl E. Braaten (London: SCM Press, 1967). Despite variations in definition, pantheism involves two central assertions: that everything that exists constitutes a unity, and that this all-inclusive unity is divine.

Fortunately, two of the speeches Kuyper gave as rector of the Free University help shed light on his perception of pantheism: "The Blurring of Boundaries" *(De verflauwing der grenzen)*, delivered in 1892 and published in English under the suggestive title "Pantheism's Destruction of Boundaries";[54] and "Evolution" *(Evolutie)*, delivered on 20 October 1899, almost exactly a year after Kuyper's visit to Princeton.[55] The argument of his speech of 1892 was that pantheism aimed at the elimination of divinely ordered boundaries in the created order. By identifying God with progress, pantheism removed the distinction between God and the world was removed, and thus all other boundaries were "blurred into mere shadows."[56] God was thus reduced to a "world-power," his conscious life dissolved in the life of humanity.[57] Except in the world of academic philosophy, where "Hegel has long been dethroned," the supremacy of this idea was everywhere apparent:

> It . . . exercises its influence upon the special sciences, predominates in our textbooks, takes the premium in our novels, glitters as tinsel in the daily press, vitiates the unction of our poets, colours the tone of conversation by *Schlagwörter*, and, in the circles of the mediocrity . . . it altogether subverts public opinion.[58]

Although scientists, including Darwin, had admitted to the inadequacies of the natural selection theory, which was based on pantheistic premises, it was taught as fact in schools and generally accepted by the non-intellectual sectors of society, instilling within them "the enthusiastic worship of progress."[59]

The dangers inherent in this removal of boundaries, Kuyper argued, were manifested in the weakening of moral awareness in personal, ecclesiastical, and political life. In personal life, where the worship of God was destroyed because God was identified with the world, character

54. Kuyper, *Pantheism's Destruction.* For an overview of reactions in the Dutch press to Kuyper's speech, see Rullmann, *Kuyper-bibliografie,* III, pp. 46-52. Warfield's reaction to it (in German translation) was very positive indeed. See his introduction to W. H. de Savornin Lohman's "Dr. Abraham Kuyper" (p. 562); A. Kuyper, *Die Verwischung der Grenzen,* trans. by W. Kolhaus (Leipzig: Deichert, 1898).

55. Kuyper, *Evolutie.*

56. Kuyper, *Pantheism's Destruction,* p. 8.

57. Kuyper, *Pantheism's Destruction,* p. 14.

58. Kuyper, *Pantheism's Destruction,* p. 4.

59. Kuyper, *Pantheism's Destruction,* p. 5.

was being damaged and skepticism was taking hold of the human heart. Because the aesthetic was allowed to take precedence over the ethical, and with the boundary between right and wrong removed, the demands of the sensual life could not but be gratified. All this explained the current lack of great characters, and the widespread sense of life's futility and dreariness, causing some to escape it in suicide. In the sphere of the church, confessional boundaries were being destroyed by the public proclamation of liberty of doctrine, spurred on by the writings of the *Vermittelungs*-theologians. In the political realm the boundary was being removed between the authorities, as the powers ordained of God, and the people, who are appointed by God to be subject to them. Thus the state was allowed to take the place of God as the highest power and the source of all morality, thereby becoming a state "before whose apotheosis every knee must bow, by whose grace alone we live, and to whose word we must all be subject."[60] This carried with it the threat of both absolutism on the part of the state and anarchy on the part of the people.

So much for Kuyper's general perception of pantheism, crucial for an understanding of his argument in the Stone Lectures. But who did he think were its chief representatives? Although he held Darwin's theory of evolution to be a concrete example of pantheism's influence in the world of science and philosophy, he associated pantheism's origins with Germany rather than Britain.[61] In his speech in Philadelphia on "The Antithesis Between Symbolism and Revelation," he suggested that in terms of philosophy, pantheism encompassed more or less the entirety of German thought from Kant to Schelling. In their enthusiasm for organic oneness and systematical conception, these thinkers had objected to the disintegration to which the French Revolution had submitted European life and thought, and, faced with an insipid Christianity, had returned to the philosophy of ancient Greece.[62] So sophisticated and well-ordered was the work of these philosophers that scholarship itself was virtually identified with the pantheistic worldview: "those who dared to oppose it were simply deemed unscientific, and, if clever, men willingly insincere, and guilty deceivers of the people."[63] Kuyper obviously considered Schleiermacher and Hegel to belong to this tradition,

60. Kuyper, *Pantheism's Destruction,* p. 28.
61. Kuyper, *Pantheism's Destruction,* p. 5.
62. Kuyper, *The Antithesis,* pp. 13-14.
63. Kuyper, *The Antithesis,* p. 14.

Hegel being its final exponent before it entered its demise in academic circles.[64]

References to leading German thinkers notwithstanding, the focus of Kuyper's critique was on the consequences of pantheism in practical life, rather than on pantheism's philosophical formulations, which he believed had become moribund. It was on this "practical" level that it found the manifold expression already alluded to: in the social and political sphere, an enthusiastic worship of progress, and with it the danger of state absolutism; in the church, the attempt to reduce the importance of doctrine; in science, the perpetuation of evolutionary theories; in art and religion, mysticism and symbolism.[65]

Kuyper's presentation of pantheism as a many-sided phenomenon of all-pervasive influence was not merely for rhetorical effect. It also provided the background against which he presented the central argument of his *Lectures on Calvinism:* that Calvinism represented an all-embracing world-view, equal in scope, coherency, and dynamism to the pantheistic world-view to which it was opposed. His conception of Calvinism reflects, therefore, the influence of pantheistic philosophy. His stress on the need for a coherent system of principles, comprehensive in scope and derived from "a single, unifying principle," was a characteristic of pantheistic monism, with its stress on the unity of all reality. In his attempt to repudiate a dualistic understanding of the world by stressing the comprehensive nature of the Calvinistic system, Kuyper demonstrated the extent to which he had been influenced by the pantheism he so violently opposed.

3.3. Evolution

It is curious, given the fact that in 1892 Kuyper seems to have thought that the evolution theory had ceased to hold sway in academic circles, that he should have paid attention to it both in his Stone Lectures and

64. Kuyper, *Pantheism's Destruction,* pp. 5, 19. Although Schleiermacher spoke of God in monotheistic as well as pantheistic terms, he committed himself to pantheism by asserting that it is the totality of things that is divine. In similar terms Hegel asserted that the divine is the totality. Recent scholarship agrees with Kuyper that Hegel's work marks the end of philosophical pantheism. See *The Encyclopedia of Philosophy,* ed. by Paul Edwards, 8 vols., vol. VI (London: Collier-Macmillan, 1967), p. 34.

65. Kuyper, *Pantheism's Destruction,* passim.

in his rectorial address of 1899.[66] The latter was a serious attack, some forty-four pages long, on evolutionary theory, not as a speculative explanation of biological phenomena but as an integrated philosophical system. It would appear, then, that by 1899 Kuyper had come to judge the threat from evolution to be more serious than he had anticipated in 1892. In his address he argued that evolutionism was responsible for the cultural, intellectual, and ethical malaise of the late nineteenth century; he opened with the lyrical phrase: "Our nineteenth century is dying away under the hypnosis of the Evolution-dogma."[67]

Kuyper's response was not unique, either in tone or imagery. John Henry Newman for example (1801-1890), while never actively engaging with Darwinian theory and never mentioning it in his publications (in contrast to the general trend among English intellectuals in the 1860s and 1870s), referred to evolutionary ideology in one of his letters, describing it as an "epidemic" that was taking a disastrous toll among Christians. Not only does Newman's diagnosis here bear resemblance to Kuyper's image of hypnosis, but Newman, like Kuyper, was confident that Christian truth would eventually prove to be an effective remedy: "It is dreadful to think of the number of souls that will suffer while the epidemic lasts; but truth is too powerful not in the end to get the upper hand."[68] If Kuyper's depiction of the malaise caused by evolutionism sounded a lot like his

66. Kuyper, *Evolutie.* This remains one of Kuyper's most highly regarded lectures. D. T. Kuiper has written that in it Kuyper demonstrated "a thorough knowledge of the findings of and controversies within contemporary science" and that he offered "a brilliant, immanent and transcendental critique of the dogmatic aspects of the theory of biological evolution and the ethical and religious conclusions connected to it by social Darwinism." From "Dutch Calvinism on the Racial Issue," *Calvin Theological Journal* 21 (1986): 51-78 (p. 68, note 45). More recently the editor of the same journal has written that the Evolution lecture is "a superb example of Kuyper's remarkable scholarship and keen instincts for the religious undercurrents and social consequences of a set of ideas that are still being fiercely debated to this day. Kuyper's prescience is stunning; often he seems to be describing our world, our century." John Bolt, "Editorial," *Calvin Theological Journal* 31 (1996): 9-10 (10).

67. Kuyper, *Evolutie,* p. 7.

68. Letter from Newman to Rev. David Brown, dated Easter Eve [4 April], 1874, published in *The Letters and Diaries of John Henry Newman,* ed. by Charles Stephen Dessain and others, 31 vols. (Oxford: Oxford University Press, 1961-1984), XXVII, p. 43. See S. L. Jaki, "Newman and Evolution," *The Downside Review* 109 (1991): 16-34 (29). Further British responses to evolutionary thought can be found in Thomas F. Glick, *The Comparative Reception of Darwinism* (Austin: University of Texas Press, 1974), pp. 3-80.

depiction of the malaise caused by pantheism in his address seven years earlier, this is because of the close connection he made between evolution and pantheism: the theory of evolution was the result of using pantheistic philosophy to interpret empirical data. Thus evolution appeared as "one of the richest thoughts of pantheism"; as pantheism's "legitimate daughter"; and, in characteristically graphic language, as a "poisonous slime upon the shore" left behind by the pantheistic stream.[69] One of the chief ways in which this toxic doctrine had displayed itself was in the so-called "social Darwinism" of contemporary society, which placed the strong over against the weak and disregarded the interests of the individual for the sake of society as a whole.[70] Its influence could not, however, be restricted to the social sphere alone, for it sought to explain, by means of a universal and absolute principle, the whole of existence, and to determine the course not only of the natural sciences but also of social and political science, law, history, ethics, and religion. As such it represented "an all-embracing system, a world-and-life-view derived from a single principle."[71] With these words Kuyper echoed the theme of his first Stone Lecture, given almost exactly a year before.

There is a striking difference, however, between the *Lectures on Calvinism* and *Evolutie* in the way Kuyper presented the evolutionary worldview as opposed to the Christian one. In the *Lectures,* Kuyper claimed that the reason Protestantism was so severely threatened by

69. Kuyper, *Pantheism's Destruction,* pp. 10, 11, 19.

70. Kuyper, *Evolutie,* p. 11.

71. *Evolutie,* p. 8. Cf. p. 24. As an example of the influence of evolutionary theory in ethics, Kuyper took Herbert Spencer's *The Data of Ethics,* 3rd ed. (London: Williams & Norgate, 1881) and in religion Ernst Haeckel's *Der Monismus als Band zwischen Religion und Wissenschaft,* 8th edition (Bonn: E. Strauss, 1899). [English edition: *Monism as Connecting Religion and Science,* trans. by J. Gilchrist (London: A. & C. Black, 1894)]. Although often associated with Darwin, the dictum "survival of the fittest" actually belongs to Spencer. In contrast to Kuyper's critique, Spencer's intention (at least early in his career) was to defend the freedom of the individual against the encroaching power of the state. See especially his *The Man versus the State* of 1854. It is true, however, that his vast *Programme of a System of Synthetic Philosophy* of 1860 was influenced, at least in part, by Darwin's *On the Origin of Species* published the previous year, and that it aimed at linking all fields of knowledge on the basis of a single principle: that evolution is a kind of progress from homogeneity to an organized heterogeneity, dependent on an unknowable force which sets the whole system in motion. His subsequent series of books issued to illustrate this theme included works on biology, sociology, psychology, education, and ethics.

modernism was because modernism had a worldview of its own, whereas Protestantism did not (LC, p. 19). In his speech on evolution the argument was reversed: "Up to now we in our Christian circles had the advantage over our opponents of being inspired by an all-encompassing and coherent faith. . . . But now, thanks to the evolution dogma, these opponents have also come to possess a comprehensive system, a worldview derived from a single principle."[72] Whereas in the Stone Lectures Kuyper suggested modernism's worldview as a model for an opposing Christian worldview, in *Evolutie* he claimed it was the Christian worldview which provided a model for modernism. A possible explanation of this discrepancy is that in the *Lectures* Kuyper was not saying that Christianity lacked a worldview but that Protestantism did; he readily conceded that Roman Catholicism possessed a clearly defined and independent worldview. In *Evolutie* he was not speaking of the worldview possessed by Protestantism but by Christianity (including Roman Catholicism). Whether or not this explanation is viable, it is clear that Kuyper held that the worldviews of Christianity and of evolution were diametrically opposed to each other, without hope of reconciliation: they were "antipoles between which neither reconciliation nor comparison is thinkable."[73] He was keen to emphasize, however, that this antithesis was not to be based on a mistrust of the scientific data produced by evolutionary scientists. In fact, the richness of such data was something he obviously welcomed and admired. He was also not opposed, in contrast to most of his Catholic and orthodox Protestant contemporaries, to the idea that one species may have evolved out of another rather than that all species had been created by the direct activity of God.[74] While holding fast to "primordial creation" over against an *"evolutio in infinitum"* he sought to do justice to "relative evolution" (LC, p. 132). For Kuyper the true conflict lay between the belief that the cosmos came into being through the creative activity of God and developed organically according to a divine plan, and the idea that the natural world originated and developed mechanically, independent of God.

Kuyper's notion of "relative evolution," or "evolutionary creation" *(evolutionistische schepping),*[75] was an attempt to acknowledge the findings of

72. Kuyper, *Evolutie,* p. 8.
73. Kuyper, *Evolutie,* p. 11.
74. Kuyper, *Evolutie,* pp. 14, 47.
75. Kuyper, *Evolutie,* p. 48.

empirical biology while maintaining the integrity of the Genesis account. His position is of particular interest because, as Ilse Bulhof has shown, among orthodox Protestant responses to evolutionary theory in the Netherlands, Kuyper's was the first to show a way of accepting the idea of progress and a form of qualified Darwinism.[76] As will become clear in Chapter Seven, in developing his doctrine of "common grace" *(gemeene gratie),* by which God restrains the effects of sin in the world, Kuyper was able to accept, on certain conditions, the results of modern science and the notion of human progress. His objection to the theory of evolution was that it had invaded and captured all areas of knowledge, including the metaphysical, and so had become a religion of its own, thanks to the likes of Herbert Spencer and Ernst Haeckel. Christians, he felt, should regard scientific theories as hypotheses, not as doctrines that told the truth about reality. He thus rejected evolutionism as a worldview, but accepted it as a scientific hypothesis, constructed with fallible human reason. This position, Bulhof claims, was "doubtless the most creative" among religious responses in the Netherlands.[77] Claude Welch, likewise, regards it as "an ingenious way of looking at evolution 'from a Christian point of view.'"[78]

In the end, Kuyper's rejection of the evolutionary worldview was not as radical as he proposed, and indeed there are clear signs of its influence on his thought. His view of world history, for instance, as we have seen, was of a continual process of development which flowed in a single stream from east to west, Calvinism representing the highest and most recent stage of development.[79] Before reaching this stage, he taught, it had passed through successive stages of Paganism, Islam, and Roman Catholicism (LC, pp. 32-34). He thus came to a position characteristic of much nineteenth-century evolutionary thought, adopted by mainstream liberalism, that humanity was involved in a process of evolutionary development from primitive to advanced stages. His purpose in presenting history in this way was clearly to infuse his audience with the inspiring thought that they, as not only Americans but Calvinists, stood at the forefront of historical

76. Ilse N. Bulhof, "The Netherlands," in Glick, pp. 269-306 (304).

77. Bulhof, p. 303. See also Bulhof's *Darwin's 'Origin of the Species': Betoverende wetenschap. Een onderzoek naar de relatie tussen literatuur en wetenschap* (Baarn: Ambo, 1988), pp. 30, 44-45.

78. Claude Welch, *Protestant Thought in the Nineteenth Century,* 2 vols. (New Haven: Yale University Press, 1985), II, p. 200.

79. See Chapter Three for a discussion of Kuyper's notion of the stream of human development.

and religious development. The privilege of such a position bore with it the responsibility to defend Calvinism against the onslaught of modernism, which was engaged in the attempt to oust Calvinism from its position of supremacy at the head of the human stream. The idea was intended to appeal to the sentiments of his audience, even at the expense of adopting Darwinian concepts of human progress.

Engaging in reasoned dialogue was not, for Kuyper, the way to respond to the impending threat from evolutionary theory. This was fruitless given the sharp division between the evolutionary and Calvinistic worldviews. Evolutionism's fundamentally religious character was to be acknowledged, and despite the benefits it had helped to bring to scientific discovery, it was to be opposed with a worldview based on Christian principles (LC, pp. 18-19). In his address on evolution he declared:

> No fascination with nor appreciation of the great beauty and richness which these studies have brought to us may allow us to have a moment's contentment with this system as a system. That system remains bad, even though in countless ways good has come out of it. We must not defend ourselves against it, but attack it.[80]

This passage, and the context in which it appears, also reflects the development of Kuyper's concept of worldview, particularly when it is compared to his speech on pantheism. Whereas in the latter the notion of worldview is not an explicit feature, it plays a pronounced and vital role in his evolution speech. Under his scathing, principled critique, the concept of evolution took on the character of a worldview encompassing the whole of reality. It is reasonable to suppose that Kuyper's first sustained and vigorous use of the worldview concept in the Stone Lectures, delivered a year before his evolution speech, accounts for this shift.

How would Kuyper's position on evolution have gone down with his colleagues of the Princeton School? Charles Hodge (1797-1878), one of the most influential of America's theologians in his day, had been vigorously opposed to evolution, based on what he considered to be Darwinism's conflict with the teachings of scripture concerning the origin of man, and with the idea of design. It was thus atheistic, even though Darwin himself was not an atheist.[81] A. A. Hodge and B. B. Warfield,

80. Kuyper, *Evolutie,* p. 50.

81. Charles Hodge, *What Is Darwinism?* (New York: Scribners, Armstrong, and Company, 1874).

however, Hodge's successors to his chair in theology, had little difficulty in accommodating Darwin's findings to the teachings of scripture. They denied that evolution necessarily involved a repudiation of design in nature. In 1880, less than two years after his father, Charles Hodge, had died, A. A. Hodge wrote: "We have no sympathy with those who maintain that scientific theories of evolution are necessarily atheistic." He did take note, however, of "the essential incongruousness of evolution and theistic philosophy."[82] Later he stressed the boundaries beyond which evolutionary theories became anti-Christian speculation, and argued that evolution must not pretend to fathom "origins, or causes or final ends," nor to exclude "design, providence, grace, or miracles." If it did so then it deserved the label "atheistic."[83] In a way similar to Kuyper, he maintained that, given these restrictions, Darwin's theory must be accepted as a potentially useful hypothesis for explaining natural development. Warfield, unlike many of his theologically conservative contemporaries, refused to accept an antithesis between creation and evolution, and argued that Darwin's agnosticism was not the inevitable result of his evolution theory.[84] He declared that evolution might supply a tenable theory of the means by which divine creation occurred. He accepted, in other words, "theistic evolution,"[85] a theory that bore close similarity to Kuyper's evolutionary creation. It was not until after Warfield's death in 1921, however, that theologians at Princeton, and conservative evangelicals in general — having since acquired the name Fundamentalists — began, along with Kuyper and the

82. A. A. Hodge, Review of Asa Gray's *Natural Science and Religion* (1880), in *Presbyterian Review* 1 (July 1880): 586, 588.

83. A. A. Hodge, "Introduction" to Joseph S. Van Dyke, *Theism and Evolution* (New York: Armstrong, 1886), pp. xv-xxii. An extract from this introduction is reprinted in M. A. Noll (ed.), *The Princeton Theology 1812-1921: Scripture, Science, and Theological Method from Archibald Alexander to Benjamin Breckinridge Warfield* (Grand Rapids: Baker, 1983), pp. 233-37.

84. B. B. Warfield, "Darwin's Arguments Against Christianity and Religion," *The Homiletic Review* 17 (1889): 9-16; "Charles Darwin's Religious Life: A Sketch in Spiritual Biography," *Presbyterian Review* 9 (1888): 569-601; *The Present-Day Conception of Evolution* (Emporia, Kans., [1895]); "Creation versus Evolution," *Bible Student* 4 (1901): 1-8; "Calvin's Doctrine of Creation," *Princeton Theological Review* 13 (1915): 190-255, reprinted in his *Calvin and Calvinism* (New York: Oxford University Press, 1931), pp. 299-306.

85. B. B. Warfield, "On the Antiquity and Unity of the Human Race" (1911), in Warfield's *Biblical and Theological Essays* (New York: Oxford University Press, 1932), pp. 235-58.

German positivist philosophers before them, to allow the notion of evolution to take on mythical proportions, as the great inclusive symbol of scientific naturalism. They began to emphasize that evolution was not merely a theory about biological development, but that it represented an entirely naturalistic worldview. As such it became the chief rallying point in their warfare with modern scientific culture.[86] Although at the time of Kuyper's visit the severity of Kuyper's attack on evolutionism as an all-embracing worldview may not have generated a positive response, the level of agreement between Kuyper and Warfield on the value of evolution as an interpretation of biological development, but also on its destructiveness if applied to the realm of metaphysics, is remarkable.

Conclusion

In expounding the concept of worldview in his first Stone Lecture, Kuyper had introduced not only the recurrent theme of all six lectures but a major thrust of his thought. The processes of history, past and present ideologies, and Calvinism itself could all be understood by recourse to this term. Contrary to common opinion among commentators on Kuyper, however, he did not employ the term in a deliberate and systematic way until his presentation of the Stone Lectures in 1898. Before this, only the bare elements of such a concept are apparent. The transition was related to the seriousness with which Kuyper viewed the threat from modernism, which increased as the end of the nineteenth century approached; but also to his reading of James Orr.

Kuyper's aim in casting modern secular ideologies in terms of all-embracing worldviews was to provide the backdrop against which to present a case for the development of an alternative, Christian worldview, based on Calvinistic principles. Although its contents would be antithetical to all other modern secular worldviews, its form would bear a strong resemblance: it was to be derived from a single unifying principle (the sovereignty of God); it was to provide answers to the same fundamental questions of human existence; and it was to be comprehensive and internally consistent. The meeting of these requirements was the

86. David N. Livingstone, "Evolution as Myth and Metaphor," *Christian Scholar's Review* 12 (1983): 11-25; George M. Marsden, *Understanding Fundamentalism and Evangelicalism* (Grand Rapids: Eerdmans, 1991), p. 147.

means by which Kuyper hoped the Calvinistic worldview would be brought up-to-date, fit to engage with contemporary issues of society, politics, and culture. To him, Calvinistic thought, developed in accordance with the demands of the late nineteenth century, could offer a comprehensive, logically cohesive alternative to modernistic thought and provide the basis for Christian cultural renewal.

In fact, however, this program borrowed liberally from the systems it purported to oppose — from pantheism the idea of coherence and unity; from evolutionism the idea of human and religious progress. Despite his emphasis on the antithesis between Calvinism and modernism, Kuyper's ideas are a testimony to the all-pervasiveness of nineteenth-century modernism, of which he himself was all too keenly aware. His aim of using the modernistic worldview as a model for his own in order to bring Calvinism up-to-date appears to have included some pitfalls he proved unable entirely to avoid.

Second Lecture: Calvinism and Religion

The aim of Kuyper's second lecture was to identify the religious principles that were central to the Calvinistic worldview and which accounted for its dynamic and transforming effect in world history. They were principles, he believed, that had had their initial impact in the sphere of religion, and only subsequently had transformed the broader fields of culture. This explains why he examined the sphere of religion first, and only after that went on to discuss the effects of these principles in spheres of politics, science, and art. For Kuyper, Calvinism represented a kind of centrifugal force that moved outwards in ever-widening circles — from its initial influence in the sphere of religion — to encompass the whole of human existence. The same outward-moving force was also evident within the sphere of religion itself. Here the fundamental ideas of Calvinism produced, in rapid succession, a distinctive form of religious belief, ecclesiastical life, and morality (LC, p. 41). Special attention will be given in this chapter to the doctrines of common grace, biblical authority, and the church, these being particularly important foundations to Kuyper's worldview that hitherto have virtually escaped historical analysis.

1. The Fundamentals of Religion

Kuyper believed that four mutually dependent, fundamental questions determined the nature of all religion (LC, p. 43): (1) does religion exist for the sake of God or for the sake of human beings? (2) does it operate directly or mediately? (3) is it partial or comprehensive? (4) is it normal or soteriological (abnormal) in nature? The discussion of Kuyper's answers to these questions will follow the same order below.

1.1. Religion Is for God's Sake

Kuyper argued that the problem with all forms of egoistic and eudaemonistic religion, as found in modern Idealistic philosophy, was that they were directed towards human interest. Religion of this kind flourished, he claimed, in adverse circumstances but was cast aside when human needs were satisfied, as could currently be observed among nominal Christians of the wealthier classes. Calvin insisted, in contrast, that although religion produces benefits for human beings, it does not exist for their sake, but for God's, who makes them religious (LC, p. 46). In doing so, Kuyper claimed, Calvin had maintained the sovereignty of God in the sphere of religion.

Kuyper's decision to begin his exposition of the specific nature of Calvinism in the sphere of religion by dealing with the doctrine of God's sovereignty, and only to end it with the doctrine of redemption, was not incidental. He considered the doctrine of God's sovereignty to be the fundamental principle of the Calvinistic worldview, and it was one he often expounded in his discussions of both political and cultural issues, and of theological matters. In doing so he was concerned to counter the idea that Calvinism was primarily a dogmatic position concerning the doctrine of redemption and of significance only to the church. The dominating theme of Calvinism, he explained, "was not, soteriologically, justification by faith, but, in the widest sense cosmologically, the sovereignty of the triune God over the whole cosmos" (LC, p. 79). For Kuyper it was this principle that explained the superiority of Calvinism over Lutheranism in terms of its transforming effect on human culture: whereas Lutheranism was preoccupied with the question of how to obtain eternal life, Calvinism was primarily concerned with establishing God's sovereignty in every sphere of life.

Kuyper's emphasis on God's absolute sovereignty was designed to draw attention to the fundamental divergence, as he saw it, between Calvinists, who held fast to this doctrine, and modernists, who rejected it. In his *E Voto Dordraceno* he declared that those who rejected this doctrine encompassed broad circles of professing Christians, including the followers of J. H. Scholten, who insisted that human beings were able to determine their own salvation.[1] In the political realm likewise, modernism had exchanged divine for human sovereignty, with disastrous consequences for the freedom of the individual (LC, pp. 85-90).

Kuyper's polemics aside, it is true that the issue of sovereignty in the religious and political sphere had become increasingly important towards the end of the nineteenth century, when traditional patterns of authority were under threat in every sphere and at every level. It was against this background that Kuyper chose the concept of God's absolute sovereignty as the starting point for all discussion of the nature and proper functioning of human authority. His according of prior place to the sovereignty of God rather than to justification by faith, thus making soteriology secondary, reflected Kuyper's reaction to the pietistic tendency to hold the salvation of the individual to the fore in worship and theology, a reaction in large part born out of his disappointment with the Brighton Movement.

1.2. Religion Operates Directly

In contrast to all non-Christian religions and some varieties of Christianity, Kuyper claimed, Calvinism held that religion did not require human mediation but realized direct communion between God and the human heart. He regarded this position to be a direct consequence of the belief that religion exists for the sake of God rather than for the sake of human beings. If religion exists to help human beings, then it is natural that people should seek human mediators. If, on the other hand, religion demands that everyone should give glory to God, the possibility of one person mediating on behalf of another is excluded. In Calvinism, Kuyper explained, God himself, in Christ, is the only mediator and it is he who enters into a direct relationship with the individual, a belief expressed in the doctrine of election. This belief had ensured the liberty of the

1. A. Kuyper, *E Voto,* II, p. 181.

individual, who was no longer bound to a human priesthood by the need for a mediator. It also accounted for the fact that in Holland, France, England, and America it had been Calvinists who had championed the cause of liberty of conscience.

Although the doctrine of election, or predestination as Kuyper preferred to call it, is often considered to be the most characteristic element of Calvinistic theology, Kuyper gave no special attention to it in his exposition of Calvinism in the Stone Lectures.[2] This doctrine did not in fact feature as prominently in his writings as might be expected, not only because of his commitment to Calvinist theology, but also because he considered it to be the *cor ecclesiae,* and central to the Reformed confession.[3] His *De gemeene gratie* provides an indication as to why this was the case. There he criticized Reformed theologians for having made predestination the chief focus of their attention, paying only scant regard to the workings of God's grace in the world outside the church, expressed in the doctrine of common grace.[4]

In emphasizing the existence of a link between predestination and political liberty, Kuyper aimed not only to liberate Reformed theology from its preoccupation with the doctrine of election, but also to counter the criticism that this doctrine was concerned primarily with questions of personal salvation. In attempting to advocate the merits of Calvinism, Kuyper was prepared to seize the initiative from Calvinism's critics, and to declare that the doctrine of predestination, which they so despised, was responsible for the political liberties of Western democracy. He was always pleased to find other internationally respected intellectuals to support him in this enterprise. George Bancroft had written in his *History of the United States* that those in history who knew themselves to have been chosen by God stood up fearlessly against tyranny; and a similar point was propounded by F. D. Maurice in his *Lectures on Social Morality.*[5] Such writers bore testimony to the

2. Kuyper's preference for the term "predestination" as opposed to "election" is explained in his *E Voto,* II, p. 166.

3. A. Kuyper, *Het calvinisme: Oorsprong,* p. 54; A. Kuyper, *De gemeene gratie,* I, pp. 1-2; A. Kuyper, *E Voto,* II, p. 194. For a translation of Kuyper's discussion of election in *E Voto,* II (pp. 158-95), see A. Kuyper, *The Biblical Doctrine of Election,* trans. by G. M. van Pernis (Grand Rapids: Zondervan, 1934).

4. A. Kuyper, *De gemeene gratie,* II, pp. 91-92, 94-95.

5. Kuyper, *Het calvinisme en de kunst,* p. 78 (note 86); Bancroft, I, p. 461; F. D. Maurice, *Lectures on Social Morality,* 2nd edition (London: 1872). Later published as

fact, however unpopular it might be among the liberal establishment, that the Calvinistic *libertatis ergo,* of such benefit to the cause of democracy, had its roots in the doctrine of predestination.[6]

1.3. Religion Is Comprehensive

For Kuyper, Calvinism held that religion was comprehensive in terms of the human faculty through which it functioned, the sphere in which it operated, and the circle of people to whom it was relevant. Modern religious philosophy, he declared, sought to ban religion from the field of the human intellect and to confine it to the emotions and the will, thus excluding religion from science and from public life. A partial view of the religious faculty had thus given rise to a partial view of the sphere of religion, with the result that religion had been removed from the center of human life and placed alongside it. The Calvinist was opposed to this trend, believing that all human faculties were a field for the operation of religion and that, because God had invested every part of his creation with laws that governed their existence, the task of all human beings was to glorify God in whatever sphere of activity they were involved. Calvinists abhorred, therefore, "a religion confined to the closet, the cell or the church" (LC, p. 53). In opposition to a dualistic way of life, they insisted on Christianity's universal scope, a belief they expressed in the doctrine of common grace (LC, pp. 52, 53, 59).

It was because of the doctrine of common grace, Kuyper declared, that Calvinism had proved able to release religion from the confines of church and confessional structures to give a powerful impulse to the development of Western society. In contrast to particular grace, he explained, by which God imparts salvation, common grace is the means by which God restrains the corruption of the world caused by sin, and allows for the development of human life and culture.[7]

Social Morality: Twenty-One Lectures Delivered in the University of Cambridge (London: Macmillan, 1886), p. 310.

6. Kuyper, *Het calvinisme en de kunst,* p. 26.

7. Kuyper, *Het calvinisme en de kunst,* II, p. 602. For theological treatments of Kuyper's doctrine of common grace in English, written by theologians associated with Princeton Seminary who were influenced by Kuyper, see C. van Til, *Common Grace,* and H. van Til, *The Calvinistic Concept.*

Kuyper's major treatment of the doctrine of common grace is his *De gemeene gratie* which was first published in a series of articles in *De Heraut.* As such it was intended for a wide readership, rather than merely for professional theologians. It was not unrelated, however, to the academic theological world of his day. The radical changes that took place in the field of theology during Kuyper's career concerned in particular the relationship between the church and the world. Whereas the gap between these two had widened considerably in Protestant theology towards the end of the eighteenth century, in the nineteenth century the general trend was for the church to "rediscover" the world, a trend largely stimulated by modernistic theology, which placed the church-world relationship firmly back onto the theological agenda. Faced with the forceful challenge to the Christian tradition from the spirit of the Enlightenment, theologians of the modernist school assumed the task of redefining the relationship between Christianity and culture.[8] As a theology student at Leiden, Kuyper had sat under the tutelage of the leading representatives of this school in the Netherlands in the form of Scholten, Rauwenhoff, and Kuenen. Although he later rejected their understanding of miracles and of scriptural authority, following his conversion to orthodox Calvinism, the questions they raised concerning the relationship of Christianity to culture remained central to his thought throughout his career.

It was soon after the high point of theological modernism in the mid-nineteenth century that Kuyper began the wide publication of his theological ideas, particularly after his launch of *De Standaard* in 1872. In contrast to the belief that man was basically good but in need of greater knowledge — a belief he considered characteristic of modernism — Kuyper insisted on the radical character of sin. It was this confession, he claimed, that provided the foundation for the doctrine of common grace: "It has not arisen out of philosophical reflection but out of the confession of the deadly character of sin."[9] For Kuyper the doctrine of common grace accounted for the existence of so much that is good in human society, despite its fallen state, and as such was aimed to provide an alternative to the modernist's belief in man's inherent goodness.

8. K. H. Roessingh, *De moderne theologie in Nederland: hare voorbereiding en eerste periode* (Groningen: Van der Kamp, 1914).

9. Kuyper, *De gemeene gratie,* I, p. 7.

It was against this theological background that Kuyper formulated his ideas on common grace. In doing so, he was not initiating a new debate but was taking a particular stand in a contemporary theological discussion of the true relationship between the church and the world. Rather than giving careful scholarly consideration to various theological positions, an activity more characteristic of his theological colleague Herman Bavinck, Kuyper's concern was to indicate in bold strokes the direction his followers should take.

The theological motives that influenced the shaping of Kuyper's doctrine of common grace were closely tied to social and political ones. His copious treatment, for instance, of the church-state relationship from the perspective of common grace in his *De gemeene gratie* was an attempt to provide a principled theological approach to a practical political issue. He formulated his ideas on common grace not only as a theologian but also as a politician, and for this reason the social and political motivation of Kuyper's doctrine also deserves attention.

Kuyper's idea that common grace allowed for the development of the powers God had invested in human culture provided the foundation for his discussion of the vocation of the Christian in the world outside the church. The Christian had a duty, he explained, to engage with human culture, to discover the divinely imparted energies at work in it, and to develop them according to God's laws. There could be no room, therefore, for cultural indifference or hostility, attitudes he claimed to be typical of anabaptist groups. From the number of times Kuyper mentions the "anabaptist danger" *(dooperse gevaar)* in *De gemeene gratie* it is clear that he regarded such attitudes as a threat not limited to anabaptist and pietistic circles, of which he became critical following his Brighton experience, but present among the largely orthodox Calvinist readership of *De Heraut.*[10] His particular criticism of this attitude was that it meant the avoidance of all forms of political involvement, for fear of worldly contamination. "Politicophobia" *(politicophobie)* was the term Kuyper used in his persistent denunciations of this phenomenon. His attacks were frequently directed against the *Réveil* tradition, represented by the Ethical theologians, who remained suspicious and critical of Kuyper's efforts towards party organization. Kuyper himself was aware

10. The index to Kuyper's *De gemeene gratie* contains over thirty references to "anabaptists" *(dooperschen)*. The adjective anabaptist *(doopers)* is not listed in the index but occurs frequently throughout the work.

of the challenge the ARP presented to the followers of the *Réveil.* With this group in mind he wrote: "We became an anti-revolutionary political party . . . in direct opposition to the politicophobia of Christian timidity."[11] He criticized the Ethicals, likewise, for their "false passivity" *(valsche lijdelijkheid)* in the area of politics.[12] It would be safe to assume that he considered the threat to effective party organization to be greater from the side of the Ethicals than from the pious orthodox Reformed groups of the sort he had become acquainted with in Beesd. Most members of these groups were not enfranchised and were averse to any kind of involvement in political debate, thus posing no effective opposition to Kuyper's political objectives. The Ethicals, on the other hand, enjoyed considerable influence in the public arena by means of journalistic organs and capable spokesmen. They were not averse to letting their voice be heard in politics, despite their firm opposition to Christian social and political organizations. Kuyper stigmatized their attitude as being akin to that of the anabaptist, and of displaying the same symptoms of politicophobia — albeit, in their case, a fear of Christian politics rather than of politics as such — a condition he seems to have considered to be on the increase: it was being "embraced by thousands and advocated by eminent men."[13] His series of articles on common grace, which appeared in *De Heraut* in the period immediately following Kuyper's conflict with Lohman (1895-1901), who sympathized with the *Réveil* tradition, was designed to provide an effective antidote to this phenomenon.

Kuyper's intention in expounding the doctrine of common grace went further than merely providing a critique of attitudes that tended towards political aloofness. His aim was also to stimulate the active participation of the anti-revolutionaries in all departments of national life. Many of the readers of Kuyper's articles on common grace had left the *Hervormde Kerk,* either in the *Afscheiding* of 1834 or in the *Doleantie* of 1886, forming in 1892 the new confederation of *Gereformeerde Kerken in Nederland.*[14] Although this confederation was granted legal status, which had originally been denied to the *Afgescheidenen,* it was faced with

11. Kuyper, *Encyclopedia,* p. 49. See also Kuyper's *Antirevolutionaire staatkunde: met nadere toelichting op 'Ons program'* (Kampen: Kok, 1916) I, pp. 593 ff.

12. Kuyper, *Antirevolutionaire staatkunde,* I, pp. 309, 314.

13. A. Kuyper, *Uit het Woord: Stichtelijke Bijbelstudiën,* series 2, vol. III, *Praktijk der Godzaligheid* (Amsterdam: Kruyt, 1886), p. 190.

14. See Chapter Two.

the question of what its position should be towards society and the state. Whereas its members had belonged to a church that enjoyed a secure and recognized position in public life, they now needed to redefine their attitude toward the world outside their circle, without the guarantee of social privilege. P. J. Hoedemaker, the leading critic from among those remaining within the *Hervormde Kerk,* reproached the *Gereformeerden* for their formation of a church outside the established church, because in doing so, he claimed, they were reducing the church to a sect and had abandoned their claim on the Dutch population as a whole. He believed that the Netherlands was essentially a Protestant country, and therefore he opposed the legal equalization of all religious groups. It was in the midst of this precarious ecclesiastical debate that Kuyper, a few years after the union of 1892, began to give broad treatment to the relationship between the church and the world in his exposition of the doctrine of common grace. His aim was to overcome the threat of social marginalization by encouraging the *Gereformeerden* to take up the position in national life that he believed was historically and culturally due to them.

Kuyper was well aware of the difficulty of this task. In his rectorial address of 1899 he remarked that in the sphere of intellectual life, despite the establishment of the Free University, "Christian principles acted only sporadically as a guiding star."[15] In his *De gemeene gratie* he explained that in the founding of independent schools, hospitals, and trade unions, the orthodox Protestants had taken their first step outside the sphere of the church into society at large, where they had been confronted with principles in direct conflict with their own. They were thus faced with a twofold decision: "we either had to draw back into our ecclesiastical circle and abandon our concern for the scientific and artistic life of the nation, or else rebuild a structure of principles in accordance with our *Gereformeerde* confession."[16] There was no doubt in Kuyper's mind that the decision to do the latter had been the right one, despite the challenges and problems it had presented. It was only the doctrine of common grace, he asserted, which declared God's rule over all life outside the church, that could provide the means by which these challenges and problems could be squarely faced.[17] It is clear,

15. Kuyper, *Evolutie,* p. 7.
16. Kuyper, *De gemeene gratie,* III, p. 7.
17. Kuyper, *De gemeene gratie,* III, p. 7.

therefore, that Kuyper was himself all too aware of the strategic and practical motivation of his doctrine and was prepared on occasions to reveal this to his followers.

His comments also help to explain why it was in the latter half of the 1890s that Kuyper began to give special attention to this doctrine, for it was around this time that his *Gereformeerde* followers began to work from a position that was becoming institutionally and politically established. The Free University and the ARP had not only survived almost two decades of existence, despite fierce opposition from several quarters, but had attracted the support and participation of a small but dedicated sector of the Dutch population, together with a number of capable and talented leaders. The coalition cabinet of anti-revolutionaries and Roman Catholics between 1888 and 1891 had served in particular to consolidate and validate the anti-revolutionary position and had created a sense, shared by ally and opponent alike, that this group was proving itself a force to be reckoned with, not only at the educational and social level, but also at the highest levels of government. Coupled with this was a growing sense among Kuyper's followers that the world around them was not such a bad place after all. They had proved it was possible to be active in modern culture and society without compromise to their principles, and they had even enjoyed a certain measure of respect from the world outside their own circle. This encouraged a less hostile and defensive attitude towards the unbelieving world, and this in turn stimulated Kuyper's advocacy of the concept of common grace, as a means both of justifying the attitude and of directing it towards positive social and political ends.

The problem faced by orthodox Protestants since becoming organizationally established, of how to relate to the world outside, was of equal if not greater importance to Kuyper's followers among the Dutch immigrant communities in the United States. They were threatened with a form of isolation that was not only religious but also cultural and linguistic. Kuyper's message to these groups during his visit to them in 1898 was clear: they were to make every effort to integrate into American society, and to take up their responsibilities as loyal American citizens.[18] Kuyper had found in his doctrine of common grace both a basis from which to address specific social problems and a means of justifying his

18. *Holland Daily Sentinel*, 28 October 1898.

approach. In both the Netherlands and America it was this doctrine which "became the linchpin for the entire transformation of consciousness Kuyper was trying to effect."[19]

1.4. Religion Is Soteriological

The fourth and final fundamental question addressed by religion was whether the condition of humankind should be regarded as "normal" or "abnormal" (LC, p. 54). In other words, was the moral condition of men and women the same as it was at their creation, and therefore normal, or had it undergone a change that had made it corrupt, and therefore abnormal? The prevalent idea, espoused by modernism, Kuyper claimed, was that humankind was normal and in a state of upward development. Calvinism, on the other hand, insisted that it was abnormal and in a state of degeneration due to humanity's fallen state. True religion could therefore only be restored soteriologically, involving both regeneration, to restore real existence, and revelation, to restore clear consciousness (LC, p. 56).

Focussing on revelation, the means by which God provided humankind with light in the darkness caused by sin, Kuyper argued that Calvin's insistence on the authority of the scriptures, expressed in his doctrine of *necessitas Sanctae Scripturae,* explained why the present-day Calvinist was opposed to the attempts made by modernistic scholars, such as Albert Schweitzer, to apply techniques of literary criticism to the biblical accounts. These attempts, he claimed, worked as a solvent on the authority of the scriptures and were based on the presupposition that the human condition was normal. If this assumption were true, religion need not be soteriological and the need for divine revelation would thereby be abolished. The Calvinist did not affirm the authority of the scriptures as a result of reasoned argument but because the Holy Spirit, who indwelt the believer, bore witness to their truth — a doctrine Calvin had expressed in his *testimonium Spiritus Sancti* (LC, pp. 56-57).

Although Kuyper's reference to modern biblical criticism was an oblique one, he was touching on a subject which during the last quarter of the nineteenth century was at the center of intense controversy, on

19. James D. Bratt, *Dutch Calvinism in Modern America: A History of a Conservative Subculture* (Grand Rapids: Eerdmans, 1984), p. 20.

both sides of the Atlantic, concerning the reliability of the biblical records and related questions regarding the authority and inspiration of scripture. This was part of a much wider debate about the relationship between faith and reason, and, more broadly still, between Christianity and modern scholarship. Kuyper was keen to address these broader parameters of the debate, and did so in his Stone Lecture on "Calvinism and Science," which will be discussed in Chapter Seven. Here the discussion will concentrate solely on his position in the debate on biblical authority, against the Dutch and American background.

Kuyper's involvement in the debate began in 1873, when he entered into a sharp conflict with J. H. Gunning. In *De Standaard* he took issue with Gunning's statement, made in an earlier issue of the same newspaper, that "God's Word is *in* the Scriptures," insisting instead that "the Bible *is* God's Word."[20] A lively debate ensued between the two theologians, both in *De Standaard* and in their correspondence, centering on the question of scriptural infallibility. Gunning insisted that the church had never maintained the infallibility of the Bible and that Kuyper's attempts to do so were totally misguided.[21]

Kuyper's most notable contribution to the debate came in his rectorial address at the Free University in 1881.[22] Its title, which translated reads, "Present-Day Biblical Criticism and Its Dubious Effect on the Church of the Living God," indicates the nature and content of his argument. In strongly polemical terms he contended that contemporary biblical criticism was "destructive of the best interests of the church . . . because it robs her of the Bible and destroys her liberty in Christ."[23] The Ethicals in particular came under severe attack, Kuyper accusing them of denying the divine inspiration of scripture. He explained, however, that his aim in this oration was merely to mark out his position in general terms, requesting that any serious criticism of his position should be

20. *De Standaard,* 23 February 1873, referring to Gunning's article in *De Standaard* of 16 February 1873. Gunning repeated his argument in a pamphlet written in response to Kuyper's *Confidentie:* J. H. Gunning, *De Heilige Schrift, Gods Woord* (Amsterdam: Höveker, 1873).

21. See the correspondence between Kuyper and Gunning published in J. H. Gunning (Jr), *Professor Dr. J. H. Gunning: leven en werken,* 2 vols. (Rotterdam, 1922-1925), especially pp. 906-7, 914-15.

22. Kuyper, *De hedendaagse Schriftcritiek;* "The Biblical Criticism of the Present Day."

23. Kuyper, "The Biblical Criticism," p. 410.

postponed until he had addressed the subject in more detail in his forthcoming *Encyclopaedie*.[24] Kuyper's request went unfulfilled, the publication of his speech unleashing a torrent of rebuke. J. J. van Oosterzee (1817-1882) for instance, a professor of theology at Utrecht, accused Kuyper of adopting a mechanical view of scriptural inspiration, a charge Kuyper was swift to deny in a series of articles in *De Heraut*.[25]

In 1881, the same year that Kuyper delivered his speech on biblical authority at the Free University, the position of the Princeton Theologians on the same issue received classic expression in an article by Warfield and A. A. Hodge.[26] As with Kuyper's speech, it was occasioned by a growing sense of alarm at the threat made to traditional Christianity by interpretations of the Bible derived from the use of techniques of higher criticism typical of German theologians. Despite differences in method and argumentation between Kuyper on the one hand and Warfield and Hodge on the other, their positions show some remarkable points of similarity. Warfield and Hodge agreed with Kuyper, for instance, on the infallibility of the scriptures and their divine inspiration: "the scriptures not only contain, but *are the word of God,* and hence all their elements and all their affirmations are absolutely errorless and binding on the faith and obedience of men."[27] Their claim, likewise, that their position was identical to that of the Reformers and in line with the traditional teachings of the church was virtually indistinguishable from that of Kuyper.

The debate that surrounded the Princeton view of scripture also bore certain similarities to that surrounding Kuyper. The leading founder of the journal in which Warfield and Hodge published their famous article, the *Presbyterian Review,* was C. A. Briggs (1841-1913), who in the late nineteenth century was one of America's foremost biblical

24. Kuyper, *De hedendaagse Schriftcritiek,* p. 54.

25. J. J. van Oosterzee, *Brief van een vriend over de ingeving van de Heilige Schrift* (1881); *De Heraut,* nos. 215-45.

26. A. A. Hodge and B. B. Warfield, "Inspiration," *Presbyterian Review* 2 (1881): 225-60. This article was republished in book form as A. A. Hodge and B. B. Warfield, *Inspiration.* With an introduction by Roger R. Nicole (Grand Rapids: Baker, 1979). For an interesting theological critique of Warfield's view of biblical inspiration from the perspective of the doctrine of the trinity, see Begbie, "Who Is This God?" pp. 261-68, 275-82. Begbie regards Warfield as "the most famous modern exponent" of biblical inspiration (p. 261).

27. Hodge and Warfield, *Inspiration,* p. 29.

scholars. He had become attracted to German higher criticism while at the University of Berlin, where he had studied for three years (1866-1869), and after his appointment to a position at Union Seminary in New York in 1874 he began to promote the use of critical methods in the study of scripture. Far from considering the application of such methods to constitute a challenge to belief in the supernatural character of biblical revelation, he wished to see the new scholarship used and interpreted by evangelical Christians, rather than monopolized by those opposed to historic Christianity.[28] It was chiefly with this end in view that he became co-editor, with A. A. Hodge, of the newly formed *Presbyterian Review* in 1880, a journal which aimed to encourage both positive and negative evaluations of biblical criticism to be expressed in open rational debate. The initial goodwill was short-lived, however, and tensions between Briggs's higher critical views and the more traditional perception of scripture held by the theologians at Princeton contributed to the journal's demise in 1889.[29] The controversy continued unabated, with Briggs insisting that it was mere assumption to maintain, as did Hodge and his Princeton colleagues, that the original texts of Scripture were inerrant, and he challenged their view that this position had been held by the Reformers and the Westminster Divines.[30] Whereas Briggs's stance can be likened to that of Gunning in the Netherlands, Warfield's response, which appeared in a series of articles between 1889 and 1894, bore resemblance to that of Kuyper.[31] Both Warfield and Kuyper took for granted that there was one system of Reformed theology, and both failed to address the historical questions raised concerning the traditional teaching of the church and the technical issues raised by the application of higher criticism to the biblical texts. Both their responses, instead, were assertive and polemical, the major difference being Warfield's use of apologetics, a means Kuyper totally eschewed. Warfield's position

28. J. B. Rogers and D. K. McKim, *The Authority and Interpretation of the Bible: An Historical Approach* (San Francisco: Harper and Row, 1979), p. 349; Bradley J. Longfield, *The Presbyterian Controversy* (Oxford: Oxford University Press, 1991), pp. 22-23.

29. Rogers and McKim, pp. 349-50; Longfield, p. 22.

30. Lefferts Loetscher, *The Broadening Church: A Study of Theological Issues in the Presbyterian Church Since 1869* (Philadelphia: University of Pennsylvania Press, 1957), p. 57.

31. Warfield's articles were later expanded and republished in B. B. Warfield, *The Westminster Assembly and Its Work* (Oxford: Oxford University Press, 1931).

won considerable support, as did Kuyper's amongst the *Gereformeerden,* mainly from the largely orthodox membership of the American Presbyterian Church. Briggs, on the other hand, was eventually tried for heresy at the General Assembly of the Presbyterian Church in 1893, and was subsequently suspended from the ministry. The Assembly disavowed responsibility for the teaching at Union and reaffirmed its commitment to the doctrine of biblical inerrancy as maintained by the church throughout the ages and taught in the Westminster Confession.[32]

The principal difference between Kuyper and Warfield on the question of biblical inspiration lay in the difference in value they attributed to apologetics. Whereas Kuyper held the view, generally associated with traditional Christianity, that faith leads to understanding, Warfield tended towards the position advocated by post-Reformation scholasticism that reason was a prerequisite to faith. Kuyper believed that the Holy Spirit moved people to accept the authority of the scriptures because of the saving message it contained, and, indeed, that the function of scripture was soteriological — to bring people to salvation (LC, pp. 56-57). As if to alert his audience to his radically different approach to theology to that of his Princeton colleagues, he declared at the outset of his Stone Lectures: "In this struggle [between the world-views of Christianity and modernism] apologetics have advanced us not one single step. Apologists have invariably begun by abandoning the assailed breastwork, in order to entrench themselves cowardly in a ravelin behind it" (LC, p. 11).[33] Warfield held, in contrast, that human reason compelled people to believe the Bible because of evidential or logical proofs of its divine character. The scriptures had therefore to be vindicated as a technically reliable guide to science and history before anyone could trust them and base their beliefs on them.[34] Whereas

32. M. G. Rogers, "Charles Augustus Briggs: Heresy at Union," in *American Religious Heretics: Formal and Informal Trials,* ed. by G. H. Shriver (Nashville: Abingdon, 1966), pp. 111-38; Loetscher, pp. 54-60; Rogers and McKim, pp. 358-61.

33. In his pantheism speech, published in America in 1893, the year after it was delivered at the Free University, Kuyper provided a blistering attack on those who resorted to apologetics in the fight against modernism. By allowing the enemy to prescribe the plan of campaign, they had lost touch with their own basis of operation and had fallen into "hopeless confusion." Kuyper, *Pantheism's Destruction,* pp. 31-32 (p. 31).

34. B. B. Warfield, "Introduction" to Francis R. Beattie's *Apologetics: Or the*

Kuyper's view of the Bible may therefore be described as functional, Warfield's was philosophical.

Before considering the historical factors that may account for the differences between Kuyper's view and those of Warfield and Gunning, brief consideration should be given to the question of a change in Kuyper's position on the infallibility of scripture. It has to be noted here that, compared to Warfield, Kuyper wrote very little on this subject, his numerous publications on doctrinal issues tending to assume rather than defend the reliability of the scriptural record. In his treatment of the doctrine of scripture in his *Encyclopaedie* of 1894, however, he did make allusions to biblical criticism, and it is here that Kuyper seems to present a somewhat different case to that in his 1881 address, indicating that he was prepared to make some concession to modern critical scholarship:

> In the four gospels, words are put into the mouth of Jesus on the same occasion which are dissimilar in form and expression. Jesus obviously cannot have used four forms at the same time, but the Holy Spirit only intended to create an impression for the church which perfectly answers to what Jesus actually said.[35]

Also, having argued that the scriptures are the starting point, the principium, of all true theology, he added that the raising of critical questions concerning the nature of scripture should not be impeded. Rather, the task of theology was to address these questions squarely, "provided it is clearly understood . . . that . . . the failure of your first attempts to resolve such critical objections can rob you of certainty of your principium, as little as success can strengthen it."[36]

The reason for Kuyper's apparent lack of concern for any harmful effects to faith engendered by critical studies lay in the emphasis he placed on the witness of the Holy Spirit, which, he explained, operated as a light irradiating from the scriptures onto the regenerate mind.[37] The miracle of regeneration, or palingenesis, wrought by the Holy Spirit was

---

Rational Vindication of Christianity (Richmond, Virginia: Presbyterian Committee of Publication, 1903).

35. Kuyper, *Encyclopaedie,* II, p. 499.
36. Kuyper, *Encyclopedia,* pp. 562-63.
37. Kuyper, *Encyclopedia,* pp. 556-57.

inseparable from the conviction, produced by the same Holy Spirit, that everything the Bible taught and revealed was divine in character.[38] Because of this, it was unnecessary to defend the authority of scripture. In the Preface to his *Encyclopedia* he wrote that the reason he had devoted considerable attention to the doctrine of scripture was that in the contemporary theological debate this doctrine was of crucial importance, and needed to be resolved in any encyclopedia that grounded itself on the authority of the Bible.[39] From the treatment Kuyper gave to the question of scripture it is clear, however, that he was only concerned to offer a doctrinal resolution to the problem rather than an apologetic one. His defense of biblical authority was limited to the approval of what he considered to be the teaching of the Reformers, which, together with Warfield, he regarded as homogeneous.

Given the concessions Kuyper was prepared to make in his *Encyclopedia,* his assertion in his second Stone Lecture that: "the Calvinist of today considers the critical analysis and the application of the critical solvent to the Scriptures as tantamount to an abandoning of Christianity itself" (LC, p. 56), may seem to represent a reversal of his position back to that of 1881. This is unlikely, however, given the fact that his *Encyclopedia* was published in English in 1898, the same year he gave the Stone Lectures. A more probable explanation is that Kuyper's generally dismissive attitude to higher criticism in both the Stone Lectures and his rectorial address was due to the polemic and programmatic style of these addresses, as opposed to the more precise, scholarly approach of his *Encyclopedia.* He may also have been deliberately gratifying his Princeton audience, which, given its well-publicized stance on biblical inerrancy, would have been eager to hear where he stood on this issue. Although he avoided entering into the controversy at a deep level, he did provide a clear indication of his position in the debate, which no doubt was aimed at winning the approval of his audience who differed from him on the place of apologetics. The quotation given above from the *Lectures,* for instance, in which he almost seems to imply that belief in the infallibility of scripture is essential to Christian belief, comes very close to the position of Warfield and Hodge. It would therefore seem safe to conclude that, despite the nuances he adds in his *Encyclopedia,* his position on biblical inspiration remained basically the same throughout

38. Kuyper, *Encyclopedia,* pp. 558-61.

39. Kuyper, *Encyclopedia,* p. ix.

his career. And despite his unwillingness to defend his position by means of apologetics, in contrast to Warfield, his doctrinal position on the authority and inspiration of scripture was in fact very close to that of his American colleague.[40]

The differences that did divide Kuyper and Warfield can be accounted for in part in terms of their respective philosophical and historical backgrounds. Kuyper's identification early in his career with the intellectual tradition represented by Groen van Prinsterer and his anti-revolutionary followers brought him into close contact with the concept of the antithesis. This concept underlay much of their thinking, writings, and activities, and provided a basis both for their mutual solidarity and for their opposition towards what they considered to be the ill effects of the Enlightenment in the life of the Dutch nation. Kuyper's acceptance and advocacy of the concept meant that all forms of rational debate, in which the aim was to convince the unbeliever of the truths of Christianity by means of intellectual argument, were alien to him. His insistence that regeneration was a prerequisite to an understanding of Christian truth was a hallmark of the anti-revolutionary tradition in which he stood. The tradition of Scottish Common Sense Realism, in contrast, with which Warfield identified, stressed the effectiveness of reason in gaining an understanding of theological truth. Warfield wrote:

> Apologetics has its part to play in Christianizing the world: and this is not a small part: nor is it merely a subsidiary or a defensive part. . . . It has a primary part to play and a conquering part. . . . Christianity . . . has been placed in the world to reason its way to the dominion of the world. . . . By reasoning it will gather to itself all its own. And by reasoning it will put its enemies under its feet.[41]

40. Rogers and McKim have little evidence to support their claim that Kuyper had a much more positive attitude to biblical criticism than did Warfield. They write: "While Hodge and Warfield were rejecting biblical criticism Kuyper and Bavinck were meeting the issue openly and constructively" (Rogers and McKim, p. 390). Rogers and McKim's interpretation of the biblical inerrancy controversy has received severe scholarly criticism, most notably in J. D. Woodbridge, *Biblical Authority: A Critique of the Rogers/McKim Proposal* (Grand Rapids: Zondervan, 1982), and *Inerrancy and the Church,* ed. by John D. Hannah (Chicago: Moody Press, 1984). In the latter volume, see especially the article by J. I. Packer, "John Calvin and the Inerrancy of Holy Scripture," pp. 143-88.

41. From Warfield's review of H. Bavinck's *De zekerheid des geloofs* (Kok: Kampen, 1901) in *Princeton Theological Review* 1 (1903): 138-43 (pp. 146-47). A discussion

It is chiefly this difference of belief in the relative effectiveness of apologetics in Kuyper and Warfield, stemming from their differences in philosophical background, that accounts for the fact that Warfield came to express criticism of Kuyper and his associates. Their tendency to make so little of apologetics was to Warfield "a standing matter of surprise."[42]

If Warfield believed the future of Christianity lay in its reasoning power, Kuyper believed it to lie in the embodiment of its principles in social organizations. For Kuyper, providing a reasoned justification for Christian belief in the authority of scripture, or any other doctrine, was a fruitless task, because of the reality of the antithesis. It also stood in the way of his strategic goals. His efforts were aimed towards the emancipation of the orthodox Protestant sector of the population, who needed to be strengthened in their commitment to the authority of scripture, not persuaded into believing it by means of intellectual argument.

Practical objectives also go some way to explaining the abovementioned difference between Kuyper and Gunning in their approaches to scripture. Whereas Kuyper was primarily concerned with the renewal of Reformed Christianity outside formal church structures, Gunning's chief concern was with spiritual renewal within the national church. Kuyper was therefore reluctant to become involved in an issue he considered of little relevance to the world outside the church, whereas Gunning believed it to be of overriding importance and significance. Indeed, Kuyper's insistence on the soteriological nature of religion, of which his doctrine of scripture was merely a part, was not aimed at making a further contribution to the Reformed doctrine of the salvation of the elect — a doctrine Kuyper regarded as having received disproportionate attention — but was designed

---

of the philosophical background of the Princeton view of biblical inspiration is contained in D. Clair Davis, "Princeton and Inerrancy: The Nineteenth-Century Philosophical Background of Contemporary Concerns," in *Inerrancy and the Church,* pp. 359-78.

42. Warfield's review of Bavinck's *De zekerheid des geloofs,* p. 144. Warfield admitted that it was not that Kuyper wanted to abolish apologetics altogether, but that he believed its use was restricted to "the narrow task of defending developed Christianity against philosophy, falsely so called. He was also willing to admit that apologetics did not have the power *in itself* to make someone a Christian or to conquer the world for Christ — only the Holy Spirit could do that. See *Selected Shorter Writings* of Benjamin B. Warfield, ed. by John E. Meeter, 2 vols. (Nutley, N.J.: Presbyterian and Reformed Publishing Company, 1973), II, pp. 95, 99.

to sharpen the perception of an antithesis between the principles of Calvinism and those of modernism. As in his interpretation of the doctrine of God's sovereignty and the doctrine of election, Kuyper's treatment of the soteriological nature of religion reflects his attempt to reformulate traditional Calvinistic doctrine in such a way as to direct the attention of his readers towards the world outside the church, and to stimulate their active engagement with it.

The issue of biblical authority is particularly revealing, finally, in that it focuses the clash of forces that was taking place between science and religion towards the end of the nineteenth century, both in Europe and the United States. Darwinian science and rationalist philosophy threatened to undermine the concept of revealed truth and belief in religious absolutes. Kuyper's reaction, as well as that of the Princeton theologians Warfield and Hodge, was to seek refuge in the concept of authority. While they insisted that this authority lay ultimately and objectively in the scriptures, it formed part of a search for authority that preoccupied a great deal of the church in the West, finding expression most notably in the bolstering of papal authority in the First Vatican Council of the Roman Catholic Church in 1870.

2. The Church

Having made its initial impact in the sphere of religion, the Calvinistic worldview had found expression in a particular understanding of the church. Throughout his career Kuyper devoted much attention to the history and doctrine of the church, and it was in this area that both his first work and his last articles were written.[43] Many of his activities were related to ecclesiastical issues, not only as church leader and professor of theology but also as politician, journalist, and educational reformer. Kuyper's concept of the church was, accordingly, a wide one, encompassing all Christian activity and influence in the world. The world was the church's sphere of activity and the church was called to establish the

43. Kuyper's first work was an unpublished paper written in 1859 on the development of papal power under Nicholas I. When Kuyper died in November 1920 he was in the process of writing a series of articles on the church for publication in *De Heraut.* See H. Zwaanstra, "Abraham Kuyper's Conception of the Church," *Calvin Theological Journal* 9 (1974): 149-81 (pp. 149-50).

sovereignty of Christ in the world.[44] Kuyper provided theological justification for this view by making a distinction between the church as institute and the church as organism. The church as institute was the visible and institutional expression of the true essence of the church, which was organic and encompassed the whole of regenerate human life (LC, p. 59). Kuyper was not always clear about how he wished to make this distinction and was prone to use the term "church" in a variety of ways that confuse the distinction he tried to make.[45] In keeping with the kind of analysis employed in this book, we will not dwell on the theoretical inaccuracies in Kuyper's ecclesiology, but will look instead at questions relating to its historical context: what was the background against which he formulated it and what did he hope to achieve by expounding it? Kuyper began his exposition in the Stone Lectures by dealing with the essence of the church, which was organic, and then with the form of the church, which was both democratic and multiform.

2.1. Organic

Kuyper acknowledged his indebtedness regarding the essence of the church to the Ethical theologians, who had "resurrected that rich organic principle in order to restore its vitality within the consciousness of the church."[46] Kuyper's adoption of this principle cannot be explained only in terms of his associations with the Ethical theologians, however, and it is likely that he borrowed the concept directly from German theologians such as Schleiermacher and Rothe, who had themselves adopted the term from German Romantic philosophy, particularly that of Schelling.[47] The organic concept in the thought of this school had a strong tendency towards monism, and this was a characteristic of Kuyper's own worldview, as noted in the previous chapter. According to Schelling, the world was one great organism, in which mankind formed a living unity, a single organism. Rothe taught, in a similar vein, that the organic unity

44. See C. H. W. van den Berg, 'Kuyper en de kerk', in *Abraham Kuyper: zijn volksdeel, zijn invloed,* pp. 146-78 (p. 146).

45. Zwaanstra, "Abraham Kuyper's Conception," p. 150.

46. Kuyper, *Predicatiën,* p. 340.

47. Kuyper's familiarity with the work of Schleiermacher, Rothe, and Schelling is evident from his detailed treatments of it in his *Encyclopaedie,* III, pp. 333-40, 376-79, and 399-403 respectively.

of the human race and of the entire cosmos would be reached in the coming kingdom of God, and Schleiermacher held that the organic life of the church was founded on regeneration.[48] All three of these ideas are echoed in the following passage from Kuyper's second Stone Lecture: "Regeneration saves the organism, itself, of our race. . . . But not before the Second Advent shall this new all-embracing organism manifest itself as the center of the cosmos" (LC, pp. 59-60). There is strong evidence, therefore, that Kuyper's concept of the church as organism was borrowed directly from German philosophical and theological thought.[49] His purpose in adopting and emphasizing the concept of the church as organism, in contrast to the church as institute, is clear. It allowed him to restrict the activity of the church as institute to its ecclesiastical offices such as the ministry of the Word and sacraments, alms-giving, and church discipline (LC, pp. 65-67), and thereby to lay stress on the far broader task of the church as organism, which was the transformation of human society by bringing it into harmony with the insights provided by the Christian faith. The formation of a Christian mind or disposition, for instance, as well as Christian social organizations, Christian science, and Christian art, came into the realm of activity belonging to the church as organism. Kuyper's ecclesiology, therefore, was designed both to reserve a large place for his own social and cultural program and to accredit this program with ecclesiastical sanction. It was also designed to oppose the idea of a state church, an idea he saw expressed in the close association between the *Hervormde Kerk* and the Dutch government, according to which the institutional church was considered the whole church. Kuyper considered this idea a consequence of one of Roman Catholicism's chief errors in history, which was to have placed all of human life under the authority of the institutional church, with the effect both of hindering

48. R. Rothe, *Dogmatiek von Dr. Rothe, aus dessen handschriftlichen Nachlasse,* ed. by D. Schenkel (Heidelberg, 1870), II, pp. 4, 34; F. D. E. Schleiermacher, *Die christliche Sitte. Sämtliche Werke* (1893), XII, p. 424; P. A. van Leeuwen, *Het kerkbegrip in de theologie van Abraham Kuyper* (Franeker: Wever, 1946), p. 118; H. Zwaanstra, "Abraham Kuyper's Conception," p. 161.

49. The distinction between the church as organism and institute can be found in the work of Albert Schweitzer. A. Schweitzer, *Die Christliche Glaubenslehre nach protestantischen Grundsätzen dargestelt* (Leipzig, 1877), II, p. 191; van Leeuwen, pp. 118-19. The influence of German organic thought can also be seen in Kuyper's sociopolitical theory. See Chapter Six.

the development of human culture and of corrupting the life of the church (LC, pp. 21, 29).[50]

In adopting and advocating the concept of the church as organism and institute, Kuyper aimed, therefore, to encourage both the Christianization of society and society's complete separation from the institutional church.[51] The Christianization of society would involve bringing all aspects of human life into conformity with Christian principles, and the separation of society from the institutional church would help to purify the church from its corrupting involvement in the world. With his doctrine of the church as organism, therefore, Kuyper aimed to forge a unifying link between the church and the world which would serve his twin aims of social and ecclesiastical renewal.

2.2. Democratic

Moving from the essence of the church to its form or manifestation, Kuyper declared that Calvinism held that the church on earth was manifested in local congregations of regenerate individuals. Within these congregations the universal priesthood of all believers operated and there were no distinctions of rank. Instead of a spiritual order endowed with special mystical powers there were only ministers who served, led, and regulated according to a presbyterian form of government, by which Christ's authority was invested in the congregation itself. While Christ's sovereignty in the church was thereby allowed to remain monarchical, the government of the church on earth was "democratic to its bones and marrow" (LC, p. 63). This applied not only within each local congregation but also between churches, such that no one church could have authority over another; churches could only be united by confederation, rather than by means of a hierarchical structure (LC, p. 63).[52]

50. See also Kuyper's *Encyclopaedie,* III, p. 341; *De gemeene gratie,* II, pp. 274-76.

51. Kuyper, *De gemeene gratie,* II, pp. 274-76.

52. Kuyper's insistence on the democratic nature of the church was closely tied to his advocacy of the so-called "voluntarist principle" in church organization, which was more akin to the ecclesiology of the English Independents than to that of Calvin. See Kuyper's *Tractaat,* pp. 27-29; and *Separatie en Doleantie* (Amsterdam: Wormser, 1890), pp. 9-13. Kuyper's admiration for the English Independents is evidenced in his "Calvinism: The Origin and Safeguard," pp. 398-410. Here he also

Kuyper's emphasis on the democratic character of church government was a conscious response to the democratization of society at large, which he both witnessed and helped encourage in his role as political leader. As early as 1873, in his *Confidentie,* he wrote that everything scripture taught regarding church government harmonized with the "democratic keynote" of the age.[53] The same principles that determined the proper government of the church, he explained, were relevant to the government of the state. In stressing the democratic character of the church, therefore, Kuyper aimed to justify his efforts to encourage the active participation of Christians in the political structures of society.

2.3. Pluriform

Kuyper's insistence on the democratic nature of church government also served to undergird his concept of the pluriformity of the church. The system of church organization by which local churches were linked only by means of confederation, he explained, allowed for differences in factors such as climate, nationality, history, and temperament to be expressed freely, with the result that the church as institute assumed a variety of forms. He admitted that this had not been taught by original Calvinism but that it was the natural outcome of the Calvinistic principle of liberty which, in the ecclesiastical sphere, allowed each local congregation to enjoy complete autonomy. The result had been a proliferation of denominations, and although such multiformity had been marred by rivalry and errors of conduct, it had proved over three centuries to be more beneficial to the growth and well-being of religious life than compulsory uniformity, which was the inescapable consequence of a hierarchical form of church government (LC, pp. 64-65).

Kuyper's commitment to the pluriformity of the church sprang,

---

links his notion of ecclesiastical and political democracy to the doctrine of election: "A church which confesses election as its *'Cor ecclesiae'* cannot be clerical, but must seek its strength in its lay members. Hence from this confession was deduced the democratic church-principle, which was soon transferred from the church to the political platform, and there called into life the liberties of Holland, the liberties of England's Whigs, and the liberties of America" (p. 666).

53. Kuyper, *Confidentie,* p. 79.

therefore, from his belief in the democratic form of church government. It also derived from his perception of the natural diversity of the material and spiritual world. All healthy life, he claimed, bore the characteristic of multiformity; uniformity could only be observed where natural differences were suppressed. An organizational unity of the church could only be maintained, therefore, if its members were homogeneous in doctrinal and spiritual disposition. In actual fact, however, the church appeared among groups of people that differed widely in all manner of respects, and this inevitably found expression in the plethora of forms in which the church was manifested (LC, pp. 64-65).[54]

Not surprisingly, Kuyper's idea of the freedom and pluriformity of the church generated fierce criticism from Roman Catholic contempories.[55] The idea was not, however, unique within his theological milieu, and again it reflects the influence of German organic thought. Both Schleiermacher and Vinet were leading spokesmen for individuality and liberty in the area of church and religion, arguing that freedom was a necessary precondition for all religious life. Schleiermacher, like Kuyper, flatly denied the desirability of the structural unity of the church, insisting instead that its organic unity was manifested in its pluriformity. They both placed the false unity of uniformity over against the true unity of pluriformity.[56] In the Netherlands, the Groningen and Ethical Schools adopted a similar position to Schleiermacher, the eminent Ethical theologian Daniël Chantepie de la Saussaye (1818-1874) becoming a chief defender of the principle of ecclesiastical liberty. Gunning also advocated this principle, even though he continued to defend the unity of the visible church. He acknowledged the natural diversity and plurality of forms in human life, and believed this to work itself out in the area of religion, but he did not agree that the multiformity of the church had to be accepted as an inevitable consequence. It is likely, in fact, that it was from Gunning that Kuyper borrowed his concept of pluriformity, although he differed from Gunning as to how it should be applied to the church.

54. Kuyper, *De gemeene gratie,* III, pp. 233-34.

55. See T. F. Bensdorp, *Pluriformiteit. Een fundamenteele misvatting van Dr. A. Kuyper of een hopeloos pleidooi: eene studie over Dr. Kuyper's pluriformiteitsstelsel. Benevens een antwoord van en aan Dr. Kuyper door denzelfden* (Amsterdam: Borg, 1901).

56. F. D. E. Schleiermacher, *Die christliche Sitte. Sämtliche Werke,* XII, pp. 133-37, 417.

Kuyper's efforts towards church reform also helped shape his notion of pluriformity. In his speech on "Uniformity: The Curse of Modern Life" in 1869 he fiercely attacked the idea of the uniformity of the church, and in his inaugural sermons at Utrecht in 1867 and Amsterdam in 1870, as well as in his *Confidentie* of 1873, he gave early indications of his preference for free churches, praising in the latter the system of free churches in North America.[57] In his Utrecht sermon he spoke of "the ruins of the once so splendid church of our fathers," and added: "Whether we are to involve ourselves in church reform or with the establishment of a new church, we are in any case called to build."[58] He struck a similar note at Amsterdam: "We do not live in agreeable circumstances. We must either rebuild or move out."[59] It would seem, therefore, that although Kuyper did not initially intend to establish new churches alongside of and in opposition to the *Hervormde Kerk*, as the *Afscheiding* had done, he nevertheless advocated from an early stage in his career the principle of freedom in determining the form of the church, and entertained the possibility, should this freedom be denied, of establishing dissenting churches. At the time of the *Doleantie* in 1886 the idea of the pluriformity of the church served to justify and defend Kuyper's involvement in the establishment of such churches outside the synodical jurisdiction of the *Hervormde Kerk*.

Kuyper's concept also reflects, finally, his response to the widescale intellectual and social diversification that took place in Europe in the second half of the nineteenth century. This was a development of which Kuyper was fully aware: the characteristic feature of the times in which he lived, he wrote in 1874, was the "specialization, differentiation and individualization" of thought and life.[60] The organizational unity of the church had been left behind in history and to try to restore it was to try to swim against the historical stream, he argued. The only viable solution was the establishment of free churches, in

57. Kuyper, *Eenvormigheid, de vloek van het moderne leven* (Amsterdam: De Hoogh, 1869), passim; *Confidentie,* p. 85.

58. A. Kuyper, *De menschwording Gods het levensbeginsel der kerk: intreerede uitgesproken in de Domkerk te Utrecht den 10den November 1867* (Utrecht: Van Peursen, 1867).

59. A. Kuyper, *'Geworteld en gegrond': de kerk als organisme en instituut: intreêrede, uitgesproken in de Nieuwe Kerk te Amsterdam, 10 Augustus 1870* (Amsterdam: De Hoogh, 1870).

60. Kuyper, *Het calvinisme: oorsprong,* p. 84. See also Kuyper, *Predicatiën,* p. 404.

which like-minded people could voluntarily be joined together.[61] Kuyper's particular sensitivity to the social and intellectual diversification of his times was due in part to the fact that it was precisely this process that threatened to marginalize the place of religion in society. He did not seek a solution in the strengthening of the legal status of the national church, as did Hoedemaker, nor in the reinforcement of the institutional authority of the church, as did the First Vatican Council, but in a corresponding diversification and decentralization of the churches: "I exalt multiformity and hail in it a higher stage of development" (LC, p. 194). In thus arguing for the pluriformity of the church, Kuyper was attempting to bring his Calvinistic worldview into conformity with the social and intellectual circumstances of the late nineteenth century, created largely by the rapid democratization and diversification of Dutch society. Although he sought to base his ecclesiology on that put forward by the Reformers, his awareness of contemporary developments, which was partly intuitive and partly informed by his reading and involvements, had a decisive influence on its expression.

Conclusion

Kuyper's second Stone lecture is the most explicitly theological of all six lectures. This should not, however, be allowed to obscure the practical objectives Kuyper had in mind in giving it. The dynamic and transforming potential of the Calvinistic worldview, which had been the theme of his first lecture, was now presented as the reason for an enquiry into the religious principles that lay at the heart of this worldview and accounted for its great potential. Set within this framework, Kuyper's discussion of theological beliefs was not so much a restatement of traditional Calvinistic doctrine as a radical reinterpretation and reapplication of it in a way that broadened its relevance to encompass the whole of human existence. The doctrines of God's sovereignty, election, redemption, and the church, all of which he believed to have been interpreted primarily in terms of their relevance to personal and ecclesiastical life, even by Reformed theologians, were given sig-

61. Kuyper, *Predicatiën,* p. 403.

nificance to the areas of life outside the church. No doubt Kuyper had his audience in mind in this enterprise. The theologians at Princeton Seminary would have been familiar with the traditional teachings of the Reformed faith. Kuyper aimed to challenge them to regard these teachings not as dogmas to be defended, preserved, and contained within the confines of the institutional church, but as dynamic principles which, once released into the world, had the power to transform it. The one exception to this pattern was the doctrine of common grace, which was not normally considered one of the essential or fundamental doctrines of Calvinism, and does not occupy a prominent position in Calvin's theology.[62] In arguing for the centrality of this doctrine in the Calvinistic worldview, Kuyper was making explicit an element that was implicit in Calvin's thought. Given the emphasis he placed on this doctrine, and the importance he attached to it, it is not without good reason that Kuyper has been named "the theologian of common grace."[63]

Kuyper's challenge to his audience in his second Stone Lecture was that it was to regard Calvinistic theology not as a set of independent doctrines, existing in isolation to each other, but as an entire system of thought that provided a particular understanding of the very fundamentals of religion. It was a consistent response to the questions raised in all religions and basic to all of human life. Its doctrines, therefore, were not dogmatic law-codes, standards of morality, or exclusive possessions of the church, but answers to universal human questions concerning the nature of the created order. Although Kuyper stressed the universality of these questions, and of the answers Calvinism provided to them, his treatment of them clearly reflects the times in which he lived. His ideas on God's sovereignty and the inspiration of scripture, for instance, reflect his concern to restore the principle of authority in the midst of intellectual and social changes which seemed to undermine traditional authority structures and to relegate religion to the realm of sentiment and private conscience. His ideas on the nature of the church, likewise, demonstrate

62. The issue of the relationship between common grace and science in Kuyper's theology is discussed in relation to Calvin in Chapter Seven of this book. For treatments of the doctrine of common grace in Calvin's theology, see Douma, pp. 205-57; Herman Kuiper, *Calvin on Common Grace* (Goes: Oosterbaan & Le Cointre, 1928).

63. H. van Til, p. 117.

how his worldview was formulated in response to contemporary political, social, intellectual, and ecclesiastical change. He aimed to show that Calvinism's theology of religion was dynamic, comprehensive, and relevant to modern life.

Third Lecture: Calvinism and Politics

It was not without precedent that Kuyper withheld the presentation of his political ideas at Princeton until after he had laid out the framework of his religious and theological principles. One of the striking features about *Ons program* (1879), his commentary on the manifesto of the ARP, is the importance he gave to setting out *a priori* the theological foundations from which the anti-revolutionary position in politics was to be derived. This feature was, indeed, typical of Kuyper's political writings, reflecting the fact that although he became heavily involved in the practical side of politics, his approach to political issues remained essentially theological throughout his career. His postponement of the subject of politics in the *Lectures* also, however, fitted the scheme of his argument. Having defined his use of the term Calvinism and laid out its fundamental religious principles in his first two lectures, Kuyper was keen to substantiate his claim that Calvinism was not merely an ecclesiastical and dogmatic movement, but a worldview that encompassed the whole of human life (LC, p. 78). Although Calvinism's initial impact was in the sphere of religion, it went on from there to transform the sphere of politics (and, subsequently, the fields of science and art, the subjects of the following two lectures).

It was the sovereignty of God, the "root principle" of the Calvinistic worldview, that for Kuyper constituted the starting point of Calvinism's approach to politics. The aim of his third Stone Lecture, accordingly, was to lay out a Calvinistic political theology in such a way as to make clear that its chief concepts were derived from its root principle (LC, p. 79). God's sovereignty found a threefold expression in human life, he explained: in the state, in society, and in the church.

1. Sovereignty in the State

1.1. The Calvinist Position

Calvinism held, Kuyper declared, that the entire human race, including all its past, present, and future generations, was intended to form an organic unity due to its common genealogy. Had sin not entered into human experience, the whole of humanity would now be joined in one world empire. But the intervention of sin had destroyed the organic unity of the human race, dividing it into groups, and had necessitated the institution of governments. For Calvinism, therefore, the state is something unnatural, not belonging to the original order of creation, and it holds as its first political principle that "God has instituted the magistrates by reason of sin" (LC, pp. 79-81). The dark side of this mechanical institution of government is the danger that, because of sin, state authority could degenerate into despotism, but the bright side is that it preserves human society from destruction through anarchy (LC, p. 81). Calvinism taught, therefore, that the state and the magistrates are to be gratefully received from the hand of God as indispensable to human life, and that people are always to be vigilant against the threat to their personal liberty that lies in the power of the state (LC, p. 81). From this first political principle, Kuyper explained, Calvinism went on to assert that "all authority of governments on earth originates from the Sovereignty of God alone" — the second Calvinist political principle. It was a principle that was applicable to all states, whatever the form of the government (LC, pp. 82-83).

Kuyper's aim in insisting on the divine origin of political sovereignty was to lay a basis from which to mount an attack on two contemporary political theories which he believed denied God's sovereignty in the political sphere. Before his opposition to these theories is considered, it is important that attention is paid to his assertion that the divine origin of human authority did not determine a particular form of government, as this involves the question of whether Kuyper was in favor of democracy on point of principle. This question is particularly pertinent in view of the fact that Kuyper and his anti-revolutionary movement are often referred to in terms of "Christian Democracy" and were indeed fundamental to the emergence of the Christian Democratic movement in the Netherlands in the second half of the twentieth century.[1]

Despite his preference for a republic, Kuyper claimed, Calvin considered a monarchy, an aristocracy, and a democracy to be possible and practical forms of government; the form of government depended on circumstances, even though the most desirable conditions would exist where people were free to choose their own magistrates. Calvin's "Commentary on Samuel" supported this assertion, Kuyper explained, where he exhorted those who enjoyed political freedom not to abuse it: "And ye, O peoples, to whom God gave the liberty to choose your own magistrates, see to it, that ye do not forfeit this favour, by electing to the positions of highest honour, rascals and enemies of God." Making a direct appeal to the sympathies of his audience, and one that accorded with his concept of America as a Calvinistic country, Kuyper pointed out that the preamble of more than one of the constitutions of member states of the United States almost literally adopted these words of Calvin, in the phrase "Grateful to almighty God that He gave us the power to choose our own magistrates" (LC, pp. 84, 192).

Kuyper's assertion that Calvin had a preference for a republican form of government was disingenuous. For in his *Institutes,* where he discussed the form a government should take, Calvin made no mention of a republic, and out of the three forms he did consider — monarchy, aristocracy, and democracy — he expressed a distinct preference for an aristocracy.[2] It is true that Calvin qualified this preference by suggesting that an aristocracy should be "modified by popular government," and the reason he gave for his preference was that, owing to men's vices or defects, it was "safer and more tolerable" for several to share in government than for one person to rule, as in the case of a monarchy. It was,

1. See Michael P. Fogarty, *Christian Democracy in Western Europe, 1820-1953* (London: Routledge and Kegan Paul, 1957), p. xv; Dirk Jellema, "Abraham Kuyper's Attack on Liberalism," *Review of Politics* 19 (1957): 472-85. Kuyper himself is reported to have once announced to the Dutch socialist leader P. J. Troelstra: "I have always been a democrat, and I hope to die a Christian democrat" (Romein, p. 157).

2. John Calvin, *Institutes of the Christian Religion,* IV.xx.8.

in fact, his penchant for the sharing of power that determined his preference for an aristocracy. But contrary to Kuyper's assertions, Calvin expressed no preference for a republic, and he even declared that democracy tended to encourage sedition.[3] Kuyper had maintained the same assertions in his rectorial address at the Free University in 1888. There he was willing to concede, however, that Calvin preserved an aristocratic trait in his political thought, and that he never opposed in principle a monarchical form of government.[4] Kuyper's portrayal of Calvin's position in the Stone Lectures was colored by his desire to declare the Calvinistic origins of the republican government of the United States and thus to recommend the benefits of Calvinism to an American audience.

In view of Kuyper's assertion of Calvin's republican bias, his avoidance of the term "democracy" in his discussion of the Calvinistic contribution to the sphere of politics in the Stone Lectures is striking, and may suggest that he did not consider it to be an important political principle. In dealing with the form of church government in his second lecture he had claimed that the democratic nature of church government provided a model for the proper functioning of government.[5] He made no attempt, however, to develop this idea in a principled way, or to relate it to political practice. His outright rejection of the label "Democrat" during his visit to Michigan, noted in Chapter Three, had to do with his supposed allegiance to the Democratic Party in the United States and not with his position on the principle of democracy. The swiftness and firmness of his response in the American press could, of course, indicate that he harbored a deep-seated aversion to the term "democratic" as a characterization of his position.

More clarity on this issue may be expected from his editorship of *De Standaard.* In 1890 he ran a two-part series in the newspaper under the title "Democratic."[6] In it he distanced himself from the charge made by Liberal and Conservative political groupings that the ARP was

3. Calvin, *Institutes.* This is not to imply that the issue of democracy in Calvin is clear-cut. For an example of the kind of debate that surrounds it, see *Calvin and Calvinism: Sources of Democracy?,* ed. with an introduction by Robert H. Kingdom and Robert D. Linder (Lexington, Mass., 1970).

4. Kuyper, *Het calvinisme en de kunst,* p. 82 (note 96). See also *Antirevolutionaire staatkunde,* I, p. 636.

5. See Chapter Five.

6. *De Standaard,* 7 and 10 March 1890.

"democratic." He wrote the series, however, to protest against allegations made by his political opponents that the ARP had associations with the Social Democrats. When his newspaper expressed support for democracy, he explained, it did not mean that it advocated the abolition of class distinctions or that the populace should have the right to regulate its own laws or that it was not obliged to obey governmental authority. To advocate any of these things would be to replace God's sovereignty with man's, and historic Calvinism had always insisted that a recognition of the sovereignty of God was more important than the form of government. Nevertheless, he claimed, in the history of Calvinism the word "democratic" had no "bad aftertaste" — a democratic form of government was just as good as any other.[7] When he used the term "democratic" to describe the anti-revolutionary position, he concluded, he did so in protest against the idea that only the moneyed sector of the populace had the right to determine the fate of everyone else. On the contrary, no organic part of the populace should be barred from participation in government. As to the form government should take in the Netherlands, the ARP supported the form that had developed in history from the time of the Dutch Republic.[8]

There is considerable ambiguity, therefore, as to Kuyper's position on the value of democracy as a political principle. His emphasis on the sovereignty of God, and thereby on the need to obey God's laws for society, has even suggested to one scholar, Dirk Kuiper, that he had theocratic as well as democratic leanings.[9] Those instances in which Kuyper does seem to advocate democracy, he insists, are driven merely by his desire to see Christians take a large enough share of power to be able to institute a form of Christian hegemony, and thus to re-Christianize society. Although Kuiper's identification of theocracy in Kuyper's thought is limited to the latter's insistence that all spheres of society should function in accordance with God's ordinances, it is nevertheless a misleading term to use with reference to Kuyper, not least because it implies that his ideas were merely reactionary, intent on salvaging as

7. *De Standaard,* 10 March 1890.

8. *De Standaard,* 10 March 1890. See also Article 6 of the Anti-Revolutionary manifesto, in *Ons program,* 2nd edition (Amsterdam: Kruyt, 1879), p. 2.

9. D. T. Kuiper, "The Historical and Sociological Development of the ARP and CDA," in *Christian Political Options* (The Hague: AR-Partijstichting, 1979), pp. 10-32 (p. 19). See also D. T. Kuiper, "Theory and Practice in Dutch Calvinism," pp. 70-72.

much as possible of a theocratic ideal, without positive principles of their own.[10] Kuyper repeatedly rejected, indeed, any suggestion that theocracy was a legitimate form of government.[11] Despite his reluctance to prescribe any particular form of government, he was clear that theocracy was not one of the options.[12] His lack of clarity regarding the desirability of democracy is unlikely, therefore, to have been caused by a longing for theocracy. It is more likely that it was connected to Lohman and the conservative wing of the ARP, who were uneasy about the possible consequences of the further democratization of Dutch society and advocated more aristocratic forms of government. As noted in Chapter Two, Lohman and his sympathizers within the ARP were opposed to the extension of the franchise, leading to their secession from the party in 1894. Kuyper, in an attempt to preserve unity following the split, and to prevent further conservative dissention, deliberately avoided proclaiming a strict allegiance to the principle of political democracy. Against this background, the *Lectures on Calvinism,* delivered only four years after the split occurred, are resolute in their avoidance of the question of democracy.

1.2. The Modernist Position

In direct opposition to the Calvinist understanding of God's sovereignty in the political realm, Kuyper declared to his Princeton audience, stood two other theories: popular-sovereignty, belonging to the French Revolution, and state-sovereignty, which had been developed more recently by German Idealist philosophers (LC, p. 85). In keeping with the argument in his first Stone Lecture that the principles of the French Revolution and those of German pantheism were chief components of the

10. D. T. Kuiper, "The Historical and Sociological Development," p. 30.

11. See, for instance, Kuyper's *Ons program,* 2nd edition, p. 46; *Lectures on Calvinism,* p. 85; *Antirevolutionaire staatkunde,* I, pp. 273-74.

12. J. Skillen suggests that the evidence from Kuyper's own political involvement indicates that he was a staunch supporter of democratic representative institutions in government on the basis of social, ideological, and political pluralism. James W. Skillen, "The Development of Calvinistic Political Theory in the Netherlands, with Special Reference to the Thought of Herman Dooyeweerd" (unpublished Ph.D. thesis, Duke University, 1973), p. 255. See also G. J. Spykman, "Pluralism: Our Last Best Hope?" *Christian Scholar's Review* X (1981): 99-115.

modernistic worldview, Kuyper argued in his third lecture that popular-sovereignty and state-sovereignty were the two main theoretical political positions of modernistic thought. Springing from the revivified humanism and rationalism of the French Revolution, both were antitheistic, dethroning God by depositing sovereignty into the hands of human beings. Before Kuyper's criticism of these positions is examined, it is important to emphasize the fact that Kuyper's chief concern in dealing with them was the issue of sovereignty. He did not submit them to a detailed theoretical critique, nor did he discuss the various emphases and nuances of their advocates. Only one issue was of overriding concern to him: did sovereignty in the state reside in God or in humanity, whether humanity be construed as "the people" or as "the state"?

This preoccupation with sovereignty reflects the fact that it was an issue of some importance in nineteenth-century Europe. Thinkers such as Machiavelli, Bodin, and Hobbes had accustomed political theorists to regard sovereignty as the essential feature of the state and to believe that there was a need in any state for one ultimate source of universal, exclusive authority, charged to make laws and uphold good order. It was within this context that Kuyper declared in his speech marking the centenary of the French Revolution in 1889 that the issue of sovereignty had become the political question of supreme importance in the nineteenth century.[13]

1.2.1. Popular-Sovereignty

For Kuyper the real evil of the French Revolution did not lie in its overthrow of the Bourbon dynasty but in its opposition to divine authority, summed up in the Revolutionaries' slogan: *ni Dieu ni maître.* As he explained in his first Stone Lecture, it was not so much indignation at abuses as the desire to substitute human sovereignty for that of God, that was the principal motive of the Revolutionaries. For this reason, the French Revolution was of a totally different nature to the three revolutions in the Calvinistic world (the Dutch Revolt against Spain, England's Glorious Revolution, and the American Revolution), which had left God's sovereignty intact (LC, pp. 86-87). From its basis in the free will

13. Kuyper, *Niet de vrijheidsboom,* p. 11. Kuyper gave special attention to the issue of sovereignty in both his *Ons program,* 2nd edition, pp. 26-39, and his *Antirevolutionaire staatkunde,* I, pp. 261-89.

of the individual person, the French Revolution had taught, sovereignty was passed on to the many, conceived of as "the people," and thus it was in the people, as the sum total of individuals, that true sovereignty resided. This theory, expressed in the notion of Social Contract, was a doctrine Kuyper considered "identical to atheism" (LC, pp. 87-88).

Kuyper's argument was a reaction to the political philosophy of Jean Jacques Rousseau (1717-1778), who argued in his *Du Contrat Social* of 1762 that the social order was based on a voluntarily agreed contract between its members, who promised to obey the "general will" *(volonté générale),* which was both infallible and sovereign.[14] Although Rousseau's work contains strongly statist and collectivist themes, Kuyper's chief concern was with its insistence that the foundation of sovereignty was in the individual, rather than in God — in other words, with its individualism. It is this concern that goes some way towards explaining why Kuyper opposed the idea of popular-sovereignty throughout his career.[15] For it was individualism, having received an initial impetus in the thought of Thomas Hobbes (1588-1679) and John Locke (1632-1704) and having been subsequently carried forward with power in the thought of Rousseau and François-Marie Voltaire (1694-1778), that lay at the heart of Dutch political liberalism, the foremost enemy of the anti-revolutionaries.[16]

Kuyper often pointed out the radically divisive effects individualism had had on the organic structure of society. In his speech at the Social Congress in 1891, for example, he contrasted the Christian desire to seek personal human dignity in the social relations of an organically

14. Jean Jacques Rousseau, *Du Contrat Social,* ed. by Ronald Grimsely (Oxford: Clarendon Press, 1972), I.vi.

15. See, for instance, his "Calvinism: The Origin and Safeguard," p. 662; *Ons program,* 2nd edition, p. 33; *Antirevolutionaire staatkunde,* I, p. 286. That Kuyper's chief objection to popular-sovereignty was with its location of sovereignty in the individual rather than God is indicated in the following passage from "Calvinism: The Origin and Safeguard": "The idea that every man by being born of a woman has a claim to a part of the political authority, and that the state has its origin in the unification of these atomistic parts, puts a limit to the sovereignty of God; it locates the source of sovereignty in man as such, and not in the mighty arm of God, and leads to the destruction of all moral authority" (p. 662).

16. The policies of the Dutch liberal statesmen Thorbecke and Samuel van Houten (1837-1930) rested on individualistic premises, van Houten being a major proponent of popular sovereignty. See E. H. Kossmann, *The Low Countries, 1790-1940* (Oxford: Oxford University Press, 1978), p. 299.

associated society with that of the vision of the French Revolution which, having destroyed the "organic tissue" of social relationships, had nothing left but "the monotonous self-seeking individual, asserting his own self-sufficiency."[17] Such individualism, which destroyed the spiritual and moral make-up of human beings as well as their social relationships, was central to the social crisis now facing Europe:

> The French Revolution, like present-day liberalism, was anti-social, and the social need that now disturbs Europe is the evil fruit of the individualism enthroned by the French Revolution.[18]

Despite liberalism's proclamation of freedom, equality, and fraternity it had encouraged a "passionate struggle for possessions" which in turn had exacerbated material inequality and class antagonism, and deprived the working classes of social and economic necessities, dignity, and justice.[19]

Kuyper's association of popular-sovereignty with liberalism by linking them both to the anti-theistic individualism of the French Revolution certainly helped to add polemic weight to his argument that both were enemies of Calvinism and destructive to the welfare of society. There are, however, some serious problems with it, which are important to note, as they help to situate Kuyper's ideas within their intellectual environment. First, it made liberalism seem more extreme than it actually was, in terms of its religious antagonism. Dutch liberalism in the second half of the nineteenth century may be taken as a typical example of what is often referred to as "continental liberalism," which was characteristically anti-clerical.[20] This trait grew during the final years of the nineteenth century in the Netherlands, where the expansion of confessional power posed an increasing threat to the survival of liberalism as a dominant political force. The corresponding growth of antagonism towards liberalism from Catholic and orthodox Protestant quarters

17. Kuyper, *The Problem of Poverty,* p. 44. See Chapter Four for a comparison of Kuyper's position here with that of Marx.

18. Kuyper, *The Problem of Poverty,* p. 44 (note 1).

19. Kuyper, *The Problem of Poverty,* pp. 43-46 (p. 44); *De Standaard,* 16 April 1872.

20. Guido de Ruggiero, *The History of European Liberalism,* trans. by R. W. Collingwood (Boston: Beacon, 1959); George H. Sabine, "The Two Democratic Traditions," *Philosophical Review* 61 (1952): 451-74.

tended, however, to overexaggerate liberalism's anti-religious stance. A second, associated, problem is that Kuyper's argument failed to distinguish between different traditions and currents within liberalism and thereby ascribed to it a monolithic character it did not possess. He made no distinction, for instance, between British, American, and continental liberalism, nor between the two broad traditions within liberalism, represented on the one hand by Locke and Baron de Montesquieu (1689-1755) and on the other by Voltaire and Rousseau.[21] It was the latter tradition, particularly that of Rousseau and his followers, that adopted popular-sovereignty and rigid anti-theism, and it was only against this variety of liberalism that Kuyper's attack may have been justified.[22] The liberalism of the former tradition had strong constitutionalist underpinnings and was almost as sharply opposed to the continental variety as was the theism of Kuyper and the anti-revolutionaries. Kuyper also failed to acknowledge, thirdly, where his own political theory coincided with, and had been influenced by, liberal positions. In terms of social contract theory, Kuyper owed liberalism very little. But in his advocacy of limited state authority, and in his rejection of absolutism in favor of individual and group freedom, there is a clear tie to aspects of the liberal tradition. Although he emphasized the Calvinistic origins of his political thought, he owed a great deal to the liberalism of Locke and Montesquieu in the formation of his views. His attachment to Edmund Burke, in addition, was due to more than their mutual condemnation of the French Revolution, even though he refused to regard the philosophy of the Whigs as liberal, insisting instead that its origins lay in English Puritanism. In Kuyper's view, Whig-based Calvinism had formed the basis of British democracy and civil liberty, and was then passed on to the founding fathers of the American Republic.[23]

21. Steven E. Meyer, "Calvinism and the Rise of the Protestant Political Movement in the Netherlands" (unpublished Ph.D. thesis, Georgetown University, 1976), pp. 234-35.

22. Even so, Rousseau was capable of expressing ideas that Kuyper would surely have approved of: "Those who consider Calvin only as a theologian fail to recognize the breadth of his genius. The editing of our wise laws, in which he had a large share, does him as much honour as his *Institutes.* Whatever revolution time may bring in our religion, so long as the love of country and liberty is not extinct among us, the memory of this great man will be held in reverence." *Du Contrat Social,* II.vii.

23. Kuyper, "Calvinism: The Origin and Safeguard," pp. 395, 677, 673-74; Meyer, pp. 236-37.

1.2.2. State-Sovereignty

Adherents of state-sovereignty, according to Kuyper, rejected the concept of "the people" as an aggregate of individuals bound by the mechanism of social contract, in favor of the idea that the state is a historically developed, organic whole. While he could agree with this idea, he firmly rejected the notion that the state was a mystical, conscious entity, possessing a sovereign will. If that were the case, all sense of right and wrong would be embodied in the laws of the state, so that the law would be considered right simply because it was law (LC, p. 89).

Although Kuyper made no explicit reference to it, his critique of state-sovereignty was directed largely against the influence of the political philosophy of G. W. F. Hegel (1770-1831). In his *Grundlinien der Philosophie des Rechts* (1821), Hegel criticized liberalism for pushing the concept of subjective personal freedom and egoistic individual interests to absurd extremes, and insisted that the state was the actualization of freedom. The subjective judgment of the individual, he insisted, was mere caprice in comparison to that of the state, of which the individual was a dependent and subordinate part.[24] It was the state, therefore, that provided the sole standard of morality and its laws were necessarily just. As a result, all people were to venerate the state as a secular deity.[25] Such thinking coincided with Kuyper's characterization of pantheism as the removal of boundaries between God and the created order, noted in Chapter Four, which in the political sphere meant the removal of boundaries between rulers and subjects: "both are dissolved in the one all-sufficient State."[26] As a consequence of this removal, he argued, the state assumed divine attributes and functions, instead of remaining a mechanical institution for the sake of sin, thus becoming a state to whose word all must be subject.[27]

Kuyper's dismissal of the concept of the self-sufficiency of the state inherent in the doctrine of state-sovereignty indicates that it was in particular the collectivist doctrines of socialism that formed the target

24. G. W. F. Hegel, *Grundlinien der Philosophie des Rechts,* ed. by Johannes Hoffmeister, 4th edition (Hamburg: Felix Meiner, 1955), pp. 207-83.

25. Hegel, *Grundlinien,* pp. 278-88. For a standard treatment of Hegel's political thought in English, see Shlomo Avineri, *Hegel's Theory of the Modern State* (Cambridge: Cambridge University Press, 1972).

26. Kuyper, *Pantheism's Destruction,* p. 26.

27. Kuyper, *Pantheism's Destruction,* pp. 26-27.

of his attack. For it was in socialism that Hegel's ideas, having been reinterpreted and modified by Karl Marx, found one of their most potent expressions, and it was socialism that posed itself as a mounting threat to Kuyper's political objectives as it grew in strength and popularity towards the end of the nineteenth century.[28] Indeed, the fact that socialism was still in its infancy during the early part of Kuyper's career accounts for the fact that in his early political writings he did not represent state-sovereignty as a serious threat to Calvinistic understandings of political sovereignty. Although in his speech on "Calvinism: The Origin and Safeguard of Our Constitutional Liberties," delivered in 1874, he challenged the notion of "the supremacy of the state," he gave no indication that he perceived this to be a threatening and fully articulated political theory.[29] It was not until 1892 that he reached this position, in his speech on pantheism.[30] By the time of the Stone Lectures, he had become acutely aware of the dangers of state absolutism — they were, he declared, "death to our civil liberties" (LC, p. 98). Despite the fact that he made no mention of socialism the evidence is strong that he perceived these dangers to be embodied chiefly in socialist doctrines. In his speech on the social question in 1891, he divided socialism into two broad strands, "social democracy" and "state socialism," and suggested that both of these strands included collectivist tendencies.[31] Social democracy advocated that the state was the housekeeper of society, he explained, commissioned with the task both of arranging the various social "families" in such a way that they were dissolved into the single family of the state, and of providing equally for the needs of each

28. R. N. Berki, *The History of Political Thought: A Short Introduction* (London: Dent, 1977), p. 179.

29. Kuyper, "Calvinism: The Origin and Safeguard," pp. 662-63.

30. Kuyper, *Pantheism's Destruction,* pp. 26-27. In his earlier addresses, state-sovereignty features chiefly in historical arguments: "'Sphere-sovereignty' defending itself against 'state-sovereignty' — that was the course of world history before the proclamation of Messianic Sovereignty. . . . When the age of ambiguity draws to a close there is no freedom; no nations; no spheres." Kuyper, *Souvereiniteit,* pp. 13-14. Kuyper's use of the term "sphere-sovereignty" is explained later in this chapter.

31. Kuyper, *The Problem of Poverty,* pp. 56-57. Kuyper's critique of socialism does not suffer as badly as his critique of liberalism from his tendency to ignore divisions within the traditions of his opponents, and he does not criticize it with the same degree of severity. This may well have been because socialism was not as intimately and directly associated with the anti-clericalism and anti-theism of the French Revolution as was liberalism.

individual. State-socialism, on the other hand, advocated the exact opposite of social democracy in its elevation of the state far above society, from where it was to lead society in a patriarchal manner.[32] Kuyper's objection to state-sovereignty was integral, therefore, to his criticism of socialism, and it grew bolder as socialism expanded.

Although Kuyper's criticism of the idea that human sovereignty should replace divine sovereignty in the political arena — whether that sovereignty be conceived of as belonging to "the people" or "the state" — had appeared in his work prior to the *Lectures on Calvinism,* his formulation and juxtapositioning of these ideas using the terms "popular-sovereignty" and "state-sovereignty" was new to the Stone Lectures. His concern in Princeton, clearly, was to show that Calvinism provided an alternative to both these options. In fulfilling this aim, he intended to demonstrate how the Calvinistic confession of God's absolute sovereignty could provide the basis for a theory of social organization that was directly relevant to the needs of modern society and could provide effective opposition to the politics of modernism. It is to this theory that we now turn.

2. Sovereignty in Society

For Kuyper, society was made up of various spheres such as the family, business, science, and art, which derived their authority not from the state, but directly from God, to whom they were accountable. The phrase he used to denote this theory, which he launched in his speech at the opening of the Free University in 1880, was "sovereignty in the individual social spheres" now often referred to by English-speaking commentators as "sphere-sovereignty."[33] He expounded this theory in his

32. Kuyper, *The Problem of Poverty,* pp. 45-46; *Geen vergeefs woord: Verzamelde deputaten-redevoeringen* (Kampen: Kok, 1951), p. 84.

33. The title of Kuyper's speech at the opening of the Free University was *Souvereiniteit in eigen kring.* This phrase cannot be easily translated into English. Literally it means something like "sovereignty in one's own sphere." The version given in the text above — "sovereignty in the individual social spheres" — is that used in the *Lectures* and is therefore sure to have had Kuyper's own approval. For the sake of conciseness, however, the term "sphere-sovereignty" will be used in this book. A. Kuyper, *Souvereiniteit.* A translated extract from Kuyper's speech can be found in *Political Order and the Plural Structure of Society,* ed. by James W. Skillen and

third Stone Lecture by making a distinction between the organic nature of society and the mechanical nature of government.

2.1. The Organic Nature of Society

Every sphere of life develops spontaneously, Kuyper argued, according to the data it received at creation. In the sphere of the family, for instance, the divinely created duality of man and woman gave rise to marriage, and from the innate power of reproduction, children are born who are naturally interrelated to each other. When these offspring marry and bear their own children, yet more ties and blood relationships are formed, and so the organic interrelatedness of human society is perpetuated in an entirely spontaneous way (LC, p. 91). The same kind of development was true for all the other spheres of society, through the exercise of powers which God had invested within nature: since these powers operated only in an organic way, the organic development of the social spheres was sustained.

In stressing the organic nature of society, Kuyper was reacting not only to individualism but to the mechanicism and scientism prevalent in the intellectual world at the end of the nineteenth century. In opposition to these theories, which taught that society was governed by neutral forces that operated in terms of cause and effect, he argued that society should instead be understood as a moral *(zedelijk)* organism, in the sense that it was held together by groups sharing common philosophical positions.[34] He obviously found it an opportune moment to stress this aspect of his social thought at the opening of the Free University[35] — an example, as he saw it, of a social institution that embodied a specific ideological position — as it provided justification for its existence. It also fitted well with his idea, based on his concept of worldview, that Roman Catholicism, humanism, and Calvinism, as the three legitimate historical traditions in Dutch society, each had the

Rockne M. McCarthy (Atlanta: Scholars Press, 1991), pp. 257-63. A slightly earlier but less developed exposition of Kuyper's idea of sphere-sovereignty can be found in *Ons program,* 2nd edition, pp. 20-35.

34. Kuyper, *Ons program,* p. 57. For discussion of this idea, see Meyer, pp. 268-69; D. T. Kuiper, *De voormannen,* pp. 166-67.

35. Kuyper, *Souvereiniteit,* p. 7.

right to organize those portions of society that adhered to their particular principles. Each group also had the right to argue that its principles should provide the ideological basis for the entire social organism, a right Kuyper did not hesitate to make use of, arguing frequently that the Calvinist tradition was most closely attuned to Dutch national character, and that it represented the historical "core" *(kern)* of Dutch society. He insisted, however, that such convictions could not be imposed by one group on any other; the organic nature of society demanded mutual recognition, and an absence of coercion or persecution.[36] It is likely that the acceptance of this idea played an important role in the creation and legitimization of *verzuiling*, the uniquely Dutch form of political and social pillarization.[37] It certainly provided the rationale for Kuyper's argument that no single sector of society could presume to represent the best interests of the entire nation, an error, he thought, of which the Liberals were particularly guilty.[38] As such it formed the basis of Kuyper's political pluralism.

Despite Kuyper's appeal (noted in the previous chapter) to scriptural teaching on the church as the source of his idea of the organic nature of society, this idea was also heavily influenced by organicist social theories, which had their roots in German historicism and Romanticism.[39] J. G. Herder (1744-1803), a leading precursor of these traditions, argued that the entire nation was a single organism made up of many organic parts. After Herder, the organicist school developed in two principal directions. The first of these, represented by Adam Müller (1779-1829), was conservative and statist, insisting, in line with Hegel, that the state was the preeminent organism and that all other spheres were to be subservient to it.[40] The other direction was liberal

36. Kuyper, *Ons program,* 2nd edition, pp. 16-21.

37. See later in this chapter for a discussion of the relationship between sphere-sovereignty and *verzuiling.*

38. *De Standaard,* 10 March 1890.

39. The influence of historicist thought on Kuyper's social theory has been suggested in the following studies, but has yet to be dealt with in depth: Dengerink, pp. 150-52; J. van Weringh, *Het maatschappijbeeld van Abraham Kuyper* (Assen: Van Gorcum, 1967), pp. 158-87; D. T. Kuiper and H. E. S. Woldring, *Reformatorische maatschappijkritiek: ontwikkelingen op het gebied van sociale filosofie en sociologie in de kring van het nederlandse protestantisme van de negentiende eeuw tot heden* (Kampen: Kok, 1980), pp. 56-66.

40. Andrew Vincent, *Theories of the State* (Oxford: Basil Blackwell, 1987), p. 27.

and pluralistic, opposed to the Hegelian view of sovereignty, and was represented by the German historian and legal theorist Otto von Gierke (1841-1921).[41] The parallels between von Gierke and Kuyper are striking, as von Gierke held that state and society must be distinguished from each other, and that society was made up of many autonomous "associations" such as schools, trade unions, and the church, each serving their own range of human needs and interests, free from interference by the state, and sovereign in their own sphere.[42] The similarities here are so close that it is possible to conclude that Kuyper derived his ideas primarily from von Gierke and his pluralist colleagues, with Groen van Prinsterer's belief in the organic nature of society as an important part of the background. No definitive link with von Gierke can be established, however, as Kuyper's works are devoid of all significant reference or allusions to him or his school. But the wealth of affinities ensures that the influence of the liberal and pluralistic strand in German organicism on Kuyper's thought can be regarded as beyond reasonable doubt.

2.2. The Mechanical Nature of Government

Having argued for the organic nature of society, Kuyper went on to outline, in contrast, the mechanical nature of government (LC, pp. 92-97). This was mainly a restatement of his claim (outlined earlier in this chapter) that Calvinism taught that governments had been instituted as a mechanical remedy to the disintegration caused by sin. What is important to point out here is the role he reserved for government, particularly as his insistence on the autonomy of the social spheres implies that this role was a severely restricted one. The state, he insisted, could not force any of the

41. This trend found repercussions in Britain, in the work of the pluralist thinkers F. W. Maitland, J. N. Figgis, and H. J. Laski, who were influenced by Gierke. Figgis helped Maitland in his translation of part of Gierke's massive work *Das Deutsche Genossenschaftsrecht,* 4 vols. (Berlin: Weidmann, 1868-1913), published under the title *Political Theories of the Middle Ages* (Cambridge: Cambridge University Press, 1988 [1900]).

42. Otto von Gierke, *Community in Historical Perspective,* trans. by Mary Fischer, ed. by Antony Black (Cambridge: Cambridge University Press, 1990). This work consists largely of extracts from the first volume of von Gierke's *Das Deutsche Genossenschaftsrecht.*

social spheres to conform to its will but, as a sphere of its own, was to occupy a place alongside all other spheres (LC, p. 97). The supremacy of the state was, however, evident in its threefold obligation to intervene in society, in order to enforce mutual respect for the boundary lines between each sphere whenever a conflict arose between spheres; to defend the powerless within a sphere whenever that sphere abused its authority; and to impose taxes for the maintenance of national unity (LC, p. 97).[43] Therefore, although the state was merely one of the social spheres, it did enjoy supremacy, and the relation between this supremacy and the sovereignty of the social spheres was to be regulated by means both of constitutional law and of representative government, aspects of statecraft that were hallmarks of Calvinism (LC, p. 98). Once again Kuyper's position came very close to that of von Gierke, who argued that the role of the state was to function as an umpire, maintaining the minimal conditions of order, determining conflicts of jurisdiction, and protecting members of one association from the encroachments of another.[44]

2.3. Sphere-Sovereignty and Verzuiling

It is not insignificant that one of Kuyper's earliest and most potent formulations of the doctrine of sphere-sovereignty coincided with the opening of the Free University in 1880. It suggests that this doctrine was of great strategic and practical importance to the realization of his objectives. In propounding the doctrine, according to which the scientific sphere, as one of the several social spheres, was autonomous, Kuyper aimed to provide the necessary justification for the establishment of a university free from political and ecclesiastical control.

Now, if the founding and development of ideologically based institutions such as the Free University during the course of the last two decades of the nineteenth and first two decades of the twentieth centuries is taken as evidence of the emergence of *verzuiling,* is it reasonable to suppose that Kuyper's doctrine of sphere-sovereignty, which lay at the foundation of the Free University, also laid the basis for the development

43. In this sense the state was "the sphere of spheres" *(de kring der kringen). Souvereiniteit,* p. 18 (cf. p. 12). See also Kuyper's *Ons program,* pp. 52, 61-62.

44. James W. Skillen and Rockne M. McCarthy, pp. 79-96. This anthology contains an extract from von Gierke's *Community.*

of *verzuiling?*[45] To investigate this question fully would take the discussion outside the scope of this book. It is important to note, however, that sphere-sovereignty in its primary meaning is not necessarily theoretically linked to *verzuiling.* Kuyper's doctrine was chiefly concerned with the existence of social spheres such as the family, education, business, and the church, whereas *verzuiling* was a phenomenon involving the arrangement of ideological groupings in society, such as Catholic, Protestant, liberal, and socialist. It could be argued, therefore, that if Dutch society had been of a more "homogeneous" nature, sphere-sovereignty would still have been practically viable whereas *verzuiling* would not have been necessary. Ever since the days of the Dutch Republic, however, Dutch society had known a roughly tripartite ideological divide between Catholics, Protestants, and humanists. Towards the end of the nineteenth century the rapid demise of the liberal establishment, the rise of the middle classes, and the birth of *laissez-faire* economic policy combined to present new opportunities to the members of confessional groups to organize their own social institutions such as schools, trade unions, and political parties. The threat from the new and powerful forces of secularization, expressed in a welter of new ideologies, encouraged the development of these organizations along confessional lines. Evidence for the existence of ideas that led to *verzuiling* may therefore be better sought in the doctrine of the antithesis, which does involve ideological and institutional divisions, as will become clear in the next chapter.

There is evidence, however, that Kuyper attached a secondary meaning to his idea of sphere-sovereignty, which was the notion that confessional or ideological groups in society were free to organize their own autonomous institutions. This was a meaning evident in Kuyper's early exposition of the doctrine in his speech at the opening of the Free University, and it reappeared in several subsequent publications. In his rectorial address of 1892, for instance, he argued that the only effective response of Protestants to pantheism's pervading influence was one of isolation, in order to consolidate forces and to develop an independent "life-sphere" *(levenskring)* on the basis of palingenesis, which would encompass all aspects of human existence.[46] "We wish to retreat behind

45. See Chapter One for an introduction to the question whether Kuyper contributed to the development of *verzuiling.*

46. Kuyper, *De verflauwing,* p. 49. The occurrence of this secondary meaning in Kuyper's fourth Stone Lecture will be discussed in the following chapter.

our own lines," he declared, "in order to prepare ourselves for the struggle ahead."[47] It is clear that Kuyper was using the concept of "sphere" *(kring)* here to refer to a social group rather than a realm of human existence, and it is his use of the term sphere in this sense that helps to provide him with the necessary rationale for the organization of independent Calvinistic institutions of the sort that contributed to the development of *verzuiling.*

It should be pointed out here that this secondary meaning of the concept of sphere-sovereignty was incompatible with the first. As noted above, Kuyper grounded his concept of sphere-sovereignty in the creational order: the spheres existed in God's original creation and had been invested with divine laws that governed their existence. This claim makes little sense if "sphere" is also understood to refer to confessional or ideological groupings, as these cannot have belonged to the original created order. The problem here in Kuyper's theory was first indicated by Herman Dooyeweerd, who was a proponent of sphere-sovereignty as a creational principle.[48] He was critical, however, of Kuyper's lack of definition as to what the various spheres of society actually were, leading to different enumerations and meanings of "spheres" in different works. It was this confusion of thought, he claimed, that prevented Kuyper from being able to provide a sound philosophical basis for his social and political theory.[49] The contention of this book is that the same confusion amounted to two usages, one creational and the other socio-ideological; that the two were irreconcilable with each other; and that this double usage is likely to have served as a stimulus to the development of *verzuiling* in Dutch society.

47. Kuyper, *De verflauwing,* p. 47. In making his argument for isolation, Kuyper was able to appeal to his predecessor Groen van Prinsterer, whose motto was "In isolation lies our strength" *(In het isolement ligt onze kracht),* p. 37.

48. H. Dooyeweerd, "Introduction," in *The Idea of a Christian Philosophy: Essays in Honour of D. H. T. Vollenhoven* (Toronto: Wedge, 1973). Published simultaneously in *Philosophia Reformata: orgaan van de vereniging voor calvinistische wijsbegeerte* 38 (1973), p. 7.

49. H. Dooyeweerd, *Roots of Western Culture: Pagan, Secular and Christian Options,* trans. by John Kraay (Toronto: Wedge, 1979), p. 54.

3. Sovereignty in the Church

The final part of Kuyper's third lecture concerns the authority of the church as opposed to that of the state — in other words, the question of the relationship between church and state. This was an issue of vital importance to Kuyper throughout his career, and he dealt with it in numerous articles, speeches, and pamphlets. In the third volume of his *De gemeene gratie,* for instance, twenty-eight out of the fifty-one collected articles from *De Heraut* addressed the issue directly. For Kuyper it was obviously an issue of some difficulty, made particularly problematic to Calvinists by the burning of Servetus and Calvin's support of government intervention in matters of religion (LC, p. 99). Added to this was the fact that in the Calvinistic Netherlands, Roman Catholics had been denied certain rights and liberties for centuries, and also that the Belgic Confession (Article 36) still entrusted to the government the task of preserving the sanctity of the church by dealing with false religion. These problematic aspects of Calvinism had to be understood, Kuyper explained, as remnants from the medieval period with its conviction that the church could only be manifested in one form and as one institution (the so-called "territorial principle"). Despite its medieval carry-overs, Kuyper was confident that Calvinism had conceded that the church could find expression in a variety of forms and that it had allowed for the flourishing of free churches. Thus, reiterating in Princeton the motto he had placed at the head of *De Heraut,* Kuyper claimed that the only system Calvinism supported was that of "a free church in a free state" (LC, pp. 99, 106).

Despite the apparent unambiguity of his advocacy of the concept of a free church (that is, free from the state), the question ought to be raised whether Kuyper was in favor of a free church in principle, or whether he merely considered it to be the only viable option. D. T. Kuiper's use of the term "theocratic" to describe Kuyper's politics, mentioned earlier in this chapter, would suggest that the latter may have been the case. In addition, Leonard Verduin has argued that Kuyper saw "no principial reason for opposing the use of force" in religious matters, and he concludes that Kuyper favored a form of Constantinian sacralism.[50] As evidence for his conclusion Verduin cites from a passage in *Ons program,* where Kuyper writes: "If coercion by the state only worked

50. Leonard Verduin, *The Reformers and Their Stepchildren* (Grand Rapids: Eerdmans, 1964), p. 79.

we would not for one moment hesitate to employ it."[51] It is clear, however, that Verduin has not paid sufficient attention to the context of Kuyper's words, which was a principled, historical argument in which he claimed that state coercion in matters of religion was antagonistic to divine principles.[52] It appears, moreover, that Kuyper argued consistently for the mutual autonomy of church and state. According to his doctrine of sphere-sovereignty, which found expression throughout his career from its inception around 1880, the church and the state form independent, co-existing spheres accountable directly to God. He even dealt explicitly with the evils of "Constantinian sacralism," both in his third Stone Lecture and in his *Pro Rege*.[53] In both places he argued that the idea that the state had the right and the competence to legislate on religious matters was a fallacy. The only appreciable difference in his argument in these two instances was that whereas in his third lecture he identified the origin of this idea in Constantine, in *Pro Rege* he traced it back to the pagan Roman Empire. After the conversion of Constantine, he explained, the pagan ideal was maintained; Christianity was merely substituted for paganism as the new state religion.[54]

There is no real basis, therefore, for doubting Kuyper's commitment to a free church on principled grounds. He was keen to stress, however, that his position did not imply that the government was exempt from all obligations towards religion. Its first obligation was an acknowledgment on the part of the magistrates that God was the source of their authority, and that they were to govern according to his ordinances. In the fulfillment of this duty they were not bound to submit to the pronouncements of any church, but to their own consciences. A Christian state might, indeed, only be realized through "the subjective convictions of those in authority" and not by legislative means. A second obligation was to tolerate the multiformity of church denominations, both because the state lacked the competence to judge on spiritual matters and because any government legislation in this area infringed on the sovereignty of the church (LC, pp. 103-4).

51. Verduin, *The Reformers and Their Stepchildren,* p. 79.

52. Kuyper, *Ons program* (original version, with supplements), p. 1121. Dengerink includes a discussion of this passage in his *Critisch-historisch onderzoek,* p. 133.

53. Kuyper, *Pro Rege of het Koningschap van Christus,* 3 vols. (Kampen: Kok, 1911-12), III, pp. 299-302.

54. Kuyper, *Pro Rege,* III, pp. 301-2; James Skillen, "The Development of Calvinistic Political Theory," p. 260.

In addressing the question of the responsibilities of the government towards the church, Kuyper was dealing with an area which had already involved him in a good deal of controversy. The argument centered on the exact wording of Article 36 of the Belgic Confession, which conceded to the civil magistracy the right to "protect the sacred ministry" and thus to "remove and prevent all idolatry and false worship." During the 1890s Kuyper repeatedly proposed that this latter phrase be eliminated from the Article. He was bitterly opposed in this venture by Hoedemaker, his former colleague at the Free University, who held to a theocratic understanding of the role of the state in matters of religion, a position which led to his resignation from the Free University in 1887. He subsequently severed his connection with Kuyper and the ARP and became an instrumental figure in the early development of the more conservatively inclined Christian Historical Union.[55] Hoedemaker argued that Article 36 should be preserved because the government was bound in its actions to the confession of the national church. Although he taught that church and state were organizationally independent, the government, where necessary, must be instructed in certain policies by the national church. He differed sharply from Kuyper on the question of whether the state could know and recognize the church as *the church,* the divinely instituted revelation of the body of Christ on earth. He agreed with Kuyper's assertion that the government did not need to be asked if it wished to tolerate the church because the church existed *"jure divino"* (LC, p. 106). But he insisted, in opposition to Kuyper, that the state must recognize the fact that God had formed the church, and that the only criterion for determining whether a state was Christian or not was whether the government granted a public and legal status to the church as a divine institution.[56]

Kuyper refused to accept that the government was obliged either to recognize the church for what it was or to judge which of the various denominations was the true church, although his position on this

55. See Chapter Two. For detailed discussions of the conflict between Hoedemaker and Kuyper, see G. J. J. A. Delfgaauw, *De staatsleer van Hoedemaker: een bijdrage tot de kennis van de christelijk-historische staatsopvatting* (Kok: Kampen, 1963), pp. 132-41; H. van Spanning, 'Hoedemaker en de antirevolutionairen', in *Hoedemaker herdacht,* ed. by G. Abma and J. de Bruijn (Baarn: Ten Have, 1989), pp. 234-45.

56. P. J. Hoedemaker, *Artikel 36 onzer Nederduitsche geloofsbelijdenis tegenover Dr. A. Kuyper gehandhaafd* (Amsterdam: Van Dam, 1901).

matter seems to have undergone some fluctuation. Early on in his public career he argued, along with Hoedemaker, that the government, as God's servant, must not only take into consideration the so-called *natural* knowledge of God but was also subject to God's *revealed* will in the scriptures. Later, however, in a series of articles in *De Heraut,* he changed his position and argued that it was impossible, as a result of all kinds of circumstances, for the government to act in accordance with God's revealed will, and could only govern by the light of the natural knowledge of God.[57] In contrast to the light of God's revealed will, the natural knowledge of God was insufficient to enable the government to judge between church confessions. By the time of the Stone Lectures, Kuyper's position had become more nuanced. There he reserved a place once again for God's revealed will in the judgments of the state, but insisted that this was to be mediated through the consciences of government officials and not through the dictates of any church:

> In order that they may govern, according to His holy ordinances, every magistrate is in duty bound to investigate the rights of God, both in the natural life and in His Word. Not to subject himself to the decision of any Church, but in order that he himself may catch the light which he needs for the knowledge of the Divine will (LC, p. 103).

Both the seriousness with which he debated the issue with Hoedemaker and the changes in Kuyper's position reflect Kuyper's attempt to come to terms with the liberal domination of Dutch politics throughout most of the nineteenth century. This attempt necessitated for him a compromise that significantly reduced the possibilities for large-scale parallelism between church and state. His concern was to reach a synthesis between what he saw as the ideal relationship, which appears to have involved a formal attachment to God's revealed will, and the prevailing conditions of the nineteenth century — the aim being to effect the accommodation of free churches and Christian organizations within the liberal state. It was in the interests of guaranteeing such freedom and accommodation that the ARP formally abandoned Article 36, regarding it as an anachronism that should be

57. Kuyper, *Ons program,* 74; L. Kalsbeek, *Contours of a Christian Philosophy: An Introduction to Herman Dooyeweerd's Thought,* ed. by Bernard and Josina Zylstra (Amsterdam: Buijten en Schipperheijn, 1975), pp. 229-30.

"interpreted historically," having greater relevance to the Middle Ages than to the nineteenth century.[58]

Conclusion

Kuyper lived in a period that had recently witnessed the capitulation of many European states to the spirit of the Enlightenment. The shift in consciousness that this had brought about was immense, and had significant political ramifications. The preeminent feature of the new politics, and the one that most concerned Kuyper, was the exalted position it gave to human beings as autonomous individuals. Governments were no longer perceived of as ruling by divine right, and society was no longer thought of as functioning according to inherent, God-given laws. Rather, society was perceived as a collection of individuals, operating in an "open market," where equal and opposing forces met in direct competition with each other. Individuals no longer needed the government to confer upon them their rights and privileges, for these were innate to them by reason of their own personal sovereignty. The government, made up of "the people," was merely to protect the rights of the individual against their violation by others. Gradually, towards the end of the nineteenth century, and under the influence of pantheism, historicism, and socialism, the idea that sovereignty was invested in the people made way for the idea that the state constituted the people and was therefore the true repository of sovereignty. It was within this intellectual environment that Kuyper formed the political ideas he presented at Princeton. The gradual shift from individualism to collectivism as the leading political trend was mirrored in his attack on political modernism, which focused initially on individualism and later came to include collectivism. Despite the fierceness of his attack, he maintained his aversion to the contention of contra-revolutionary politics that a return to the old order would benefit contemporary circumstances. He even admired some revolutions (noted in Chapter Three) and did not wish to deny the obvious benefits

58. A. Kuyper, *De gemeene gratie,* III, pp. 288-89. In 1905 the synod of the *Gereformeerde* churches abandoned the phrase in Article 36 which prescribed that the government was to eliminate false religion. Those that did agree to this found it difficult to remain within the main body of the *Gereformeerde* churches and of the ARP (see Meyer, p. 264).

that had come as a result of the French Revolution. The name anti-revolutionary was designed to point to an alternative agenda for political change and thus bore with it the notion of progression.

The basis for this alternative was Kuyper's idea of sphere-sovereignty. Although he often stressed its distinctiveness, it borrowed liberally from other theories, particularly from organicist ones and from certain forms of liberalism. It was developed primarily as a theoretical justification for the founding of independent Christian institutions, while also serving as the intellectual foundation for the ARP's position on the autonomy of church and state. Most importantly, it provided the rationale for social and political pluralism, which was Kuyper's answer to the liberal domination of politics. Insofar as this pluralism coincided with Kuyper's notion of religious or ideological pluralism it helped to lay the basis for the development of *verzuiling,* which came about chiefly as a result of the sweeping social changes that had reached full momentum in the Netherlands by the end of the nineteenth century.

Kuyper on receiving his doctorate of theology
from Leiden University in 1862.
Source: Free University, Amsterdam.

Johanna Schaay (1842-1899), Kuyper's fiancée, who sent him a copy of Charlotte Yonge's *The Heir of Redclyffe* in 1862. The couple was married in 1863 and had eight children. Source: Free University, Amsterdam.

The novelist Charlotte M. Yonge (1823-1901), whose work was influenced by the Oxford movement leader, John Keble (1792-1866).
Source: Free University, Amsterdam.

Kuyper as member of parliament between 1874 and 1877. In 1875 Kuyper attended a mass rally in Brighton, organized as part of a series of revival meetings held in Britain led by American evangelists Dwight Moody, Ira Sankey, and Robert Pearsall Smith.

Source: Free University, Amsterdam.

A°. 1872. N°. 1.

DE STANDAARD.

Maandag 1 April.

Abonnementsprijs per drie maanden: Voor Amsterdam ƒ 2.27½. — Franco per post ƒ 2.75.

BUREEL: Nieuwendijk L 76. Amsterdam. Administrateur J. H. KRUYT

Enkele Nummers 3 Ct. aan het Bureel. Prijs der Advertentiën 15 Cents per gewone regel.

Amsterdam, 1 April 1872.

First edition of Kuyper's daily newspaper *De Standaard.*

Source: Free University, Amsterdam.

Kuyper's Roman Catholic political colleague Herman Schaepman (1844-1903).
Source: Free University, Amsterdam.

Sketch of Kuyper at his writing desk in 1892 by Jan Veth.
Source: Free University, Amsterdam.

Kuyper at Princeton after receiving an honorary doctorate in law from the university on 22 October 1898.
Source: Free University, Amsterdam.

The luxury steamship *R. M. S. Lucania,* which took Kuyper across the Atlantic from Liverpool to New York in August 1898.
Source: Free University, Amsterdam.

Benjamin B. Warfield (1851-1921), Professor of Didactic and Polemic Theology at Princeton from 1887 to 1921. He was nicknamed the "American Kuyper."

Source: Princeton Seminary Archives.

Cover of the program of Kuyper's visit to Cleveland, Ohio, which included an address entitled "The Political Principles of Calvinism." In Cleveland, as elsewhere in the United States, Kuyper was given a rapturous welcome.

Source: Free University, Amsterdam.

Cleveland's Welcome
HOLLAND'S FOREMOST CITIZEN.
PROFESSOR ABRAHAM KUYPER, D. D., LL.D.
STATESMAN, THEOLOGIAN, LITERATEUR,
Old Stone Church, Tuesday, November 15, 1898.

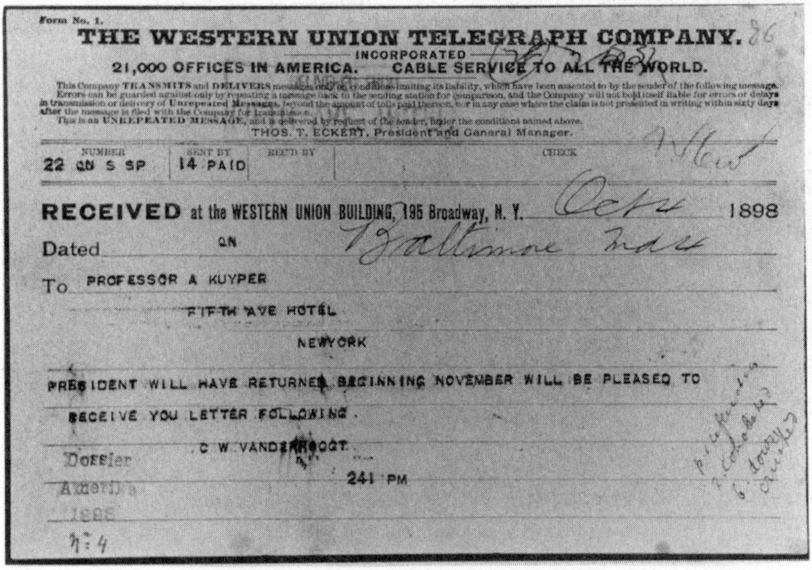

Form No. 1.

THE WESTERN UNION TELEGRAPH COMPANY.

INCORPORATED

21,000 OFFICES IN AMERICA. CABLE SERVICE TO ALL THE WORLD.

This Company TRANSMITS and DELIVERS messages only on conditions limiting its liability, which have been assented to by the sender of the following message. Errors can be guarded against only by repeating a message back to the sending station for comparison, and the Company will not hold itself liable for errors or delays in transmission or delivery of Unrepeated Messages, beyond the amount of tolls paid thereon, nor in any case where the claim is not presented in writing within sixty days after the message is filed with the Company for transmission.

This is an UNREPEATED MESSAGE, and is delivered by request of the sender, under the conditions named above.

THOS. T. ECKERT, President and General Manager.

NUMBER	SENT BY	REC'D BY	CHECK
22 QN S SP	14 PAID		

RECEIVED at the WESTERN UNION BUILDING, 195 Broadway, N. Y. Oct 4 1898

Dated ON Baltimore Md

To PROFESSOR A KUYPER

FIFTH AVE HOTEL

NEWYORK

PRESIDENT WILL HAVE RETURNED BEGINNING NOVEMBER WILL BE PLEASED TO RECEIVE YOU LETTER FOLLOWING.

C W VANDERHOOGT

241 PM

Dossier

Amerika

1898

N° 4

A telegram sent to Kuyper on 4 October 1898 informing him that the U.S. President, William McKinley (1843-1901), was willing to meet him at the White House.

Source: Free University, Amsterdam.

Kuyper was often satirized by the Dutch press. In the cartoon at the left, entitled "Abraham the Mighty," Kuyper's ruthless and bombastic traits were caricatured. The cartoon below stems from Kuyper's period as Prime Minister, when he held the portfolio for internal affairs. It suggests that Kuyper's willingness to make trips abroad reflected a lack of concern for social issues at home. The cartoon was accompanied by the caption: "The Minister of the Interior at work."

Source: Free University, Amsterdam.

De Minister van Binnenlandsche Zaken aan het werk.

Kuyper as Prime Minister in 1905, wearing ceremonial attire. He was elected to office in 1901, three years after he gave the Stone Lectures at Princeton.
Source: Free University, Amsterdam.

Kuyper presiding at a sitting of the Dutch coalition cabinet of 1901-1905, made up of representatives of the Antirevolutionary and Roman Catholic political parties.
Source: Free University, Amsterdam.

Kuyper at work in his study at home in The Hague, where he lived from 1901 until his death in 1920.

Source: Free University, Amsterdam.

Fourth Lecture: Calvinism and Science

Kuyper's career spanned a period that witnessed a revolution in science, the rise of the modern university, and the birth of the "scientific culture," which has been predominant in the life of Western nations ever since. It was only natural, therefore, given his desire to revitalize Calvinism by bringing it in line with the demands of modern life, and to encourage the social emancipation of the orthodox Protestants, that he should be concerned with question of the relationship between Christianity and science. Although fascinated and enthralled by the wealth of new scientific discovery and technological innovation, which he welcomed with enthusiasm, his interest and involvement in the scientific world did not stem from personal interests alone but was part of his concern for the transformation of Dutch society by means of independent Christian institutions.

Kuyper was no philosopher of science in the strictly academic sense. Although he provided a substantial theological and philosophical rationale for his position he never developed a systematic philosophy of science *(Wissenschaftslehre)*.[1] Nevertheless, his ideas on science and their embodiment in the Free University are largely responsible for the fact that, out of all the countries in the Western world, the Netherlands was the one in which evangelical Protestantism suffered the least serious

1. The term "science" is used here, and throughout this chapter, in the way Kuyper used it (see section 1 of this chapter).

decline in intellectual influence during the heyday of science and secularization in the first half of the twentieth century.[2] His ideas also provided the foundations for the philosophy of science developed by the later generation of neo-Calvinist thinkers, represented chiefly by Herman Dooyeweerd, known as the *Wijsbegeerte der Wetsidee,* usually translated into English as the "Philosophy of the Cosmonomic Idea," which still enjoys considerable influence in the work of philosophers associated with the neo-Calvinistic, or "Kuyperian" school of thought.[3]

Although not a philosopher of science, Kuyper remained throughout his career closely involved with the academic world of his day, not only as a writer of academic theology, but also as founder of the Free University and as its Rector Magnificus and Professor of Theology. As Prime Minister one of his main achievements was his facilitating the establishment of the Netherlands' first college of advanced technology *(Technische Hoogeschool)* in Delft in 1905 (now Delft University).[4] In the United States his ideas on science have had marked influence among American evangelicals, and today form one of the most significant points of reference around which evangelical scholars gather. Indeed, the international Kuyperian school owes more of its body of thought to Kuyper's ideas on science than to those on other areas, including politics.

2. George Marsden, "The Collapse of American Evangelical Academia," in *Faith and Rationality,* ed. by Alvin Plantinga and Nicholas Wolterstorff (Notre Dame: University of Notre Dame Press, 1983), p. 247; Mark A. Noll, *The Scandal of the Evangelical Mind* (Grand Rapids: Eerdmans; London: IVP, 1994), p. 216. Noll regards the Kuyperian intellectual tradition as an exception to the "scandal" of evangelical avoidance of rigorous academic enterprise (see review of Noll's book by Peter Somers Heslam in *Anvil* 14 [1997]: 67-69). Ray Anderson makes a similar point with regard to theology in his essay "Evangelical Theology," in *The Modern Theologians,* ed. by David F. Ford, pp. 480-98 (494).

3. This philosophy received its classic articulation in Dooyeweerd's monumental *De wijsbegeerte der wetsidee,* 3 vols. (Amsterdam: Paris, 1935-1936). English translation: *A New Critique of Theoretical Thought,* 4 vols. (Philadelphia: Presbyterian and Reformed Publishing Company, 1953-1958). Shorter and more accessible expositions can be found in his *In the Twilight of Western Thought: Studies in the Pretended Autonomy of Philosophical Thought* (Nutley, N.J.: The Craig Press, 1972) and in his *Roots of Western Culture.* See also D. T. H. Vollenhoven, *Het calvinisme en de reformatie van de wijsbegeerte* (Amsterdam: Paris, 1933). See also Del Ratzsch, "Abraham Kuyper's Philosophy of Science," *Calvin Theological Journal* 27 (1992): 277-303.

4. C. de Ru, *De strijd over het hoger onderwijs tijdens het ministerie-Kuyper* (Kampen: Kok, 1953).

Although science came after politics in Kuyper's exposition of the relevance of Calvinism for modern culture in his Princeton lectures, the significance of Kuyper's ideas on science, particularly as they were expressed in these lectures, was certainly not secondary to that of his ideas on politics. In terms of relevance to his immediate audience, his views on science were paramount, as the question of the relationship between Christianity and science was high on the agenda at Princeton, and, indeed, in the American intellectual world as a whole, at the time of Kuyper's visit. Warfield was chiefly responsible for the interest in this subject at Princeton, and he, along with Kuyper, influenced a great deal of evangelical scientific thought. This influence has remained up to the present day; most American evangelical thinkers today belong either to the school of Warfield or to that of Kuyper.[5]

There were four chief points in the argument Kuyper presented at Princeton: Calvinism fostered love for science; it restored science to its domain; it advanced the liberty of science; and it provided the solution to the conflict in science. The last of these represented the climax of his argument, and it includes the most significant and enduring elements of his thinking on science. Before he launched into his argument proper he explained to his audience what he meant by the term "science," and it is important to take note of this before proceeding.

1. What Is Science?

Kuyper did not take "science" to mean what was commonly understood by the English "sciences" and the French *"sciences exactes."* This would be to limit the meaning of the term to the natural sciences, he explained, whereas his usage encompassed the whole of human knowledge, including the humanities.[6] Kuyper's usage, instead, was equivalent to that of the German *Wissenschaft* or the Dutch *Wetenschap,* the term he used

5. Marsden observes: "In almost every field today, evangelical scholars are divided into two camps . . . the Warfieldians and the Kuyperians." In *Understanding Fundamentalism and Evangelicalism* (Grand Rapids: Eerdmans, 1991), p. 151.

6. The *Oxford English Dictionary* noted in 1933 that the use of the word "science" to refer only to the natural and physical sciences, to the exclusion of the humanities, was a fairly recent phenomenon, recording its first appearance in 1867. *Oxford English Dictionary* (Oxford: The Clarendon Press, 1933), IX, p. 222.

in his Dutch edition of the Stone Lectures.[7] The second usage of the term Kuyper wished to reject was that which denoted empiricism. This, he declared, was merely the perception and observation of phenomena, and could only become science if it went on to discover the universal laws, and thereby the principles, that governed the whole range of observable phenomena. A similar argument (in similar words) had been propounded by James Orr: "The mind . . . is not content with fragmentary knowledge, but tends constantly to rise from facts to laws, from laws to higher laws, from these to the highest generalizations possible."[8] Charles Hodge, Warfield's predecessor at Princeton, also maintained the breadth of the scope of science. As early as 1873 Hodge had criticized the current trend towards limiting the meaning of science from its original, etymological meaning of "knowledge" to "the ordered phenomena which we recognize through the senses." This trend, he claimed, tended to encourage scientists to undervalue all science that was not based on the evidence of the senses.[9]

Kuyper's understanding of the meaning of science was designed to oppose agnosticism. This trend, given its name by Thomas Henry Huxley (1825-1895) in 1869, and based on the Kantian distinction between the phenomena and the noumena of science, taught that all scientifically accessible knowledge is limited to the realm of observable phenomena. The scientist knows that underlying all such phenomena are certain essential qualities, or noumena, that affect them in some way, but these are inaccessible to observation. Thus Herbert Spencer in England and John Fiske in America, who made much of this idea, spoke of a great "Force" or "Power" behind the universe.[10] Fully fledged agnosticism went further than this, however, claiming that positive science, dealing with phenomena, gave us knowledge whereas other areas, such as religious or moral absolutes, were noumena and therefore belonged to the realm of the unknowable. So widely were these views on science and

7. A. Kuyper, *Het calvinisme: zes Stone-lezingen in october 1898 te Princeton (N.-J.) gehouden* (Amsterdam: Höveker & Wormser, 1898), passim.

8. Orr, *The Christian View of God,* p. 6. Orr appealed to *Der alte und der neue Glaube* by the great Tübingen biblical critic D. F. Strauss (1808-1874) in making this argument — even though in this book, Strauss's last (1872), he accepted scientific materialism, rejected life after death, and espoused Darwinian evolution.

9. Charles Hodge, *What Is Darwinism?* (New York: Scribners, Armstrong, and Company, 1874).

10. Like Spencer, Fiske was a keen defender of Darwinism.

religion adopted in Western culture that the century after 1869 has been called "the age of agnosticism."[11]

Kuyper was clearly not unnerved by the predominance of this trend. He was confident, indeed, that human thought inevitably strove to find answers to questions as to the origin, interconnection, and destiny of observable things. Evidence of this quest could be seen in the fact that evolution theory had rapidly come to dominate all branches of science, not just the observation of biological phenomena (LC, p. 113). Although agnosticism denied vast areas of scientific investigation to the researching subject, agnostic scientists were finding it impossible to restrict their field of enquiry to empirical phenomena, due to the unescapable desire within the human spirit to search for the meaning of the cosmos in all its inner relations.[12] By defining science in its broadest, most comprehensive sense, both Kuyper and Hodge were pleading for the retention of the scientific status of the "spiritual sciences" (including theology), and of the metaphysical dimensions of science. For them these areas were fully within the scope of scientific study, and were open to rigorous academic enquiry. They thus sought to oppose the rising tide of materialism, which they regarded as a threat to Christianity, encompassing as it did the false doctrines of agnosticism and evolutionism.[13]

2. Love for Science

2.1. Leiden University

Kuyper's argument that Calvinism fostered love for science included an illustration from history that captures him in one of his most romantic flights of historical interpretation. It concerned the siege of Leiden in 1573-1574 during the Eighty Years' War between Spain and the Netherlands. This episode, he declared, was a struggle between the Duke of Alva and Prince William of Orange over the future course of world history. The siege having ended in a heroic victory for William's forces,

11. Marsden, "The Collapse," pp. 245-46.

12. Kuyper, *Encyclopedia,* p. 91.

13. Hodge's pamphlet *What Is Darwinism?* concluded with the answer: "it is atheism" (p. 177).

the States of Holland presented the citizens of Leiden, as a tribute to their tenacity and patriotism, with a university, rather than with wealth or honors. Richly endowed with chairs, this university was able to attract some of the greatest scientists in Europe and helped to infuse the whole nation with a love for science, evidenced by the fact that the telescope, the microscope, and the thermometer had all been invented in the Netherlands, allowing for the birth of modern empirical science. The establishment of such a fine university could only have been possible in a country in which there already existed a great love for science. For Kuyper the entire episode represented "a glorious page" in the history of Calvinism (LC, p. 110), and he used it to confront his audience with a vivid and arresting, if not entirely convincing, illustration of his argument that Calvinism fostered love for science.

2.2. The Doctrine of Decrees

If the illustration of the argument owed its appeal to Kuyper's imaginative and visionary talents in expounding Calvinism's illustrious history, the argument itself was theological rather than historical and was based on the Calvinistic doctrine of decrees. In keeping with this doctrine, he explained, the Calvinist believed the cosmos to be subject to divine ordinances and to be directed by them according to a pre-established plan (LC, p. 115). From this doctrine was derived the belief in foreordination, according to which the cosmos was not "a plaything of caprice and chance" but manifested unity, stability, and regularity. Kuyper was confident that this belief, fundamental to the very possibility of science, was integral to modern scholarship. Adherents of the evolutionary school, for instance, showed almost unanimous agreement that the cosmos reflected the kind of unity and stability taught by Calvinism, rather than the chance and disorder characteristic of Arminianism (LC, p. 115).[14] Thus, despite his fierce opposition to modern philosophical systems, Kuyper was prepared to bring them to Calvinism's defense whenever he felt it expedient, in order to strengthen his case. Following the pattern he established in his lecture on religion, he expounded traditional Calvinistic doctrine in such a way as to demonstrate its contemporary cultural significance. He managed to place

14. Kuyper cited Henry Thomas Buckle's *History of Civilization in England,* 5 vols. (Leipzig: Brockhaus, 1865), as belonging to this scholarly consensus.

the doctrine of decrees, despised by his opponents as the very belief that had thwarted the development of science, at the heart of the scientific impulse in the modern era.

The argument that Calvinism fostered love for science was not only useful in demonstrating the relevance of Calvinism to modern life, but also in stimulating the enthusiastic pursuit of science, as a mark of being a true Calvinist with an authentic faith. This, Kuyper explained, did not only apply to those who were able to pursue a professional scientific career; during the heyday of Calvinism the need for unity, stability, and order in thought, knowledge, and worldview was evident among wide circles of the common people (LC, p. 117). As a leader who through his daily and weekly articles in *De Standaard* and *De Heraut* aimed to educate his followers, the majority of whom had no access to study at the university level, Kuyper no doubt cherished this thought. While his plea for the scholarly, disciplined pursuit of science was directed towards a small Calvinistic élite, he insisted that this élite, once educated, was to provide leadership for the rest. Persistently in *De Standaard* he argued for the rigorous scientific training and scholarly formation of potential Calvinistic leaders, who would eventually be able to interpret contemporary issues on behalf of the less well-educated.[15] Kuyper's explicit purpose in making this argument was often to appeal for funds to support the Free University, where such training could take place; the Calvinist's love for science could not be satisfied without proper funding. As the Free University was entirely dependent on private patronage, the effectiveness of his argument is partly reflected in the fact that a steady stream of financial contributions flowed, over a period of decades, from a sector of the population that enjoyed few opportunities for higher education and belonged largely to the underprivileged lower middle classes.

In terms of stimulating scientific involvement among his Princeton audience, which belonged to the American Calvinistic élite, Kuyper was preaching to the converted. Its members were deeply committed to the development of a scientifically based culture, the founding of Princeton University two years before Kuyper's visit testifying to their enthusiasm for non-theological scientific education and research. Involvement and leadership in the academic world was, in fact, a characteristic of a good deal of American evangelicalism, such that it is possible to speak of the "Evangelical love affair with Enlightenment

15. See, for instance, *De Standaard,* 7 August 1891.

science."[16] Kuyper's proposition that it was essential Calvinistic doctrine that fostered such a love affair would, therefore, have been met at Princeton with warm approval.

Three years after the Stone Lectures, and just a few months before he became Prime Minister, Kuyper gave a fuller and riper treatment to the significance of God's decrees for the scientific impulse in *De Heraut*.[17] There he argued that since all created things originated in God's thought, it was God's thought that formed the nucleus and essence of all created things and prescribed their means of existence, development, and function. Because of this, the entire created order was "a visible curtain behind which the exalted workings of divine thought shines forth."[18] Human beings, made in the image of God, had been given both the capacity and the mandate to recognize these thoughts, to understand them, to think about them, and to integrate them into a unified system. In doing so they were thinking God's thoughts after him, the result of which activity is the development of science.[19] In proclaiming the idea that the vocation of the scientist was to think God's thoughts after him, Kuyper sought to dispel two popular misconceptions. The first of these was that the divine mind was clearly discernible only in the scientific results produced by Christians. Kuyper's argument was designed to show that all true science is revelatory of the divine, not only the science of professing Christians. Christians should therefore engage fully with the work of non-Christian scientists. In the second place, he hoped to dispose of the idea that within the scientific community it was only theologians who could discover and examine God's thoughts. Instead, all scientists, whatever their discipline and whether they recognized it or not, were engaged in this activity: their true vocation lay in making God's thoughts their own. Kuyper's intention was that Christian scientists would find within this concept a powerful stimulus to their scientific endeavors: their vocation, just as much as that of theologians, was to make a study of divine things.

16. Marsden, *Understanding*, p. 122.

17. *De Heraut*, 5 May–9 July 1901, published in A. Kuyper, *De gemeene gratie in wetenschap en kunst* (Amsterdam: Höveker & Wormser, 1905).

18. Kuyper, *De gemeene gratie*, p. 5.

19. *De gemeene gratie*, p. 8. Kuyper had noted, in his speech at the founding of the Free University in 1880, that the business of science was to think God's thoughts after him, but the point was made only in passing. See Kuyper, *Souvereiniteit*, p. 19. He returned to a discussion of this proposition in his *Pro Rege*, III, pp. 408-18.

3. The Domain of Science

The second element in Kuyper's argument for the significance of Calvinism for science was that it restored science to its domain. After the medieval fixation on the celestial sphere, and following the renewal of interest in the writings of Aristotle, it was Calvinism that had reopened the entire cosmos for scientific study, by means of its cosmological understanding of redemption and its doctrine of common grace (LC, p. 117).

3.1. Cosmic Redemption[20]

Christendom had been guilty, Kuyper explained, of a dualistic conception of regeneration, the result of which had been the rupture of the life of nature from the life of grace. An exclusive concentration on eternal things had led to a neglect of the temporal realm, Christ's redemption being conceived of only in terms of the salvation of the soul. Its cosmic significance and scope had been thereby disregarded.[21] For Kuyper the destiny of creation was not to be understood as the salvation of souls, but as "the restoration of the entire cosmos." This "wide, comprehensive, cosmical meaning of the gospel" had been apprehended by Calvin, he argued, who had put an end to contempt for the world and neglect of temporal things (LC, pp. 119-20). Calvinism, consequently, reserved no place for the notion that to concentrate on the study of nature was to be preoccupied with vain or idle things, but was able to agree with Humanism on the value of secular life.

The concept of cosmic redemption was clearly fundamental to Kuyper's interpretation of Calvinism. He even went so far as to call it Calvinism's "dominating principle" (LC, p. 118). It is curious, therefore, that the *Lectures* are the only place in his works where he argues the significance of this belief for the development of science.[22] Elsewhere

20. The term "cosmic redemption" is not one employed by Kuyper himself. It is used here as a shorthand means of referring to his position.

21. Kuyper held that the cosmic significance of Christ's salvation was taught by the following passages of scripture: John 1:1-4; Matthew 19:28; Romans 8:19-23; Colossians 1:16-20; Revelation 4:11 (LC, pp. 119-20).

22. Kuyper does make a "provisional remark" to this effect in his *Encyclopedia*, but provides no further explanation (p. 182).

he draws a distinction between the regeneration of the human soul and that of the entire created order, thus speaking of a twofold rebirth *(tweeërlei wedergeboorte),* but the relevance of this distinction to scientific discovery receives no mention.[23] The doctrine of common grace probably provided him with adequate theological grounds for his plea for the pursuit of science. This suggestion is supported by the fact that in the Stone Lectures he infers that belief in the cosmic scope of Christ's redemption is the *principle* from which the *dogma* of common grace is derived (LC, p. 118). For Kuyper, belief in the cosmic scope of Christ's redemption allowed the entire created order to be seen as the field of God's grace.

3.2. Common Grace[24]

Common grace provided Kuyper with the solution to an important problem that was inherent in constructing a Christian approach to science: how was it possible, given the fact that regeneration provides the only salvation from the destructive power of sin, that great talents and virtues could be found among the unregenerate? Why was it, for instance, that the great works of heathen civilizations, such as those of Plato and Cicero, were fascinating and instructive to both Christians and non-Christians alike, and that the "virtues of the heathen" often surpassed those of Christians in their attractiveness? Whereas the answer typical of Roman Catholicism was that as a result of the fall only the suitability of human beings for the celestial sphere had been lost, their own nature remaining almost unimpaired, Calvinism insisted on the absoluteness of sin and its effects on human nature, but held that these effects were kept in check by common grace, so as to allow the proper functioning of society and the flourishing of human talent. Life outside the church thereby came to be seen as fully belonging to God and worthy of special study, kindling a new love for all areas of scientific research

23. Kuyper, *E Voto,* II, p. 233; A. Kuyper, *Van de voleinding,* 4 vols. (Kampen: Kok, 1929-1931), II, p. 295. See also Kuyper's *De gemeene gratie,* II, pp. 637, 648, 650, where Kuyper makes a distinction between Christ as mediator of creation and Christ as mediator of redemption.

24. Kuyper's doctrine of common grace was introduced in Chapter Five as a vital component of his worldview.

—which were able to "throw new light on the glories of the entire cosmos" (LC, p. 126).

Kuyper's exposition of the doctrine of common grace in relation to science reveals the importance he attached to the effect of sin on the intellect. As a result of the fall, he argued, Adam lost the perfect understanding of the nature and coherence of the universe he had originally possessed. His state thus became comparable to that of a bird that inhabits the precincts of a beautiful palace: the bird sees the stones and the woodwork, the plaster and the colors, but it does not understand the design, nor the architectural motif, nor the function of the various parts of the building. Human beings, likewise, are able to see the components of creation but are unable to discern the identity of its architect. They therefore cannot understand the universe in its unity, origin, and destiny. Due to the intervention of common grace, however, they are able, through observation, experiment, imagination, and thought, to gain understanding of the outward nature of the created order. Thus it was that Plato, Aristotle, Kant, and Darwin were able to shine as "stars of the first magnitude."[25]

Kuyper's argument reflects the influence of Calvin's doctrine of the total depravity of human nature *(corruptio totalis),* which taught that no area of human life escaped the corruption of sin, and therefore the need of restoration through God's grace in Jesus Christ.[26] In the area of the intellect, accordingly, sin had produced such a darkening of reason that only muddled notions were possible. Calvin formulated this teaching in opposition to the classical medieval scholastic view of sin and the intellect: the scholastic *lumen naturale,* the natural light of reason, he taught, was "blind" or "extinguished."[27] The difference between Calvin's position and that of scholasticism goes some way to explain the disagreement between Kuyper and Warfield on the subjects of science and apologetics, as will become clear later in this chapter. Here it is important to note Kuyper's dependence on Calvin for the positive value he accorded to the works of the unregenerate intellect. Speaking of the study of law, philosophy, logic, medicine, and mathematics, Calvin wrote: "we cannot read the writings of the ancients on these subjects without great

25. Kuyper, *De gemeene gratie,* pp. 11-17 (p. 12).

26. John Calvin, *Institutes of the Christian Religion,* I.i.1, cf. II.i.9. Calvin's doctrine is reflected in the Heidelberg Catechism (1563), which states that man's nature is "wholly incapable of doing any good and inclined to all evil" (Lord's Day III, 8).

27. Calvin, *Institutes,* II.i.9; II.ii.18, 24.

admiration. We marvel at them because we are compelled to recognise how pre-eminent they are."[28] God was the source of these gifts, he explained, and therefore to depreciate or ignore them would show deep ingratitude to the giver. Although Calvin thus stressed the depravity of human reason, he did not for that reason reject non-Christian thought out of hand. He declared, indeed, that the "admirable light of truth" shining in the works of pagan and secular writers demonstrates that reason, even if apostate, "is nevertheless clothed and ornamented with God's excellent gifts."[29] There is, therefore, a subtleness about Calvin's attitude to non-Christian culture and science. While wanting to avoid ingratitude to God for the gifts he had distributed outside the church, he also did not wish to consider these gifts merely in themselves and esteem them as purely human achievements. When he occasionally spoke of God's common grace, therefore, he did so in order to avoid both a denial of human depravity and a depreciation of what God bestows by his spirit on those outside the circle of faith.[30] Calvin did not, however, propound the concept of common grace in the systematic, principled way that is found in Kuyper's work, and sometimes he expressed the same idea simply by speaking of God's providence, kindness, mercy, and gentleness, and of his grace to all and to few.[31] Although Calvin's ideas thus provided Kuyper with a solution to the problem of the value of non-Christian science, they did not do so by means of a fully fledged doctrine of common grace, as Kuyper's appeal to Calvin implies. Calvin's perspective did, however, provide Kuyper with a means to oppose dualism, which appears as a major concern in his fourth Stone Lecture. To Kuyper, a dualistic mentality, characteristic not only of Roman Catholicism but of much orthodox Protestantism, posed itself as one of the chief obstacles in his attempt to encourage Christian involvement in science and the subsequent development of a specifically Christian kind of science. This was another reason for his opposition to pietism, which, he claimed, favored a withdrawal from the study of the

28. Calvin, *Institutes,* II.ii.15.

29. Calvin, *Institutes,* II.ii.15.

30. See, for instance, *Institutes,* II.ii.17. See also Jacob Klapwijk, "Rationality in the Dutch Neo-Calvinist Tradition," in *Rationality in the Calvinian Tradition,* ed. by Hendrik Hart, Johan van der Hoeven, and Nicholas Wolterstorff (Lanham, Maryland: University Press of America, 1983), pp. 93-131 (pp. 99-100); and H. Kuiper, *Calvin on Common Grace* (Goes: Oosterbaan & Le Cointre, 1928).

31. Calvin, *Institutes,* II.ii.14; I.v.14; III.iii.25.

secular sciences in favor of the study of scripture and doctrine. The doctrine of common grace, which stood in close association with the authentically Calvinistic belief in the cosmic scope of Christ's redemption and in man's total depravity, provided Kuyper both with a solution to the chief intellectual problems in the relationship between Christianity and science, and with an incentive and justification for the active Christian pursuit of scientific learning.

4. The Liberty of Science

For Kuyper, Calvinism had advocated, both in theory and in practice, the complete autonomy of science. Whereas in the early Middle Ages science had been embodied in a *respublica litterarum* (a commonwealth of learning), the scientific sphere had gradually become attached to the sphere of the church, which exercised the right to legislate on truth and error both inside and outside its institution. The pressure this imposed on science often found expression in persecution. By insisting, however, that the church withdraw from the domain of common grace and be restricted to the domain of particular grace, Calvinism was able to relieve this pressure, and helped provide a safe haven to persecuted scientists (LC, p. 129).

Kuyper's argument reflects his involvement in the Schools Question and in the founding of the Free University.[32] In his conflict with the Ethicals over his plans to establish the Free University, A. W. Bronsveld had publicly expressed his opposition to the plans on the basis that they lacked historical precedent.[33] Provoked by the fierceness of Bronsveld's criticism, Kuyper published a sharply polemical yet thoroughly researched pamphlet in which he presented a detailed historical and legal argument as an apologia for the establishment of an independent university, free from political or ecclesiastical control.[34] He made much of the medieval idea of the university as an autonomous institution, embodied in the original Italian universities, and claimed Bronsveld's assertion that Oxford University was founded by the state to be a mis-

32. See Chapter Two for an account of this involvement.

33. A. W. Bronsveld, *De bede van Dr. A. Kuyper afgewezen door Dr. A. W. Bronsveld* (Utrecht: Breyer, 1880).

34. A. Kuyper, *'Strikt Genomen': Het recht tot universiteitsstichting staatsrechtelijk en historisch getoetst* (Amsterdam: Kruyt, 1880).

handling of the facts.[35] Kuyper had more than historical arguments to justify to his opponents the establishment of a "free" university, independent of church and state. The theory of sphere-sovereignty was also part of his arsenal.[36] In his speech at the opening of the Free University in 1880, he explained that it was from this idea that the new university had been born.[37] A free university was indeed a logical necessity if the principle of sphere-sovereignty was to be applied consistently to the field of science, because other societal spheres, such as the church and the state, were incompetent to have jurisdiction over the sphere of science. This incompetence was evident in practice; entrusting the universities into the hands of the state had allowed them to be dominated by liberalism masquerading as neutrality. The same was true of the state schools, which had become "the sectarian schools of the modernists."[38]

The prevailing idea, represented by Kuyper's political opponent in the Schools Question, Kappeyne van de Coppello, was that education and science had to be free of religious and ideological presuppositions, and that the best way of guaranteeing such was to keep them within the jurisdiction of the neutral state. Kuyper believed just the opposite: that science could only be free if it was allowed to develop according to the underlying principles and presuppositions on which it was based, and that the best way of ensuring this was to liberate it from all ecclesiastical and political control. He declared at the founding of the Free University:

> Our science will not be "free" in the sense of "detached from its principles." . . . Freedom in the realm of science is . . . that everyone is free to build on the foundation of his own principles.[39]

35. Kuyper appealed to Rudolf Ackermann's two-volume *A History of the University of Oxford* (London: Ackermann, 1814) to challenge Bronsveld's suggestion that King Alfred was responsible for the establishment of Oxford University, citing from it the following passage: "the most eminent modern antiquarians appear to have agreed, that this venerated monarch had no share whatever in the establishment of this seat of learning" (I, p. xix). (*'Strikt Genomen',* p. 90). Kuyper also found support for his argument in V. A. Huber, *The English Universities,* trans. and ed. by Frances W. Newman, 2 vols. (London: William Pickering, 1843), I, p. 13 (*'Strikt Genomen',* p. 6).

36. For a summary of Kuyper's theory of sphere-sovereignty see Chapter Two, and for a discussion of how this theory functioned in his political thought, see Chapter Six.

37. Kuyper, *Souvereiniteit,* p. 24.

38. Kuyper, *Ons program,* pp. 214-15.

39. Kuyper, *Souvereiniteit,* p. 29.

Kuyper's argument at Princeton for the autonomy of science must, therefore, be seen as an extension of his struggle in the Netherlands for the freedom of education. The issue of the underlying principles in science and that of science's proposed neutrality were both hotly debated in the Netherlands, and were fundamental to his argument at Princeton. These issues will feature prominently in the remainder of this chapter.

5. The Conflict in Science

The inevitable consequence of the freedom of science was conflict between scientific schools holding opposing principles. Kuyper's purpose in the final part of his fourth lecture was to show how Calvinism provided the resolution of this conflict. In fulfilling this aim he presented the ideas that have been of such great influence on evangelical thinking about the nature of scholarship and research.

The conflict was not, he emphasized, between science and faith, as no such conflict existed; all science presupposed faith and proceeded from it. The true conflict was that between opposing underlying presuppositions, which at its most fundamental level was the conflict between Christian and non-Christian principles. This conflict manifested itself in the division between those scientists who believed the cosmos to be in an abnormal (fallen) state and those who believed it to be in a normal (unfallen) state.[40] The former group, whom Kuyper called the "Abnormalists," believed that as a result of the fall a disturbance had taken place in the natural ordering of the cosmos which could only be put right by means of the supernatural act of regeneration. "Normalists," on the other hand, believed the cosmos to be in a state of eternal evolution from its potential to its ideal. They denied the existence of sin and the supernatural, insisting instead on a natural interpretation of all phenomena. Two scientific systems, therefore, both of which aimed to incorporate the whole of existence, stood in fierce opposition to each other and actively sought to undermine the foundations of the other. Any attempt to reach a compromise between the two inevitably

40. See Chapter Five for an explanation of Kuyper's use of the terms "normal" and "abnormal" in relation to the sphere of religion.

involved a betrayal of consistency and scientific integrity (LC, pp. 132-34).

Kuyper sought the explanation of this conflict, and its resolution, in what he considered to be the Calvinistic understanding of human consciousness. If the normal state of affairs had not been destroyed, he explained, human consciousness would have operated in the same way for all people. But because of the intervention of sin and the need for regeneration there were two kinds of consciousness: that of the regenerate and that of the unregenerate, the former of which held to the abnormal state of things, and the latter to the normal (LC, p. 137). Now, if the human consciousness is the *primum verum,* the starting point of all knowledge, it must be the starting point from which all science proceeds. And because of the twofold division in consciousness, the science of Normalists and that of Abnormalists must be fundamentally at odds with each other. For this reason, both groups sense an obligation to construct "a scientific edifice for the whole cosmos" that is in harmony with their own consciousness (LC, p. 138). Thus the Calvinistic way of solving the conflict of principles, Kuyper explained, was not to push science aside, nor to undervalue it, but to construct a science that accorded with its principles.

A more thorough and scholarly treatment of the conflict in science can be found in Kuyper's *Encyclopaedie* of 1894. There he devoted considerable space to pointing out areas that were common to both forms of science. These included those aspects of both the natural and the human sciences that were chiefly concerned with empirical investigation by means of measurement and observation. These stood at the lower levels of science, in which there were no essential differences between the scientific reasoning of the regenerate and the unregenerate.[41] But as soon as science ventured into areas that dealt with impalpables, palingenesis exerted its influence and science developed along two separate paths.[42] The inclusion of such qualifications did not, however, detract from the main thrust of his argument, which corresponded to that in his *Lectures:* that the divine act of regeneration split humanity in two, causing

41. Kuyper, *Encyclopedia,* p. 168.

42. This explains Kuyper's belief in the futility of apologetics, which concerned the "impalpable phenomenon" of faith. See Kuyper's *Encyclopedia,* p. 160. Chapter Five includes a discussion of Kuyper's position on apologetics in comparison to that of Warfield.

an unbridgeable divide in human consciousness which in turn effected an antithesis in science. "Two kinds of people" inevitably produced "two kinds of science."[43]

Kuyper's position contrasted sharply with that of mainstream liberalism, which, as noted in the case of Kappeyne van de Coppello, was committed to the supposed neutrality and objectivity of science. It is arguably for this reason that Kuyper's idea that science is not religiously neutral but is determined by certain prescientific convictions or presuppositions came to be one of the most characteristic features of neo-Calvinistic thought, and has remained so up to the present day.[44] In North America, as noted in Chapter One, this aspect of neo-Calvinism came to be known as "principled thinking" and is responsible for providing much of the motivation behind the school of thought that seeks to expose and engage with what it considers to be the presuppositions and starting points of modern theoretical thought.[45] In both his *Lectures* and his *Encyclopaedie* Kuyper's argument for the religious foundations of science laid the necessary basis for the central thesis in his theory of science: that all science is divided in two according to the twofold division in human consciousness— between the regenerate and the unregenerate—and because of this the development of an independent and comprehensive science based on Christian principles is an absolute necessity.

It is clear, therefore, that Kuyper, in stressing the existence of this conflict, stimulated and defended the development of an independent Calvinistic school of thought within the scientific sphere. All the findings of modern science had to be studied and assimilated, divested of their underlying premises, and incorporated into a scholarship based firmly

43. Kuyper, *Encyclopedia,* pp. 150-76. Although W. J. Wieringa is right to point out that there are differences between the line of Kuyper's argument in the *Lectures* and that in his *Encyclopaedie,* Kuyper's position in each is clearly the same in essence. W. J. Wieringa, 'De Vrije Universiteit als bijzondere instelling, 1880-1890', in *Wetenschap en rekenschap 1880-1890: een eeuw wetenschapsbeoefening en wetenschapsbeschouwing aan de Vrije Universiteit* (Kampen: Kok, 1980), pp. 11-43.

44. Albert Wolters, "Dutch neo-Calvinism: Worldview, Philosophy and Rationality," in H. Hart et al., pp. 113-31 (pp. 123-24).

45. James Bratt writes: "for decades 'principled thinking' was the distinguishing characteristic of all Kuyperians, both in Europe and America." From *Dutch Calvinism in Modern America: A History of a Conservative Subculture* (Grand Rapids: Eerdmans, 1984), p. 17.

on Christian principles. It was an objective which almost certainly contributed to the development of *verzuiling,* particularly given that Kuyper believed the only way for such an independent school of thought to flourish was through the establishment of separate scientific institutions. He drew encouragement in this idea from what he regarded as a growing recognition in European countries that the religious and ideological division of higher education was a necessity. In Belgium, he noted, the *Université Libre* of Brussels had been founded by "unbelieving Normalists," and in Switzerland the University of Freiburg had been created to embody Roman Catholic principles, as was the case in Ireland with the University of Dublin. In France, Roman Catholic faculties operated in fierce opposition to the faculties of State Universities, and in the Netherlands the Free University of Amsterdam had been instituted for the development of science based on Calvinistic principles (LC, p. 140).[46] Although the Catholic institutions Kuyper cited here were, in fact, under episcopal authority, his solution to the demand for the liberty of science and its resulting conflict in principles lay in the establishment of institutions of learning based on fundamental religious convictions, but free from church as well as state control.[47]

The suggestion that it is in the presentation of this "solution" that some of the ideological origins of *verzuiling* may be found is given weight by the fact that, in proposing this solution in the Stone Lectures, Kuyper used the term "sphere" in the sense of ideological groupings, as opposed to "spheres of human life" such as politics, science, and art, which belonged to the original created order.[48] This occurs in a passage in which he predicts that, although "the curse of uniformity" was still preva-

46. Kuyper restricted his examples to Europe, but could, for instance, have included reference to the Catholic University of America in Washington, established as a papal university in 1889 by Pope Leo XIII.

47. The University of Dublin, which was opened in 1854 by its creator John Henry Newman, foundered in 1882, partly because attempts to obtain a government charter, necessary for the right to award degrees, failed in the face of the refusal of the Irish bishops to allow the university to become autonomous. Charles Stephen Dessain, *John Henry Newman,* 3rd edition (Oxford: Oxford University Press, 1980), pp. 88-109 (pp. 105-7). Newman's vision for a Catholic university is articulated famously in his *The Idea of a University,* ed. by I. T. Ker (Oxford: Clarendon, 1976), first published in 1873.

48. The two different senses in which Kuyper used the word "sphere" are noted in Chapter Six, along with the fact that they are logically incompatible.

lent,[49] despite the emerging ideological diversification of science, this curse would eventually be broken, allowing Roman Catholic, Calvinistic, and Evolutionary principles to give rise to "separate *spheres* of scientific life, which would flourish in a multiformity of universities" [my emphasis] (LC, p. 141). Although Kuyper did not use the term *kring* (sphere) in this passage in the Dutch version of the Stone Lectures, he did speak of the same three systems of principles producing "their own scientific life" *(een eigen wetenschappelijk leven),* which conveyed the same idea of independent schools of scientific thought embodied in their own independent institutions.[50] Kuyper's ideas on the antithesis in science thus provide additional evidence for the suggestion made in this book that some of the origins of *verzuiling* can be found in Kuyper's thought, even though he did not propose or necessarily intend the vertical divisions in society that later became a dominant feature of Dutch national life.

Before considering the context of his ideas on the conflict in science and its solution, it is worth noting that Kuyper, in listing the Free University along with what he saw as comparable manifestations in other countries of the trend towards scientific multiformity, bequeathed international status and significance on his own project for higher education in the Netherlands. He thereby released his solution to the conflict from what might otherwise have been a suspicion that it rested on ideas applicable only to the particular circumstances in the Netherlands or to Kuyper's own career. Obviously acutely aware of the need to demonstrate the relevance of his ideas to a foreign audience, and keen that its members should sense the universal validity and dynamism of Calvinistic principles, Kuyper avoided specific reference in his Stone Lectures to his own particular social, educational, political, and ecclesiastical projects and struggles in the Netherlands. The mention he made of the Free University was an exception, but it was made in a way that highlighted its international significance. It also helped to bolster one of the central aims of his *Lectures:* to demonstrate that Calvinism could no longer be dismissed as an out-of-date system of dogma, but represented a dynamic force for positive change in the modern world, and this at a time when, as will be seen below, the university was increasingly perceived as both the center and the leader of culture.

49. Kuyper's language and argument here is reflected in the title of his speech of 1869 *Eenvormigheid, de vloek van het moderne leven* (Uniformity, the curse of modern life).

50. Kuyper, *Het Calvinisme: zes Stone-Lezingen,* p. 134.

6. The Conflict and Solution in Context

Kuyper's perception of the conflict in science and its solution can be comprehended only within the context of his times, as a response to one of the most important questions that faced Christianity in the latter half of the nineteenth century: how can religious faith be reconciled with the discoveries of modern science? His response was, of course, one of many, and in order to be able to interpret it within its context it will be compared with that of Warfield, Kuyper's host at Princeton.

6.1. Warfield

To Warfield, Kuyper's view of science was sheer folly. He agreed with the predominant opinion of the scientific establishment of his time that science was an objective, unified, and cumulative enterprise of the whole of humanity. There could be no difference in kind, therefore, between the work of regenerate and unregenerate scientists. Employing the same metaphor as Kuyper in order to criticize him directly, he argued that, rather than both types of scientist constructing a separate building, they "work side by side at the common task and the common edifice takes gradually fuller and truer outlines."[51] He did not wish to deny that there was a difference between the results produced by Christian and non-Christian scientists, but for him this was not a difference between two types of science but in the quality of their findings: "It is not a different kind of science that they are producing. . . . It is only a better scientific outlook, and the better scientific product."[52] Despite their differences, both sorts of scientist were striving towards erecting "one edifice of truth."[53]

This belief in a unified corpus of knowledge may be added to the reasons suggested in Chapter Five as to why Warfield so strongly differed

51. See B. B. Warfield's review of Herman Bavinck's *De zekerheid des geloofs* (The certainty of faith) (Kampen: Kok, 1901), *Princeton Theological Review* 1 (1903): 138-48 (145); Marsden, *Understanding*, p. 123. Although Warfield noted Kuyper's view of science in 1898 (in his introductions both to Kuyper's *Encyclopaedie* and to W. H. de Savornin Lohman's "Dr. Abraham Kuyper" [p. 562]), he refrained from any evaluation of it.

52. Warfield's review of Bavinck, *De zekerheid des geloofs*, pp. 145-46.

53. Warfield's review of Bavinck, *De zekerheid des geloofs*, p. 146.

from Kuyper on the value and effectiveness of apologetics. But apart from the need to provide an epistemological basis for arguments for or against apologetics, why, historically speaking, should Kuyper and Warfield have disagreed so sharply about the unity of science? Many factors comprise the answer to this question, but one aspect in particular deserves special attention for the light it throws on their respective positions: the difference in their attitudes towards the Enlightenment and revolution.

Kuyper and the anti-revolutionaries followed Groen van Prinsterer in associating the Enlightenment with the secularization of intellectual and cultural life that had been on the increase in Western Europe ever since the end of the eighteenth century. They regarded the revolutionary changes that had taken place to have been characterized by "unbelief." Thus Kuyper spoke of a fundamental antithesis between two competing worldviews — that of Calvinism on the one hand, grounded on the principle of God's sovereignty, and that of the Enlightenment on the other, grounded on humanistic and naturalistic principles.[54] Calvinists in the United States, however, together with their evangelical allies, had supported the American Revolution, and this profoundly influenced the way later generations of evangelicals perceived the Enlightenment and modern science. Although they opposed certain aspects of eighteenth-century thought, they were on the whole its chief proponents, at least as far as it stood committed to the pursuit of reason and scientific thought. This ambivalent but essentially affirmative attitude towards the Enlightenment can best be accounted for in terms of the fact that neither radical revolution nor Enlightenment skepticism had taken deep root in American culture. The American Revolution was staged, in fact, chiefly by advocates of the moderate Enlightenment associated with Newton and Locke. Moreover, Scottish Common Sense thought, which maintained its influence in American intellectual circles (including those at Princeton) during most of the nineteenth century, had helped to encourage a synthesis of the three great strands in American thought — modern empirical scientific ideas, the self-evident principles of the American Revolution, and evangelical Christianity.[55] In contrast to Dutch Calvinists, therefore, American

54. See Chapter Four.

55. Marsden, *Understanding*, pp. 127-28; Henry F. May, *The Enlightenment in America* (New York: Oxford University Press, 1976), p. xvi and passim.

evangelicals were on the whole committed to the Enlightenment idea of an empirically based rationality, without any sense that this might be inconsistent with their religious principles. In fact, they hailed objective science as one of Christianity's most trusted allies, because the laws it sought to discover provided evidence of God's benevolent design. For most American evangelical scientists and theologians, scientific reasoning firmly supported the Christian faith, and as a matter of principle they were deeply involved in scientific culture.[56]

This propitious relationship between science and Christianity faced a severe challenge with the rise of the scientific revolution associated with Darwin's *The Origin of Species* of 1859. The supposedly neutral scientific method, instead of supporting Christian doctrine, demonstrated considerable opposition to it, providing a series of alternative explanations for the apparent order of the universe without reference to a divine creator. Thus the means Protestant Christianity employed to accommodate new scientific knowledge as a result of the first scientific revolution, associated with the Enlightenment, was rapidly destroyed by the second, associated with Darwin.[57]

Despite the severity of the challenge of this revolution to orthodox Christianity, and its effectiveness in beginning a trend that would play an important role in effecting the virtual dissolution of the evangelical marriage to science in the early decades of the twentieth century, the Princeton theologians maintained their confidence in the possibility of objective, neutral science and in its value in supporting the claims of Christianity. In 1871, for instance, Charles Hodge claimed that the solution to the apparent conflict between science and religion was simply to "let science take its course, assured that the Scriptures will accommodate themselves to all well-authenticated facts in time to come, as they have in the past."[58] Warfield maintained his confidence that any structures that would help promote true science would also, in the long run, help to promote true religion.

56. Theodore Dwight Bozeman, *Protestants in an Age of Science: The Baconian Ideal and Antebellum American Religious Thought* (Chapel Hill: University of North Carolina Press, 1977), pp. 71-100.

57. James Ward Smith, "Religion and Science in American Philosophy," in *The Shaping of American Religion,* ed. by James Ward Smith and A. Leland Jamison (Princeton: Princeton University Press, 1961), pp. 402-42.

58. Charles Hodge, *Systematic Theology* (New York: Scribners, 1872-1873), I, p. 57.

By the last decade of the nineteenth century the Princeton theologians were part of a dying breed, although, due to their confidence in the potential of science to support and promote Christianity, they did not see themselves as taking an heroic last stand. Rather, they believed themselves to be representing a position that offered bright prospects for the continuance of the synthesis between Christianity and objective science. In the meantime, however, the general trend towards the isolation of the sciences from all religious considerations continued to grow, such that by the early twentieth century it was becoming increasingly difficult for conservative evangelicals to express their religious convictions within their scientific disciplines. American academia had indeed one science, and evangelical Christianity had no part in it. The naturalistic definition of science (outlined in the first section of this chapter) was in the process of being transformed from a methodology into a dominant academic worldview, and it was becoming increasingly fashionable for intellectuals to turn their backs on the Christian faith.[59]

The crux issue at stake between Kuyper and Warfield was at heart epistemological: does it follow, because all human minds are of the same essential structure, that the regenerate and the unregenerate know in essentially the same way? Their varying answers to this question turned largely on their different notions about the acquisition of knowledge, which they derived from their respective philosophical backgrounds. Kuyper, who, though critical of the German Idealist tradition was nevertheless influenced by it,[60] conceived of knowledge in terms of the organic relationships it involved between creator, cosmos, and the knowing subject. The practice of science, therefore, presupposed certain convictions about the fundamental structures of the universe. For this reason knowledge did not come in isolated packages but was understood by the subject in the context of other beliefs he or she held. Warfield, on the other hand, stood in the Baconian tradition with his insistence that knowledge was gained by considering evidence and reaching conclusions based on that evidence. Thus knowing was primarily dependent on observation, not on other things known to the subject or upon the worldview belonging to the subject. An item of knowledge, once established by science on the basis of evidence, was in principle accessible to all rational people regardless of other beliefs they might hold. It was an

59. Marsden, *Understanding*, pp. 144-45.

60. See Chapter Four.

ideal particularly suited to the United States, a nation founded on principles drawn largely from the moderate Enlightenment, and it contrasted sharply with Kuyper's critique of Enlightenment ideals, which presented themselves as a greater threat to Christianity in the Netherlands than in the United States.[61]

Against this background, Kuyper's aim in insisting on the twofold division in science at Princeton was to encourage American Calvinists to end their infatuation with Enlightenment science and to develop their own kind of science within their own independent institutions as a means of providing effective opposition to the influence of the modernistic worldview. It was an attempt born out of Kuyper's belief in the superiority of the Calvinistic worldview and out of his confidence in Calvinism's potential to transform modern society. It failed in its objective, however, at least as far as Warfield and his followers were concerned, and was largely responsible for the divergence between Warfieldian and Kuyperian trends in American evangelicalism, which continues today. As was the case with his concept of America as a battleground between the traditions of Hamilton and Jefferson, Kuyper's application of the antithesis idea, relevant to his objectives within the Dutch situation, was not fitted to the American context, where Christian and Enlightenment traditions coexisted without open conflict.

6.2. *The Warfare Metaphor*

Kuyper's use of military imagery in arguing that the true conflict in science was not between science and religion but between two kinds of science reflects the fact that ever since the publication of Darwin's masterwork of 1859, "all Europe was in ferment over the conflict between science and religion."[62] Kuyper's outright denial of this conflict was motivated in part by his rejection of and opposition to pietism, which was only too ready to highlight the existence of the conflict. Indeed, the concept of a conflict between science and religion was partly the result

61. Marsden, "The Collapse," p. 253. Marsden's work is used in this chapter as a generally reliable account, despite the challenge issued to it in Donald Fuller and Richard Gardiner, "Reformed Theology at Princeton and Amsterdam in the Late Nineteenth Century: A Reappraisal," *Presbyterion* 21 (1995): 89-117.

62. Owen Chadwick, *Newman* (Oxford: Oxford University Press, 1983), p. 73.

of the hostile reaction of Christian groups (particularly pietistic ones) to the new discoveries of Darwinian science. A number of recent historical studies have shown convincingly, however, that in the early decades after the publication of *The Origin* the "warfare" metaphor was used primarily by ardent anti-Christian polemicists in characterizing the relationship between Christianity and Darwinism.[63] They claimed that traditional Christianity had always opposed modern science and that the current debate was simply the most recent recurrence of the age-old warfare between science and religion. They heralded a new age in which scientific enquiry would be freed from religious constraint. Supreme among these polemicists was T. H. Huxley, nicknamed "Darwin's Bulldog," who frequently employed the warfare metaphor in his attacks on Christianity. As noted earlier in this chapter, he represented the new group of intellectual "agnostics" who believed that all beliefs that could not be substantiated scientifically should be rejected. Thus the older science, which had accepted the existence of religious truth, had to be disbanded and its advocates driven out of the scientific community.[64]

This was the intellectual context in which Kuyper formulated his view that there was no warfare between science and faith, but between Christian and non-Christian science. His use of the warfare metaphor reflected not only his opposition to pietism and his concept of the antithesis, but the vocabulary and imagery of the agnostic-dominated science versus religion debate, into which he wished to introduce an alternative view. Even his exaggerated rhetoric that in the contemporary academic world normalists were "turning us [Abnormalists] out into the street" (LC, p. 139) gains some plausibility when placed beside Huxley's polemic about ousting those who refused to become agnostics from the academic community. In the face of allegations that Christianity not only hindered but opposed free scientific enquiry, Kuyper dismissed the debate entirely, claiming it to have no substance whatever, because the supposed conflict did not in fact exist: "Notice I do not speak of a conflict between faith and science. Such a conflict

63. James R. Moore, *The Post-Darwinian Controversies: A Study of the Protestant Struggle to Come to Terms with Darwin in Great Britain and America, 1870-1900* (Cambridge: Cambridge University Press, 1979); Peter J. Bowler, *Evolution: The History of an Idea* (Berkeley: University of California Press, 1984); *Darwinism and Divinity: Essays on Evolution and Religious Belief* ed. by John Durant (Oxford: Basil Blackwell, 1985).

64. Neil C. Gillespie, *Charles Darwin and the Problem of Creation* (Chicago: University of Chicago Press, 1979), pp. 152-53; Marsden, *Understanding*, pp. 140-41.

does not exist. Every science in a certain degree starts from faith" (LC, p. 131). The conflict that did exist was exactly the one Kuyper's opponents denied, that is, between two kinds of science. His insistence on the existence of this conflict should be understood, therefore, as a deliberate attempt to relocate the scientific debate from being between science and Christianity to being between Christian and non-Christian science. This was important to his aim of stimulating the development of a specifically Christian ("Calvinistic") science, because the popular notion of a conflict between science and faith was to him a major obstacle, both to devout Christians becoming involved in the scientific world and to scientists taking the Christian faith seriously.[65]

6.3. The Secularization of the University

Kuyper's argument for the significance of Calvinism to science culminated in his advocacy of the free development of science, based firmly on a plurality of ideological positions, and embodied in autonomous scientific institutions. This solution — which may be termed "scientific pluralism" — may be viewed both as a reflection of and an alternative to the prevailing trend towards the secularization of science and the university. This is particularly the case in his advocacy of the absolute freedom of science from ecclesiastical control, as well as in his belief that university education was a key instrument in the struggle for the intellectual and social emancipation of the orthodox Protestant sector of the population. These were important elements in the movements towards the reform of higher education in most Western European countries in the latter half of the nineteenth century.[66] Ever since the Middle Ages, university education in the Western world had been under the aegis of the church, and one of its principal purposes had been to prepare young men for an ecclesiastical career. The latter half

65. These concerns are apparent in Kuyper's *Encyclopedia,* p. 140.

66. See David Bebbington, "The Secularization of British Universities since the Mid-Nineteenth Century," and George M. Marsden, "The Soul of the American University: An Historical Overview," both in *The Secularization of the Academy,* ed. by George M. Marsden and Bradley J. Longfield (New York: Oxford University Press, 1992), pp. 259-77 and pp. 9-45 respectively. See also Marsden's *The Soul of the American University: From Protestant Establishment to Established Nonbelief* (New York: Oxford University Press, 1994).

of the nineteenth century witnessed, however, the increasing professionalization of university education, such that the role of university tutor came to be distinct and autonomous from that of an officer in the church, and one in which the "academic freedom" of each individual tutor began to develop into a guiding principle — a development that was accompanied by the increasing specialization of the sciences. Whereas during the seven preceding centuries, higher education had simply meant expertise in classics, law, and medicine, the last quarter of the nineteenth century saw the development of new, specialized disciplines, stimulated by the demands of an emerging industrialized and technological society. As governments saw the value of technological research and development for the advancement of a modern economy, they gradually became the chief sponsors of much of the new science and thus were able in increasing measure to set its agenda. The result was that universities developed into an arm of the state rather than of the church.[67] It was in reaction to this development that Kuyper argued for the freedom of science in its own sphere, as part of his doctrine of sphere-sovereignty.

Closely tied to the emergence of the industrial economy was the rise of the middle classes, which benefited most directly from the fruits of industrialization. These began to sense ever more clearly the value of specialized technical (non-classical and non-theological) studies as an important means of social advancement. Kuyper's call for a university with an explicitly Reformed *(Gereformeerd)* constitution was simultaneously a call for a university for a specific social group, the Protestant lower middle classes *(kleine luyden),* and also for one which had aspirations to teach and carry out research over a broad range of fields, including the natural sciences. This indicates his awareness of the growing potential both of the social class to which most of his followers belonged and of the specialized technological sciences to effect change in society. Kuyper promoted, therefore, the same disestablishment of science, together with its corollaries, professionalization and specialization, that were part of the trend towards the secularization of science. But he did this in a way that aimed to make possible a commitment both to Christianity and to modern science.

67. Jan Marius Romein, *Universiteit en maatschappij in de loop der tijden* (Leiden: Brill, 1947).

Conclusion

Providing an effective antidote to ideological secularization in the arena of science was not going to be easy, and Kuyper's lecture reveals that one of the main obstacles he perceived was the pietism of many orthodox Protestants, which made them naturally suspicious of, or at least indifferent towards, involvement in science. His arguments for the significance of Calvinism for science reveal how he sought to overcome the obstacles: by going back to the religious roots of science; by claiming that the vocation of the scientist was to think God's thoughts after him; by presenting science as a God-given duty and a cultural mandate; by claiming science to be a divine invention, capable of proclaiming God's glory and controlled by eternal decrees; by relocating the debate between scientists from that between science and belief towards that between Christian and non-Christian science; by appealing to elements of Calvin's theology and to the history of Calvinism; by confronting and denouncing dualism; and by presenting the conflict in science as worldwide, of immeasurable significance to the future of human civilization.

The last of these arguments, concerning the international scope of the conflict, cannot be explained only as part of Kuyper's attempt to appeal to a foreign audience. It reveals that his solution, scientific pluralism, was not simply a product of his efforts towards the emancipation of the Protestant lower middle classes but was part of his vision for the emancipation of the Christian intellect in the Western world. This vision emerged within a situation in which the whole of Western intellectual thought had been deeply influenced by various forms of positivism, such as that expressed in agnosticism, which served to end the dominance of explicitly Christian values in science. It indicates Kuyper's hope (which reappeared in his final Stone Lecture) that the revival of an all-embracing and strident Calvinism would not be restricted to the Netherlands but would become the leaven in the lump of the entire Western intellectual world.

Two aspects of Kuyper's lecture, finally, are of particular importance to an overall understanding of the nature of Kuyper's neo-Calvinistic worldview. The first is the way he employed Calvin's theology. As demonstrated in this chapter, Kuyper's appeal to Calvin involved giving systematic expression to implicit elements of his theology and presenting them in a form directed towards the achievement of specific practical goals, such as the founding of the Free University. Kuyper's doctrines of the antithesis, common grace, and sphere-sovereignty, to name three of the most important ones, were thus derivations from elements of Calvin's theology which originally had none of the coherence and significance that Kuyper attached to them. These derivations served as the basis for every stage in his argument for scientific pluralism. More than any other of his Stone Lectures, his lecture on science reveals how he employed the full constellation of his neo-Calvinistic doctrines to argue for the transformation of modern culture.

The second aspect is Kuyper's relationship to the Enlightenment, which serves to clarify some of the differences between his and Warfield's attitude to modern science. Kuyper's lecture is one of the clearest demonstrations of the anti-revolutionary nature of his worldview, and thereby of his indebtedness to Groen van Prinsterer. Although he formulated the conflict in science by employing images (such as the warfare metaphor) that were particular to his time and gave it fresh theological grounding, it was nevertheless in essence the same fundamental conflict Groen had propounded using the contradistinction "unbelief and revolution." Kuyper made no reference to Groen in his lectures at Princeton, appealing only to Calvin and historical Calvinism as the origin of his thought, but his vision of science was as much anti-revolutionary as it was neo-Calvinistic. The existence of both these ingredients helps to explain the significance he attached to the religiously held principles which, he believed, lay at the foundation of all scientific endeavor. It is this particular attaching of significance that has proved the most lasting aspect of his scientific legacy.

Fifth Lecture: Calvinism and Art

Kuyper's career was a broad one, but it did not encompass the arts. In his Stone Lectures on religion, politics, and science he was dealing with areas in which he had been actively and creatively engaged for a number of years as clergyman, politician, theologian, and Rector Magnificus. In the realm of art, however, he spoke as an "outsider" — as someone not directly involved. This, together with the fact that he occasionally manifested hostility towards certain forms of art, particularly drama, has contributed to the fact that his ideas on art have been virtually neglected in scholarly research.[1]

It is striking, therefore, that Kuyper's influence in this field should have been so effective and enduring, although it has to be said that this influence has worked more in terms of art theory and criticism than in terms of art production.[2] It is equally striking that he should have addressed

1. The only serious treatment of Kuyper's ideas on art is that by the British theologian Jeremy Begbie, in his *Voicing Creation's Praise: Toward a Theology of the Arts* (Edinburgh: T. & T. Clark, 1991). As Begbie deals with the ideas of a number of other neo-Calvinist thinkers, comparing them to those of Paul Tillich, his treatment of Kuyper is inevitably limited in scope. See my review in *Theology* 44 (1991): 388-89.

2. Kuyper's influence in the field of art theory is reflected chiefly in the work of Hans Rookmaaker and Calvin Seerveld, but also in that of Nicholas Wolterstorff. See, for instance, Hans Rookmaaker's *Modern Art and the Death of a Culture* (London: IVP, 1970). This book so impressed Malcolm Muggeridge that he made it his *Observer* book of the year in 1971 (Begbie, *Voicing Creation's Praise,* p. 127); Calvin Seerveld,

the subject of art at all, given the fact that serious treatments of the arts that go beyond moral critique are rare in the history of Protestantism.[3]

Although Kuyper was not involved in the arts, he did take them seriously and appreciated their value. He lectured at the Free University in both aesthetics and the history of Dutch literature;[4] he paid particular attention to the novel in a lengthy series of articles in *De Heraut*;[5] he published a collection of prints made of original paintings of biblical scenes, and provided a commentary;[6] he corresponded with Joseph Israels (1824-1911), a famous Dutch impressionist painter of the Hague School;[7] and he wrote extensively on the relationship between theology and the arts.[8] It will become clear in what follows, however, that the reason Kuyper took the arts seriously was that he took religion seriously. His interest was inspired not so much by a concern for the arts in themselves — his ideas run counter to "art for art's sake" — but in art as an expression of religion.

As in the case of Kuyper's understanding of "science," his use of the term "art" encompassed much more than is usually understood by

---

A Christian Critique of Art (St. Catharines, Ontario: The Association for Reformed Scientific Studies, 1962), and *Rainbows for the Fallen World* (Toronto: Tuppence Press, 1980); Nicholas Wolterstorff, *Art in Action: Towards a Christian Aesthetic* (Grand Rapids: Eerdmans, 1980). See Begbie, *Voicing Creation's Praise,* pp. 127-41, for a treatment of Rookmaker and Seerveld.

3. Begbie, *Voicing Creation's Praise,* pp. xv-xvi. See also Begbie's essay "Christ and Cultures: Christianity and the Arts," in *The Cambridge Companion to Christian Docrine,* ed. by Colin Gunton (Cambridge: Cambridge University Press, 1997), pp. 101-18 (101).

4. His lecture notes for these courses are kept in KA: LB; P2 and LG; P12.

5. *De Heraut,* 1901; 10 February, 24 February, 10 March, 7 April, 5 May, 19 May, 2 June.

6. A. Kuyper, *Modern Masters as Interpreters of Holy Writ: A Series of Seventy-two Mezzogravures from the Work of Some of the Leading Modern Painters.* With an introduction by The Right Reverend Arthur Foley Winnington-Ingram, D.D., Lord Bishop of London. 2 vols (London: Gresham Publishing Company, n.d.).

7. Letters from Joseph Israels to Kuyper can be found in KA; *Brieven,* nos. 6884, 7213, 7262, 7317.

8. Apart from in his lecture at Princeton, Kuyper dealt with this subject at length in the following publications under his name: *Het calvinisme en de kunst; Encyclopaedie,* III, pp. 331-38, 341-43; *De gemeene gratie in wetenschap en kunst* (published as articles in *De Heraut* between 5 May and 14 July 1901); *Pro Rege,* III, pp. 470-580. Out of these, *Het calvinisme en de kunst* is the most important regarding the relationship between Calvinism and art, and for this reason it will receive more attention in this chapter than the others. Kuyper's final discussion of art, in *Pro Rege,* contains no elements that are new to his thought, and will therefore be left out of the discussion.

the term, at least in English-speaking contexts. It is clear from his Stone Lecture on art that his use of the term included painting, architecture, music, poetry, and drama, and is therefore roughly equivalent to the term "the arts" in English. This should be taken into account when the word "art" is used in this book. Kuyper's lecture also dealt with the *theory* of art, or "aesthetics," an area in which he lectured at the Free University. At the outset of his lecture he proposed to concentrate on "the Beautiful and the Sublime in its eternal significance, and upon art as one of the richest gifts of God to mankind" (LC, p. 143), explaining that the concepts of "the Beautiful" and "the Sublime" were central to the traditional study of aesthetics, and belonged to the terminology of modern aesthetics.[9] This chapter will therefore include a historical examination of Kuyper's aesthetics.

1. The Democratization of Art

Kuyper was ambivalent about the upsurge of interest in art among the masses. Whereas on the one hand it amounted to the "almost fanatical worship of art," and encouraged the proliferation of mediocre works, on the other hand it encouraged the ennoblement of ordinary life and provided a welcome respite from the current infatuation with wealth and the intellect (LC, p. 143). Increasing materialism and rationalism had brought atrophy to the human heart, threatening to "reduce the life of the emotions to freezing-point." An antidote was sought in the gratification of the artistic instinct, simply as a means of survival: "in this cold, irreligious and practical age the warmth of this devotion to art has kept alive many higher aspirations of the soul" (LC, p. 143).[10]

From these remarks it is clear that Kuyper did not have in mind the development of a particular type or school of art, as has been sug-

9. The importance of these terms to Kant, the founder of modern aesthetics, is clearly evident in his *Observations on the Feeling of the Beautiful and the Sublime,* which appeared in 1764.

10. In an article in *De Standaard* of 31 August 1903 Kuyper again expressed a qualified approval of the wide-scale renewal of interest in the arts, and contrasted it to the barrenness of rationalism, but now he believed the latter to be on the wane: "The period of dry intellectualism lies behind us. To be practical, before everything else, was then the watchword, and every guilder spent on decoration and ornamentation was considered wasted money."

gested, but a general and large-scale movement towards the popularization of art — or, in his words, its "democratization" and "vulgarization."[11] One of the ways he characterizes this movement is particularly helpful in identifying it in his cultural context. He spoke about the widening circle of the population that sought enjoyment by means of music and theatre, a demand that could increasingly be met because "the easy means of communication between the nations imparts such an international character to our best singers and players, that the finest artistic enjoyments are now brought for almost no price within the reach of an ever-widening class" (LC, p. 142). The development in the history of the performing arts that most closely matches Kuyper's characterization followed the invention of the phonograph or gramophone by Thomas Edison in 1877; although he is likely also to have been referring to the increased opportunities for international musical tours brought about by improvements in rail and sea travel. The appearance of the gramophone, and the mass production of gramophone records that soon followed, allowed large numbers of people to gain easy and relatively inexpensive access to the kind of music that had hitherto been patronized exclusively by a small wealthy minority. As a new and exciting medium of entertainment, unhindered by national and linguistic boundaries, the gramophone brought the work of the world's greatest orchestras and soloists within easy reach of a broad, international public.[12]

Kuyper was not alone in his mixed response to the popularization of art. As early as 1870 John Ruskin had voiced similar feelings of appreciation and concern towards the same trend:

11. Roel Kuiper's suggestion that this passage of the Stone Lectures illustrates Kuyper's unfavorable reaction to the reception of "modern art" (for example the movements towards naturalism and impressionism, whose representatives in Dutch literature were known as the *Tachtigers* by the Dutch middle class at the end of the nineteenth century is without foundation. Roel Kuiper, 'Esthetiek en atrophie', *Transparant: Orgaan van de vereniging van christen-historici* 1, (1990): 16-21 (16).

12. The November 1898 edition of the British journal *The Musical Times* gave expression to some of the excitement and enthusiasm with which the new invention was received: "As to the newest Edison phonograph, we can say from practical knowledge that it is a very wonderful instrument . . . whose use will give much pleasure and not a little amusement." Cited in Percy A. Scholes, *The Oxford Companion to Music,* 9th edition (London: Oxford University Press, 1955), pp. 421-22.

> there is no limit to the good which may be effected by rightly taking advantage of the powers we now possess of placing good and lovely art within the reach of the poorest classes. Much has been already accomplished; but great harm has been done also . . . by forms of art definitely addressed to depraved tastes.[13]

Ruskin's and Kuyper's concern reflects a strand of thought that was prevalent in intellectual circles in the second half of the nineteenth century, in which comments on art and artists tended to center around what could be considered "good taste," true art being whatever measured up to certain standards of taste. As there was disagreement, however, on what these standards should be, no scientific study of art or artists could proceed very far, and many forms of art were not considered "true art." In 1898 Leo Tolstoy (1828-1910) went so far as to exclude from art those symphonies and paintings that appealed to the more sensual and decadent tastes, including some of the most respected works of Wagner and Michelangelo.[14]

What is distinctive about Kuyper's perspective within this climate of opinion is the connection he made between the democratization of art and the "atrophy" caused by the dominating influences of money and of barren intellectualism. This was an expression of the contrast he made, together with other professors at the Free University, between the material and the spiritual, the ideal and the real, an antithesis that pervaded Kuyper's aesthetics, as will become clear later on.[15] A one-sided preoccupation with material things had so thwarted spiritual life many people were seeking relief in art as a new kind of religion. Kuyper's perception of art as a new form of popular religion partly explains why he should have chosen to address the subject of art in his Stone Lectures, even though he denied that this had motivated his decision (LC, pp. 142, 143). As has already become evident in previous

13. John Ruskin, *Lectures on Art. Delivered before the University of Oxford in Hilary Term, 1870,* 6th edition (London: George Allen, 1892), p. 13.

14. Leo Tolstoy, *What Is Art?,* trans. by Aylmer Maude (Oxford: Oxford University Press, 1930).

15. Jan Woltjer (1849-1917), Professor of Classical Philology at the Free University from 1881 to 1917, made much use of the same antithesis in his philosophical work. See, for instance, his 'Ideëel en Reëel', in *Verzamelde redevoeringen en verhandelingen,* I (Amsterdam: N. V. Dagblad, De Standaard, 1931), pp. 178-235.

chapters, not only was Kuyper sensitive to the development of new trends in thought and society, particularly those manifest at a popular level, but he tended to characterize these in religious terms, portraying them as consciously hostile and antagonistic to Calvinistic principles. This gave him the opportunity to demonstrate that Calvinism provided a viable alternative worldview for ordinary people in contemporary society.

2. The Prejudice

Kuyper was keen not only to portray art in religious terms but to address what he regarded as "a deeply rooted prejudice" that Calvinism was incapable of producing notable works of art or of contributing to art's development (LC, p. 144). It was a prejudice he addressed not only at Princeton but on a number of occasions throughout his career, most notably in his articles in *De Standaard* and in his rectorial address on "Calvinism and Art" in 1888.[16] In the latter he introduced his subject by referring to a report published in Germany three years earlier on Dutch ecclesiastical life, in which the author expressed his surprise that at the Free University of Amsterdam he was able to attend a lecture on aesthetics.[17] This, Kuyper pointed out, was a testimony to the fact that the idea that Calvinism and art were mutually incompatible was still alive and well, even among well-meaning commentators. It was in the hope of correcting this misunderstanding that he had chosen the subject of his address.[18] The same motive lay behind his articles on art in *De Standaard.* One of the earliest of these, published in 1873, was written in response to an article published in an artistic journal the same year, which had ridiculed Calvinism for its lack of artistic creativity and had claimed that the great artists of the Golden Age in Dutch culture during the seventeenth century were masters *in spite of* their Calvinism. Kuyper retaliated with an appeal to Bilderdijk, a poet

16. Kuyper, *Het calvinisme en de kunst.*

17. Kuyper, *Het calvinisme en de kunst,* p. 5. The publication to which Kuyper was referring was J. Gloel, *Holland's Kirchliches Leben. Bericht über eine im Auftrag des Köninglichen Domdekenetenstifts zu Berlin unternommene Studienreise nach Holland* (Wittenberg: Herrose, 1885).

18. Kuyper, *Het calvinisme en de kunst,* p. 5.

of the Dutch *Réveil,* whom he admired as a truly Calvinistic poet, ending his tirade with the sigh: "This restless hostility towards the Calvinistic name!"[19] Thirty-five years later Kuyper was still challenging the same attitude, this time refuting the charge that Calvinism had always been opposed to theatre, and that this was due to hostility towards it on the part of Calvin himself.[20] Whether or not it was thanks to Kuyper, it seems that towards the end of his career there was some hope among Kuyper's followers in the Netherlands that the indictment against Calvin and Calvinism when it came to art had been revoked. In 1915 it was noted in a *Gereformeerde* weekly that the truth had "finally come to light" after centuries of prejudice, that Calvinism was in no way hostile to the arts.[21]

Three points can be drawn from Kuyper's treatment of the prejudice he sought to address. First, it does appear from the concrete examples he gave that the hostility towards Calvinism when it came to the arts was real rather than imagined. This is supported by the fact that dismissals of Calvinism by contemporary non-Calvinist writers and theologians tended to single out its attitude towards the enjoyment of the arts as a focus of attack. Albrecht Ritschl (1822-1889), for instance, wrote that "Calvin . . . combatted everything that pertained to the gay and free joyousness of life and luxury."[22] It is clear, secondly, that his desire to remove a perceived prejudice was another reason why Kuyper addressed the arts at all. Given his aim of presenting Calvinism as a worldview of all-embracing proportions — embracing even the arts — it is understandable that he should have been concerned about the prevailing opinion that Calvin and Calvinism were hostile to the arts. If his case for Calvinism was to have any credibility, he needed to counter this opinion, showing that Calvinism had sus-

19. *De Standaard,* 27 August 1873. Kuyper's regard for Bilderdijk was noted in Chapter Three.

20. *De Standaard,* 4 June 1908.

21. 'Calvijn en de kunst', *Oude paden: weekblad voor de verbreiding der gereformeerde beginselen ten dienste van kerk en volk,* 29 October 1915. Critical treatments of the prejudice against Calvinism in the field of the arts can also be found in Emile Doumergue, "Calvin: Epigone or Creator?" in his *Calvin and the Reformation: Four Studies* (New York: Revell, 1909), pp. 50-52, and Simon J. de Vries, "Calvin's Attitude Towards Art and Amusements," *The Calvin Forum* 17 (1952): 101-7.

22. Albrecht Ritschl, *Geschichte des Pietismus,* 3 vols (Bonn: Marcus, 1880-1886), I, 76.

tained, and still could sustain, a positive impact on the development of the arts. Because of this, his lecture on Calvinism and art was the most crucial of all the six lectures he gave at Princeton if his argument was to be carried. Thirdly, his treatment suggests that he felt it necessary to provide an apology for his decision to deal with the arts, and in doing so was obviously aware that he was addressing an area hitherto virtually disregarded by Calvinist theologians. He thereby unwittingly leaves the reader with the impression that the so-called prejudice against Calvinism's relationship with the arts was to some extent justified.

Having identified the prejudice as the chief object of his critique, Kuyper was now in a position to address the three main questions of his lecture: why did Calvinism not develop its own form of ecclesiastical art? what is the place of art in the Calvinistic worldview? and what has Calvinism done for the advancement of art? Addressing the first of these questions involved Kuyper in a discussion of the relationship between art, religion, and symbolism, to which we shall now turn.

3. Art, Religion, and Symbolism

It was because Calvinism was such a highly advanced form of religion that it had proved unable to develop an independent style of art. In making this argument, Kuyper appealed to the insights of Hegel and Eduard von Hartmann (1842-1906). Hegel had argued that it was only in its lower, sensual, stages of development that religion needed the support of art in order to liberate the human spirit. Once religion had reached a higher form of development, however, such liberation could be found only in the spiritual realm.[23] The same argument was put forward "even more emphatically" by Eduard von Hartmann (LC, p. 148, cf. p. 67). He declared, Kuyper noted, that the more religion progresses

23. Kuyper was evidently referring to a passage from Hegel's *Encyklopädie der Philosophischen Wissenschaften in Grundrisse* (Berlin, 1845), which he reproduced in full in his *Het calvinisme en de kunst,* p. 80 (note 91). The key sentence, for Kuyper, was the following: *'Aber die schöne Kunst ist nur eine Befreiungsstufe, nicht die höchste Befreiung selbst'.* In the Stone Lectures he rendered this in somewhat contracted form as: "beautiful art is not its [the human spirit's] highest emancipation" (LC, p. 148).

towards maturity the more it will free itself from the bonds of art, because art is unable to express the essence of religion.[24]

Although Kuyper resorted to the insights of modern philosophy, he could have appealed directly to Calvin. In several of his works Calvin had pointed out that under the New Covenant inaugurated by Christ, many of the artistically elaborate ceremonies of the Old Testament had been abolished or radically simplified. He even went so far as to say that the use of musical instruments in worship was suited for those "yet tender, like children," who had been trained under the law, but was no longer necessary since Christ's coming, when religion had left behind its stage of infancy.[25] He also believed, as indeed did Kuyper, that the process could be reversed should there be a decline in the vitality and purity of religion; he wrote that for the first five hundred years of the church's history, when "religion was still flourishing, and a purer doctrine thriving, Christian churches were commonly empty of images. It was when the purity of the ministry had somewhat degenerated that they were first introduced for the adornment of the churches."[26] Kuyper had ample grounds, therefore, to appeal to Calvin in his argument that the vitality of religion and artistic forms of worship stood in a negatively proportional relationship to each other. That he appealed to Hegel and von Hartmann instead was a reflection of his attempt to give contemporary intellectual credibility to traditional Calvinistic thought. The argument itself was foundational to Kuyper's thinking on the arts, and it provided him with a means of judging current trends in the relationship between art and religion. In a passage that echoes Calvin's use of the "childhood" metaphor noted above, Kuyper expressed his dismay at current attempts to reestablish symbolical forms of worship in the church:

> The fact that in these days our Calvinistic churches are deemed cold and *unheimisch* [gloomy], and a reintroduction of the symbolical in our places of worship is longed for, we owe to the sad reality that the

24. Kuyper's appeal was to von Hartmann's *Aesthetik,* 2 vols., II, pp. 458, 459.

25. See, for instance, *Calvin's Commentaries,* on Psalm 33:2; Psalm 81:2; Exodus 15:20. Calvin was not against the playing of musical instruments outside the context of church services, where it "may minister to our pleasure, rather than our necessity." Because of this valuable function, it was "not to be thought altogether superfluous nor should it be condemned" (Commentary on Genesis 4:20).

26. Calvin, *Institutes,* I.xi.13.

> pulsebeat of the religious life in our times is so much fainter than it was in the days of our martyrs.... Second childhood, in your old age, is a painful, retrograde movement. The man who fears God, and whose faculties remain clear and unimpaired, does not on the brink of age return to the playthings of his infancy. (LC, p. 149)

Two clues help identify the "reintroduction of symbolism" to which Kuyper was referring. The first comes in a passage at the start of his *Lectures:*

> In her Thirty-nine Articles, the Church of England is strictly Calvinistic, even though in her Hierarchy and Liturgy she has abandoned the straight paths, and has met with the serious results of this departure in Puseyism and Ritualism. (LC, p. 16)

Ever since Edward Pusey (1800-1882) had joined it in 1835, the Oxford Movement had come to be associated, at least in the public mind, with his name. This was reflected in the nickname "Puseyism" given to the movement by those outside it and here employed by Kuyper.[27] The second clue lies in the fact, noted in Chapter Three, that the lecture he gave before the Historical Presbyterian Society in Philadelphia after his visit to Princeton, titled "The Antithesis between Symbolism and Revelation," was to a large extent a criticism of "the current of symbolical religion, which of late is becoming almost dominant in England, and now already in a considerable degree menaces our Calvinistic churches."[28] Kuyper was evidently referring to the reintroduction of symbolism into the liturgy of the churches of the Anglican communion, a development that was in large part a consequence of the Oxford

27. R. W. Church, an adherent of the Oxford Movement and one of its early historians, recorded in 1897 that this derogatory term was used widely on the European continent: "this nickname, partly from a greater smoothness of sound, partly from an odd suggestion of something funny in it, came more into use than others; and the terms *Puseismus, Puséisme, Puseista* found their way into German lecture-halls and Paris salons and remote convents and police offices in Italy and Sicily; indeed in the shape of *pouseismos* it might be lighted on in a Greek newspaper." R. W. Church, *The Oxford Movement. Twelve Years, 1833-1845* (London: Macmillan, 1897), p. 183.

28. Kuyper, *The Antithesis.* Kuyper set his entire address against the background of the ritualistic trend in England, devoting his introduction to a characterization of this movement.

Movement. It was a development that found support in the kind of argument expressed by John Henry Newman in the following passage, written to make the case that the outward and visible aspects of worship should not be disregarded in favor of the inward and spiritual. It is a passage that reads almost as if it were directed against Kuyper himself:

> There is no such thing as abstract religion. When persons attempt to worship in this (what they call) more spiritual manner, they end, in fact, in not worshipping at all. . . . What will the devotion of the country people be, if we strip religion of its external symbols, and bid them seek out and gaze upon the Invisible? Scripture gives the *spirit,* and the Church the *body,* to our worship; and we may as well expect that the spirits of man might be seen by us without the intervention of their bodies, as suppose that the Object of faith can be realised in a world of sense and excitement, without the instrumentality of an outward form to arrest and fix attention, to stimulate the careless, and to encourage the desponding.[29]

Kuyper and his colleagues on the editorial board of *De Heraut* reacted to such reasoning, and the influence it had on Anglican worship, with considerable alarm, *De Heraut* carrying regular reports on the development of the symbolistic and ritualistic trend in the Church of England.[30] Obituaries of some of the influential figures in this movement did, however, display a large degree of personal sympathy and respect for their causes,[31] and Kuyper never lost his admiration for traditional

29. J. H. Newman, *Parochial and Plain Sermons,* 8 vols., 1873 edition, II, pp. 74-75; cf. IV, p. 176.

30. These reports appeared in *De Heraut* between 7 December 1877 and 2 November 1902. A report in *De Standaard* during Kuyper's visit to America commented that "ritualism was being discussed in England more than ever before" (6 November 1898).

31. The following obituaries appeared in *De Heraut:* E. B. Pusey, 5 November 1882; J. H. Newman, 21 September 1890, 19 October 1890; H. P. Liddon, 19 October 1890. The mixture of criticism and regret is exemplified in the following passage from the obituary of Newman: "Following his death both friend and foe have paid tribute to his honest character. But it is regrettable that a man of such rich gifts as Newman should have given himself to initiating a contra-reformation" (*De Heraut,* 21 September 1890). A similar tone was sounded by Warfield in his review of the third volume of H. P. Liddon's *Life of Edward Bouverie Pusey,* 4 vols. (London: Longmans, Green & Company, 1894): "Here we have a picture of a good man's unwearied

Anglican liturgy, first instilled by his reading of Charlotte Yonge's *The Heir of Redclyffe.*[32] His chief concern for the Church of England was that the reintroduction of symbolism would inevitably lead to doctrinal indifference because the motive behind it was rooted in German pantheistic thought.[33] He illustrated such indifference by relating a visit he had made to an Anglican service led by an advocate of the symbolical movement:

> I still remember how once I felt shocked by the church performances of a distinguished adherent of the new system, who in private conversation made no secret whatsoever to me of his absolute apostasy from the Christian faith, and whom three days later I saw mounting the pulpit, solemnly reading what in the Book of Kings is written about Elijah's miracles, and thereupon leading the collects of the Book of Common Prayer. I confess frankly that I felt unable to explain such a bold contrast of personal conviction and outward performance.

Kuyper went on to relate how this clergyman later explained to him that he was able to take part in Christian worship on the basis of its poetic qualities, rather than because it expressed any essential reality.[34]

It was his notion that the symbolical movement was rooted in German pantheism that explains why Kuyper should have been so preoccupied with a movement largely contained within the Anglican Church. As noted in Chapter Four, the advance of pantheistic thought

---

and generally useful efforts to do good, mingled, of course, with the evils which grew out of the nature of his religious opinions." *The Presbyterian and Reformed Review* 7 (1896): 347-50 (349).

32. The effect this novel had on Kuyper was noted in Chapter Two. Kuyper's appreciation of Anglican forms of worship is particularly apparent in his major liturgical work *Onze Eeredienst* (Kampen: Kok, 1911), where he wrote that the Church of England was "much more highly developed liturgically" than the Reformed churches of the Netherlands (p. 492).

33. As noted in Chapter Four, Kuyper's main objection to pantheism was that it tried to abolish the boundary between God and the world. Symbolism, similarly, sought to abolish the distinction between the infinite and the finite, the eternal and the temporal realms. See A. Kuyper, *The Antithesis,* p. 15.

34. Kuyper, *The Antithesis,* pp. 17-18. An emphasis on ritual at the expense of doctrine was of major concern to evangelicals within the Church of England, who responded in part through the founding of evangelical theological colleges at Oxford and Cambridge. See Peter Somers Heslam, "Evangelical Anglicanism," pp. 1-16.

was something he considered to be a threat to Western Christianity as a whole. For Kuyper, therefore, it was only a matter of time before the pantheism that had already manifested itself in the Anglican Church would take firmer hold in the Calvinistic churches of the Netherlands and the United States: "There exists an undeniable affinity between the, as yet, feeble symbolical action in our own churches and the dark ritualistic cloud pending over Great Britain."[35]

Kuyper's establishment of a link between symbolism in liturgy and indifference in doctrine by assigning them a common source in German pantheism suggests that it was the maintenance of doctrinal purity, rather than the fortunes of art, that was his chief feason for dealing with symbolism in his lecture on art at Princeton. Moreover, it enabled him, in characteristic fashion, to reduce the entire issue to a clash of antithetical principles — Calvinism on the one hand versus pantheism on the other: "The principle of Symbolism and that of Calvinism are just the reverse of one another. An abyss is gaping between them" (LC, p. 21). Kuyper's case for a concrete link between symbolism and pantheism is, however, unconvincing. Not only is his evidence largely anecdotal, but if the danger of symbolism was doctrinal indifference, his use of the ritualistic trend in England as his chief example is somewhat problematic, given that the Oxford Movement did wish to see a restoration of traditional Christian doctrine within the historic church and a rejection of pantheism.

The fact that Kuyper was one of the earliest Dutch representatives of the Liturgical Movement is a further sign of the lack of precision which characterized his critique. This movement, which developed simultaneously in several Western countries, advocated the restoration of beauty and form to a post-Reformation liturgy which in many parts of the Reformed and Anglican world had become dull and uninspiring.[36]

35. Kuyper, *The Antithesis,* p. 9.

36. Kuyper's insistence on beauty as a requirement for all genuinely religious worship is expressed in his *Onze Eeredienst* (pp. 73-91), and in his *De gemeene gratie in wetenschap en kunst* (pp. 77-78). For a discussion of Kuyper's role in stimulating the rise of the Liturgical Movement in the Netherlands, see Peter Staples, *The Liturgical Movement in the Netherlands Reformed Church, 1911-1955. With Special Reference to the Anglican Dimension* (Utrecht: Interuniversitair Instituut voor Missiologie en Oecumenica, 1983), pp. 28-33; J. F. Lescrauwaet, *De liturgische beweging onder de Nederlandse Hervormden in oecumenisch perspektief: Een fenomenologische en kritische studie* (Bussum: Paul Brand, 1957); E. van der Schoot, *Hervormde eredienst: De liturgische*

This was, also however, one of the chief goals of the advocates of the restoration of symbolism, as Kuyper himself acknowledged when he spoke of those who advocated the reform of a Calvinistic liturgy that had became "cold and *unheimisch*." On this point, as on others, he was clearly more concerned with differences in underlying premise than with the similarity of practical results.

Despite the problems inherent in Kuyper's perspective on the relationship between art, religion, and symbolism, an intellectual basis for it can be found in his doctrine of sphere-sovereignty. If, according to this doctrine, art and religion occupy their own autonomous spheres, then it follows that for the healthy development of each it is necessary that both are free from interference from the other — a freedom that symbolism threatened to undermine. The close association Kuyper made between symbolism and pantheism also finds support in the doctrine of sphere-sovereignty. Given that, in his view, pantheism sought the elimination of the boundaries between spheres, pantheism inevitably gave rise to symbolism in which the division between the spheres of art and religion was blurred. Sphere-sovereignty also supported Kuyper's endorsement of Hegel's and von Hartmann's argument that the more developed the form of religion, the more liberated it is from dependence on the trappings of art. Although he made no mention of it, Kuyper's doctrine of sphere-sovereignty is foundational to his approach to the arts.

4. The Place of Art in the Calvinistic Worldview

It was Kuyper's attempt to address this question that elicited his presentation of a Calvinistic theology of art — a "Calvinistic aesthetics."[37] Important to the analysis of this book is the way he handled Calvin's ideas and how he contrasted his approach with those of idealism and empiricism, the two major trends in contemporary aesthetics.

---

ontwikkeling van de Nederlandse Hervormde Kerk ('s-Gravenhage: Boekencentrum, 1950).

37. Begbie's theological study of Kuyper's ideas on art in the Stone Lectures is based almost entirely on this section of the fifth lecture. See Begbie, *Voicing Creation's Praise,* pp. 96-99.

4.1. Calvin's Aesthetics

In presenting a Calvinistic aesthetics, Kuyper was aware of two problems: Calvin's frequent disparagement of the arts, and the fact that aesthetics did not exist as an independent field of enquiry during the period of Calvinism's ascendancy. With regard to the first, he made a distinction between Calvin's criticism of the abuse of art and his ideas on its proper use, explaining that he would only be concerned with the latter. This was a significant restriction, as it allowed Kuyper to set to one side the very passages in Calvin's works from which many commentators had concluded that Calvin was opposed to the arts in themselves. Kuyper dealt with the second problem only in his rectorial address on art in 1888, but the solution he drew there underlies his argument in the Stone Lectures. Since Calvin took God's revelation in the scriptures as the starting point for his thought, Kuyper explained, the solution was to discover what perspective the biblical worldview offered as to the significance of art.[38] Kuyper went on to develop a theory of art and beauty based on the biblical concept of "glory" (δοξα), which for him included concepts of God's radiance, perfection, splendor, and "divinity" (θειοτης). This glory was impressed upon all of God's creation, such that beauty was the shining through of God's glory in both spiritual and material things.[39] As a result of the fall, the original beauty of creation was lost, despite the intervention of common grace, only to be restored in and through Jesus Christ: "Christ . . . is the canon and ideal of all beauty."[40]

Having thus formulated a biblical framework for his aesthetics, given here in its briefest outline, Kuyper was in a position to apply it to a consideration of art itself, and in particular to the question which had dominated all discussions of art since Plato: is art an imitation of nature, or does it transcend nature? It was this question that preoccupied Kuyper in his various treatments of art, including that in the Stone Lectures, his

38. Kuyper, *Het calvinisme en de kunst,* p. 10.

39. This thought is closely akin to Kuyper's idea that all created things contain and reflect God's thoughts, an idea he used to stimulate the pursuit of science, as shown in Chapter Seven.

40. Kuyper, *Het calvinisme en de kunst,* p. 12. Begbie sums up Kuyper's position thus: "Beauty must therefore now be understood in the light of Jesus Christ, through whom all things were created, and in whom creation is restored to its intended beauty." Begbie, *Voicing Creation's Praise,* p. 97.

argument being that for Calvin the true vocation of art was not to imitate nature but to "reveal to us a higher reality than is offered to us by this sinful world" (LC, p. 154). In other words, art has the function of reminding human beings of the lost beauty of paradise and of anticipating the future glory of the new heavens and the new earth.[41] Although this was not the entirety of what he called Calvin's "system of aesthetics," it was this insight that Kuyper believed to be "the heart of the matter" (LC, p. 154).[42]

Kuyper's presentation of a system of Calvinistic aesthetics, possessing a core principle, is revealing. It illustrates a characteristic of his thought already noted at several points in this book: that he was prepared to improvise on Calvin's thought in those areas where Calvin did not explicitly formulate a position — in this case because aesthetics as such did not exist in Calvin's time. In doing so he developed, from scriptural themes and a few of Calvin's scattered insights, an approach to the arts that corresponded to the general intellectual trend of his own day, with its emphasis on systems and principles — but which went much further than Calvin in addressing the question of art's vocation. Kuyper wanted to address the issue on behalf of Calvinism because such questions of systems and principles dominated contemporary discussions of aesthetics.

4.2. Calvinistic Aesthetics versus Idealism and Empiricism

Kuyper declared that "the forms and relations exhibited by nature are and ever must remain the fundamental forms and relations of all actual reality, and an art which does not watch the forms and motions of nature nor listens to its sounds, but arbitrarily likes to hover over it, deteriorates into a wild play of fantasy." This was a position he claimed was "all too often forgotten by idealists" (LC, p. 154). These words indicate where

41. Herman Bavinck held a similar position, emphasizing that this function of art gave it a prophetic character, as it allowed creaturely beauty to lift beholders above the conflicts of life and point them towards the glory yet to be revealed. See H. Bavinck, 'Van schoonheid en schoonheidsleer', in *Verzamelde opstellen* (Kampen: Kok, 1921), pp. 262-80. Cf. Begbie, *Voicing Creation's Praise,* p. 99.

42. The other tenets of this "system," which Kuyper seems to have derived mainly from Calvin's commentaries on Genesis (4:20) and Exodus (20:4), were that art was to be esteemed as a gift of the Holy Spirit, and that the purpose of art was to glorify God, to ennoble human life, and to give pleasure (LC, p. 153).

Kuyper's ideas on art stood in relation to others of his time. The trend towards idealism in aesthetics, which had Kant as its chief founder, was a reaction against the Platonic idea, that the artist does not create but limits himself to imitating — the so-called principle of "mimesis" (μιμησις). Accordingly, the emphasis in Platonic aesthetics was on the object rather than on the subject; earthly "reality" conditions the artist, who contemplates it and then represents the more genuine and constant heavenly reality, of which the terrestrial version is but a pallid reflection.[43] Idealistic aesthetics aimed to supplant art viewed as mimesis with art understood as creation. As a result, the divine world became more human and immediate, and the beautiful, although it still preserved its former transcendental nature, acquired a new character that allowed it to be equated with art.

Kuyper's insistence on the beautiful as an objective reality determined his opposition to idealism. But this did not mean that he was ready to lend unreserved support to realism, or, as Kuyper called it in his Stone Lectures, "empiricism." In opposition to idealism it emphasized the mimesis proncìple, believing the task of the artist to be not creation but the imitation of nature. Kuyper was as dismissive of this idea as he was of idealism, and his criticism of it both defines his understanding of the true vocation of art and demonstrates an important connection between his ideas on art and those on science.

For Kuyper, the attempt to limit art to the imitation of nature was to make the same mistake committed by scientists when they confined their research to observation, computation, and the accurate recording of facts:

> For even as science has to ascend from the phenomena to the investigation of their inherent order, to the end that man, enriched by the knowledge of this order, may propagate nobler species of animals, flowers and fruits, than nature, herself, could produce, so also it is the vocation of art, not merely to observe everything visible and audible, to apprehend it, and reproduce it artistically, but much more to discover in those natural forms the order of the beautiful, and, enriched by this higher knowledge, to produce a beautiful world that transcends the beautiful of nature. (LC p. 154)

43. Hence Plato's well-known doctrine of art as imitation of an imitation, and his ensuing condemnation of art as lacking creativity. See Plato's *Republic,* Book Ten.

Just as Kuyper's opposition to empiricism in science was part of his opposition to scientific positivism, manifested in particular in agnosticism, so his opposition to empiricism in art was part of his opposition to artistic positivism. The connection between empiricism in art and positivism in science is found in the writings of Auguste Comte (1798-1857), where art is reduced to a "fact," as science is considered able to eliminate all metaphysical claims. It was an idea reflected in the terms "naturalism," "verism," and "realism," which were gradually introduced into the aesthetics of positivism.[44]

Kuyper did not fully accept the aesthetics either of idealism or of realism, indicating instead that Calvinistic aesthetics occupied an independent position between these two alternatives. What he was able only to indicate at Princeton, he had spelt out in greater detail in his rectorial address on art in 1888, where it is evident that he possessed firsthand knowledge of the arguments put forward by contemporary idealist and empiricist aestheticians.[45] The critique of these two schools that Kuyper offered in this address cannot be discussed in detail here, but it is important to note that he believed that by regarding God's glory as manifest in both spiritual and material phenomena, the antithesis between idealism and empiricism falls away. For, he explained, in seeking the essence of the beautiful only in the realm of the spirit or in the realm of matter, both schools sacrificed one realm of the beautiful for the other. If, however, God's glory was reflected in both material and spiritual phenomena, then true beauty was manifest in both spheres: "A color, a tone, or a line can be beautiful in itself just as much as a character-trait, a disposition, a thought or a deed."[46]

Thus it is clear that, while rejecting idealism and realism as total

44. The use of such terms in aesthetics, albeit with changes in meaning, has survived to the present day. See *Encyclopedia of World Art,* 17 vols. (New York: McGraw-Hill, 1959-1987), V, pp. 48-49.

45. Kuyper reckoned those belonging to the empiricist school to include Helmholtz, Pfau, and Semper and those of the idealist school to include Schelling, Solger, Seising, Kostlin, Zimmerman, and von Hartmann. That Kuyper kept abreast with new developments in aesthetics is illustrated by the fact that von Hartmann's work *Aesthetik,* to which Kuyper refers, was published in 1888, the same year as he delivered his rectorial address. See *Het calvinisme en de kunst,* p. 71 (notes 61 and 62).

46. Kuyper, *Het calvinisme en de kunst,* p. 17.

explanations of the function of art, Kuyper was prepared to integrate a synthesis of their insights into an alternative vision that he felt was true to Calvinism.[47] This is reflected in the question Kuyper posed at the start of his lectures on aesthetics in the academic year 1884-1885 at the Free University: "Does our University, and our research in this field . . . only have to repeat what others have said . . . or can our own lines, our own principle, our own school of thought, our own position be found in this area also?"[48] His aim was evidently to stimulate the development of a consciously and unashamedly Calvinistic aesthetics. In his efforts to fulfill his vision he developed a theology of art that he claimed rather anachronistically to be "Calvin's aesthetics" but was in fact more his own preliminary perspectives on a subject that had not previously received attention, either in Calvin's theology or in that of Calvinistic theologians. By placing his position in the midst of a contemporary debate, Kuyper was demanding intellectual credibility for it, he was attempting to bring Calvinism up-to-date, and he was aiming to show that Calvinism, even in the area of the arts, enjoyed an independent position. Calvinism could therefore be regarded as a truly viable alternative to the modern constellation of worldviews.

It is clear from the above discussion that for Kuyper there was a close connection between aesthetics and theology. Indeed he derived his aesthetics from his theology. This is reflected in the fact that he, as a professor of theology and, more importantly, as someone driven by religious concerns, should have thought it worthwhile to lecture on aesthetics. In a circular he distributed to new students of theology, aesthetics appeared as an integral part of the curriculum. It stipulated a good "aesthetic development" as a formal requirement, along with competence in ancient and modern languages, for proceeding from preliminary to advanced studies in theology. The reason given was that "the life of art is more closely allied to the religious life than the life of the intellect. The relation between languages and theology is no stonger than that between aesthetics and theology."[49]

47. Kuyper, *Het calvinisme en de kunst,* pp. 18, 73 (note 68).

48. From Kuyper's lecture notes, in KA; LB; P2. These notes, unfortunately very fragmentary, indicate that Kuyper's course on aesthetics included sections on the definition of art and of beauty and on the history of aesthetics.

49. A. Kuyper, *Method van Studie,* published in J. C. Rullmann, *Kuyper-bibliographie,* II, pp. 263-65.

5. Calvinism's Contribution to the Development of the Arts

5.1. In Principle: Common Grace

Kuyper's chief aim in the penultimate subsection of his lecture on art was to determine whether the liberation of art from the bonds of the church was merely accidental, or whether it proceeded from Calvinistic principle. Calling upon von Hartmann once again, he argued that it was because of Calvinism's higher religious development that it was able to overcome symbolical religion and thus to break the tutelage of the church in the sphere of the arts.[50] But this was not the only factor responsible for art's emancipation; also involved was the Calvinistic doctrine of common grace.

Kuyper's rendering of the significance of this doctrine with respect to the arts appears to have been leveled against any idea that there should be a specifically Christian art, the existence of which one would expect Kuyper to affirm, given his advocacy of Christian science in his previous Stone Lecture. Against the idea of a specifically Christian art, or at least against the idea that true, genuine art can only be found in specifically Christian art, Kuyper appealed to Calvin's statement that God imparts the liberal arts promiscuously to believers and unbelievers alike.[51] Restricting the enjoyment of art to the regenerate, Kuyper explained, would make it a product of particular grace, whereas both history and experience taught that the highest artistic instincts were natural gifts that flourished by virtue of common grace. It was in Greece, in fact, rather than in ancient Israel, that the fundamental laws for art, which remained forever valid, had been revealed. Kuyper's insistence here that the fundamentals of Greek art provided the fun-

50. Kuyper cited the following from von Hartmann (LC, p. 159): "It is pure spiritual religion which with one hand deprives the artist of his specifically religious art, but which, with the other, offers him, in exchange, a whole world, to be religiously animated." The quote is taken from von Hartmann's *Aesthetik,* II, p. 459.

51. See Calvin's commentary on Genesis 4:20. There is a slight difference between the English and the Dutch versions of the Stone Lectures at this point. The English version, which predates the Dutch, places Calvin's position in contrast to the idea of there being a specifically Christian art; the Dutch version against the idea that true, genuine art can only be found in Christian art (see LC, p. 160; *Het calvinisme: zes Stone-lezingen,* pp. 155-56).

damentals for all subsequent art production, whether that art be produced by Christians or non-Christians, stands in stark contrast to his insistence that the starting point for all science was human consciousness, which was either regenerate or unregenerate, and had a determining influence on the presuppositions and conclusions of the scientist. There is no deliberate mention of "two kinds of art" to complement his idea of "two kinds of science." Three historical reasons may be suggested to account for this discrepancy.

The first is that Kuyper, as someone intimately involved in academia, was more closely acquainted with trends in science that challenged Christian fundamentals than with those within the arts. This is demonstrated in the Stone Lectures themselves where, in his lecture on science, he showed himself to be well informed about scientific schools that imperiled Christian belief, such as agnosticism, whereas in his lecture on art he makes no mention of any artistic school imposing a similar threat. His opposition to the rise of symbolism, as noted earlier, had more to do with his concern for the realm of religion, particularly the correct functioning of liturgy, than for the realm of art. In the realm of aesthetics Kuyper was prepared to concede that the two leading trends of idealism and realism provided valuable insights compatible with his alternative Calvinistic aesthetics. Both the omission of a plea for the development of a specifically Christian art and of any characterization of potential opposition to such a development are uncharacteristic of Kuyper's argument at Princeton, and indicate that, compared to his acute awareness of contemporary trends in religion, politics, and science, his familiarity with developments in the arts was inadequate. This was not true of his knowledge of aesthetics, in which he did advocate an alternative approach, but this discipline did not concern the production of art as such, and besides, Kuyper's treatment of it was more in terms of a branch of theology than an independent discipline.[52]

The second, related reason was the relative strategic importance of providing an independent alternative in the areas of politics and science to one in the arts. Kuyper fought persistently for the establishment of independent political and scientific institutions, believing this to be the only way the orthodox Protestants in the Netherlands could be free to organize their own lives, and to make an impact on society at

52. Kuyper, *Encyclopaedie,* III, p. 343.

large. Both the Anti-Revolutionary Party and the Free University were founded toward this end. In the area of the arts, Kuyper made no attempt to pursue similar projects, and there is no evidence that independent schools or societies for the arts that sought to embody religious principles in their productions were so much as contemplated. His first serious treatment of the arts came in his rectorial address of 1888, a decade after he had consolidated plans for the ARP and the Free University. Kuyper clearly felt that, in terms of effecting social change, politics and science were more important than the arts, and it was partly for this reason that he failed to make any efforts towards providing a Christian alternative in the arts.

Lastly, not only was Kuyper's motivation stronger in social terms for the posing of an antithesis in science rather than in art, but also in intellectual terms. As pointed out in the previous chapter, Kuyper's ideas on the duality of science can be interpreted against the background of the rise of positivism in the philosophy of science towards the end of the nineteenth century and an accompanying optimism on the part of many scientists and intellectuals about the potential benefits to civilization that could be reaped from a wholehearted pursuit of an objective, neutral science. Kuyper's insistence on the role of ideologically determined presuppositions in the results of science can be understood as a response to such optimism, and as evidence of the extent to which he considered it a threat to the place of Christianity in the arena of scientific discovery and debate. No similar intellectual threat was posed to society from the direction of the arts. Although ideas hostile to Christianity, such as nihilism, had begun to find expression in the arts by the end of the nineteenth century, no one proposed that the arts could provide a radically new order and a means of solving all manner of problems in human society, as was thought to be the vocation of science.

The reasons given here may help to explain why Kuyper thought differently about science than about art, but they do not solve the inconsistency between the two approaches, an inconsistency that weakens his attempt to present an internally coherent worldview. If he intended to take a different line on art than on science, it seems odd that he never explained why this should be the case.

5.2. In Practice: Painting

Kuyper's aim in the final part of his lecture was to demonstrate how Calvinism had actually advanced the development of the arts in history. Conscious of the need to draw his examples from forms of art that could be appreciated by an international audience, he deliberately avoided any reference to the poetry and literature of the Netherlands, concentrating instead on music and painting, which were unrestricted by language. With respect to painting, Kuyper was more explicit as to how specific aspects of Calvinistic belief influenced the work of artists, and for this reason his comments on painting only will be considered here.

It is not surprising, given the international fame of the Dutch School, that Kuyper should have selected the Glorious Age of Dutch art in the late sixteenth and seventeenth centuries, which included the work of Rembrandt and Vermeer, to argue for the influence of Calvinism in the area of painting. His argument was not, he insisted, that the universally acknowledged brilliance of this school of art was due to its members being staunch Calvinists, as not all of them were. It was rather that Calvinism formed the context within which they worked, influencing their perceptions of the world they sought to represent, whether or not they adhered to a confessional faith. The concept of common grace and the love of liberty accordingly encouraged them to have regard for commonplace human existence and its new-found independence and dignity outside the bounds of the institutional church.[53] Likewise, the idea of election by free grace had encouraged Dutch artists to portray the hidden importance of the seemingly small and insignificant. Here Kuyper has been said to have come to his "most decisive insight" in his ideas on art.[54] He declared:

53. Kuyper claimed support for this thesis in the work of Hippolyte Taine and Moriz Carrière, two art historians who were "far from sympathizing with Calvinism" (LC, p. 166). See H. Taine, *Philosophie de l'art dans les Pays Bas,* 2 vols. (Paris: Germer Baillière, 1869), II, p. 148; and M. Carrière, *Die Kunst in Zusammenhang mit der Culturentwickelung,* 5 vols. (Leipzig: Brockhaus, 1873-1880), IV, p. 308.

54. Calvin Seerveld, *A Christian Critique of Art* (St. Catharines, Ontario: Association for Reformed Scientific Studies, 1963), p. 50. Seerveld develops Kuyper's insight in an attempt to suggest criteria for a Christian critique of art.

> If a common man, to whom the world pays no special attention, is valued and even chosen by God as one of his elect, this must lead the artist also to find a motive for his artistic studies in what is common and of every-day occurrence, to pay attention to the emotions and the issues of the human heart in it. . . . Thus far the artist had only traced upon his canvas the idealized figures of prophets and apostles, of saints and priests; now, however, when he saw how God had chosen the porter and the wage-earner for Himself, he found interest not only in the head, the figure and the entire personality of the man of the people, but began to reproduce the human expression of every rank and station. (LC, p. 166)[55]

The sufferings of Christ, Kuyper went on, which hitherto had been conceived only in relation to the pains of his crucifixion, came to include, in a mystical sense, the general sufferings and hardships of humankind. Thus Rembrandt's chiaroscuro demonstrates his grasp of the richness of ordinary human life, in all its sober reality.[56]

Kuyper had once again seized upon what seemed to him a powerful means of recommending Calvinism to a foreign audience and of challenging the prejudice against both the Calvinist doctrine of predestination and Calvinism's relationship to the arts. He did not have to labor to establish the greatness of the Dutch School, as this was internationally recognized, but by ascribing this greatness to Calvinism, and particularly to a belief closely associated with the despised doctrine of predestination, he sought to illustrate Calvinism's credibility and preeminence to the world at large. In doing so, not only his

55. Kuyper's argument that the doctrine of election undergirded Calvinism's championing of democracy (for which he found support in the work of G. Bancroft and F. D. Maurice) was noted in Chapter Five.

56. In support of this interpretation of Rembrandt's chiaroscuro Kuyper once again appealed to Taine's *Philosophie de l'art dans les Pays-Bas* (pp. 164-65). John Ruskin was far from sharing this interpretation. He wrote that in as much as artists are searchers after truth, Rembrandt belongs to the lowest class of artists who only perceive and imitate evil: "they delight in the beggary and brutality of the human race; their colour is for the most part subdued or lurid, and the greatest spaces of their pictures are occupied by darkness." From John Ruskin, *The Stones of Venice,* 3 vols. (London: Routledge, 1907), II, pp. 206-7. Despite such sharp criticism, Ruskin did acknowledge that Rembrandt's strength lay in his rendering of human character. See *Selections from the Writings of John Ruskin* (London: Blackfriars, [n.d.]), p. 167.

triumphalism, but also his nationalism, which has been noted at other points in this book, are all too evident. His treatment reflects traces of the type of nationalistic sentiment which was on the increase towards the end of the nineteenth century.[57] These traces can be found in particular in those comments that highlight the worldwide supremacy of the Dutch School: his comment, for instance, that it had produced "those wondrous art-productions which still immortalize its fame, and which have shown the way to all the nations for new conquests" (LC, p. 167).[58] Once again Kuyper betrays a desire to highlight the significance of the Netherlands, a small nation, within the wider world. In preceding lectures he had pointed to the constitutional liberties which, having taken root in Dutch soil, had been transplanted to the New World where they had helped to make the United States great. The scientific discoveries made at Leiden University, likewise, were of international significance to the development of modern science, which had revolutionized the life of Western nations. Here, in his final lecture on the significance of Calvinism for the various spheres of life, he aimed to show that, even in so unlikely a field as the arts, a small, Calvinistic country had led the world and pointed the way ahead.

Conclusion

This lecture is more about religion than about art. At every stage it is clear that religious and theological concerns, rather than artistic ones, dominate the argument. It would, therefore, have offered little in the way of practical guidance to the interested artist. This can be contrasted with his lectures on politics and science, which, though equally theolog-

57. See Nico Wilterdink, "The Netherlands Between the Greater Powers: Expressions of Resistance to Perceived or Feared Foreign Cultural Domination," in *Within the US Orbit: Small National Cultures vis-à-vis the United States,* ed. by Rob Kroes (Amsterdam: Free University Press, 1991), pp. 13-31.

58. A similar note is sounded in his *Encyclopaedie:* "the same Calvinistic Holland that had censured church art saw the rise of a general human school of art which has not yet been surpassed" (III, p. 342). Expressions of nationalistic sentiment permeated the elaborate celebrations in July 1906 of the third centenary of Rembrandt's birth, which received extensive coverage and comment in *De Standaard* (see, for instance, *De Standaard,* 17 July 1906).

ical, clearly have a practical dimension, aimed at stimulating specific kinds of political and scientific activity. The message is clear in Kuyper's lecture on art that Calvinism has a vocation in the realm of the arts, but it is unclear how this vocation should be fulfilled. That art has the task of reflecting the beauty of the lost paradise and the coming kingdom of glory may have been an attempt to provide the basis for a Calvinistic aesthetics, but it has little bearing on the kind of art that may be considered consistent with Christian principles. Some guidelines can be extracted, and will be outlined in brief below, but there is a general lack of clarity and consistency, particularly when the argument in this lecture is compared to that in his lecture on science, which takes a substantially different line. The resulting ambiguity may well have contributed to the fact that, compared to the achievements of Kuyper's followers in the area of science and politics, those in the production of and performance of the arts were unimpressive. By allowing what he perceived as a prejudice against Calvinism to dominate his argument, he forfeited the opportunity to present a vision for the renewal of the arts along Calvinistic lines. The impression given is almost that once the prejudice had been removed the struggle for the acknowledgment of Calvinism's contribution to the arts would be over. But correcting a misunderstanding is not the same as presenting a program for change.

It was, however, as a theologian, and not as an artist or art critic, that Kuyper was invited to Princeton, and his audience was made up not of artists but of the faculty and students of a theological seminary. The significance of Kuyper's lecture should, therefore, be sought more in the fact *that* he addressed the arts, and did so in a positive way, avoiding moral questions, than in *what* he actually had to say about them, especially in view of the fact that in Protestant circles scholarly treatments of the arts were a rarity, and that there had often been a tendency within them to marginalize the arts, or even to stigmatize them. In this sense, Kuyper may be credited with helping to remove the ban under which the arts had been held among his followers. The removal of this ban may be a chief reason why in Kuyperian circles, in contrast to many others within the Protestant tradition, thoughtful and scientific treatments of the arts have proliferated.

It should be added, however, that it is not his specific ideas on art that are responsible for the flourishing of neo-Calvinistic discussions of art and aesthetics, but his idea of worldview and its role in shaping culture. Hans Rookmaaker's book *Modern Art and the Death of a Culture,* for instance, makes much use of this latter idea, interpreting art as an expression of the worldview held by the artist.[59] Seen in this light, the leading motifs of the neo-Calvinistic school of art probably owe more to Kuyper's ideas on science than to those on art, however strange this may seem.

That Kuyper was able to display a positive approach to the arts was largely due to his doctrine of common grace, which in this lecture, in contrast to his lecture on science, is emphasized at the expense of his doctrine of the antithesis, which plays no significant role. This discrepancy is one of the clearest indications of what is perhaps the central tension in Kuyper's thought between the antithesis and corresponding isolation on the one hand, and common grace and corresponding engagement and accommodation on the other. It was a tension Kuyper never resolved, and a comparison of his Stone Lecture on art with that on science demonstrates how it led to flaws in the overall coherence of his thought.

Even though common grace rather than the antithesis plays a determinative role in Kuyper's lecture on art, to the extent that "Calvinistic art" would seem an anomaly, it is possible to extrapolate from Kuyper's arguments the characteristics he would consider art would have to possess if it were to be true to Calvinism. They are listed here along with the specific doctrine from which Kuyper derives them: free from political and ecclesiastical control, because of the doctrine of sphere-sovereignty; beautiful, because God has placed the stamp of his glory on all created things, a belief derived from the doctrine of God's sovereignty; in obedience to classical norms, because of common grace; attentive to the significance of the commonplace and the ordinary, because of the doctrine of election. Although it apparently was not Kuyper's intention, it is possible that his application of theology to the arts could have provided the rudimentary criteria for a specifically Christian critique of art.

Kuyper's chief concern, instead, was to challenge a prejudice. This was of overriding importance to his aim of demonstrating that Calvinism did not represent an exclusively theological and ecclesiastical movement but was an all-embracing worldview. It probably was due, in fact, to Kuyper's sense of the strength of the prejudice that he decided to address the arts at all; if he could show that Calvinism had a unique perspective

59. See footnote 2 of this chapter.

here, of all places, it would greatly strengthen his case for Calvinism as a worldview that embraced all aspects of culture.

Kuyper also wanted to bring the Calvinistic worldview up-to-date, and to show that it still offered a viable alternative. This helps explain why he argued his case in constant reference to contemporary trends, which in this lecture included the democratization of art in society and the rise of symbolism in the churches. In order to present a Calvinistic perspective on such movements, he tended to reduce whatever trend it was to an underlying motivating principle to which Calvinism was opposed. Thus the democratization of art was a result of materialism, and symbolism in worship was a product of pantheism. This illustrates the kind of culture critic Kuyper was. Although his knowledge of such trends was based on his familiarity with a broad range of primary sources, he rarely engaged in detailed analysis and criticism of them but used a considerable amount of intuition, and not a little polemical verve, to characterize them in their general lines and in their fundamental positions.

Sixth Lecture: Calvinism and the Future

Kuyper's sixth and final Stone Lecture was a conclusion to the series. His aim in the preceding five lectures had been to "eradicate the wrong idea that Calvinism represented an exclusively dogmatical and ecclesiastical movement" by pointing out its achievements in every department of life:

> Calvinism . . . raised our Christian religion to its highest spiritual splendour; it created a church order, which became the preformation of state confederation; it proved to be the guardian angel of science; it emancipated art; it propagated a political scheme, which gave birth to constitutional government, both in Europe and America; it fostered agriculture and industry, commerce and navigation; it put a thorough Christian stamp upon home-life and family-ties; it promoted, through its high moral standard, purity in our social circles; and to this manifold effect it placed beneath Church and State, beneath society and home-circle a fundamental philosophic conception strictly derived from its dominating principle, and therefore all its own. (LC, p. 171)

Kuyper's objective at Princeton was not, however, merely to win a case in the interpretation of history and so to challenge a prejudice against Calvinism. Above all he wished to make an appeal, on the basis of what Calvinism had achieved in the past, for effective Calvinistic activity in the future—for the carrying forward of the work begun in the sixteenth century. This was an aim he disclosed at the outset of his lectures, where he urged his audience to consider Calvinism's achievements, and to decide on the basis of them "whether it will do to banish any longer this God-given Calvinism to the archives of history, and whether it is so much of a dream to conceive that Calvinism has yet a blessing to bring and a bright hope to unveil for the future" (LC, pp. 39-40). It was towards the possibility of this future "blessing" and "bright hope" that Kuyper wished to point his audience in his final lecture. The possibility could only become reality if appropriate action was taken, and his sixth lecture represents an exhortation to the sort of activity that would secure the influence of Calvinism in years to come. Calvinism's achievements in the past, outlined in the first five lectures, were not to be dwelt on for their own sake but were to inspire and inform further vigorous activity. It was at this point that Kuyper's lectures shed a good deal of their apologetic style and took on something of the nature of a party-political address aimed at outlining a specific program of action. As such, the concern of his last lecture was chiefly with the current state of affairs, rather than with circumstances that might have been envisioned in the future. It was by bringing his vision of the past triumphs of Calvinism to bear on the present situation that Kuyper developed a program for Calvinistic activity in the future. The title of the lecture — "Calvinism and the Future" — needs, therefore, some clarification. It suggests that it was primarily concerned either with the specific interpretation, or vision, of the future provided by Calvinism, or with the likely course Calvinism would take in the future, whereas neither of these is true. In stimulating the desired response, Kuyper sought to indicate Calvinism's potential, not so much to interpret or predict the future, but to affect its course. In doing so he devoted considerable space to a characterization of the current circumstances.

Although this lecture was not concerned with the prediction of future events, it does invite questions about the nature of Kuyper's expectations about the future, and particularly whether they were optimistic or pessimistic. Did he really expect, for instance, that Calvinism, which in his estimation had been in the vanguard in the development of world civilization, would prove able to steer the whole of humanity towards a brighter future, or would its blessings be limited to those who belonged to its own circle of adherents? The final section of this chapter will seek to address this question.

1. Malaise

In order to emphasize the need for the development of Calvinism in the future, Kuyper depicted the sorry state of current affairs. Drawing his characteristic distinction between the material and the spiritual aspects of human life, he argued that the recent rapid improvements in the material aspects, especially in the form of modern comforts, health, travel, and communications, were unable to improve the spiritual side of human life, which was in a state of serious decline: "the hypertrophy of our external life results in a serious atrophy of the spiritual" (LC, p. 172).[1] This decline was expressed in a general sense of discontent, in complaints about impoverishment, degeneracy, and petrification, and in the extreme pessimistic philosophies of Schopenhauer and Nietzsche. The latter's demand for the *Übermensch* was an example of "the cry of despair wrung from the heart of humanity by the bitter consciousness that it is spiritually pining away" (LC, p. 173).[2] As a whole, he concluded, it was fitting that the parallel was often drawn between the current times and the golden age of the Roman Empire, "when the external brilliance of life likewise dazzled the eye, notwithstanding that the social diagnosis could yield no other verdict than 'rotten to the very core'" (LC, p. 173).

Kuyper's language and imagery of widespread malaise, decadence, and decline reflect the mode of thought that developed in the 1890s which is often referred to as the *fin de siècle*. The chief features of this trend — the general melancholic awareness that a great age was coming to a close, the sense of tiredness, lethargy, and depression, the longing for escape from prevailing circumstances, either in death or by means of a hedonistic pursuit of immoral forms of pleasure (hence the term "*la belle époque*" or the "gay nineties")[3] — can all be found in Kuyper's typification of the nature of the malaise:

1. See also Kuyper's *De gemeene gratie*, I, p. 456. His claim that such atrophy was a root cause of the democratization of art was discussed in Chapter Eight.

2. Kuyper was one of the first intellectuals in the Netherlands to pay attention to Nietzsche, in his speech on pantheism in 1892. *Kuyper-bibliografie*, III, p. 47.

3. For discussions of this trend with particular reference to the Netherlands, see Jan Romein, *Op het breukvlak van twee eeuwen*, 2 vols. (Leiden: Brill, 1967), I, passim; Bettina Polak, *Het fin de siècle in de Nederlandse schilderkunst: de symbolistische beweging, 1890-1900* ('s-Gravenhage: Nijhoff, 1955).

> Anarchism and Nihilism but too plainly demonstrate that there are thousands upon ten thousands who would rather demolish and annihilate everything, than continue to bear the burden of present conditions. . . . Money, pleasure, and social power, these alone are the objects of pursuit; and people are constantly growing less fastidious regarding the means employed to secure them. . . . In the midst of the weariness of life, what can restrain the disappointed from taking refuge in suicide? (LC, pp. 173, 179)[4]

Kuyper's comparison of the current decline with that of the Roman Empire reflected a central theme of decadence and decay in the thought of the *fin de siècle,* which drew comparisons between the current paradoxical state of affairs and the coexistence of refined glory and crude decadence that had characterized the latter days of both the Byzantine empire and the *ancien Régime.* Many artistic works of the period reflected this theme, particularly in autumnal motifs such as those that feature in the music of Claude Debussy and in the writings of Oscar Wilde. These can be found in Kuyper's concept of the stream of development in world civilization (see Chapter Three), according to which life in Europe had become "frostbound and dull," in contrast to the energy and vitality of American life. As he put it at the start of the Stone Lectures: "You are yet in your Springtide, — we are passing through our Fall" (LC, p. 9); and at the end: "On the American continent, in a younger world, a relatively healthier tone of life prevails than in senescent Europe" (LC, p. 173).

The cultural pessimism typical of the 1890s, reflected in this understanding of civilization, prefigured the leading arguments in Oswald Spengler's *Untergang des Abendlandes* (1918-1922), according to which contemporary Western culture represented the final, uncreative phase in the history of civilization, the phase of decay, winter, or old age. It generally took the form of a conscious reaction against positivism and the self-satisfied optimism attached to material progress, seeking to replace the latter with the subjective and the mystical, a fact that helps to explain the rise in Nietzsche's popularity in the 1890s.[5] Kuyper was keenly aware of this trend, especially in Germany, where "Nietzsche is

4. *De Heraut* carried several anxious reports about the rise of Nihilism, particularly in Russia. See, for instance, *De Heraut,* 14 September 1879 and 29 August 1880.

5. H. Stuart-Hughes, *Consciousness and Society: The Reorientation of European Social Thought, 1890-1930* (Brighton: Harvester Press, 1979), pp. 33-42; Polak, pp. 1-6.

the author whose works are being most eagerly devoured" (LC, p. 178). The youth of Germany in particular, he declared in 1892, regarded this philosopher as a rising star, and "devoured, cited and adulated him."[6] As noted above, Kuyper found Nietzsche's "cry of despair" fitting for the state of affairs at the end of the nineteenth century, and he emphasized that Nietzsche perceived a decline into mediocrity, rather than progress, to be characteristic of modern culture.[7] It is clear, therefore, that Kuyper was not only acutely aware of but was prepared to go along with the general pessimism that prevailed in the intellectual and artistic spheres of his day, even if this meant going as far as endorsing the pessimistic evaluations of Schopenhauer and Nietzsche, of nihilism and anarchism.

2. Diagnosis

In diagnosing the cause of the malaise, Kuyper presented an argument consistent with his idea of the centrality of the religious sphere in all human thought and culture. The cause lay, he argued, in the "spiritual degeneration" that had characterized the end of the eighteenth century and for which the church was largely responsible. Neglecting its duties towards the whole of human existence, the church had allowed the tone of life to become "vapid and common-place, ignoble and base at heart," a condition reflected in the literature of the period. It was against this background, Kuyper asserted, that the French Revolution had broken out, attempting as it did to reorder society on the assumption that human nature continues in its uncorrupted state (LC, pp. 175-76). In a similar way, the philosophical and cultural pessimism that characterized the contemporary *fin de siècle* was not the cause but the manifestation of the malaise. For Kuyper it was religion rather than philosophy that was responsible for the state of society, and even though he characterized the whole of "modern life" and indeed all of "modernistic" thought by recourse to the terms "French Revolution," "pantheism," and "evolu-

6. Kuyper, *De verflauwing,* p. 5. Here Kuyper noted with alarm that Nietzsche's popularity was also growing in France (p. 65, note 3). Three years later he declared it had become common among Western youth in general — they "followed him and idolized him," he observed, despite the fact that he had gone mad. *De Heraut,* 5 May 1895.

7. Kuyper, *De verflauwing,* p. 66 (note 4). Here Kuyper appealed to Hugo Kaats, *Die Weltanschauung Nietzsche,* 2 vols. (Dresden and Leipzig, 1892), in his typification of Nietzsche's views.

tionism" (see Chapter Four), he did not consider these philosophies to be the cause of the malaise, but its symptoms. The importance of an accurate interpretation of these symptoms was something Kuyper wished to stress: "only a correct diagnosis can lead to an effective treatment" (LC, p. 175). It was to this treatment or remedy that he turned his attention for the rest of the lecture. First, however, he outlined the remedies provided by Protestantism and Catholicism. Although he felt that they had proved ineffective, he was prepared to voice his appreciation of their attempts. His assessment of them is particularly deserving of consideration as it helps to situate Kuyper's remedy within the context of his times and so to shed light on his presentation of Calvinism.

3. Ineffective Remedies

3.1. Protestantism

Protestant thinkers and theologians from Schleiermacher to Ritschl had made great and noble efforts, Kuyper claimed, to promulgate altruism and mysticism in the hope of bringing new life and warmth to a Christianity that had grown cold and uninspiring (LC, pp. 180, 187-88).[8] The emphasis on altruism had stimulated great initiative and devotion in the cause of philanthropy, evangelism, and mission, whereas the revival of mysticism had encouraged the liberation of the spiritual life from the constraints imposed on it by biblical criticism. Despite Kuyper's appreciation of these efforts, he criticized them sharply for their acceptance of empiricism and rationalism, and their adoption of a "crass dualism." Accordingly, followers of this trend had come to accept the findings of biblical criticism and had become estranged from Christian doctrine, in some cases going as far as to express a preference for spiritualism and Buddhism. Even though they generally wished to hold the name of Christ in honor, it was not the traditional Christ of the church they aimed to preach, but the so-called historical Jesus, whom they claimed to have rediscovered (LC, pp. 180-82).

Kuyper's specific criticism of the altruistic tendency was that it reduced Christianity to a concern for human welfare, resulting in a denial of

8. Kuyper's use of the term "altruism" (coined by August Comte) coincided with the idea expressed in utilitarian and positivistic philosophy that love for one's neighbor was the source and criterion for all morality.

the divinity of Christ and his work of salvation, as found in the preaching of so-called "liberal missionaries" (LC, pp. 187-88). His criticism of the mystical trend centered on mysticism's reclusive nature, which involved an avoidance of contact with the world and a consequent inability to take a positive stand in human affairs. It could not, therefore, be expected to bring about a reversal in the spirit of the age (LC, p. 189).[9] This was exemplified in the fact that "not Bernard of Clairvaux but Thomas Aquinas, not Thomas à Kempis but Luther have ruled the spirits of men" (LC, p. 188).

Kuyper's mention of Friedrich Schleiermacher and Albrecht Ritschl (1822-1889) is important in identifying the trends with which he was engaging.[10] It was clearly Schleiermacher's stress on the role of mystery, imagination, and feeling in the functioning of religion to which Kuyper was reacting in his criticism of the mystical trend, particularly as this emphasis involved a reinterpretation of scripture and traditional doctrine on the basis of mystical religious feeling.[11] Ritschl's insistence that ethics, rather than feeling, lay at the heart of religion, indicates that it was towards Ritschl's ideas that Kuyper was turning in his criticism of altruism.[12]

9. The strength of Kuyper's opposition to the mystical trend is evident in his *De gemeene gratie,* I, p. 154; II, pp. 250, 387.

10. Kuyper's discussion of Schleiermacher in his *Encyclopaedie* was noted in Chapter Five. Ritschl's ideas were criticized in over twenty articles in *De Heraut* between 13 August 1882 and 23 June 1901.

11. See Schleiermacher's *The Christian Faith,* ed. by H. R. Mackintosh and J. S. Stewart (Edinburgh: T. & T. Clark, 1928, 1960), pp. 12, 54, 385. Translation of F. D. E. Schleiermacher, *Der Christliche Glaube: nach den Grundsätzen der evangelischen Kirche im Zusammenhange dargestelt* (1821/1822). See edition by Martin Redeker, 2 vols. (Berlin: de Gruyter, 1960).

12. See A. Ritschl, *The Christian Doctrine of Justification and Reconciliation,* trans. by H. R. Mackintosh and A. B. Macaulay (Edinburgh: T. & T. Clark, 1900 [1874]). Although Ritschl followed Schleiermacher in his attempt to extract the essence of Christianity from religious experience, he denounced mysticism and pietism as individualistic, amoral, and not distinctively Christian (see *The Christian Doctrine,* pp. 451, 448). Ritschl's emphasis on the importance of altruism was shared by Herbert Spencer (1820-1903) and Ernst Haeckel (1834-1919), two thinkers Kuyper associated with revolutionism (see Chapter Four), along with the majority of nineteenth-century Idealistic thinkers. James Orr was among the first and most important critics of Ritschl in Britain, arguing that Ritschlianism was opposed to orthodox Christianity and had to be rejected on intellectual grounds because it restricted the role of reason in Christian thought and experience. See James Orr, *The Ritschlian Theology and the Evangelical Faith* (London, 1897); *Ritschlianism: Expositionary and Critical Essays* (London: Hodder & Stoughton, 1903); *The Christian View of God,* pp. 405-8.

It cannot, however, only have been the ideas of German academic theologians such as Schleiermacher and Ritschl that motivated Kuyper's argument, as it is clear that he perceived mysticism and altruism to be powerful trends within Protestantism, not limited to the world of scholarship. As noted in Chapter Two, the Ethical theologians in the Netherlands, with whom Kuyper had come into conflict early in his career, were influenced by Schleiermacher in their acceptance of a critical approach to scripture and their emphasis on personal experience, rather than on reason, in the proper functioning of religion. The same was true of American liberal theologians, such as Washington Gladden (1836-1918) and Walter Rauschenbusch (1861-1918), with whom the members of Kuyper's audience were in constant dispute. The essence of the Christian faith, they and their followers insisted, was life, not doctrine, and the future of Christianity could be assured by stressing the ethical. Whereas Calvinism, together with other traditional theologies, had concentrated on the judicial aspects of the divine-human relationship, Jesus had emphasized the fatherhood of God and the brotherhood of humankind. Their commitment to the ethical and social implications of Christianity, which they shared (together with the Dutch Ethical theologians) with Ritschl, found many expressions at the popular level, such as in Charles M. Sheldon's best-seller *In His Steps,* published in 1896.[13] It also helped to stimulate the proliferation of the educational, philanthropic, and missionary activity that became characteristic of Western Christendom in the last quarter of the nineteenth century.[14] Kuyper was an enthusiastic advocate of such activity, and formulated his ideas on mission and philanthropy in the Dutch colonies in his so-called Ethical Policy, which became part of official government policy in 1901, at the start of his term of office as Prime Minister.[15] His reservations regarding humanitarian initiatives were due, therefore, not to any aversion to such efforts in themselves but to the altruistic

13. George M. Marsden, *Understanding Fundamentalism and Evangelicalism* (Grand Rapids: Eerdmans, 1991), pp. 34-35.

14. See Stephen Neill, *A History of Christian Missions* (Penguin: London, 1964), pp. 322-96.

15. See Peter Heslam, "The Christianization of the East Indies: The Ideas of Abraham Kuyper on Dutch Colonial Policy," *Reflection: An International Reformed Review of Missiology* 2 (1989): 13-17. For a fuller treatment, see Peter Heslam, "De kerstening van Indië: Denkbeelden van A. K. over de Nederlandse koloniale politiek, 1871-1879" (unpublished paper, Hull University, 1988).

thought that so often motivated them, which he regarded as an expression of values more akin to secular humanism than to Christianity.

The mystical trend also had a corollary outside the bounds of strictly theoretical thought in late nineteenth-century Europe, particularly in the flourishing of esoteric forms of religious expression, including, as Kuyper suggested, spiritualism and occultism and in Eastern religions such as Buddhism and Hinduism.[16] A new interest in Plato emerged, and in the Netherlands new translations appeared of mystical writers such as Thomas à Kempis.[17] The Buddhist concept of "Nirvana" found a place in the Dutch language,[18] and the Dutch novelist Frederik van Eeden, who became enthralled with theosophy and spiritualism, encouraged his readers to consult Alfred Sinnet's *Esoteric Buddhism,* a book that became as popular in the Netherlands as *Isis Unveiled* by the theosophist Helena Blavatsky.[19] In Britain, W. R. Inge, who delivered his Bampton Lectures at Oxford in 1899 on the subject of Christian mysticism, wrote in 1933 that his lectures had coincided with the beginning of a great revival of interest in the subject, after a century in which mysticism had been held in dishonor in British circles, in contrast to the respect given to it on the continent by thinkers as dissimilar as Hegel and Schopenhauer.[20] Inge linked the revival of interest in mysticism to the birth of the new science of psychology, pointing out that in all leading countries, but especially in America, a plethora of well-documented studies had appeared on "religious experience."[21] It may well be that

16. Polak, pp. 3-6; C. Aalders, *Spiritualiteit vroeger en nu* ('s-Gravenhage: Boekencentrum, 1969), pp. 139-42.

17. A Dutch translation of Thomas à Kempis' *De imitatione Christi* appeared in 1898 by Mathijs Acket, and soon became very popular. A new translation followed in 1908 by Willem Kloos (1859-1938), a leading poet of the *Tachtigers.*

18. Justus van Maurik, *Anarchisten: klucht in drie bedrijven* (Amsterdam: 1895), p. 55.

19. See Frederik van Eeden's contribution in *De Nieuwe Gids,* I (1891), pp. 1-15; Alfred Percy Sinnet, *Esoteric Buddhism,* 6th ed. (London: Chapman & Hall, 1888); Helena Petrovna Hahn Blavatsky, *Isis Unveiled: a Master-key to the Mysteries of Ancient and Modern Science and Technology,* 2 vols. (London: The Theosophical Publishing Company, 1910).

20. W. R. Inge, *Christian Mysticism. Considered in Eight Lectures Delivered before the University of Oxford (The Bampton Lectures 1899),* 7th edition, with a new Preface (London: Methuen, 1933), pp. v-vi.

21. Inge, *Christian Mysticism* p. vii. One of the earliest of such studies was William James's influential *The Varieties of Religious Experience: A Study of Human Nature. Being the Gifford Lectures on Natural Religion, Delivered at Edinburgh in 1901-1902* (London: Longmans, 1902).

Kuyper had recognized the strength of this trend in the United States and was therefore especially keen to address it on his visit to that country, even though it was Paris that had become the Western center for mysticism, occultism, and spiritualism.

There is ample evidence, therefore, that Kuyper was indeed engaging with trends of some significance in terms of scope, dynamism, and international influence. These characteristics explain the intensity of his opposition to them, along with the fact that they enjoyed popular support, even though they were philosophically conceived. As noted in connection with other trends in previous chapters, Kuyper had a particular interest in and concern for tendencies and movements that had both intellectual and popular expression. It was an interest that reflects the fact that he himself was a leader of such a movement, and aimed to communicate his ideas at both the intellectual and the popular level.

His portrayal of these trends also served to emphasize the weakness, as he saw it, of contemporary Protestantism, caused by its lack of a comprehensive and consistent worldview. As a result, it was being banned from all spheres of human culture, except from those on which the predominant culture placed no exclusive claim. Ethics and religion were two such areas, which was why it was developing primarily in these two directions, seeking as it did to avoid confrontation.[22] Without a worldview of its own, Kuyper concluded, contemporary Protestantism was powerless to help procure relief from the suffocating effects of the malaise.

It is clear that Kuyper's criticism of these trends was theological, aimed at weaknesses in their intellectual foundations rather than in their practical expressions, for which he reserved some admiration. He insisted that they were based on a theology that undermined the authority of the scriptures, challenged orthodox Christian teaching on sin and redemption, regarded Christ as no more than a religious genius, and indulged in a mysticism opposed to the workings of the intellect. All this was evidence of the extent to which Protestantism had given way to the pantheistic spirit of the age and had made a radical break with true Christianity.[23] Such a theology was utterly powerless to restore modern life to a stable foundation (LC, pp. 182-83). By associ-

22. Kuyper, *Encyclopaedie,* 2nd edition, I, pp. 535-36.
23. Kuyper, *The Antithesis,* p. 11.

ating altruism and mysticism with pantheism Kuyper had once again couched Calvinism's opposition to modern Protestantism in terms of a clash of conflicting underlying principles, even though due recognition had to be given to the latter's practical achievements.

3.2. Roman Catholicism

If Protestantism was unable to provide a remedy to the malaise, could help be expected from Roman Catholicism, which had displayed tremendous energy and vitality in the latter half of the century (LC, p. 183)? Kuyper was keen to point out what a valuable ally Roman Catholicism was in Calvinism's struggle against atheism and pantheism. It was precisely those fundamental Christian doctrines held in common by both traditions, he explained, that were now under attack from modernism: "in this conflict Rome is not an antagonist, but stands on our side" (LC, p. 183). He was not prepared, however, to rely on Roman Catholicism for triumph in this struggle, and the reasons he gave were twofold. First, South America and southern Europe, having been controlled by Roman Catholicism for centuries, both found themselves in a pitiful state of affairs politically, economically, and socially, particularly compared to the situation in Protestant-dominated North America and Northern Europe (LC, pp. 184-85). His second reason was derived from his evolutionary view of world history and religion, discussed in Chapter Four. To look to Roman Catholicism for leadership, he argued, would be to take a step backwards in the process of history: "Rome's world- and life-view represents an older and hence lower stage of development in the history of mankind. Protestantism succeeded it, and hence occupies a spiritually higher standpoint" (LC, p. 186). Here Kuyper combined nineteenth-century ideas of heliotropic development with those of evolutionary theory to defend his claim that Calvinism was a more advanced and thereby superior form of religion than Roman Catholicism. It was an argument formed within the context of the increasing organization and institutionalization within both the orthodox Protestant and Catholic sectors of the Dutch population, such that in almost every area of society reciprocal Protestant and Catholic institutions and organizations developed almost simultaneously. Although this brought with it the desire on both sides for political cooperation and alliance, it also strengthened the sense of competition and rivalry that had characterized relations between Dutch Catholics and Protestants for centuries.

Kuyper was not, however, paying an empty compliment in his admiration of modern Catholicism, and although he made no explicit reference to Dutch Roman Catholicism at Princeton, the appreciation he expressed there for the work done by Catholics in the struggle against modernism stemmed from his close contact with Catholic social and political activity in the Netherlands, as well as his acquaintance with developments within Catholicism in Europe in general. The latter was dominated, just as much as orthodox Protestantism in the Netherlands, by opposition to the forces that drew their strength from the Enlightenment, expressed both in the ultramontane revival and the subsequent rise of Catholic political parties.[24] Kuyper reserved enthusiastic admiration for the efforts of the leaders of these developments in England, N. P. Wiseman (1802-1865) and H. E. Manning (1808-1892), the first two Archbishops of Westminster following the restoration of the Catholic hierarchy in England in 1851 (LC, p. 185). He no doubt felt a certain kinship with them, for they had gone to great lengths to make Roman Catholicism more socially conscious and to bring English Catholics into the full stream of national life, goals towards which Kuyper strove on the part of Dutch Protestants. They also, like Kuyper, concentrated on education as the means to achieve emancipation, and Manning matched the enthusiastic welcome Kuyper gave to Pope Leo XIII's social encyclicals *Immortale Dei* (1885) and *Rerum novarum* (1891).[25] In the Netherlands, likewise, Herman Schaepman, the ultramontane priest and political leader of the Dutch Catholics, saw the need to mobilize political support for Catholic aims, such as the freedom to run their own schools, if the emancipation of Catholics was to succeed, and that this would entail forming a well-organized party with a political program.[26] As he expressed it himself, his aim was "to make Catholics into a political power in the Netherlands" and

24. J. A. Bornewasser, 'Christendom en Aufklärung: over geschiedenis en interpretatie', in *Tussentijds: Theologische Faculteit Tilburg, bundel opstellen bij gelegenheid van haar erkenning*, ed. by H. H. Berger et al. (Tilburg: Hart van Brabant, 1974), pp. 24-45.

25. Kuyper, *Het sociale vraagstuk,* pp. 49-50. Here Kuyper admits: "It must be recognized, to our shame, that Roman Catholics are far ahead of us in the study of the social question, *very* far ahead" (p. 49).

26. Kuyper's cooperation with the Catholics under Schaepman on the Schools Question was discussed in Chapter Two.

"to employ every means to form Catholics into a party-organization."[27] In 1883, three years after becoming the first priest to enter the Dutch parliament, he published a Catholic party program.[28] It insisted on the necessity for a disciplined party organization and an alliance with the Anti-Revolutionaries, rather than the Liberals, if the Catholics were to make any real achievements.[29] *Rerum novarum* was in many ways a vindication of Schaepman's efforts, with its acceptance of the necessity of using the apparatus of modern political and social debate to achieve Catholic objectives.[30] By the end of the century Schaepman had won over most Dutch Catholics to his approach: Catholic trade unions had been founded, effective political organizations had been established at every level, and great achievements had been made in education.[31] In 1887 he succeeded, in collaboration with Kuyper, in securing the extension of the franchise, and a year later the Netherlands' first confessional coalition cabinet that took office, consisting of Anti-Revolutionaries and Catholics.[32] In 1901 Kuyper acted as Prime Minister in the second confessional coalition cabinet that took office. By the turn of the century, therefore, the Dutch Catholic world had replaced conventional ultramontanism with rigorous organizational activity in order to secure for itself a place of freedom within the Dutch state.

Against this background it is understandable that Kuyper should have seen Roman Catholicism as a valuable ally in obtaining the objectives towards which he worked throughout his career. He was conscious of the fact that, without the support of Catholics, his objectives, particularly in the field of education, had little chance of success. It was not his concept of the pluriformity of the church, therefore, that inspired the accommodating attitude towards Roman Catholicism he expressed in his final Stone Lec-

27. The quotations are from Schaepman's letters to Willem Nuyens (co-editor with Schaepman of the journal *De Wachter*), 2 December 1881 and 4 March 1884, cited in G. Puchinger, *Ontmoetingen met Nederlandse politici* (Zutphen: Terra, 1981), p. 25.

28. Hermanus Johannes Aloysius Maria Schaepman, *Eene katholieke partij; proeve van een program* (Utrecht: Van Rossum, 1883).

29. Schaepman, *Eene katholieke partij,* p. 67.

30. Michael Wintle, *Pillars of Piety: Religion in the Netherlands in the Nineteenth Century, 1813-1901* (Hull: Hull University Press, 1987), p. 50.

31. In 1896 Schaepman managed to unite Dutch Catholics in the *Rooms-Katholieke Staatspartij* (Roman Catholic National Party), whose social program was based on the guidelines given in *Rerum novarum.*

32. In 1888 the parliament of 100 members had 26 Roman Catholics, 27 anti-revolutionaries, and one conservative, making possible the coalition cabinet under the anti-revolutionary Aeneas baron Mackay.

ture, but his pragmatism in striving towards specific social and political goals. This pragmatism, and that of Schaepman, was of considerable historical significance, as it laid the basis for the cooperation between Protestant and Catholic parties which has dominated Dutch politics for most of the twentieth century, and gave rise to the politically powerful Christian Democratic representation in the Dutch parliament. The fact that in Princeton Kuyper couched his appreciation of modern Catholicism in terms of its value as an alliance partner against the modernistic spirit of the age, rather than as an aide in the achievement of political emancipation for the orthodox Protestants, is to be understood as part of his attempt to encourage a sense of the scale and scope of the struggle against modernism, and of its principled character. Although Catholicism was unable to provide a remedy for the malaise, its principles were antagonistic to those of modernism and were thus a support to the objectives of Calvinism.

4. The Only Effective Solution

At the start of his lectures Kuyper had explained that his purpose would be to present Calvinism as "the only decisive, lawful, and consistent defence for Protestant nations against encroaching, and overwhelming Modernism" (LC, p. 12). It was in keeping with this purpose that at the end of his lectures he argued, by way of conclusion, that the only hope of a recovery from the malaise was a "return to Calvinism" (LC, p. 190). But what did Kuyper envisage in such a return? Clearly he did not mean a return to Reformed creeds, in the hope of establishing a single Reformed church organization — this would have been in conflict with his idea of the pluriformity of the church and of the universality of Calvinism's relevance. He declared:

> I am far from cherishing so crude, so ignorant, so unhistorical a desire. . . . Such an identification of my program with the absorption of one Church by another would be at variance with the whole tendency of my argument. Not ecclesiastically, confined to a narrow circle, but as a phenomenon of universal significance, have I commended to you the Calvinism of history. (LC, pp. 191, 192)

Kuyper reduced to four points what he believed this return to Calvinism would entail. As summarizing and concluding points, they reflect both Kuyper's principal objectives in lecturing at Princeton and, due to the summary nature of the *Lectures,* the four leading tenets in his overall program. All four points have featured in various ways in previous chapters, but the way they are presented in Kuyper's final lecture demands further attention.

First, Calvinism should no longer be ignored where it existed, but strengthened in places where its historical influence was still evident. In making this request, Kuyper was making a petition to his American audience in particular, for the United States was just the kind of place he had in mind — a country, he believed, in which the historical influence of Calvinism was indisputable. Although its influence in contemporary America was under threat, Calvinism's residual workings could still be detected, for instance, in the tradition of opening prayers in the Houses of Congress and in the schools, in the decentralized and autonomous character of local government, in the esteem in which women were held, in the championship of free speech, and in the freedom of conscience (LC, pp. 192-93).

Kuyper's aim in underlining the Calvinistic origin of these and other social virtues was to challenge the popular idea, particularly prevalent amongst nineteenth-century liberals, that these virtues were derived from the humanism of the French Revolution. The same aim motivated his argument in *De Standaard* in 1901, where he criticized his liberal political opponents for basing their opposition to the Christian coalition cabinet on the assumption that history began with the birth of modern liberalism.[33] Once again, however, more seems to have been at stake for Kuyper than the correct interpretation of history. He saw the attempt to "humanize" the origins of modern civilization as part of a large-scale effort to "divert the current of life into French revolutionary or German-pantheistic channels" (LC, p. 193). This concern was, of course, grounded in his idea of the continually evolving stream of human life, which had reached its high point in Calvinism. Now it was being diverted along the inevitably degenerative lines of modern humanism. It is this aspect of Kuyper's thought that is likely to explain why, despite his stress on the universal significance of the Calvinistic worldview, he appears to lack any vision for the potential of Calvinism outside those geographical areas in which it had already enjoyed significant influence. There is, for instance, no call for Calvinism to be introduced in those countries or areas that had hitherto escaped its influence. He certainly allowed for the possibility that the benefits of Calvinism, once recognized and renewed, could be carried further westwards by the stream of history

33. *De Standaard,* 6 September 1901.

from their current resting place on the Pacific coast of North America (LC, p. 34). But there is no indication that the Calvinistic worldview should be introduced, or Calvinistic activity encouraged, on a global scale, and indeed in introducing his Stone Lectures he explained that his purpose was to present Calvinism as the only defense of *Protestant* nations against the threat of modernism (LC, p. 12). In spite of his insistence on Calvinism's universal scope and relevance, which he ascribed to the universality of God's ordinances, upon which Calvinism was based, when it came to translating the Calvinistic vision into practical activity he was only prepared to consider doing so in areas defined by the Calvinistic stage in the process of historical development. This apparent discrepancy is part of the more fundamental tension in Kuyper's thought between his "universalistic" and "particularistic" tendencies, which surfaced in his treatments of science and art at Princeton, and will be returned to briefly later in this chapter.

What Kuyper actually meant by the strengthening of Calvinism where its remains could be found was not spelled out. Given, however, the contents of his previous lectures, he is likely to have meant the reinforcing of a Calvinistic perspective in the various spheres of life. In countries such as the United States, the Netherlands, and England, the Calvinistic influences left behind by history presented themselves to him as the neglected foundations of modern civilization, demanding urgent consolidation and support.

Kuyper's second request was that Calvinism's principles should be rediscovered by means of diligent historical study and built into a coherent system of thought. This, he believed, had not yet been undertaken, as Calvinism had never received systematic expression, not even in its original formulations:

> Since Calvinism arose not from an abstract system, but from life itself, it was never, in the century of its prime, presented as a systematic whole. The tree blossomed and yielded its fruit, but without any one having made a botanic study of its nature and growth. Calvinism, in its rise, rather acted than argued. But now this study may no longer be delayed. Both the biography and biology of Calvinism must now be thoroughly investigated and thought out. (LC, p. 194)[34]

34. The importance Kuyper attached to a thorough study of historical Calvinism is underlined by the fact that he repeated the plea in a series of fourteen

Kuyper had good grounds for his assertion that original Calvinism was not presented in a systematized form. Two recent monographs on John Calvin, by William Bouwsma and Alister McGrath, point out that the commonly held notion that Calvin was a systematic theologian in the sense that he aimed at arranging Christian theology into a coherent and unified "system" has no grounding in history and reflects a later preference for system in the Reformed theological tradition.[35] Kuyper certainly shared this preference, and his desire to formulate Calvinism in terms of a coherent "life-system" derived from a single, unifying principle reflects the extent to which he was influenced by nineteenth-century monism. As McGrath points out, the very idea of a "central dogma" in Calvin's religious thought has its origins in the monistic thought of the Enlightenment, rather than in the theology of the sixteenth century.[36] The influence of such monism exerted itself most directly on Kuyper through the work of J. H. Scholten, whose predilection for system, coherence, and principle in his approach to Reformed theology never ceased to impress Kuyper, despite his opposition to the contents of Scholten's theology.[37]

Kuyper's aim in encouraging a thorough study of Calvinism was not only in order that it might acquire systematic form. It was also so that, having "lost its place in the hearts of the people . . . the outside world may come to know it" (LC, pp. 192, 193). Publicizing Calvinism was, of course, something Kuyper pursued with vigor, not only in his writings on church history and theology, but in his politics, his aesthetics, his ideas on science, and in his journalism. Although he was advocating, in the first instance, serious scholarly research, it is clear that he expected the results of this kind of study to increase the knowledge and credibility of Calvinism outside its own direct circle. This was an expression of his

---

articles in *De Heraut* titled "The Task of the Future" *('De taak der toekomst')*, published in 1899 and 1900.

35. William J. Bouwsma, *John Calvin: A Sixteenth Century Portrait* (New York: Oxford University Press, 1988), p. 5; Alister E. McGrath, *A Life of John Calvin: A Study in the Shaping of Western Culture* (Oxford: Basil Blackwell, 1990), pp. 147-48.

36. McGrath writes: "there is no 'hard core,' no 'basic principle,' no 'central premise,' no 'essence' of Calvin's religious thought." McGrath, *A Life of John Calvin*, p. 149. A similar case is made in C. Partee, "Calvin's Central Dogma Again," *Sixteenth Century Journal* 18 (1987): 191-99.

37. Gerrit Brillenburg Wurth, *J. H. Scholten als systematisch theoloog* ('s-Gravenhage: Van Haeringen, 1927), p. 197. See also Chapter Two of this book.

desire to see an improvement in the standing of Calvinism in the eyes of the world at large, even though this was not coupled with an expectation that new converts would be gained. The strengthening and consolidation of Calvinism by means of rigorous academic work would increase the reverence in which Calvinism was held, and this in turn would help facilitate its social program. In this sense, Kuyper's vision for the future of Calvinism was influenced by his role as leader of a movement for the social and intellectual emancipation of the Calvinistic sector. Serious research into historical Calvinism would not only help to discover its principles, but would demonstrate to the non-Calvinist world its right to self-expression in society at large.

Kuyper's third request is of considerable importance to an understanding of the Stone Lectures, and of Kuyper's thought as a whole: "the development of the principles of Calvinism in accordance with the needs of our modern consciousness, and their application to every department of life" (LC, p. 194). Once again it was Scholten who first drew Kuyper's attention to the need for Calvinism to be made relevant to contemporary modes of thought, an objective Kuyper claimed had motivated all his work.[38] It is this self-confessed objective that provided the starting point for the discussion in this book, which centers on the question of how Kuyper's thought was related to the social and intellectual environment at the end of the nineteenth century. It was an objective, once put into practice, that brought Kuyper severe criticism from would-be followers and opponents alike, who reproached him for having broken with traditional Calvinism. Not only conservative Protestants, but modernistic theologians such as B. D. Eerdmans and C. B. Hylkema, condemned Kuyper's "Modern Orthodoxy" or "Neo-Calvinism" for giving totally new meanings to traditional Reformed concepts. Eerdmans even went so far as to declare:

> Through Kuyper's influence a large sector of our nation is brought to a new way of thinking, and to the acceptance of ideas, which it will probably hear from no one but from him. Dr. Kuyper is a man of "progress." . . . But his theology is not Reformed. That he presents it as such is one of the means by which this progress is achieved. Without doing so his followers would lose faith in him.[39]

38. Kuyper, *Encylopaedie,* 2nd edition, I, p. vi.

39. B. D. Eerdmans, 'De theologie van Dr. A. Kuyper', *Theologisch Tijdschrift* 43 (1909): 209-37 (237).

Ernst Troeltsch, who, as noted in Chapter One, billed Kuyper's *Lectures* the *"Manifest des modernen Calvinismus,"* claimed that "in all these questions [pluriformity of the church and political pluralism] Neo-Calvinism has drifted far away from Calvin — a fact which Kuyper tried in vain to conceal."[40] Hendrikus Berkhof has pointed out that this criticism of Kuyper is unfounded, and he attributes it to Troeltsch's unfamiliarity with Kuyper's Dutch works, in which Kuyper explains his distance from Calvin.[41] Berkhof's argument is weakened by the fact that he fails to cite instances from Kuyper's works to support his claim, and it is important to emphasize that any distance Kuyper did acknowledge between his ideas and those of Calvin was only in terms of the application of Calvin's theology to questions that had not yet arisen in Calvin's day.[42] Kuyper never expressed a desire to add to or to take away from Calvin or traditional Calvinism, but only that, in dealing with the epistemological questions raised by Protestant philosophers since Kant, a modern Calvinistic theory of knowledge needed to be developed.[43]

It was not only in the area of philosophy, however, that Calvinism had to undergo modernization. Calvinism had to be brought up-to-date and made relevant through the application of its principles in all scientific disciplines. Kuyper's confidence in the viability of this undertaking was based on his belief that all the human sciences could be reduced to underlying principles. The modernization of Calvinism with respect to the sciences would therefore begin with the question of whether the principles currently employed in the methodology of these sciences were "in agreement with the principles of Calvinism, or were at variance with their very essence" (LC, p. 194). It was Kuyper's firm conviction that these principles were in direct contradiction to those of Calvinism, a conviction that helped to motivate his idea of two kinds of science.

Kuyper's fourth and final request was something of a postscript, albeit of no lesser importance than the preceding three: that those who

40. Ernst Troeltsch, *The Social Teaching of the Christian Churches,* 2 vols., trans. by Olive Wyon (New York: Harper & Row, 1960), II, p. 676.

41. Hendrikus Berkhof, *Two Hundred Years of Theology,* p. 109.

42. See *Publicatie van den Senaat der Vrije Universiteit, in zake het onderzoek ter bepaling van den weg die tot de kennis der Gereformeerde beginselen leidt* (Amsterdam: Wormser, 1895), pp. 13-14. Although this publication was officially written by the Senate of the Free University, the style and contents are characteristic of Kuyper, who was one of the Senate's members.

43. *Publicatie van den Senaat,* p. 14.

subscribed to the Calvinistic faith should cease to be ashamed of their confession, but should find the courage to put into practice "in word, deed, and whole manner of life" what they confessed to be true (LC, p. 195). This was Kuyper's final summons for a strident and self-confident Calvinism, undeterred by the stigma often attached to it. Conscious of the immense benefit it had been historically to both the church and the world, Calvinism was to lift its head up high in the face of all mounting opposition. It was a plea that encapsulated much of what Kuyper hoped to achieve in visiting the United States, and it demonstrates the extent to which his message was formulated as a response to the way he believed Calvinism was normally perceived, which involved an underestimation of its relevance to the areas of human life outside the church. He aimed to replace a feeling of insignificance and low self-esteem with a sense of historical pride, and confidence in the value of a worldview based firmly on Calvinistic principles.

Kuyper's four requests reflect the causes for which he worked during most of his career. As such they form a kind of "autobiographical program" — Kuyper himself had sought to strengthen Calvinism where it already existed, particularly through his journalism and political leadership in the Netherlands; he had made Calvinism a subject of intense study, and had done much to publicize it; he had attempted to modernize it and apply it to the various spheres of life outside the church, founding the Free University and organizing the ARP with this specific purpose in mind; and he had encouraged his followers in the churches of the *Doleantie* to be consciously and unashamedly Calvinistic.

5. Optimistic or Pessimistic?

Kuyper's argument that Calvinism was the only effective remedy for a situation of widespread malaise does not necessarily imply that he believed Calvinism would in actual fact bring about a significant turn of events. Although, as noted above, he admitted at the start of his Stone Lectures that his aim would be to demonstrate that Calvinism held out a blessing and a hope for the future, he did not indicate whether he believed this blessing would ever be realized in practice. This raises the question whether his perception of the future was optimistic or pessimistic. It is a question that has recently taken on added significance with the publication of two doctoral dissertations, by R. Kuiper and Chris

A. J. van Koppen (introduced in Chapter One). Whereas Kuiper argues that Kuyper's nationalism, based on his vision of the Netherlands as a Calvinistic country, stressed in optimistic and even triumphalist tones the role of the Netherlands in the international situation, van Koppen maintains that this same vision inspired a "heartfelt pessimism about the future of the Netherlands." Kuyper believed, van Koppen argues, that Dutch Calvinism had had its day, and after enjoying its high point between 1572 and 1795, was now in a state of terminal decline. The Netherlands was therefore doomed to disappear from the international scene, most likely through annexation by Germany.[44]

It is important to emphasize in addressing this debate that Kuyper, in arguing for a return to Calvinism, did not predict that such a return would entail the adoption of Calvinistic doctrine by large numbers of people. To do so would have jeopardized both his belief in the pluriformity of the church, which he considered both inevitable and desirable, and his argument that "the Calvinistic confession is so deeply religious, so highly spiritual that, excepting always periods of profound religious commotion, it will never be realized by the large masses, but will impress with a sense of its inevitability only on a relatively small circle" (LC, p. 191). For Kuyper the quality of the Calvinistic faith was far more important than the quantity of those who embraced it, a fact which probably reflects his disappointment that the *Doleantie* had not attracted a greater number of supporters.

All this only concerns, however, the fate of Calvinism as a church confession, and not as a worldview possessing transforming power outside the ecclesiastical sphere. How did Kuyper expect this worldview to fare in the age-long struggle between Christianity and paganism? There is a note of alarm and *angst* in Kuyper's perception of the future course of this conflict, and it has to do with what he saw as the rise of the Asian races. He took this development to be a sign that the final conflict prophesied in the Book of Revelation may be imminent:

> A closely drawn curtain hides the future; but Christ has prophesied to us on Patmos the approach of a last and bloody conflict, and even

44. R. Kuiper, *Zelfbeeld en wereldbeeld: antirevolutionairen en het buitenland, 1848-1905* (Kampen: Kok, 1992), pp. 243-48; Chris A. J. van Koppen, *De Geuzen van de negentiende eeuw: Abraham Kuyper en Zuid-Afrika* (Wormer: Immerc, 1992), pp. 233-36 (235).

> now Japan's gigantic development in less than forty years has filled Europe with fear for what calamity might be in store for us from the cunning "yellow race" forming so large a proportion of the human family. . . . The Asiatic question is in fact of most serious import. (LC, p. 198)

The significance Kuyper attached to Asia in terms of the future was not only stimulated by his views on racial intermingling or his interest in world developments, which always remained keen, but was an example of the influence of the myth of heliotropic development on his understanding of history. The development of humanity and civilization, accordingly, which had begun in Asia, would also reach its final climax on that continent, having circled the globe in a westwards direction. Kuyper would probably have been less concerned about the pagan threat from Asia, particularly from Japan, had he had more confidence in the state in which Christianity found itself at the end of the nineteenth century. As it was, however, contemporary Christian thought was full of the very pagan ideals and aspirations espoused by its opponents (LC, p. 198). He therefore refrained, when he came to concluding his lectures, from exhorting his audience to move out into the battle against the forces of paganism. He certainly employed the military imagery of a conflict of diametrically opposed principles, which he had used to effect earlier in his lectures, but at the conclusion of the series he sounded no note of triumphalism, and the imagery used was more of defense than of attack; he claimed, for instance, to know of "no firmer bulwark than Calvinism" against encroaching paganism (LC, p. 199). Indeed, he justified his uncertainty as to the future prospects of Calvinism by claiming that it was up to God's sovereign will alone "whether or not the tide of religious life rise high in one century, and run to a low ebb in the next." Unless, therefore, "God send forth His Spirit," the present low ebb of religious life would decline yet further "and fearfully rapid would be the descent of the waters" (LC, p. 199). What mattered, he argued, was preparedness, and attentiveness to the movement of God's spirit:

> You remember the Aeolian Harp, which men were wont to place outside their casement, that the breeze might wake its music into life. Until the wind blew, the harp remained silent, while, again, even though the wind arose, if the harp did not lie in readiness, a rustling of the breeze might be heard, but not a single note of ethereal music delighted the ear. Now, let Calvinism be nothing but such an Aeolian

> Harp,— absolutely powerless, as it is, without the quickening Spirit of God— still we feel it our God-given duty to keep our harp, its strings tuned aright, ready in the window of God's Holy Zion, awaiting the breath of the Spirit. (LC, p. 199)

With these words Kuyper ended his Stone Lectures. It remains a somewhat surprising ending, particularly given the four points he had just made, and the fact that much of his argument in the preceding lectures had been intended to inspire vigorous activity. The offensive line of his earlier argument appears to have been exchanged for a passive— one might almost say "quietistic"— awaiting of the breath of the Holy Spirit. Given, however, the context of this passage, it is likely that what Kuyper meant by keeping the strings "tuned aright" on the Aeolian Harp of Calvinism, was the carrying out of the kind of activity he had advocated in his lectures and given in summary form in his final lecture: a strengthening of Calvinism where it already existed; Calvinism's systematization and publication; its modernization, and an application of its principles to all areas of life; a restoration of courage and self-confidence among those who subscribed to a Calvinist confession. However, while this kind of activity would doubtless serve to strengthen specifically Calvinistic culture, Kuyper failed to hold out any assurance that the potential of Calvinism to brighten the future prospects of general culture would be realized in practice.

The same lack is found in other publications by Kuyper that express his vision of the future. These emphasize Calvinism's vocation to spread its benefits to the wider world, but at the same time entertain little hope that the fulfillment of this vocation would bring about a lasting deliverance from the malaise in non-Calvinistic culture. In *De gemeene gratie,* for instance, written around the same time as the Stone Lectures, Kuyper explained that, unlike earlier periods of decline in history, the current situation represented a permanent and universal decline into apostasy, which would culminate in the appearance of the Antichrist.[45] He was optimistic, in contrast, about the vitality, dynamism, and prospects of

45. Kuyper, *De gemeene gratie,* I, pp. 415-25, 431, 432; II, p. 412. Other examples of Kuyper's pessimism regarding general human culture can be found in his *Encyclopaedie,* III, p. 340; *Pro Rege,* III, pp. 350-53; *Predicatiën,* pp. 14-15; *Welke zijn de vooruitzichten voor de studenten der Vrije Universiteit?* (Amsterdam: Kruyt, 1882), pp. 28, 29; *Maranatha: rede ter inleiding van de deputaten-vergadering gehouden te Utrecht op 12 mei 1891* (Amsterdam: Wormser, 1891), pp. 6-8.

Calvinism itself. In 1872 he wrote: "Calvinism is livening up, is branching out its roots, is becoming a powerful force."[46] Two years later he reported that "our Calvinism is alive and contains the power of development," and in 1891 that Calvinism in the Netherlands had "trebled in strength," and had once again become a power to be reckoned with. Its vitality would be preserved in future generations because, in accordance with traditional Calvinistic practice, it would be invested in organizations based on Reformed principles.[47] Even after the high point of his career, Kuyper's optimism about the future of Dutch Calvinism continued unabated. In a speech in 1912 he explained how the Calvinistic sector of the Dutch population had been delivered, like the Israelites in Egypt, from its bondage to liberalism, and was now well on its way to its promised land.[48]

It would seem, therefore, that Kuyper's pessimism about life outside the Calvinistic camp was matched by his optimism about life within it. Despite his generally confident and triumphalist attitude towards Calvinism's potential for the transformation of culture, when it came to considering its ability to bring about actual change on a broad scale he was defensive, and modest in his expectations. He seems even to have encouraged an attitude which, if not quietistic, certainly seems to come close to being introspective, and hesitant in its engagement with the world outside the Calvinistic circle. Although he was keen to increase the significance of Calvinism in the spheres of society outside the church, and thus to contribute towards a remedy for the all-pervading malaise, he does not seem to have entertained any expectation that this would make a significant difference to the general state of modern European culture, which was in irrevocable decline. This tension between optimistic and pessimistic strands in Kuyper's teaching helps explain the discrepancy between the interpretations of Kuiper and van Koppen, noted earlier. Kuiper's analysis considers Kuyper's perception of the vocation of the Netherlands, as a Calvinistic nation, in the wider world,

46. *De Standaard,* 1 November 1872.

47. Kuyper, "Calvinism: The Origin and Safeguard," p. 674; *De Standaard,* 19 October 1891.

48. A. Kuyper, *Uit het diensthuis geleid* (Kampen: Kok, 1912), pp. 7, 16-18. See also *Der jongelingen sieraad is hun kracht: feestrede bij het jubileum van den Bond van Gereformeerde Jongelingsvereenigingen op 30 april 1913 te 's-Gravenhage gehouden* (Kampen: Kok, 1913), pp. 3, 21, 23.

a perception that was characterized by unbridled optimism. Van Koppen is concerned more with Kuyper's vision of the actual realities of the future situation in the Netherlands and Europe, which, because of the decline of Calvinistic influence since the rise of liberalism, was decidedly pessimistic.

Kuyper's optimism regarding the future of Calvinistic culture and his pessimism about the prospects of non-Calvinistic culture also helps to explain two important aspects of his message to America discussed earlier in this book. The first is his plea that American Calvinists should end their "love affair" with Enlightenment science and develop instead their own kind of science within their own scientific institutions.[49] Only by developing an independent scientific culture would Calvinistic science be free from the general demise of science. This position would not have impressed Warfield, not only because he insisted on the unity of science but because he believed in the final triumph of Christianity in the realm of science (as in all areas of human culture). In voicing his criticism of Kuyper and Bavinck he argued that the effects of regeneration in the world would continue to increase, to the extent that the reason of the regenerate, employed in the pursuit of science, would ultimately conquer the whole of human life.[50] This triumph would be due to the influence of Calvinism, which was able to offer bright prospects for the future of human culture: "Calvinism thus emerges to our sight as nothing more or less than the hope of the world."[51]

The second aspect is his buoyant tone about the future of the United States.[52] Whereas in the Netherlands and Europe the high point of Calvinism was a thing of the past, in the United States there was still a real possibility that a revived Calvinism would be able to influence the

49. See Chapter Seven. Kuyper's pessimism regarding the prospects of non-Calvinistic science is particularly evident in his *Encyclopaedie.* Despite the great advances in scientific knowledge and expertise, increasing naturalism, materialism, and epicurism would eventually result in the demise of science (*Encyclopaedie,* III, p. 340).

50. This helps explain Warfield's confidence in the value of apologetics, discussed in Chapter Five. *Princeton Theological Review* 1 (1903): 138-43 (146-47).

51. B. B. Warfield, "Calvin as a Theologian" — a collection of addresses given in 1909 and published as an appendix to Warfield's *Calvin and Augustine,* ed. by Samuel G. Craig (Philadelphia: The Presbyterian and Reformed Publishing Company, 1956), pp. 481-507 (507).

52. See Chapter Three.

course of this young and vibrant country, which after all had been founded on Calvinistic principles. This idea is likely to have inspired his argument, expressed with particular poignance in his speech in Holland, Michigan, that the future development of Calvinistic principles lay not in Europe but in America, and that America's prospects of a bright future were guaranteed by the operation of these principles.

It is worth pointing out, finally, that Kuyper's doubts concerning the prospects of Calvinism outside the bounds of its historical influence, his emphasis on the smallness of Calvinism's future following, and his defensiveness and introspection when it came to considering its actual influence outside its own circle, may well have contributed to the formation of a Calvinistic "pillar" in Dutch society, and thus to the pattern of *verzuiling.* It is, in any case, likely that his argument fostered a "pillarized" *("verzuild")* mentality, which accepted isolation and internal cohesion rather than "horizontal" engagement and influence. The fact that his pessimistic vision of Calvinism's future influence coexisted with arguments that laid claim to Calvinism's potential to transform the whole of human culture points to the fundamental tension in Kuyper's thought — a recurrent theme throughout this book, and expressed at its most basic level in the dichotomy between his ideas of antithesis and of common grace. The final passage of the Stone Lectures is added evidence that this was a tension Kuyper himself was unable to resolve.

Conclusion

As several important conclusions have already been drawn in the previous two sections, it remains only to point out that Kuyper's final lecture highlights the extent to which he was influenced by trends in contemporary thought and culture. Although he was severely critical of pessimism, for instance, particularly in its anarchistic and nihilistic manifestations, he was obviously affected by the *fin de siècle* mentality, to the extent both of endorsing Nietzsche's cry of despair about the circumstances of his time and of presenting a negative vision of the future of European culture. His admiration for and criticism of the altruistic and mystical tendencies demonstrate his particular interest in movements with an intellectual and a popular expression. His appreciation of contemporary developments in Roman Catholicism points to his pragmatism when it came to finding potential allies in the struggle against the spirit of the age. His enthusiastic advocacy of the systematization and modernization of Calvinism betrays the influence of the kind of monistic thought that was typical of much nineteenth-century theology. His idea that humanity and religion developed in a westward direction towards its final destination in Asia was an expression of nineteenth-century ideas on evolutionary and heliotropic development. Even his desire to give the impression, reflected in the title of the lecture, that Calvinism had a vision of the future is indicative of the extent to which he was influenced by the idea of progress. The lecture itself shows, however, that Kuyper was too preoccupied with the present to become distracted by speculations about the future.

Conclusion

Before drawing some final conclusions it is fitting that we should end the discussion of the Stone Lectures by giving some consideration to their reception in the United States. As Chapter Three makes clear, Kuyper himself was received by his American audiences with jubilant appreciation, but as yet no attention has been paid, in this book or elsewhere, to reactions towards the Lectures following their publication. The result of this enquiry will help to indicate whether or not Kuyper succeeded in getting his message across, or whether it fell on deaf ears, especially once the excitement of his visit had died down. Another question that warrants brief discussion is that of the direction of future research on Kuyper. Several new and significant areas deserving of detailed investigation have been uncovered in this book, but for reasons of space have not been developed here. Much historical and theological research on Kuyper remains to be done; Kuyper studies are still in their infancy.

1. Reception of the *Lectures*

1.1. Warfield

The analysis of Kuyper's position *vis-à-vis* Warfield would not be complete without some examination both of Warfield's reaction to the

Stone Lectures, and of their influence on his thought. Not only was Warfield the most eminent and influential member of Kuyper's Princeton audience, but the comparisons made in this book between his and Kuyper's views have provided fruitful means of situating Kuyper's ideas within the theological and intellectual context of his times.

Contrary to what might be expected, if only the difference between Warfield and Kuyper on the relationship between faith and rationality and its repercussions for apologetics and science are taken into account, Warfield was very enthusiastic indeed about Kuyper's Stone Lectures. Having had a hand in the preparation of the proofs, he was familiar with their contents before they were given, but even so he regretted not being able to attend one of the series.[1] He valued in particular the breadth and scope of Kuyper's thought, and he felt a great affinity with its general drift. In the Lectures, Warfield wrote, Kuyper had expounded "with the utmost breadth and forcefulness the fundamental principles of Calvinism," thus becoming "one of our own prophets, to whose message we have a certain right."[2] Only two years after the publication of his two critical discussions of Bavinck and Kuyper's views on science and human reason, Warfield wrote to Kuyper:

> I have always delighted in your theological writings: the point of view from which you survey doctrine is so high and the prospect you take is so wide, — the richness of your thought, the comprehensiveness of your grasp, and the broad sweep of your mind, as you deal with these high themes, are ever my delight and admiration. There are minor matters, of course, in which I should take issue with your constructions: but these are mere nothings. — I rejoice I feel myself in full accord with the great march of your thought and I never consult your books without deriving from them both instruction and inspiration.[3]

Such a positive response to Kuyper's work, despite the admission of some disagreement, lay behind the invitation Kuyper received in 1912 from Warfield and his Princeton colleagues to return to Princeton later that year to give an address at the centenary celebrations of the founding of

1. Letter from Warfield to Kuyper, 19 October 1898. KA; *Brieven,* no. 6271.

2. Warfield's "Introduction" to *The Work of the Holy Spirit* by A. Kuyper (New York: Funk & Wagnalls, 1900), pp. xxv-xxxiv (xxv, xxvi).

3. Letter from Warfield to Kuyper, 15 April 1905. KA; *Brieven,* no. 7053. Warfield's criticisms of Kuyper and Bavinck were discussed in Chapter Seven.

the Theological Seminary.[4] As late as 1919, twenty-one years after the event, Warfield was still complimenting Kuyper on his "thoroughly admirable and wide-minded Stone Lectures."[5] It is clear, therefore, that Warfield was among those deeply impressed by the Stone Lectures and the general theological position they represented.

But did Warfield allow his admiration for Kuyper's understanding of Calvinism to influence his own thoughts on that subject? In exploring this question it has to be borne in mind that although Warfield was a prolific theologian within the Calvinistic tradition, he did not pay as much attention to the subject of Calvinism as did Kuyper, the main corpus of his work covering the fields of biblical interpretation and apologetics. However, in Warfield's most significant and poignant treatments of Calvinism, published in 1908 and 1909, Kuyper's influence is so evident that it almost takes the form of plagiarism.[6] In the first of these treatments he sought to define Calvinism, and did so in almost exactly the same way as Kuyper did in his first Stone Lecture. Calvinism was far broader, he wrote, than merely the teachings of John Calvin or the theology of the Reformed churches, as it encompassed:

> the entire body of conceptions, theological, ethical, philosophical, social, political, which, under the influence of the master mind of John Calvin, raised itself to dominance in the Protestant lands of the post-Reformation age, and has left a permanent mark not only upon the thought of mankind, but upon the life-history of men, the social order of civilized peoples, and even the political organization of states.[7]

He also followed Kuyper in claiming that the central source of Calvinism was a specific type of religious consciousness, from which emanated a particular type of theology and a particular ecclesiastical, social, and political organization:

4. Letter from Warfield to Kuyper, 18 January 1912. KA; *Brieven,* no. 7851. Kuyper was obliged to decline the invitation because of prior commitments. See Letter from Warfield to Kuyper, 16 February 1912. KA; *Brieven,* no. 7854.

5. Letter from Warfield to Kuyper, 7 November 1919. KA; *Brieven,* no. 8620.

6. B. B. Warfield, "Calvinism," in *The New Schaff-Herzog Encyclopedia of Religious Knowledge,* ed. by Samuel Macauley Johnson (New York: Funk and Wagnalls, 1908); Warfield, "Calvin as a Theologian" [1909], published as an appendix to B. B. Warfield, *Calvin and Augustine,* ed. by Samuel G. Craig (Philadelphia: Presbyterian and Reformed, 1956).

7. Warfield, "Calvinism," p. 353.

> Although Calvinism has dug a channel through which not merely flows a stream of theological thought, but also surges a wave of human life — filling the heart with fresh ideals and conceptions which have revolutionized the conditions of existence — yet its fountain-head lies in its . . . religious consciousness. For the roots of Calvinism are planted in a specific religious attitude, out of which is unfolded first a particular theology, from which springs on one hand a special church organization, and on the other a social order, involving a given political arrangement.[8]

The extent to which Warfield was borrowing here, almost word-for-word, from the *Lectures* is apparent when the above quote is compared with the following passage from Kuyper:

> Calvinism is rooted in a form of religion which was peculiarly its own, and from this specific religious consciousness there was developed first a peculiar theology, then a special church-order, and then a given form for political and social life. . . . Calvinism made its appearance . . . to populate the world of the human heart with different ideals and conceptions. (LC, p. 17)

Warfield was also indebted to Kuyper's Stone Lectures for his argument that Calvinism represented the purest, and thereby the most superior and advanced, form of religion. In unequivocal terms he declared: "Calvinism conceives of itself as simply the more pure theism, religion, evangelicalism, superseding as such the less pure."[9] A year later, in the second of the two publications mentioned above, he developed the same argument further. There he went as far as to deny that there were many varieties, or kinds, of religion, within which Calvinism presented itself as a viable option. He insisted, instead, that there was only one type, within which Calvinism was the most perfect expression; apparent varieties of religion were merely better or worse expressions of the same thing. Although, in contrast to Kuyper, his argument does not resort to themes borrowed from the idea of heliotropic development, his notion of a development in religion from less pure to purer forms shows remarkable resemblance to Kuyper's argument in the Stone Lectures.[10]

8. Warfield, "Calvinism," p. 354.
9. Warfield, "Calvinism," p. 356.
10. Warfield, "Calvin as a Theologian," pp. 492-93, 497. The influence of the heliotropic myth on Kuyper's thought was introduced in Chapter Three.

Warfield was also borrowing from Kuyper in suggesting that, because Calvinism was "religion at the height of its conception," it offered the best prospects for the future of Christianity.[11]

These four ideas — that Calvinism represented a broad movement in society and culture, not restricted to the church or doctrine; that it emanated outwards from its central source in the religious consciousness; that this religious consciousness represented the purest and most advanced stage in the development of religion; and that Calvinism offered the best prospects for the future of Christianity — are key concepts in Kuyper's thought, and they received their clearest and most coherent expression in the Stone Lectures. Warfield's use of them indicates that, although he failed to acknowledge it, his perception of Calvinism was largely indebted to Kuyper's exposition of it at Princeton. This helps to explain why Kuyper's influence in North America, as Hendrikus Berkhof has pointed out, has worked partly *through* the Princeton Theology (rather than merely in opposition to it), despite the division of the Kuyperian and Princetonian schools on key issues of epistemology.[12] There is evidence, in fact, that despite this division, Warfield was partly persuaded by Kuyper's insistence on the radical influence of worldview on scientific enterprise. In his review of Orr's published Stone Lectures for the academic year 1903-4, Warfield spoke in glowing terms of Orr's notion of an irreconcilable conflict between the Christian and the modernistic or "evolutionary" view of the world.[13] He praised Orr for having the courage "to recognize and assert the irreconcilableness of the two views and the impossibility of a compromise between them; and to undertake the task of showing that the Christian view in the forum of science itself is the only tenable one."[14] Three years on from publishing his criticisms of Kuyper's views on science, it appears, therefore, that Warfield came round to acquiescing in Kuyper's view — a view that owed much to James Orr in the way it was formulated at Princeton. The

11. Warfield, "Calvin as a Theologian," p. 497.

12. Hendrikus Berkhof, *Two Hundred Years of Theology,* p. 109.

13. B. B. Warfield, review of James Orr's *God's Image in Man, and Its Defacement, in the Light of Modern Denials* (London: Hodder and Stoughton, 1905), *The Princeton Theological Review* 4 (1906): 555-58.

14. Warfield, review of Orr, *God's Image in Man,* p. 555. The well-known American Evangelical theologian Gresham Machen (1881-1937), who was a former pupil of Warfield and a close adviser, made much of the same division of worldviews in his work. See, for instance, his *Christianity and Liberalism* (New York: Macmillan, 1923).

transformation was not, of course, complete, and Warfield continued to defend the value of apologetics in scientific debate. He did so, however, in more sober, less triumphalistic tones, and began to lay greater stress on the testimony of the Holy Spirit in his approach to scripture. [15]

1.2. American Reviews

Reviews of the *Lectures* appeared in four leading Protestant theological journals in the United States. The most significant of these was published in the journal of which Warfield was editor, the *Presbyterian and Reformed Review,* which carried reviews of a number of Kuyper's Dutch and English works, both before and after his visit to Princeton, all of them appreciative in their general tone.[16] The author stressed Kuyper's presentation of Calvinism as a preeminently cosmological rather than soteriological religion, based on an understanding of palingenesis as the restoration of the entire cosmic order, not only of the sinful human heart.[17] He was obviously both convinced of, and enthusiastic about, the potential benefit the publication of Kuyper's Stone Lectures would bring to American Presbyterianism as a whole, going so far as to suggest that a great service would be done by someone who bought up an entire edition, and ensured that a copy came into the hands of each of the younger generation of Reformed ministers. The book had appeared at a timely moment, he explained, in the midst of widespread slander and travesty of Calvin and Calvinism from those who

15. See, for instance, Warfield's "Apologetics," in *The New Schaff-Herzog Encyclopedia,* I, pp. 232-38, and his "The Deity of Christ," in *The Fundamentals* (Chicago: Testimony, 1910), I, pp. 22, 27-28; Harriet Harris, "After Liberalism: Fundamentalism in a Post-Liberal Context," *Theology* 100 (1997): 340-48 (343-44).

16. Henry Colin Minton, Review of *Calvinism: The L. P. Stone Lectures for 1898-1899: Six Lectures Delivered in the Theological Seminary at Princeton* by A. Kuyper (New York: Revell, [1899]), *The Presbyterian and Reformed Review* 11 (1900): 536-39; G. Vos, Review of *De verflauwing der grenzen* by A. Kuyper (Amsterdam: Wormser, 1892), *The Presbyterian and Reformed Review* 4 (1893): 330-32; Henry Colin Minton, Review of *Encyclopedia of Sacred Theology: Its Principles* by A. Kuyper, trans. by J. Hendrik De Vries. With an introduction by Benjamin B. Warfield (New York: Charles Scribner; London: Hodder and Stoughton, 1898), *The Presbyterian and Reformed Review* 10 (1899): 677-85; Timothy G. Darling, Review of *The Work of the Holy Spirit* by A. Kuyper (New York: Funk & Wagnalls, 1901), *The Presbyterian and Reformed Review* 12 (1901): 499-506.

17. Henry Colin Minton, Review of *Calvinism,* p. 537.

had only the slightest conception of who Calvin was and of what Calvinism had done in history. It had demonstrated that Calvinism was a *Weltanschauung* that could challenge any other, and that it had "left an impress in every sphere of human thought and in every department of human life, which the advancing ages only accentuate, and which the course of time can never erase."[18] The thrust of Kuyper's message had obviously made an impact on the writer of this review, who echoed its triumphalism.

A very different tone was sounded in the review published in *The Reformed Church Review,* where the author criticized Kuyper's claim for the universality of Calvinism, declaring that this was inconsistent with Calvinism's fundamental doctrine that the majority of human beings were not elect, but reprobate since birth.[19] The writer was obviously keenly out of sympathy with the theological foundations of Kuyper's thought as a whole, basing his criticisms on the insights of liberal theology, and thus proposing that Kuyper would most likely consider him to be an incorrigible devotee of the "mystical element of modernism."[20] His criticisms are perceptive, despite their bias, and highlight the same fundamental tension in Kuyper's thought that has been identified at various points earlier in this book, between its "universalistic" and its "particularistic" aspects. The review is also valuable evidence that the reception of Kuyper's ideas in America was not characterized solely by unbridled enthusiasm.

The confidence in the value of Kuyper's Stone Lectures for American Presbyterianism expressed in the first review was also evident in that published in the *Hartford Seminary Record* in 1900.[21] Its author hailed Kuyper as "one of the most original and forceful minds of our time" and acknowledged with particular gratitude his emphasis on the role of the early Dutch colonists in laying the basis of American civilization. Similar notes of appreciation were sounded in the fourth and final review, published the same year in *The Methodist Review,* the journal in which Kuyper's pantheism speech had appeared seven years earlier.[22] In this review,

18. Henry Colin Minton, Review of *Calvinism,* p. 539.

19. Review of *Calvinism: The L. P. Stone Lectures for 1898-1899,* in *The Reformed Church Review* 4 (1900): 273-77 (275). The author of this review, and of the two mentioned below, was left anonymous.

20. Review of *Calvinism,* in *The Reformed Church Review,* p. 276.

21. Review of *Calvinism: The L. P. Stone Lectures for 1898-1899,* in *Hartford Seminary Record* 10 (1900): 265-66.

22. Review of *Calvinism: The L. P. Stone Lectures for 1898-1899,* in *The Methodist Review* 82 (1900): 174; Kuyper, "Pantheism's Destruction."

as in the other three, it was Kuyper's conception of the comprehensive scope of the Calvinistic worldview that most impressed the author and called forth his comment, concluding that Kuyper was the ablest intellectual force in the religious life of the Netherlands.

In general, therefore, the reception of Kuyper's *Lectures* in the United States was positive, although it was mixed with severe but perceptive criticism. The fact that evaluations centered on the concept of Calvinism as an all-embracing worldview indicates that Kuyper had managed to communicate the core of his message, and indeed that this concept was perceived to be his most significant and original contribution to the theological debate, of great potential profit to Reformed religion in America.

2. Final Conclusions

In drawing final conclusions in this book it will be helpful if some of the most important findings of preceding chapters are summarized. Although this will inevitably involve the risk of repetition, it will allow broader conclusions to be drawn from the points already made.

2.1. The Modernization of Calvinism

The motive behind many of the ideas Kuyper presented at Princeton was to bring Calvinism up-to-date — to modernize it — by making it relevant to the social and intellectual circumstances in Europe and America in the late nineteenth century. This he sought to accomplish in a variety of ways.

2.1.1 Vision of America

At the heart of Kuyper's America-vision lay the idea that Calvinism, particularly Dutch Calvinism, was responsible for the fact that the United States had become the greatest country on earth. Influenced strongly by prevailing notions of a Christian America and of heliotropic development, it was an argument designed to display not only the modern relevance of Calvinism but its superiority, as reflected in the fact that America had become the most modern and advanced country in the world. His aim was to counter criticism, particularly from his conservative and liberal political opponents, that Calvinism was culturally sterile and outdated, and that it was the humanism and liberalism of the French Revolution that were responsible for the great social virtues of modern America.

2.1.2 *Worldview*

In his deliberate and self-conscious employment of the concept of worldview, adopted from contemporary German philosophy but mediated through James Orr, Kuyper found a means to characterize current ideologies in such a way as to be able to present Calvinism as an alternative worldview, and one that had equal validity to the others because it possessed the same essential characteristics: it was derived from a single unifying principle; it provided answers to the fundamental questions of human existence; it was comprehensive and internally consistent. Although, in carrying this out, he intended to demonstrate the contemporary intellectual relevance of the Calvinistic worldview rather than to change its content, he borrowed liberally from those systems and ideologies towards which, he claimed, the Calvinistic worldview was antithetically opposed — particularly pantheism and evolutionism. Moreover, his attempt to present Calvinism as a worldview, or "life-system," reflected the predilection for systems in theoretical thought that was characteristic of nineteenth-century monism. His use of secular worldviews as a model for his own served, therefore, to weaken his case for the distinctiveness of the Calvinistic worldview.

2.1.3 *Neo-Calvinist*

Kuyper's treatment of traditional Reformed doctrine amounted to a radical reinterpretation and reapplication of its central tenets. His aim was to emphasize its significance for the whole of human existence, and thereby to challenge Reformed theologians, not least those at Princeton itself, to regard it not as a collection of independent dogmas of chief importance to the church and to private morality, but as a system of dynamic and creative principles, able to provide consistent answers to the most fundamental questions of human existence, and to transform human life and culture. Thus the doctrine of common grace, which is not a major element in traditional Calvinistic theology, became, under the influence of Kuyper's objectives, a doctrine of overriding and central importance. His insistence on the centrality of this doctrine in the Calvinistic worldview was an attempt to make explicit an element that was implicit in Calvin's thought, and to give systematic expression to an aspect of Calvin's theology that had none of the coherence Kuyper ascribed to it. He then used this doctrine, along with other derivations he made from Calvin, such as the antithesis and sphere-sovereignty, to further the achievement of specific practical goals. Although he stressed the universality of Calvin's answers to fundamental religious questions, his treatment of them reflects his sensitivity to the circumstances in which he lived, which were marked by sweeping intellectual, ecclesiasical, social, and political change.

The general way in which Kuyper handled traditional Calvinist doctrine was consistent with his plea for both the continuity and development of Calvinistic principles in relation to modern circumstances. In this sense it reflects the conservative reaction to Enlightenment thought that swept through many parts of the Christian intellectual world of the West during Kuyper's lifetime, and which included such diverse figureheads as J. H. Newman, Groen van Prinsterer, and B. B. Warfield. It also, however, reflects the influence of the liberal agenda itself: Kuyper's insistence on the modernization of Calvinism was more indebted to J. H. Scholten than to Groen van Prinsterer. This partly accounts for the fact that some of the severest criticisms to be unleashed against Kuyper's program from within Reformed circles were that he had broken with traditional Calvinism, despite his assurances that he aimed to modernize only the *application* of Calvin's theology, not its contents. The result of this modernization may justifiably be called "neo-Calvinism" and cannot be taken as an accurate and reliable guide to the theology of John Calvin.

2.1.4 Anti-Revolutionary

The modernness of Kuyper's vision is also reflected in the term "anti-revolutionary," which stood in contrast to the "contra-revolutionary" stance of many of his Catholic and conservative political colleagues. It was a designation that implied a rejection of the underlying principles of the French Revolution, not of the improved circumstances this revolution had brought about. It offered, moreover, a program of equally far-reaching reform, based on principles entirely antithetical to those of the French Revolution but nevertheless progressive and forward-looking.

This desire contributed to the fact that much of Kuyper's thought reflects the leading ideas of late nineteenth-century European thought.

It was Kuyper's insistence on the conflict in science, however, that demonstrated most clearly that despite his attempts at modernization, he was serious in his opposition to Enlightenment principles. This accounts for much of the difference between Kuyper and Warfield on the question of the relationship between Christianity and science. Kuyper's views on science may be regarded, in fact, as one of the clearest examples of what he meant by anti-revolutionary, as they combined a conscious rejection of modernistic principles in science with a commitment to involvement in modern science, and an appreciation of its potential.

2.1.5 Popular Movements

Kuyper's aim of demonstrating the relevance and universality of the Calvinistic worldview also helps to explain why he was so acutely aware of contemporary cultural and religious trends, particularly those expressed at a popular level, such as the democratization of art and the reintroduction of symbolism in liturgy. His determination to show that Calvinism was able to provide a particular perspective on such movements often led him to characterize them in terms of the principles on which he believed they were based, thus providing an opportunity to expound opposing Calvinist principles. The democratization of art, for instance, was a result of materialism, and symbolism in worship was a product of pantheism. The kind of cultural criticism that characterized Kuyper's work was not uninformed, but it gave little priority to detailed analysis. It relied on a considerable amount of intuition, and an ability to characterize contemporary trends in broad and impressionistic terms in order to draw attention to the underlying principles.

2.2. The Elimination of a Prejudice

Much of Kuyper's argument in the Stone Lectures for the significance of Calvinism in the modern world was motivated by his desire to redress what he saw as a prejudice against Calvinism — that it represented a purely ecclesiastical and dogmatic movement of no relevance to current intellectual and social concerns. This motive helped to provide the Lectures with a unifying theme and contributed to the persuasive style of the polemics. It also meant that they were often preoccupied with correcting a misunderstanding rather than with explaining and developing a new and alternative way ahead. This is particularly notable in his lecture on art, in which his determination to dispel the traditional stigma that Calvinism was opposed to the arts and had thwarted artistic creativity precluded any meaningful attempt to provide a specifically Christian approach to the arts. In addressing the prejudice he hoped to convince his critics of the significance of Calvinism, and thereby to win the right to social, cultural, and intellectual self-expression. He also hoped to replace the feeling of insignificance and low self-esteem among his followers with a sense of historical pride that would inspire confidence in the value and effectiveness of the Calvinistic worldview.

2.3. A Fundamental Tension

A comparison of Kuyper's perspectives on art with those on science highlights a fundamental tension in his thought between "universalistic" and "particularistic" aspects. Whereas his approach to the arts was largely governed by his concept of common grace, his ideas on science rested chiefly on his doctrine of the antithesis. It was a tension that encouraged isolation on the one hand and engagement and accommodation on the other, reflected in the fact that although Kuyper advocated the separate development of Christian and non-Christian science within separate and independent institutions, he advocated no such division in the area of the arts. Likewise, despite his insistence on Calvinism's universal scope and relevance, his vision for the future of Calvinism was largely restricted to those geographical areas in which Calvinism had had an influence in the past, and he entertained pessimistic projections about the future of general culture in these parts, despite his insistence on Calvinism's potential to influence human culture. It was, therefore, a tension that led to serious inconsistencies, not only in his thought but also in his activities. There are features of Kuyper's treatment, both of art and of the future, that ensure, however, that these inconsistencies are limited in their effects on the coherence of his thought. Even though he failed to present a case for Calvinistic art, to complement his argument for Calvinistic science, it is possible to reconstruct from his arguments the characteristics he would expect art to possess if it were true to Calvinism. In this sense he did manage to construct a Calvinistic approach to art, however preliminary and rudimentary this may have been. In terms of his vision for the future of Calvinism, his pessimism was partly an expression of his realism when it came to considering the likely influence of Calvinism in practice, rather than doubts as to its universal relevance and potential.

2.4. An Originator of Verzuiling?

There are aspects of Kuyper's thought that may have been partly responsible for the development of *verzuiling*—most notably his concept of sphere-sovereignty, his idea of a twofold division in science, and his thoughts concerning the future of Calvinism. The most significant of these in terms of its influence on anti-revolutionary social theory and practice was the concept of sphere-sovereignty. Even though it does not appear to have been his explicit intention, he associated this concept with ideological groupings in society as well as with spheres of human existence, despite the fact that these two ideas are incompatible if sphere-sovereignty is held to be a creational principle. Kuyper's propagation of this concept in the context of arguing for ideological and organizational pluralism almost certainly encouraged the emergence of a pillarized form of social organization among orthodox Protestants, which played an important part in the development of *verzuiling*. Although there is not sufficient evidence to suggest that the development of *verzuiling* was one of Kuyper's express aims in his advocation of sphere-sovereignty, it is clear that this idea provided theoretical justification for the emergence of a pillarized form of social organization. The chief aim of sphere-sovereignty was to provide a rationale for social and political differentiation, which was Kuyper's answer to the liberal domination of politics, and to encourage the social and political emancipation of the orthodox Protestant sector of the population —all at a time when the Netherlands and Europe as a whole were experiencing rapid social change.

2.5. Further Research

The conclusion drawn above on the question of the origins of *verzuiling* in Kuyper's thought leaves unanswered the question as to whether this form of social organization was a consequence of Kuyper's activities. It is possible that he did not advocate social pillarization as a point of principle, but encouraged it in practice, either intentionally or as an inevitable consequence of his efforts towards encouraging the development of an independent orthodox Protestant "sphere" in Dutch social life. The theoretical and practical significance and influence of the inconsistencies in Kuyper's thought need to be examined and evaluated in detail, in order that the question of the origins of *verzuiling* may be divested of all notions that assume a connection between Kuyper and the initial stages of pillarization, which characterize much of the *verzuiling* literature. The whole question needs to be reappraised on the basis of an understanding of the entire scope of Kuyper's thought, towards which this book seeks to make a contribution. The significance of the question is largely due to the importance of *verzuiling* for the shape of Dutch society during most of the twentieth century, even though the focus of attention in sociological studies of the Netherlands may now be turning towards the social processes that occurred after the high point of *verzuiling* (collectively referred to as *ontzuiling*). In the fresh reflection on the development of Dutch society in the twentieth century that the twenty-first century will bring (stimulated by a new sense of distance) the issue of *verzuiling* and its origins cannot fail to occupy a prominent place. Likewise, the new wave of interest in the origins and development of *apartheid* in South Africa since its official dismantlement demands that greater clarity is reached, especially as the exact nature of any link between *verzuiling* and *apartheid* requires further elaboration.[23]

A second important and valuable area of enquiry to surface from the investigations carried out in this book is that of influences on Kuyper's ideas from the contemporary world of thought. Although the preceding chapters identify a number of sources of such influence, it is a question that demands fuller treatment. The chief obstacle to this enquiry is the popular and impressionistic style of most of Kuyper's works, which partly accounts for the fact that references to the thought of others to whom he was indebted or to whom he was reacting are rare. Conclusions may therefore have to remain tentative, as in the discussion in

23. Recent discussions of the way in which Kuyper's ideas were used to support *apartheid* can be found in P. J. Strauss, "Abraham Kuyper, Apartheid and Reformed Churches in South Africa in Their Support of Apartheid," *Theological Forum* 23 (1995): 4-27; and J. J. Lubbe, "'n Bok vir Asasel? In gesprek oor 'n Suid-Afrikaanse aanklag teen Abraham Kuyper," *Nederduitse gereformeerde teologiese tydskrif* 37 (1996): 257-85.

Chapter Six of the possible influence of Otto von Gierke on Kuyper's political pluralism: although the similarities in their position are striking, no direct influence can be established with any certainty. Nevertheless, further significant discoveries could be made, and the influence particularly of German thinkers and theologians on Kuyper's thought, which has been traced in this book, could be investigated in greater detail (a task facilitated by the fact that discussions of their ideas appear in his *Encyclopaedie*).

A third prospect to emerge from this book for the future of Kuyper studies is the value of an historical and contextual approach to Kuyper's thought. As the survey of secondary literature on Kuyper in Chapter One shows, most studies of Kuyper's ideas aim to synthesize them, rather than contextualize them. They tend also to treat them as a finished product, rather than tracing their development over time. Their approach, in other words, is systematic rather than historical. While there are undoubtedly strengths in this approach, its weakness is evident in the way that the *Lectures* has traditionally been handled. Often the ideas it contains are used to clarify positions Kuyper maintained in his earlier writings, the summary-like characteristic of the *Lectures* lending itself easily to this kind of treatment. C. Augustijn, the current Professor of Church History at the Free University of Amsterdam, rightly points out the misconceptions of Kuyper's thought that have resulted from this sort of approach: "The great studies aim to present a synthesis of Kuyper's thought but in fact offer only a tangle of raked-together ideas."[24] Much of the confusion, he argues, is because Kuyper's ideas belonging to the period 1890-1910 are projected backwards onto his earlier thought. Augustijn calls for a serious analysis of Kuyper's thought that gives due attention to the historical development of his ideas and objectives.[25]

This book has been written in response to that call. Hopefully it is only the first of many explorations of Kuyper's ideas within the context in which they were formed, involving a comparative fremework, and focusing on their chief motivations. It leaves much scope for the same

24. C. Augustijn, 'Kuypers theologie van de samenleving', in Augustijn et al. (eds.), *Abraham Kuyper*, pp. 34-60 (60). Augustijn considers Kuyper's concept of the antithesis to be a particular case in point. See also C. Augustijn, 'Kuyper en de antithese', in *Kerkhistorische opstellen aangeboden aan prof. dr. J. van den Berg* (Kampen: Kok, 1987), pp. 143-56.

25. Augustijn, 'Kuypers theologie', p. 60.

kind of analysis to be applied to areas not yet fully explored. An encouraging sign, perhaps, is that the dissertation on which this book is based (which employs the same analytical approach) has stimulated at least two such explorations — both by the American historian James Bratt.[26] Bratt's articles reflect the argument he made in his review of this earlier work, that its analysis and conclusions point Kuyper studies towards a promising future.[27] This is certainly to be hoped, as it is now over a decade since Augustijn launched his appeal.

2.6 The Question of Christianity and Culture

Kuyper's Lectures were an attempt to answer one of the most crucial questions that has faced Christianity throughout its history, the question of the relationship between Christianity and culture.[28] He sought to provide an answer to this question that was distinctly different from the solutions provided by his contemporaries. By and large, these took the form of pietism or modernism.

2.6.1 Pietism

Kuyper's conversion, which marked the beginning of his career as an orthodox Protestant theologian and politician, was directly influenced by his contact with Dutch pietism. His decision, likewise, to organize the anti-revolutionaries into a well-coordinated and disciplined political party, and to work for the establishment of the Free University, occurred soon after his encounter with the Brighton movement, which was strongly influenced by American evangelical pietism. Many of his educational, social, and political initiatives were carried out in reaction to

26. James D. Bratt, "Abraham Kuyper, American History, and the Tensions of Neo-Calvinism," in *Sharing the Reformed Tradition: The Dutch–North American Exchange, 1846-1996,* ed. by George Harinck and Hans Krabbendam (Amsterdam: VU Uitgeverij, 1996), pp. 97-114; and "Abraham Kuyper, J. Gresham Machen en de veelvormigheid van het calvinisme," *Radix* 23 (1997): 27-43.

27. James D. Bratt, "In the Shadow of Mt. Kuyper: A Survey of the Field," *Calvin Theological Journal* 31 (1996): 51-66 (63-64).

28. H. Richard Niebuhr famously categorizes the types of answers that have been given to this question in his *Christ and Culture* (New York: Harper & Brothers, 1951).

the tendency among many Protestant groups, particularly those associated with the *Réveil* and the *Afscheiding,* to be dismissive or suspicious of the kind of organizational activities Kuyper advocated, considering them to be a sign of worldliness and compromise.

Irrespective of the fact that they were living in a culture permeated by Christian values, Kuyper's pietistic contemporaries held that the institutions of culture, being part of the fallen world, were essentially opposed to Christ. Although Christ offered to all human beings the choice to be either a part of his kingdom or of the world around them, obedience to him required submission to the laws administered by the institutions of society, as all believers were subject to two moralities and were citizens of two opposing worlds. Although in Christian history Lutherans have been the chief exponents of this position, many pietistic groups have attempted to solve the problem of Christianity and culture in this manner. This includes those groups in the Netherlands and America that had an early influence on the shape of Kuyper's thought.

2.6.2 Modernism

The major formative influence on Kuyper immediately preceding his initial encounter with pietism was that of theological modernism, of the sort promulgated at Leiden during his student years. After rejecting it in favor of orthodox Protestantism, he spent the rest of his career in fierce opposition to its effects and in open conflict with its representatives. Although he was most concerned with its Dutch exponents, he was always keen to point out that they were part of a much wider movement in European religious thought, not least so as to encourage a sense of the significance, scope, and relevance of his alternative. Schleiermacher, one of the movement's chief founders, sought to solve the problem of Christianity and culture by insisting that Christ is the great hero of culture whose teachings represent the greatest human achievement, and who enters into culture in order to add an aura of infinite meaning to all temporal tasks.[29] Under Schleiermacher's influence, modernist thinkers,

29. F. D. E. Schleiermacher, *On Religion: Speeches to Its Cultured Despisers,* trans. by Richard Gouter (Cambridge: Cambridge University Press, 1988). Barth's criticism of Schleiermacher focused on this aspect of his thought. See Barth's *From Rousseau to Ritschl: Being the Translation of Eleven Chapters of "Die Protestantische Theologie im 19. Jahrhundert"* [1947] (London: SCM Press, 1959), pp. 387-91.

far from demanding a separation from culture, tended to identify Christianity with culture. The movement reached its climax in the latter half of the nineteenth century, particularly under the influence of Ritschl, against whom Kuyper leveled much of his anti-modernist criticism. Ritschl's emphasis on the ethical obligations of Christian faith was an expression of the idea that Christ's kingdom encompassed the whole of humanity, and that Christians were called upon to strive for the attainment of a perfect human society rather than to separate themselves from the world in the manner advocated by pietism and asceticism.[30] Only through involvement in public service for the sake of the common good was it possible for someone to be a true follower of Christ and a member of his kingdom.[31] It was, in fact, largely by means of his notion of the kingdom of God that Ritschl achieved a complete reconciliation of Christianity and culture.[32]

These ideas, widespread in Europe during the latter half of the nineteenth century, have dominated discussions of culture from a Protestant perspective ever since, reflected in the fact that, since Barth, they have often been referred to as "Culture-Protestantism."[33] It was Kuyper's opposition to them in their early stages that motivated much of his criticism of Scholten and his followers, but also of the Ethical theologians, who, despite their orthodox affinities, were sympathetic to the ideas of both Schleiermacher and Ritschl.

2.6.3 Kuyper's Alternative

In contrast to the Culture-Protestantism of modernists and Ethicals, Kuyper held to the radical distinction between God's work in Christ and the work of human beings in culture. Together with his pietistic contemporaries, he held that the whole of creation, including human nature, was fallen and perverted, but he opposed their attempts to advocate cultural withdrawal, claiming that Christianity (particularly in its most advanced, Calvinistic, form) was the very means by which culture could

30. Albrecht Ritschl, *Geschichte des Pietismus,* 3 vols. (Bonn: Marcus, 1880-1886), passim.

31. A. Ritschl, *The Christian Doctrine of Justification and Reconciliation: The Positive Development of the Doctrine,* trans. by H. R. Mackintosh and A. B. Macaulay (Edinburgh: T. & T. Clark, 1900 [1874]), pp. 661-62.

32. Ritschl, *The Christian Doctrine,* p. 284.

33. Karl Barth, *From Rousseau to Ritschl,* Chapter III.

be transformed according to God's ordinances. Common grace served as the theological justification for this argument, providing as it did the necessary bridge across the gap created by the antithesis between the world corrupted by sin and Christ's work of re-creation. Despite its corruption, creation was still under the sovereign rule of God, who restrained the destructive effects of the fall and called his followers to fulfill the cultural mandate he had entrusted to them. Human nature, once good, had not become absolutely or essentially bad as a result of the fall, even though every part of it had become corrupt—that is, warped, twisted, and misdirected. Culture, therefore, was not inherently evil but was perverted good, and the solution to the problem of Christianity and culture was not withdrawal from fallen creation in anticipation of the coming of a new order in the future, but a radical conversion and renewal of that creation in the present.

It was this view that influenced Kuyper's vision of history. History was not the story of a rising church or Christian culture in the midst of a dying pagan civilization, a view characteristic of pietism. Neither was it a course of merely human events, as proposed by modernism. Rather, it was the dynamic interaction of God and humankind, the story of divine deeds and human response. It is this that explains (in part) Kuyper's overriding concern for the present, with all its opportunities for reformation, rather than with future speculations—for him the eschatological future was the eschatological present. He did not live so much in expectation of a final termination of culture as in an awareness of God's power to transform it. Despite his pessimism about the current state of culture, he held to a vision of what human culture could be like through the activity of the Holy Spirit working in the lives of Christ's followers—it could be radically transformed to the glory of God.

His criticism of pietism, therefore, was that it failed to see redemption as a matter not only of the personal life of the soul but as encompassing the whole of creation. In contrast, his opposition to modernism was based on its refusal to recognize fully the fallenness of creation; and he insisted instead that earthly life was in an abnormal state, requiring Christ's unique work of redemption to restore it to its original normality. His alternative was a scheme in which creation, fall, and redemption were each conceived of in the broadest possible sense, encompassing the entire cosmos. It is this alternative that has been particularly influential in the formation of the neo-Calvinist school of thought, in which it forms the basis of the concept of worldview, and is generally regarded as the feature that distinguishes the Calvinistic or "Reformational" worldview from all other Christian worldviews, which all limit the scope of creation, fall, and redemption in some way.[34]

In presenting this alternative, Kuyper hoped to demonstrate that Calvinism enjoyed an independent position in the contemporary debate on the question of the relationship between the church and the world, a debate which had recently been revived under the influence of modernistic theology. In contrast to modernism's belief in the inherent goodness of man and human culture, Kuyper insisted on the radical character of sin, explaining the goodness of culture to be a result of common grace, which keeps the effects of sin in check. Likewise, in contrast to the objection of many orthodox Protestants that there was little value in scientific, political, and artistic involvement, given that the human intellect, human structures of authority, and human artistic talents were radically affected by the corruption of creation, Kuyper's concept of common grace maintained that this corruption had been kept under severe restraint, thus allowing Christ's redemption to take effect through the works of his followers. To Kuyper, the tendency towards dualism characteristic of much orthodox Protestantism posed itself as one of the chief obstacles to his attempt to encourage Christian engagement with culture. The doctrine of common grace, which stood in close association with belief in the cosmic scope of creation, fall, and redemption, provided him with the only sound solution to the problem of Christianity and culture, and supplied an incentive and justification for active Christian pursuit of cultural renewal.

Kuyper's alternative was influenced in many significant respects by the times in which he lived. The solution he worked out is therefore a part of history and cannot be applied directly to today's circumstances. Its value, however, lies in the seriousness with which it sought to address the question of the relationship between Christianity and culture from an orthodox, biblical perspective. In doing so, he provided a solution that was so broad in its scope, distinctive in its emphasis, lasting in its influence, and successful in its practical consequences, that it deserves ongoing study and reflection.

34. See, for instance, Albert M. Wolters, *Creation Regained: A Transforming View of the World* (Leicester: InterVarsity Press, 1986), pp. 1-11 (10); Paul Marshall, *Thine Is the Kingdom: A Biblical Perspective on the Nature of Government and Politics Today* (Basingstoke: Marshall Morgan & Scott, 1984), pp. 20-38; Arthur F. Holmes, *Contours of a World View* (Grand Rapids: Eerdmans, 1983), pp. 3-91.

Bibliography of Cited Material

1. Archives

Historisch Documentatiecentrum voor het Nederlands Protestantisme (1880-heden), Vrije Universiteit, Amsterdam: Kuyper Archief (KA).

Princeton Theological Seminary: Stone Lectures Collection.

Heritage Hall, Calvin College, Grand Rapids: Correspondence A. Kuyper—G. Vos.

2. Published Archive Material

Briefwisseling Kuyper-Idenberg. Edited by J. de Bruijn and G. Puchinger. Franeker: Wever, 1985.

Briefwisseling van Mr. G. Groen van Prinsterer met Dr. A. Kuyper 1864-1876. Edited by A. Goslinga. Kampen: Kok, 1937.

Briefwisseling van Mr. G. Groen van Prinsterer IV (1866-1876). Edited by A. Goslinga and J. L. van Essen. 's-Gravenhage: Zuid-Hollandsche Boek-en Handelsdrukkerij, 1967.

Handelingen van de Tweede Kamer der Staten Generaal, 1848-1905.

3. Newspapers

The Banner of Truth

Chicago Tribune

Cleveland Leader

Cleveland Plain Dealer
The Daily Inter-Ocean
The Daily Princetonian
De Heraut
De Hollandse Amerikaan
De Hope
De Standaard
De Wachter
Grand Rapids Democrat
Grand Rapids Herald
The Herald
Holland Daily Sentinel
Oude Paden. Weekblad voor de verbreiding der Gereformeerde beginselen ten dienste van kerk en volk, 29 (1915).
Zondagsblad van De Standaard

4. Primary and Secondary Literature

C. Aalders. *Spiritualiteit vroeger en nu.* 's-Gravenhage: Boekencentrum, 1969.

R. Ackermann (ed.). *A History of the University of Oxford.* 2 vols. London: Ackermann, 1814.

D. Adair. *Fame and the Founding Fathers: Essays by Douglas Adair.* Edited by Trevor Colbourn. New York: Norton, 1974.

C. A. Admiraal. 'Abraham Kuyper en de Amerikaanse Revolutie', *Spiegel Historiael* 11 (1976): 426-33.

C. A. Admiraal. 'De Amerikaanse reis van Abraham Kuyper: een verwaarloosd aspect uit de geschiedschrijving over Kuyper', in *Historicus in het spanningsveld van theorie en praktijk: opstellen aangeboden aan Dr. H. Klompmaker ter gelegenheid van zijn veertigjarig studieleiderschap bij de opleiding M.O.-Geschiedenis.* Edited by C. A. Admiraal, P. B. M. Blaas, and J. van der Zande, pp. 111-64. Leiderdorp: Leidse Onderwijsinstellingen, 1985.

Charles W. Akers. "Calvinism and the American Revolution," in *The Heritage of John Calvin: Heritage Hall Lectures 1960-1970.* Edited by John H. Bratt, pp. 158-76. Grand Rapids: Eerdmans, 1973.

David Alton. *Faith in Britain.* London: Hodder & Stoughton, 1991.

C. Augustijn, J. H. Prins, and H. E. S. Woldring (eds.). *Abraham Kuyper: zijn volksdeel, zijn invloed.* Delft: Meinema, 1987.

C. Augustijn. 'Kuyper en de antithese', in *Kerkhistorische opstellen aangeboden aan prof. dr. J. van den Berg,* pp. 143-56. Kampen: Kok, 1987.

C. Augustijn. 'Kuypers theologie van de samenleving', in Augustijn (ed.), *Abraham Kuyper: zijn volksdeel, zijn invloed,* pp. 34-60. Delft: Meinema, 1987.

Shlomo Avineri. *Hegel's Theory of the Modern State.* Cambridge: Cambridge University Press, 1972.

George Bancroft. *History of the United States of America,* 6 vols. New York: Appleton, 1882-1884.

Karl Barth. *From Rousseau to Ritschl: Being the Translation of Eleven Chapters of "Die Protestantische Theologie im 19. Jahrhundert"* (1947). London: SCM Press, 1959.

Herman Bavinck. "Recent Dogmatic Thought in the Netherlands," *The Presbyterian and Reformed Review* 10 (1892): 209-28.

H. Bavinck. 'Van schoonheid en schoonheidsleer', in *Verzamelde opstellen* by H. Bavinck, pp. 262-80. Kampen: Kok, 1921.

Herman Bavinck. "The Future of Calvinism," *The Presbyterian and Reformed Review* 17 (1894): 1-37.

Herman Bavinck. *Christelijke wereldbeschouwing,* 3rd edition. Kampen: Kok, 1929.

David Bebbington. *Patterns in History: A Christian Perspective on Historical Thought.* Leicester: Apollos, 1990.

David Bebbington. "The Secularization of British Universities since the Mid-Nineteenth Century," in *The Secularization of the Academy,* edited by George M. Marsden and Bradley J. Longfield, pp. 259-277. New York: Oxford University Press, 1992.

Jeremy Begbie. "Christ and Cultures: Christianity and the Arts," in *The Cambridge Companion to Christian Doctrine,* edited by Colin Gunton, pp. 101-18. Cambridge: Cambridge University Press, 1997.

Jeremy S. Begbie. "Creation, Christ and Culture in Dutch Neo-Calvinism," in *Christ in Our Place: The Humanity of God in Christ for the Reconciliation of the World. Essays Presented to James Torrance,* edited by Trevor Hart and Daniel Thimell, pp. 113-32. Exeter: Paternoster, 1989.

Jeremy Begbie. *Voicing Creation's Praise: Toward a Theology of the Arts.* Edinburgh: T. & T. Clark, 1991.

Jeremy Begbie. "Who Is This God?—Biblical Inspiration Revisited," *Tyndale Bulletin* 43 (1992): 259-82.

T. F. Bensdorp. *Pluriformiteit. Een fundamenteele misvatting van Dr. A. Kuyper of een hopeloos pleidooi: eene studie over Dr. Kuyper's pluriformiteitsstelsel. Benevens een antwoord van en aan Dr. Kuyper door denzelfden.* Amsterdam: Borg, 1901.

C. H. W. van den Berg. "Kuyper en de kerk," in Augustijn et al., eds., *Abraham Kuyper: zijn volksdeel, zijn invloed,* pp. 146-78. Delft: Meinema, 1987.

Hendrikus Berkhof. *Two Hundred Years of Theology: Report of a Personal Journey.* Grand Rapids: Eerdmans, 1989.

R. N. Berki. *The History of Political Thought: A Short Introduction.* London: Dent, 1977.

Helena Petrovna Hahn Blavatsky. *Isis Unveiled: a Master-key to the Mysteries of Ancient and Modern Science and Technology,* 2 vols. London: The Theosophical Publishing Company, 1910.

J. C. H. Blom and C. J. Missert (eds.). *Broeders sluit u aan: Aspecten van verzuiling in zeven Hollandse gemeenten.* Amsterdam: De Bataafsche Leeuw, 1985.

Charles Bloomberg. *Christian-Nationalism and the Rise of the Afrikaner Broederbond in South Africa, 1918-1948.* Bloomington: Indiana University Press, 1989.

John Bolt. "Editorial," *Calvin Theological Journal* 31 (1996): 9-10.

J. A. Bornewasser. 'Christendom en Aufklärung: over geschiedenis en interpretatie', in *Tussentijds: Theologische Faculteit Tilburg, bundel opstellen bij gelegenheid van haar erkenning,* edited by H. H. Berger et al. Tilburg: Hart van Brabant, 1974.

William J. Bouwsma. *John Calvin: A Sixteenth Century Portrait.* New York: Oxford University Press, 1988.

Peter J. Bowler. *Evolution: The History of an Idea.* Berkeley: University of California Press, 1984.

Theodore Dwight Bozeman. *Protestants in an Age of Science: The Baconian Ideal and Antebellum American Religious Thought.* Chapel Hill: University of North Carolina Press, 1977.

James D. Bratt. "Abraham Kuyper, American History and the Tensions of Neo-Calvinism," in *Sharing the Reformed Tradition: The Dutch–North American Exchange, 1846-1996,* edited by George Harinck and Hans Krabbendam, pp. 97-114. Amsterdam: VU Uitgeverij, 1996.

James D. Bratt. "Abraham Kuyper, J. Gresham Machen en de veelvormigheid van het calvinisme," *Radix* 23 (1997): 27-43.

James D. Bratt. *Dutch Calvinism in Modern America: A History of a Conservative Subculture.* Grand Rapids: Eerdmans, 1984.

James D. Bratt. "In the Shadow of Mt. Kuyper: A Survey of the Field," *Calvin Theological Journal* 31 (1996): 51-66.

T. B. F. H. Brinkel, J. de Bruijn, and A. Postma (eds.). *Het Kabinet-Mackay: Opstellen over de eerste Christelijke coalitie (1888-1891).* Baarn: Arbor, 1990.

A. W. Bronsveld. *De bede van Dr. A. Kuyper afgewezen door Dr. A. W. Bronsveld.* Utrecht: Breyer, 1880.

Colin Brown. *History and Faith: A Personal Exploration.* Leicester: InterVarsity Press, 1988.

A. Th. Bruggemann-Kruijff and others (eds.). *De taak van de universiteit.* Amsterdam: Van Gorcum, 1978.

J. de Bruijn. *Abraham Kuyper: leven en werk in beeld: een beeldbiografie.* Amsterdam: Historisch Documentatiecentrum voor het Nederlands Protestantisme (1880-heden), 1987.

J. de Bruijn (ed.). *Dooyeweerd herdacht: Referaten gehouden op het Dooyeweerd-symposium op 18 november aan de Vrije Universiteit.* Amsterdam: Free University Press, 1995.

J. de Bruijn (ed.). *Een land nog niet in kaart gebracht: aspecten van het protestants-christelijk leven in Nederland in de jaren 1880-1940.* Amsterdam: Historisch Documentatiecentrum, 1987.

Elton J. Bruins. "'An American Moses': Albertus C. van Raalte as Immigrant Leader," in *Sharing the Reformed Tradition: The Dutch-North American Exchange, 1846-1996,* edited by George Harinck and Hans Krabbendam, pp. 19-34. Amsterdam: VU Uitgeverij, 1996.

Henry Thomas Buckle. *History of Civilization in England,* 5 vols. Leipzig: Brockhaus, 1865.

Ilse N. Bulhof. "The Netherlands," in *The Comparative Reception of Darwinism,* edited by Thomas F. Glick, pp. 269-306. Austin: University of Texas Press, 1974.

Ilse N. Bulhof. *Darwin's "Origin of the Species": Betoverende wetenschap. Een onderzoek naar de relatie tussen literatuur en wetenschap.* Baarn: Ambo, 1988.

David B. Calhoun. *Princeton Seminary,* 2 vols. Edinburgh/Pennsylvania: Banner of Truth, 1996.

John Calvin. *Commentaries* on Genesis, Exodus, Samuel, the Psalms.

John Calvin. *Institutes of the Christian Religion* (1559 edition), edited by John T. McNeill. Translated by Ford Lewis Battles, 2 vols. London: SCM Press, 1960.

Douglas Campbell. *The Puritan in Holland, England, and America: An Introduction to American History,* 2 vols. London: Osgood McIlvaine, 1892.

Stanley Carlson-Thies. "The Meaning of Dutch Segmentation for Modern America," in *Sharing the Reformed Tradition: The Dutch–North American Exchange, 1846-1996,* edited by George Harinck and Hans Krabbendam, pp. 159-75. Amsterdam: VU Uitgeverij, 1996.

Stanley Carlson-Thies and James Skillen (eds.). *Welfare in America: Christian Perspectives on a Policy in Crisis.* Grand Rapids: Eerdmans, 1996.

Moriz Carrière. *Die Kunst in Zusammenhang mit der Culturentwickelung,* 5 vols. Leipzig: Brockhaus, 1873-1880.

Moriz Carrière. *Die philosophische Weltanschauung der Reformationszeit in ihren Beziehungen zur Gegenwart.* Leipzig: Brockhaus, 1887.

Owen Chadwick. *Newman.* Oxford: Oxford University Press, 1983.

Owen Chadwick. *The Victorian Church,* 2nd edition, 2 vols. London: SCM Press, 1987.

Jonathan Chaplin and Brian Walsh. "Dooyeweerd's Contribution to a Christian Philosophical Paradigm," *Crux* 19 (1983): 8-22.

R. W. Church. *The Oxford Movement: Twelve Years, 1833-1845.* London: Macmillan, 1897.

Kelly James Clark (ed.). *Philosophers Who Believe: The Spiritual Journeys of Eleven Leading Thinkers.* Downers Grove, Illinois: IVP, 1993.

Roy Clouser. *The Myth of Religious Neutrality: An Essay on the Hidden Role of Religious Beliefs in Theories.* Notre Dame: University of Notre Dame Press, 1991.

J. D. Collins. *A History of Modern European Philosophy.* Milwaukee, 1954.

Graham Cray. "A Gospel for Our Culture," in *To Proclaim Afresh: Evangelical Agenda for the Church,* edited by Gordon Kuhrt, pp. 119-32. London: SPCK, 1995.

A. B. Cramp. "Economic Ethics," in *New Dictionary of Christian Ethics and Pastoral Theology,* edited by David J. Atkinson and David H. Field, pp. 115-21. Leicester: IVP, 1995.

H. Daalder. "Consociationalism, Center and Periphery in the Netherlands," in *Mobilization, Center-Periphery Structures and Nation-Building,* edited by P. Torsvik, pp. 181-240. Bergen: Universitetsforlaget, 1981.

H. Daalder. 'Politicologen, sociologen, historic en de verzuiling', *Bijdragen en mededelingen betreffende de geschiedenis der Nederlanden* 100 (1985): 52-64.

Timothy G. Darling. Review of *The Work of the Holy Spirit* by A. Kuyper (New York: Funk & Wagnalls, 1901), *The Presbyterian and Reformed Review* 12 (1901): 499-506.

D. Clair Davis. "Princeton and Inerrancy: The Nineteenth-Century Philosophical

Background of Contemporary Concerns," in *Inerrancy and the Church,* edited by John D. Hannah, pp. 359-78. Chicago: Moody Press, 1984.

G. J. J. A. Delfgaauw. *De staatsleer van Hoedemaker: een bijdrage tot de kennis van de christelijk-historische staatsopvatting.* Kampen: Kok, 1963.

J. D. Dengerink. *Critisch-historisch onderzoek naar de sociologische ontwikkeling van het beginsel der 'Souvereiniteit in Eigen Kring' in de negentiende en twintigste eeuw.* Kampen: Kok, 1948.

Charles Stephen Dessain. *John Henry Newman,* 3rd edition. Oxford: Oxford University Press, 1980.

Charles Stephen Dessain and others (eds.). *The Letters and Diaries of John Henry Newman,* 31 vols. Oxford: Oxford University Press, 1961-1984.

Isaäc Arend Diepenhorst. *Historisch-critische bijdrage tot den leer van den christelijke staat.* Amsterdam: Noord-Hollandsche Uitgevers Maatschappij, 1943.

P. A. Diepenhorst. *Dr. A. Kuyper.* Haarlem: De Erven Bohn, 1931.

Harry van Dijk. *Groen van Prinsterer's Lectures on Unbelief and Revolution.* Jordan Station, Ontario: Wedge, 1989.

Herman Dooyeweerd. *In the Twilight of Western Thought: Studies in the Pretended Autonomy of Philosophical Thought.* Nutley, N.J.: The Craig Press, 1972.

Herman Dooyeweerd. "Introduction," in *The Idea of a Christian Philosophy: Essays in Honour of D. H. T. Vollenhoven.* Toronto: Wedge, 1973. Also published in *Philosophia Reformata: orgaan van de vereniging voor calvinistische wijsbegeerte* 38 (1973).

Herman Dooyeweerd. 'Kuyper's wetenschapsleer', *Philosophia reformata: orgaan van de vereeniging voor calvinistische wijsbegeerte* 4 (1939): 193-232.

Herman Dooyeweerd. *Roots of Western Culture: Pagan, Secular and Christian Options.* Translated by John Kraay. Toronto: Wedge, 1979.

Herman Dooyeweerd. *A New Critique of Theoretical Thought,* 4 vols. Philadelphia: Presbyterian and Reformed Publishing Company, 1953-1958.

Herman Dooyeweerd. *De wijsbegeerte der wetsidee,* 3 vols. Amsterdam: Paris, 1935-1936.

Emile Doumergue. "Calvin: Epigone or Creator?" in *Calvin and the Reformation: Four Studies.* New York: Revell, 1909.

John Durant (ed.). *Darwinism and Divinity: Essays on Evolution and Religious Belief* Oxford: Basil Blackwell, 1985.

Paul Edwards (ed.). *The Encyclopedia of Philosophy,* 8 vols, VI. London: CollierMacmillan, 1967.

B. D. Eerdmans. 'De theologie van Dr. A. Kuyper', *Theologisch Tijdschrift* 43 (1909): 209-37.

J. J. Rammelman Elsevier-Kuyper. *Herinneringen uit de kinder- en jongelingsjaren van Dr. A. Kuyper. Bijeenvergaderd door zijn eenig overgebleven zuster.* Kampen: Kok, 1921.

Encyclopedia of World Art, 17 vols. New York: McGraw-Hill, 1959-1987.

Grote Winkler Prins Encyclopaedie, 20 vols. Amsterdam: Elsevier, 1976.

J. P. Feddema. 'De houding van Dr. A. Kuyper ten aanzien van de Eerste Wereldoorlog', *Antirevolutionaire staatkunde: maandelijks orgaan van de Dr. Abraham*

Kuyperstichting ter bevordering van de studie der anti-revolutionaire beginselen 32 (1962): 163-64.

Sinclair B. Ferguson and David F. Wright (eds.). *New Dictionary of Theology.* Leicester: InterVarsity Press, 1988.

John Fiske. *The Beginnings of New England, or the Puritan Theocracy in Its Relations to Civil and Religious Liberty.* Boston: Houghton Mifflin, 1897.

John Fiske. *The Dutch and Quaker Colonies in America,* 2 vols. London: Macmillan, 1899.

Michael P. Fogarty. *Christian Democracy in Western Europe, 1820-1953.* London: Routledge and Kegan Paul, 1957.

Michael P. Fogarty. *Phoenix or Cheshire Cat? Christian Democracy Past, Present . . . and Future?* Ware: Christian Democrat Press, 1995.

John M. Frane. *Cornelius van Til: An Analysis of His Thought.* Phillipsburg, N.J.: Presbyterian and Reformed Publishing Company, 1995.

Donald Fuller and Richard Gardiner. "Reformed Theology at Princeton and Amsterdam in the Late Nineteenth Century: A Reappraisal," *Presbyterion* 21 (1995): 89-117.

Geen vergeefs woord: Verzamelde deputaten-redevoeringen. Kampen: Kok, 1951. No editor. Commissioned by the Doctor Abraham Kuyperstichting.

H. G. Geertsema and others (eds.). *Herman Dooyeweerd 1894-1977: Breedte en actualiteit van zijn filosofie,* Kampen: Kok, 1994.

Otto von Gierke. *Community in Historical Perspective.* Translated by Mary Fischer, edited by Antony Black. Cambridge: Cambridge University Press, 1990.

Otto von Gierke. *Das Deutsche Genossenschaftsrecht,* 4 vols. Berlin: Weidmann, 1868-1913.

Otto von Gierke. *Political Theories of the Middle Ages.* Cambridge: Cambridge University Press, 1988 (1900).

Neil C. Gillespie. *Charles Darwin and the Problem of Creation.* Chicago: University of Chicago Press, 1979.

Thomas F. Glick. *The Comparative Reception of Darwinism.* Austin: University of Texas Press, 1974.

J. Gloel. *Holland's Kirchliches Leben. Bericht über eine im Auftrag des Köninglichen Domdekenetenstifts zu Berlin unternommene Studienreise nach Holland.* Wittenberg: Herrose, 1885.

Arthur de Gobineau. *Essai sur l'inégalité des races humaines.* Paris, 1853. Translated as *The Inequality of Human Races.* With an Introduction by Dr. Oscar Levy, editor of the authorized English version of Nietzsche's works. London: Heinemann, 1915.

Bob Goudzwaard. *Idols of Our Time.* Downers Grove, Illinois: InterVarsity Press, 1984.

Bob Goudzwaard. *Capitalism and Progress: A Diagnosis of Western Society.* Grand Rapids: Eerdmans, 1979.

Sander Griffioen (ed.). *What Right Does Ethics Have? Public Philosophy in a Pluralistic Culture.* Amsterdam: Free University Press, 1990.

William Elliot Griffis. *The Story of New Netherland: The Dutch in America.* Boston: Houghton Mifflin, 1909.

J. H. Gunning, Jr. *Professor Dr. J. H. Gunning: leven en werken,* 2 vols. Rotterdam, 1922-1925.

J. H. Gunning. *De Heilige Schrift, God's Woord.* Amsterdam: Höveker, 1873.

Ernst Haeckel. *Der Monismus als Band zwischen Religion und Wissenschaft,* 8th edition. Bonn: E. Strauss, 1899. English edition: *Monism as Connecting Religion and Science.* Translated by J. Gilchrist. London: A. & C. Black, 1894.

Robert T. A. Handy. *A Christian America: Protestant Hopes and Historical Realities.* New York: Oxford University Press, 1971.

John D. Hannah (ed.). *Inerrancy and the Church.* Chicago: Moody Press, 1984.

George Harinck. 'Drie Nederlandse theologen zien Amerika', *Transparant* 6 (1995): 34-42.

Harriet Harris. "After Liberalism: Fundamentalism in a Post-Liberal Context," *Theology* 100 (1997): 340-48.

Hendrik Hart and Brian J. Walsh (eds.). *An Ethos of Compassion and the Integrity of Creation.* Lanham, Maryland: University Press of America, 1995.

Hartford Seminary Record. Review of *Calvinism: The L. P. Stone Lectures for 1898-1899: Six Lectures Delivered in the Theological Seminary at Princeton* (New York: Revell, 1899) by A. Kuyper, 10 (1900): 265-66.

Eduard von Hartmann. *Aesthetik,* 2 vols.

Eduard von Hartmann. *Religionsphilosophie,* 2 vols.

T. Heemskerk (ed.). *Gedenkboek, opgedragen door het feestcomité aan Prof. Dr. A. Kuyper, bij zijn vijf en twintigjarig jubileum als hoofdredacteur van 'De Standaard', 1872-1897.* Amsterdam: Herdes, 1897.

G. W. F. Hegel. *Encyklopädie der Philosophischen Wissenschaften in Grundrisse.* Berlin: 1845.

G. W. F. Hegel. *Grundlinien der Philosophie des Rechts,* 4th edition, edited by Johannes Hoffmeister. Hamburg: Felix Meiner, 1955.

R. D. Henderson. "How Abraham Kuyper Became a Kuyperian," *Christian Scholar's Review* 22 (1992): 22-35.

J. Hendriks. *De emancipatie van de gereformeerden: sociologische bijdrage tot de verklaring van enige kenmerken van het gereformeerde volksdeel.* Alphen aan den Rijn: Samson, 1971.

Peter Somers Heslam. "Abraham Kuyper's Lectures on Calvinism: An Historical Study." Unpublished D.Phil. dissertation, Oxford University, 1993.

Peter Heslam. "The Christianization of the East Indies: The Ideas of Abraham Kuyper on Dutch Colonial Policy," *Reflection: An International Reformed Review of Missiology* 2 (1989): 13-17.

Peter Heslam. "De Kerstening van Indië: Denkbeelden van Abraham Kuyper over de Nederlandse koloniale politiek, 1871-1879." Unpublished paper, Hull University, 1988.

Peter Heslam. "The Politics of Abraham Kuyper in Historical Perspective," *Christianity and History* 8 (1991): 9-12.

Peter Heslam. Review of *Voicing Creation's Praise: Toward a Theology of the Arts* (Edinburgh: T. & T. Clark, 1991) by Jeremy Begbie. In *Theology* 44 (1991): 388-89.

Peter Somers Heslam. Review of *The Scandal of the Evangelical Mind* (Grand Rapids: Eerdmans/Leicester: IVP, 1994) by Mark A. Noll. In *Anvil* 14 (1997): 67-69.

A. A. Hodge. "Introduction" to Joseph S. van Dyke, *Theism and Evolution* pp. xv-xxii. New York: Armstrong, 1886.

A. A. Hodge and B. B. Warfield. "Inspiration," *Presbyterian Review* 2 (1881): 225-60. Republished in book form as A. A. Hodge and B. B. Warfield, *Inspiration.* Introduction by Roger R. Nicole. Grand Rapids: Baker, 1979.

A. A. Hodge. Review of Asa Gray's *Natural Science and Religion* (1880), *Presbyterian Review* 1 (July 1880).

Charles Hodge. *Systematic Theology.* New York: Scribners, 1872-1873.

Charles Hodge. *What Is Darwinism?* New York: Scribners, Armstrong, and Company, 1874.

P. J. Hoedemaker. *Artikel 36 onzer Nederduitsche geloofsbelijdenis tegenover Dr. A. Kuyper gehandhaafd.* Amsterdam: Van Dam, 1901.

Rosemarijn Hoefte and Johanna C. Kardux (eds.). *Connection Cultures: The Netherlands in Five Centuries of Transatlantic Exchange.* Amsterdam: Free University Press, 1994.

P. Hoekstra. 'The American Party System', *Anti-revolutionaire staatkunde: driemanndelijksch orgaan* 7 (1933): 61-82.

Arthur F. Holmes. *Contours of a World View.* Grand Rapids: Eerdmans, 1983.

F. B. Hough. *American Constitutions.* Albany: Weed Parsons, 1872.

V. A. Huber. *The English Universities.* Trans. and ed. by Francis W. Newman. London: 1843.

Cornelius Huisman. *Nederlands Israel: het natiebesef der traditioneel-gereformeerden in de achttiende eeuw.* Dordrecht: Van den Tol, 1983.

W. R. Inge. *Christian Mysticism. Considered in Eight Lectures Delivered before the University of Oxford (The Bampton Lectures 1899),* 7th edition. London: Methuen, 1933.

Jaarverslag van de Vereniging voor Hooger Onderwijs op Gereformeerde Grondslag, vol. 19.

S. L. Jaki. "Newman and Evolution," *The Downside Review* 109 (1991): 16-34.

William James. *The Varieties of Religious Experience: A Study of Human Nature. Being the Gifford Lectures on Natural Religion, Delivered at Edinburgh in 1901-1902.* London: Longmans, 1902.

Dirk Jellema. "Abraham Kuyper's Attack on Liberalism," *Review of Politics* 19 (1957): 472-85.

Dirk Jellema. "Kuyper's Visit to America in 1898," *Michigan History* 42 (1958): 227-36.

D. M. Johnston and C. Sampson (eds.). *Religion, the Missing Dimension of Statecraft.* New York: Oxford University Press, 1994.

J. de Jong. *Van batig slot naar ereschuld.* Groningen, 1990.

Hugo Kaats. *Die Weltanschauung Nietzsche,* 2 vols. Dresden and Leipzig, 1892.

L. Kalsbeek. *Contours of a Christian Philosophy: An Introduction to Herman Dooyeweerd's Thought,* edited by Bernard and Josina Zijlstra. Amsterdam: Buijten en Schipperheijn, 1975.

Immanuel Kant. *Observations on the Feeling of the Beautiful and the Sublime* (1764).

P. Kasteel. *Abraham Kuyper.* Kampen: Kok, 1938.

R. T. Kendall. *The Influence of Calvin and Calvinism Upon the American Heritage.* London: Evangelical Library, 1976.

Robert H. Kingdom and Robert D. Linder (eds.). *Calvin and Calvinism: Sources of Democracy?* Lexington, Mass., 1970.

Jacob Klapwijk. "Rationality in the Dutch Neo-Calvinist Tradition," in *Rationality in the Calvinian Tradition,* edited by Hendrick Hart, Johan van der Hoeven, and Nicholas Wolterstorff, pp. 93-131. Lanham, Maryland: University Press of America, 1983.

Wayne Allen Kobes. "Sphere Sovereignty and the University: Theological Foundations of Abraham Kuyper's View of the University and Its Role in Society." Unpublished Ph.D. thesis, Florida State University, 1993.

Chris A. J. van Koppen. *De Geuzen van de negentiende eeuw: Abraham Kuyper en Zuid-Afrika.* Wormer: Immerc, 1992.

E. H. Kossmann. 'De groei van de anti-revolutionaire partij, in *Algemene Geschiedenis der Nederlanden,* 12 vols. Edited by J. A. van Houtte and others, vol. XI, pp. 1-22. Utrecht: De Haan, 1948-1958.

E. H. Kossmann. *The Low Countries, 1790-1940.* Oxford: Oxford University Press, 1978.

H. Krabbendam. 'Zielenverbrijzelaars en zondelozen: Reacties in de Nederlandse Pers op Moody, Sankey en Pearsall Smith, 1874-1878', *Documentatieblad voor de Nederlandse kerkgeschiedenis na 1800* 34 (1991): 39-58.

J. M. van der Kroef. "Abraham Kuyper and the Rise of Neo-Calvinism in the Netherlands," *Church History* 17 (1948): 316-34.

Rob Kroes (ed.). *Within the U.S. Orbit: Small National Cultures vis-à-vis the United States.* Amsterdam: Free University Press, 1991.

D. T. Kuiper. "Dutch Calvinism on the Racial Issue," *Calvin Theological Journal* 21 (1986): 51-78.

D. T. Kuiper. "The Historical and Sociological Development of the ARP and CDA," in *Christian Political Options,* pp. 10-32. The Hague: AR-Partijstichting, 1979.

D. T. Kuiper and H. E. S. Woldring. *Reformatorische maatschappijkritiek: ontwikkelingen op het gebied van sociale filosofie en sociologie in de kring van het nederlandse protestantisme van de negentiende eeuw tot heden.* Kampen: Kok, 1980.

D. T. Kuiper. *De voormannen: een sociaal-wetenschappelijke studie over ideologie, conflict en kerngroepvorming binnen de gereformeerde wereld in Nederland tussen 1820 en 1930.* Kampen: Kok, 1972.

Herman Kuiper. *Calvin on Common Grace.* Goes: Oosterbaan & Le Cointre, 1928.

R. Kuiper. *Zelfbeeld en wereldbeeld: antirevolutionairen en het buitenland, 1848-1905.* Kampen: Kok, 1992.

Roel Kuiper. 'Esthetiek en atrophie', *Transparant: orgaan van de vereniging van christen-historici* 1 (1990): 16-21.

A. Kuyper. *Antirevolutionaire staatkunde: met nadere toelichting op 'Ons program',* 2 vols. Kampen: Kok, 1916.

A. Kuyper. *The Antithesis Between Symbolism and Revelation.* Amsterdam and Pretoria: Höveker and Wormser; Edinburgh: T. & T. Clark, 1899.

A. Kuyper. *Bedoeld noch gezegd: schrijven aan Dr. J. H. Gunning.* Amsterdam: Kruyt, 1885.

A. Kuyper. *Het beroep op het volksgeweten: rede ter opening van de algemeene vergadering der 'Vereeniging voor Christelijk Nationaal-Schoolonderwijs, gehouden te Utrecht, den 18 mei 1869.* Amsterdam: Blankenberg, 1869.

A. Kuyper. "The Biblical Criticism of the Present Day," *Bibliotheca Sacra* 61 (1904): 409-42, 666-88.

A. Kuyper. *The Biblical Doctrine of Election.* Translated by G. M. van Pernis. Grand Rapids: Zondervan, 1934.

A. Kuyper. *Bilderdijk in zijn rationale beteekenis,* Rede gehouden te Amsterdam op 1 oktober 1906. Amsterdam: Höveker & Wormser, 1906.

A. Kuyper. *Calvinism* [Copy of Stone Lectures held in Princeton Theological Seminary Archives].

A. Kuyper. "Calvinism and Art." Translated by J. Hendrik de Vries, *Christian Thought* 9 (1892).

A. Kuyper. *Het calvinisme en de kunst: rede bij de overdracht van het rectoraat der Vrije Universiteit op 20 October 1888.* Amsterdam: Wormser, 1888.

A. Kuyper. *Het calvinisme: oorsprong en waarborg onzer constitutioneele vrijheden: een Nederlandsche gedachte.* Amsterdam: Van der Land, 1874.

A. Kuyper. *Het calvinisme: zes Stone-lezingen in October 1898 te Princeton (N.J.) gehouden.* Amsterdam: Höveker & Wormser, 1899.

A. Kuyper. *Calvinism: Six Stone-lectures.* Amsterdam: Höveker & Wormser; New York: Revell; Edinburgh: T. & T. Clark; London: Simpkin, Marshall, Hamilton, 1899.

A. Kuyper. *Calvinism: The L. P. Stone Lectures for 1898-1899: Six Lectures Delivered in the Theological Seminary at Princeton.* New York: Revell, 1899.

A. Kuyper. "Calvinism: The Origin and Safeguard of Our Constitutional Liberties." Translated by J. H. de Vries. *Bibliotheca Sacra* (July and October 1895): 385-410, 645-74.

A. Kuyper. *Christianity and the Class Struggle.* Translated with a Preface by Dirk Jellema. Grand Rapids: Piet Hein, 1950.

A. Kuyper. *Confidentie: schrijven aan den weled. heer J. H. van der Linden.* Amsterdam: Höveker, 1873.

A. Kuyper. *The Crown of Christian Heritage: Six Lectures Delivered at Princeton University Under Auspices of the L. P. Stone Foundation.* With an Introduction by Vishal Mangalwadi. Landour, Mussoorie: Nivedit Good Books, 1994.

A. Kuyper. *Dagen van goede boodschap,* 4 vols. Amsterdam: Wormser, 1887-1888.

A. Kuyper. "The Deity of Christ." In *The Fundamentals.* Chicago: Testimony, 1910. I, pp. 22, 27-28.

A. Kuyper. *Eenvormigheid, de vloek van het moderne leven.* Amsterdam: De Hoogh, 1869.

A. Kuyper. *Encyclopaedie der heilige godgeleerdheid,* 3 vols. Amsterdam: Wormser, 1894.

A. Kuyper. *Encyclopedia of Sacred Theology: Its Principles.* Translated by J. Hendrik de

Vries, with an introduction by Benjamin B. Warfield. New York: Charles Scribner; London: Hodder and Stoughton, 1898.

A. Kuyper. *Evolutie: rede bij de overdracht van het rectoraat aan de Vrije Universiteit op 20 October 1899 gehouden.* Amsterdam: Höveker & Wormser, 1899.

A. Kuyper. "Evolution." Translation coordinated by Clarence Menninga, *Calvin Theological Journal* 31 (1996): 11-50.

A. Kuyper. *De gemeene gratie,* 3 vols. Amsterdam: Höveker & Wormser, 1902-1905.

A. Kuyper. *De gemeene gratie in wetenschap en kunst.* Amsterdam: Höveker & Wormser, 1905.

A. Kuyper. *'Geworteld en gegrond': de kerk als organisme en instituut: intreêrede, uitgesproken in de Nieuwe Kerk te Amsterdam, 10 Augustus 1870.* Amsterdam: Hoogh, 1870.

A. Kuyper. *De hedendaagse Schriftcritiek in hare bedenkelijke strekking voor de Gemeente des levenden Gods: rede, bij het overdragen van het rectoraat der Vrije Universiteit, gehouden den 20sten october 1881.* Amsterdam: Kruyt, 1881.

A. Kuyper. *Honig uit den rotssteen,* 2 vols. Amsterdam: Wormser, 1880-1883.

A. Kuyper (ed.). *Institutie, ofte onderwijsinghe in de Christelicke religie. In vier boeken beschreven door Johannes Calvinus. Nu van nieuws uyt het Latijn en François getrouwelick overgeset door Wilhelmus Corsmannus. Herdruk van de uitgave van Paulus Aertz van Ravesteyn 1650 te Amsterdam.* Doesburg: Van Schenk Brill, 1889.

A. Kuyper. *Johannes à Lasco: opera tam edita quam inedita recensuit vitam auctoris enarravit,* 2 vols. Amsterdam: Muller, 1866.

A. Kuyper. *Der jongelingen sieraad is hun kracht: feestrede bij het jubileum van den Bond van Gereformeerde Jongelingsvereenigingen op 30 april 1913 te 's-Gravenhage gehouden.* Kampen: Kok, 1913.

A. Kuyper. *Keep Thy Solemn Feasts.* Grand Rapids: Eerdmans, 1928.

A. Kuyper. *Lectures on Calvinism: Six Lectures Delivered at Princeton University Under Auspices of the L. P. Stone Foundation.* Grand Rapids: Eerdmans, 1931. Reprinted in 1978, 1983, and 1987.

A. Kuyper. *Maranatha: rede ter inleiding van de deputaten-vergadering gehouden te Utrecht op 12 mei 1891.* Amsterdam: Wormser, 1891.

A. Kuyper. *De menschwording Gods het levensbeginsel der kerk: intreerede, uitgesproken in de Domkerk te Utrecht den 10den November 1867.* Utrecht: Van Peursen, 1867.

A. Kuyper. *Methode van Studie,* published in J. C. Rullmann, *Kuyper-bibliographie,* 3 vols. Kampen: Kok, 1937. II, pp. 263-65.

A. Kuyper. *Het modernisme: een Fata Morgana op christelijk gebied.* Amsterdam: De Hoogh, 1871.

A. Kuyper. *Modern Masters as Interpreters of Holy Writ: A Series of Seventy-two Mezzogravures from the Work of Some of the Leading Modern Painters.* With an introduction by The Right Reverend Arthur Foley Winnington-Ingram, D.D., Lord Bishop of London. 2 vols. London: Gresham Publishing Company, (n.d.).

A. Kuyper. *Niet de vrijheidsboom maar het kruis: toespraak ter opening van de tiende deputatenvergadering in het eeuwjaar der Fransche Revolutie.* Amsterdam: Wormser, (1889).

A. Kuyper. *Om de oude wereldzee,* 2 vols. Amsterdam: Van Holkema & Warendorf, (1907-1908).

A. Kuyper. *Ons program,* 2nd edition. Amsterdam: Kruyt, 1879. [Translated extracts are in *Political Order and the Plural Structure of Society,* ed. by James W. Skillen and Rockne M. McCarthy (Atlanta: Scholars Press, 1991) pp. 235-57].

A. Kuyper. *Onze eeredienst.* Kampen: Kok, 1911.

A. Kuyper. *Pantheism's Destruction of Boundaries.* [n.p., n.pub., 1893]. Reprinted from an article with the same title in *Methodist Review* 75 (1893): 520-37, 762-78.

A. Kuyper. *Parlementaire redevoeringen,* 4 vols. Amsterdam: Van Holkema & Warendorf, 1908-1910.

A. Kuyper. *Plancius-rede.* Amsterdam: Kruyt, 1884.

A. Kuyper. *Predicatiën in de jaren 1867 tot 1873, tijdens zijn predikantschap in het Nederlands Hervormde Kerigenootschap, gehouden te Beesd, te Utrecht en te Amsterdam.* Kampen: Kok, 1913.

A. Kuyper. *Principles of Sacred Theology.* Grand Rapids: Baker, 1980.

A. Kuyper. *The Problem of Poverty.* Edited with an Introduction by James W. Skillen. Washington/Grand Rapids: The Center for Public Justice/Baker, 1991.

A. Kuyper. *Pro Rege of het Koningschap van Christus,* 3 vols. Kampen: Kok, 1911-1912.

A. Kuyper. *Rome en Dordt.* Amsterdam: De Hoogh, 1879.

A. Kuyper. *Separatie en Doleantie.* Amsterdam: Wormser, 1890.

A. Kuyper. *Het sociale vraagstuk en de christelijke religie.* Amsterdam: Wormser, 1891.

A. Kuyper. *Souvereiniteit in eigen kring. Rede ter inwijding van de Vrije Universiteit, den 20sten October 1880 gehouden in het Koor der Nieuwe Kerk te Amsterdam door Dr. A. Kuyper.* Amsterdam: Kruyt, 1880. [Translated extracts can be found in Skillen and McCarthy, pp. 257-63].

A. Kuyper. *'Strikt Genomen': Het recht tot universiteitsstichting staatsrechtelijk en historisch getoetst.* Amsterdam: Kruyt, 1880.

A. Kuyper. *To Be Near to God.* Grand Rapids: Eerdmans & Sevensma, 1918.

A. Kuyper. *Tractaat van de reformatie der kerken, aan de zonen der reformatie hier te lande op Luther's vierde eeuwfeest aangeboden.* Amsterdam: Höveker, 1883.

A. Kuyper. *Tweeërlei Vaderland: ter inleiding van de zevende jaarvergadering der Vrije Universiteit.* Amsterdam: Wormser, 1887.

A. Kuyper. *Uit het diensthuis geleid.* Kampen: Kok, 1912.

A. Kuyper. *Uit het Woord,* 3 vols. Amsterdam: Kruyt, 1873-1879.

A. Kuyper. *Uit het Woord: Stichtelijke Bibelstudiën,* series 2, 3 vols., III *(Praktijk der Godzaligheid).* Amsterdam: Kruyt, 1886.

A. Kuyper. *Varia Americana.* Amsterdam: Höveker & Wormser, 1899.

A. Kuyper. *De verflauwing der grenzen: rede bij de overdracht van het rectoraat aan de Vrije Universiteit, oktober 1892.* Amsterdam: Wormser, 1892.

A. Kuyper. *Die Verwischung der Grenzen.* Translated by W. Kolhaus. Leipzig: Deichert, 1898.

A. Kuyper. *Van de voleinding,* 4 vols. Kampen: Kok, 1929-1931.

A. Kuyper. *E Voto Dordraceno: toelichting op den Heidelbergschen Catechismus,* 4 vols. Amsterdam: Wormser, 1892-1895.

A. Kuyper. *Wat moeten wij doen: het stemrecht aan ons zelven houden of den kerkeraad machtigen?* Culemborg: Blom, 1867.

A. Kuyper. *Welke zijn de vooruitzichten voor de studenten der Vrije Universiteit?* Amsterdam: Kruyt, 1882.

A. Kuyper. *Het werk van den Heiligen Geest.* Kampen: Kok, 1888-1889.

A. Kuyper. *When Thou Sittest in Thy House.* Grand Rapids, Eerdmans, 1929.

A. Kuyper. *Women of the New Testament.* 6th ed. Grand Rapids: Zondervan, 1979.

A. Kuyper. *The Work of the Holy Spirit.* With an introduction by B. B. Warfield. New York: Funk & Wagnalls, 1900. Republished Grand Rapids: Eerdmans, 1975.

A. Kuyper. *De zegen des Heeren over onze kerken: rede ter inleiding op het gebed voor het samenkomen der gereformeerde kerken in generale synode. gehouden in de Noorderkerk te Middelburg, op 10 augustus 1896.* Amsterdam: Wormser, 1896.

H. S. S. Kuyper. *Een half jaar in Amerika.* Rotterdam: Daamen, 1907.

H. S. S. Kuyper and J. H. Kuyper. *Herinneringen van de oude garde.* Amsterdam: Ten Have, 1922.

McKendree R. Langley. *The Practice of Political Spirituality: Episodes from the Public Career of Abraham Kuyper, 1879-1918.* Jordan Station, Ontario: Paideia Press, 1984.

Harm Jan Langman. *Kuyper en de volkskerk: een dogmatisch-ecclesiologische studie.* Kampen: Kok, 1950.

P. A. van Leeuwen. *Het kerkbegrip in de theologie van Abraham Kuyper.* Franeker: Wever, 1946.

J. F. Lescrauwaet. *De liturgische beweging onder de Nederlandse Hervormden in oecumenisch perspektief: Een fenomenologische en kritische studie.* Bussum: Paul Brand, 1957.

A. Lijphart. *The Politics of Accommodation: Pluralism and Democracy in the Netherlands,* 2nd edition. Berkeley: University of California Press, 1975.

David N. Livingstone. "Evolution as Myth and Metaphor," *Christian Scholar's Review* 12 (1983): 11-25.

Richard Lints. "Two Theologies or One? Warfield and Vos on the Nature of Theology," *Westminster Theological Journal* 54 (1993): 235-53.

Henry Cabot Lodge. *Alexander Hamilton.* Boston: 1892.

Lefferts Loetscher. *The Broadening Church: A Study of Theological Issues in the Presbyterian Church Since 1869.* Philadelphia: University of Pennsylvania Press, 1957.

Bradley J. Longfield. *The Presbyterian Controversy.* Oxford: Oxford University Press, 1991.

J. van Lonkhuyzen. "Abraham Kuyper: A Modern Calvinist," *Princeton Theological Review* 19 (1921): 131-47.

J. J. Lubbe. "'n Bok vir Asasel? In gesprek oor 'n Suid-Afrikaanse aanklag teen Abraham Kuyper," *Nederduitse gereformeerde teologiese tydskrif* 37 (1996): 257-85.

Stephen E. Lucas. "The Plakkaat van Vertalinge: A Neglected Model for the American Declaration of Independence," in *Connection Cultures: The Netherlands in Five Centuries of Transatlantic Exchange,* edited by Rosemarijn Hoefte and Johanna C. Kardux, pp. 187-207. Amsterdam: Free University Press, 1994.

J. Gresham Machen. *Christianity and Liberalism.* New York: Macmillan, 1923.

Margaret Mare and Alicia C. Percival. *Victorian Best-seller: The World of Charlotte Yonge.* London: Harrap, 1948.

George Marsden. "Fundamentalism as an American Phenomenon: A Comparison with English Evangelicalism," *Church History* 46 (1977): 215-32.

George M. Marsden. "The Collapse of American Evangelical Academia," in *Faith and Rationality,* ed. by Alvin Plantinga and Nicholas Wolterstorff, pp. 219-64. Notre Dame: University of Notre Dame Press, 1983.

George M. Marsden. "The Soul of the American University: An Historical Overview," in *The Secularization of the Academy,* edited by George M. Marsden and Bradley J. Longfield, pp. 9-45. New York: Oxford University Press, 1992.

Geroge M. Marsden. *The Soul of the American University: From Protestant Establishment to Established Nonbelief.* New York: Oxford University Press, 1994.

George M. Marsden. "The State of Evangelical Christian Scholarship," *The Reformed Journal* 37 (1987): 12-16.

George M. Marsden. *Understanding Fundamentalism and Evangelicalism.* Grand Rapids: Eerdmans, 1991.

Paul A. Marshall, Sander Griffioen, and Richard J. Mouw. *Stained Glass: Worldviews and Social Science.* Lanham, Maryland: University Press of America, 1989.

Paul Marshall. *Thine Is the Kingdom: A Biblical Perspective on the Nature of Government and Politics Today.* Basingstoke: Marshall Morgan & Scott, 1984.

Martin E. Marty. *Righteous Empire: The Protestant Experience in America.* New York: Dial Press, 1970.

Karl Marx. *Die Frühschriften,* edited by S. Landshut, pp. 525-60. Stuttgart: Kröner, 1971.

F. D. Maurice. *Lectures on Social Morality,* 2nd edition. London: 1872. Later published as *Social Morality: Twenty-One Lectures Delivered in the University of Cambridge.* London: Macmillan, 1886.

Justus van Maurik. *Anarchisten: klucht in drie bedrijven.* Amsterdam, 1895.

Henry F. May. *The Enlightenment in America.* New York: Oxford University Press, 1976.

Alister E. McGrath. *Bridge-building: Effective Christian Apologetics.* Leicester: IVP, 1992.

Alister E. McGrath. *A Life of John Calvin: A Study in the Shaping of Western Culture.* Oxford: Basil Blackwell, 1990.

Alister E. McGrath. *A Passion for Truth: The Intellectual Coherence of Evangelicalism.* Leicester: Apollos, 1996.

C. T. McIntire (ed.). *The Legacy of Herman Dooyeweerd.* Lanham, Maryland: University Press of America, 1995.

John E. Meeter and Roger Nicole. *A Bibliography of Benjamin Breckinridge Warfield 1851-1921.* Phillipsburg, N.J.: Presbyterian and Reformed Publishing Company, 1974.

M. Merthelot. *Les Origines de l'Alchimie.* Paris: Librairie des Sciences et des Arts, 1938.

The Methodist Review. Review of *Calvinism: The L. P. Stone Lectures for 1898-1899: Six*

Lectures Delivered in the Theological Seminary at Princeton by A. Kuyper (New York: Revell, 1899), 82 (1900): 174.

Steven E. Meyer. "Calvinism and the Rise of the Protestant Political Movement in the Netherlands." Unpublished Ph.D. thesis, Georgetown University, 1976.

J. Richard Middleton and Brian J. Walsh. *Truth Is Stranger Than It Used to Be: Biblical Faith in a Postmodern Age.* London: SPCK, 1995.

John Stuart Mill. *Utilitarianism, Liberty and Representative Government.* London: Dent, 1910.

Henry Colin Minton. Review of *Calvinism: The L. P. Stone Lectures for 1898-1899: Six Lectures Delivered in the Theological Seminary at Princeton* by A. Kuyper (New York: Revell, 1899), *The Presbyterian and Reformed Review* 11 (1900): 536-39.

Henry Colin Minton. Review of *Encyclopedia of Sacred Theology: Its Principles,* by A. Kuyper, translated by J. Hendrik de Vries. With an introduction by Benjamin B. Warfield (New York: Charles Scribner; London: Hodder and Stoughton, 1898), *The Presbyterian and Reformed Review* 10 (1899): 677-85.

John Clover Monsma. *What Calvinism Has Done for America.* Chicago: [n.p.], 1919.

James R. Moore. *The Post-Darwinian Controversies: A Study of the Protestant Struggle to Come to Terms with Darwin in Great Britain and America, 1870-1900.* Cambridge: Cambridge University Press, 1979.

Marianne L. Mooijweer. 'Een voorlijke ertgenaam van Nederland: Abraham en Henriette Kuyper over Amerika', *Spiegel Historiael* 24 (1989): 310-15.

Richard Mouw. *Called to Holy Worldliness.* Minneapolis: Fortress, 1980.

Richard Mouw. "Dutch Calvinist Philosophical Influences in North America," *Calvin Theological Journal* 24 (1989): 101-13.

Stephen Neill. *A History of Christian Missions.* Penguin: London, 1964.

Lesslie Newbigin. *Foolishness to the Greeks: The Gospel and Western Culture.* London: SPCK/Grand Rapids: Eerdmans, 1986.

Lesslie Newbigin. *Proper Confidence: Faith, Doubt and Certainty in Christian Discipleship.* London: SPCK, 1995.

New Catholic Encyclopedia, 4 vols. New York: McGraw-Hill, 1967.

J. H. Newman. *Parochial and Plain Sermons,* 1834-1842, 8 vols. London: Longmans, Green & Company, 1901.

J. H. Newman. *The Idea of a University.* Edited by I. T. Ker. Oxford: Clarendon, 1976.

H. Richard Niebuhr. *Christ and Culture.* New York: Harper & Brothers, 1951.

Mark A. Noll. *A History of Christianity in the United States and Canada.* Grand Rapids: Eerdmans, 1992.

Mark A. Noll. *The Scandal of the Evangelical Mind.* Grand Rapids: Eerdmans/Leicester: IVP, 1994.

Mark A. Noll (ed.). *The Princeton Theology 1812-1921: Scripture, Science, and Theological Method from Archibald Alexander to Benjamin Breckinridge Warfield.* Grand Rapids: Baker Book House, 1983.

Jan Willem Schulte Nordholt. *Triomf en tragiek van de vrijheid: de geschiedenis van de Verenigde Staten van Amerika.* Amsterdam: Meulenhoff, 1985.

Jan Willem Schulte Nordholt. *De mythe van het Westen: Amerika als het laatste wereldrijk.* Amsterdam: Meulenhoff, 1992.

Jan Willem Schulte Nordholt. *The Myth of the West: America as the Last Empire.* Translated by Herbert H. Rowen. Grand Rapids: Eerdmans, 1995.

Oliver O'Donovan. *Resurrection and Moral Order: An Outline for Evangelical Ethics.* Leicester: IVP/Grand Rapids: Eerdmans, 1986.

James H. Olthuis. "On Worldviews," in *Stained Glass: Worldviews and Social Science,* edited by Paul A. Marshall, Sander Griffioen, and Richard J. Mouw, pp. 26-40. Lanham, Maryland: University Press of America, 1989.

J. J. van Oosterzee. *Brief van een vriend over de ingeving van de Heilige Schrift.* 1881.

James Orr. *The Christian View of God and the World as Centring in the Incarnation.* Being the Kerr Lectures for 1890-1891, 4th edition. Edinburgh: Andrew Elliot, 1897. First published in 1893.

James Orr. *God's Image in Man, and Its Defacement, in the Light of Modern Denials.* London: Hodder and Stoughton, 1905.

James Orr. *The Ritschlian Theology and the Evangelical Faith.* London: [n.p.], 1897.

James Orr. *Ritschlianism: Expositionary and Critical Essays.* London: Hodder & Stoughton, 1903.

Oxford English Dictionary, IX. Oxford: Clarendon, 1933.

J. I. Packer. "John Calvin and the Inerrancy of Holy Scripture," in *Inerrancy and the Church,* edited by John D. Hannah, pp. 143-88. Chicago: Moody Press, 1984.

C. Partee. "Calvin's Central Dogma Again," *Sixteenth Century Journal* 18 (1987): 191-99.

Alvin Plantinga. "A Christian Life Partly Lived," in *Philosophers Who Believe: The Spiritual Journeys of Eleven Leading Thinkers,* edited by Kelly James Clark, pp. 45-82. Downers Grove, Illinois: IVP, 1993.

Bettina Polak. *Het fin de siècle in de Nederlandse schilderkunst: de symbolistische beweging, 1890-1900.* 's-Gravenhage: Nijhoff, 1955.

L. Praamsma. *Let Christ Be King: Reflections on the Life and Times of Abraham Kuyper.* Jordan Station, Ontario: Paideia Press, 1985.

Ronald H. Preston. *Church and Society in the Late Twentieth Century: The Economic and Political Task.* London: SCM Press, 1983.

Publicatie van den Senaat der Vrije Universiteit, in zake het onderzoek ter bepaling van den weg die tot de kennis der Gereformeerde beginselen leidt. Amsterdam: Wormser, 1895.

G. Puchinger. *Abraham Kuyper: De jonge Kuyper (1837-1867).* Franeker: Wever, 1987.

G. Puchinger. *Kuyper-herdenking 1987 (de religieuze Kuyper): vijf opstellen en lezingen van de herdenking van de honderdvijftigste geboortedag van Abraham Kuyper, 29 oktober 1987.* Kampen: Kok, 1987.

G. Puchinger. *Ontmoetingen met anti-revolutionairen.* Zutphen: Terra, 1981.

G. Puchinger. *Ontmoetingen met Nederlandse politici.* Zutphen: Terra, 1981.

J. van Putten. *Zoveel kerken zoveel zinnen: een sociaal-wetenschappelijke studie van verschillen in behoudendheid tussen Gereformeerden en Christelijke Gereformeerden.* Kampen: Kok, 1968.

R. S. Rait. *Memorials of Albert Venn Dicey. Being Chiefly Letters and Diaries.* London: Macmillan, 1925.

A. J. Rasker. *De Nederlandse Hervormde Kerk vanaf 1795: haar geschiedenis en theologie in de negentiende en twintigste eeuw,* 2nd edition. Kampen: Kok, 1981.

Del Ratzsch. "Abraham Kuyper's Philosophy of Science," *Calvin Theological Journal* 27 (1992): 277-303.

The Reformed Church Review. Review of *Calvinism: The L. P. Stone Lectures for 1898-1899: Six Lectures Delivered in the Theological Seminary at Princeton* by A. Kuyper (New York: Revell, 1899), 4 (1900): 273-77.

Simon Jan Ridderbos. *De theologische cultuurbeschouwing van Abraham Kuyper.* Kampen: Kok, 1947.

Albrecht Ritschl. *The Christian Doctrine of Justification and Reconciliation: The Positive Development of the Doctrine.* Translated by H. R. Mackintosh and A. B. Macaulay. Edinburgh: T. & T. Clark, 1900 (1874).

Albrecht Ritschl. *Geschichte des Pietismus,* 3 vols. Bonn: Marcus, 1880-1886.

Albrecht Ritschl. *Theologie und Metaphysik.* Bonn: Marcus, 1887.

R. E. L. Rodgers. *The Incarnation of the Antithesis: An Introduction to the Educational Thought and Practice of Abraham Kuyper.* Durham: Pentland Press, 1992.

K. H. Roessingh. *De moderne theologie in Nederland: hare voorbereiding en eerste periode.* Groningen: Van der Kamp, 1914.

J. B. Rogers and D. K. McKim. *The Authority and Interpretation of the Bible: An Historical Approach.* San Francisco: Harper and Row, 1979.

M. G. Rogers. "Charles Augustus Briggs: Heresy at Union," in *American Religious Heretics: Formal and Informal Trials,* edited by G. H. Shriver, pp. 111-38. Nashville: Abingdon, 1966.

Jan Marius Romein. *Universiteit en maatschappij in de loop der tijden.* Leiden: Brill, 1947.

Jan Marius Romein. *Op het breukvlak van twee eeuwen,* 2 vols. Leiden: Brill, 1967.

Peter van Rooden. *Religieuze regimes: Over godsdienst en maatschappij in Nederland, 1950-1990.* Amsterdam: Bert Bakker, 1996.

Peter van Rooden. 'Studies naar lokale verzuiling als toegang tot de geschiedenis van de constructie van religienze verschillen in Nederland', *Theoretische Geschiedenis* 20 (1993): 439-54.

Hans Rookmaaker. *Modern Art and the Death of a Culture.* London: InterVarsity Press, 1970.

R. Rothe. *Dogmatiek von Dr. Rothe, aus dessen handschriftlichen Nachlasse,* edited by D. Schenkel. Heidelberg: 1870.

Jean Jacques Rousseau. *Du Contrat Social,* edited by Ronald Grimsely. Oxford: Clarendon Press, 1972.

C. de Ru. *De strijd over het hoger onderwijs tijdens het ministerie-Kuyper.* Kampen: Kok, 1953.

Guido de Ruggiero. *The History of European Liberalism.* Translated by R. W. Collingwood. Boston: Beacon, 1959.

A. A. van Ruler. *Kuyper's idee eener christelijke cultuur.* Nijkerk: Callenbach, 1938.

J. C. Rullmann. *Abraham Kuyper: een levensschets.* Kampen: Kok, 1928.

J. C. Rullmann. *Kuyper-bibliografie,* 3 vols. Kampen: J. H. Kok, 1923-1940.
John Ruskin. *Lectures on Art. Delivered before the University of Oxford in Hilary Term, 1870,* 6th edition. London: George Allen, 1892.
John Ruskin. *Selections from the Writings of John Ruskin.* London: Blackfriars, (n.d.).
John Ruskin. *The Stones of Venice,* 3 vols. London: Routledge, 1907.
R. A. Russell. "Herman Dooyeweerd," in *New Dictionary of Christian Ethics and Pastoral Theology,* edited by David J. Atkinson and David H. Field, p. 317. Leicester: IVP, 1995.
George H. Sabine. "The Two Democratic Traditions," *Philosophical Review* 61 (1952): 451-74.
Philip Sampson, Vinay Samuel, and Chris Sugden (eds.). *Faith and Modernity.* Oxford: Regnum/Paternoster, 1996.
J. W. Sap. *Wegbereiders der revolutie: calvinisme en de strijd om de democratische rechtsstaat.* Groningen: Wolters-Noordhoff, 1993.
Witsius H. de Savornin Lohman. *Dr. Abraham Kuyper.* Haarlem: H. D. Tjeenk Willink, 1889. English translation: "Dr. Abraham Kuyper," *The Presbyterian and Reformed Review* 36 (1898): 561-609.
Hermanus Johannes Aloysius Maria Schaepman. *Eene katholieke partij; proeve van een program.* Utrecht: Van Rossum, 1883.
M. P. C. M. van Schendelen (ed.). *Consociationalism, Pillarization and Conflict-Management in the Low Countries.* Published as a special-theme edition of *Acta Politica* (1984) I.
F. D. E. Schleiermacher. *Der Christliche Glaube: nach den Grundsätzen der evangelischen Kirche im Zusammenhange dargestelt,* edited by Martin Redeker, 2 vols. Berlin: de Gruyter, 1960 (1821/1822).
F. D. E. Schleiermacher. *Die christliche Sitte. Sämtliche Werke* XII. 1893.
F. D. E. Schleiermacher. *The Christian Faith.* Translated and edited by H. R. Mackintosh and J. S. Stewart. Edinburgh: T. & T. Clark, 1928, 1960.
F. D. E. Schleiermacher. *On Religion: Speeches to its Cultured Despisers.* Translated by Richard Gouter. Cambridge: Cambridge University Press, 1988.
Percy A. Scholes. *The Oxford Companion to Music,* 9th edition, pp. 421-22. London: Oxford University Press, 1955.
J. H. Scholten. *Het evangelie naar Johannes: kritisch historisch onderzoek.* Leiden: Engels, 1864.
L. W. G. Scholten, C. Smeenk, and J. Waterink (eds.). *Dr. A. Kuyper: gedenkboek uitgegeven bij gelegenheid van de herdenking op 29 oktober 1937 van het feit, dat Dr. A. Kuyper honderd jaar geleden te Maassluis geboren werd.* Kampen: Kok, 1937.
E. van der Schoot. *Hervormde eredienst: De liturgische ontwikkeling van de Nederlandse Hervormde Kerk.* 's-Gravenhage: Boekencentrum, 1950.
Schrift en historie: gedenkboek bij het vijftig-jarig bestaan der georganiseerde Antirevolutionaire Partij 1878-1928. [No editor. Commissioned by the *Doctor Abraham Kuyperstichting.*] Kampen: Kok, 1928.
G. J. Schutte. 'De ere Gods en de moderne staat: het antwoord van de Anti-Revo-

lutionaire Partij op de secularisatie en democratisering van Nederland: antithese, souvereiniteit in eigen kring en gemene gratie', *Radix* 9 (1983): 73-104.

G. J. Schutte. 'Over '86 en '92 en daarna: Kuypers gereformeerde wereld herdacht', *Bijdragen en mededelingen betreffende de geschiedenis der Nederlanden* 110 (1995): 515-47.

A. Schweitzer. *Die Christliche Glaubenslehre nach proteztantischen Grundsätzen dargestelt.* Leipzig: 1877.

Peter Sedgwick, "Theology and Society," in *The Modern Thelogians: An Introduction to Christian Theology in the Late Twentieth Century,* edited by David F. Ford, pp. 286-305. 2nd ed. Oxford: Blackwell, 1997.

Calvin Seerveld. *A Christian Critique of Art.* St. Catharines, Ontario: The Association for Reformed Scientific Studies, 1962.

Calvin Seerveld. *Rainbows for the Fallen World.* Toronto: Tuppence Press, 1980.

Alfred Percy Sinnet. *Esoteric Buddhism.* 6th ed. London: Chapman & Hall, 1888.

James W. Skillen. "The Development of Calvinistic Political Theory in the Netherlands, with Special Reference to the Thought of Herman Dooyeweerd." Unpublished Ph.D. thesis, Duke University, 1973.

James W. Skillen and Stanley W. Carlson-Thies. "Religion and Political Development in Nineteenth-Century Holland," *Publius: The Journal of Federalism* 12 (1982).

James W. Skillen and Rockne M. McCarthy (eds.). *Political Order and the Plural Structure of Society.* Atlanta: Scholars Press, 1991.

James Skillen. *Recharging the American Experiment: Principled Pluralism for Genuine Civic Community.* Grand Rapids: Baker, 1994.

James Ward Smith. "Religion and Science in American Philosophy," in *The Shaping of American Religion,* edited by James Ward Smith and A. Leland Jamison, pp. 402-42. Princeton: Princeton University Press, 1961.

H. van Spanning. 'Hoedemaker en de antirevolutionairen', in *Hoedemaker Herdacht,* edited by G. Abma and J. de Bruijn. Baarn: Ten Have, 1989.

Herbert Spencer. *The Data of Ethics,* 3rd ed. London: Williams & Norgate, 1881.

Oswald Spengler. *Untergang des Abendlandes* (1918-1922). Translated as *The Decline of the West* (1926-1929).

G. J. Spykman. "Pluralism: Our Last Best Hope?" *Christian Scholar's Review* 10 (1981): 99-115.

Peter Staples. *The Liturgical Movement in the Netherlands Reformed Church, 1911-1955, with Special Reference to the Anglican Dimension.* Utrecht: Interuniversitair Instituut voor Missiologie en Oecumenica, 1983.

J. Stellingwerff. *Dr. Abraham Kuyper en de Vrije Universiteit.* Kampen: Kok, 1987.

J. Stellingwerff. *D. H. Th. Vollenhoven (1892-1978): Reformator der wijsbegeerte.* Baarn: Ten Have, 1992.

Alan Storkey. *Foundational Epistemologies in Consumption Theories.* Amsterdam: Free University of Amsterdam Press, 1993.

Alan Storkey. *Transforming Economics.* London: SPCK, 1986.

Elaine Storkey. "Dooyeweerd's Anthropology: The Male-Female Dimension," in

Christian Philosophy at the Close of the Twentieth Century, edited by Sander Griffioen and Bert M. Balk, pp. 85-92. Kampen: Kok, 1995.

P. J. Strauss. "Abraham Kuyper, Apartheid and Reformed Churches in South Africa in Their Support of Apartheid," *Theological Forum* 23 (1995): 4-27.

H. Stuart-Hughes. *Consciousness and Society: The Reorientation of European Social Thought, 1890-1930.* Brighton: Harvester Press, 1979.

Siep Stuurman. *Verzuiling, kapitalisme en patriarchaat: aspecten van de ontwikkeling van de moderne staat in Nederland.* Nijmegen: Socialistische Uitgeverij, 1983.

Hippolyte Taine. *Philosophie de l'art dans les Pays Bas,* 2 vols. Paris: Germer Baillière, 1869, II.

Cornelius van Til. *Common Grace.* Philadelphia: Presbyterian and Reformed Publishing Company, 1947.

Henry R. van Til. *The Calvinistic Concept of Culture.* Grand Rapids: Baker, 1959.

Paul Tillich. *Perspectives on 19th and 20th Century Protestant Theology,* edited by Carl E. Braaten. London: SCM Press, 1967.

Leo Tolstoy. *What Is Art?* Translated by Aylmer Maude. Oxford: Oxford University Press, 1930.

Ernst Troeltsch. *Die Soziallehren der christlichen Kirchen und Gruppen,* 16 vols. Tübingen: Mohr, 1922.

Ernst Troeltsch. *The Social Teaching of the Christian Churches,* 2 vols. Translated by Olive Wyon. New York: Harper &: Row, 1960.

Radoslav A. Tsanoff. *Ethics,* revised edition. New York: Harper, 1955.

Frank van den Berg. *Abraham Kuyper.* Grand Rapids: Eerdmans, 1960.

Henry van der Goot (ed.). *Life Is Religion: Essays in Honour of H. Evan Runner.* St. Catharines, Ontario: Paideia Press, 1981.

Leonard Verduin. *The Reformers and Their Stepchildren.* Grand Rapids: Eerdmans, 1964.

Andrew Vincent. *Theories of the State.* Oxford: Basil Blackwell, 1987.

D. T. H. Vollenhoven. *Het calvinisme en de reformatie van de wijsbegeerte.* Amsterdam: Paris, 1933.

G. Vos. Review of *De verflauwing der grenzen* by A. Kuyper (Amsterdam: Wormser, 1892), *The Presbyterian and Reformed Review* 4 (1893): 330-32.

Jasper Vree. *De Groninger Godgeleerden: de oorsprongen en de eerste periode van hun optreden (1820-1843).* Kampen: Kok, 1984.

Simon J. de Vries. "Calvin's Attitude Towards Art and Amusements," *The Calvin Forum* 17 (1952): 101-7.

Simon J. de Vries. *Bible and Theology in the Netherlands,* 2nd edition. New York: Peter Lang, 1989.

B. B. Warfield. "Apologetics," in *The New Schaff-Herzog Encyclopedia of Religious Knowledge,* edited by Samuel Macauley Johnson. New York: Funk and Wagnalls, 1908. Republished in B. B. Warfield, *Studies in Theology.* New York: Oxford University Press, 1932.

B. B. Warfield. *Calvijn als theoloog en de stand van het Calvinisme in onzen tijd.* Translated by C. M. E. Kuyper, with a preface by H. Bavinck. Kampen: Kok, 1919.

B. B. Warfield. *Calvin and Calvinism.* New York: Oxford University Press, 1931.

B. B. Warfield. "Calvin as a Theologian" [1909]. Published as an appendix to B. B. Warfield, *Calvin and Augustine,* edited by Samuel G. Craig, pp. 481-507. Philadelphia: Presbyterian and Reformed, 1956.

B. B. Warfield. "Calvinism," in *The New Schaff-Herzog Encyclopedia of Religious Knowledge,* edited by Samuel Macauley Johnson. New York: Funk and Wagnalls, 1908. Republished in B. B. Warfield, *Calvin and Calvinism.* New York: Oxford University Press, 1931.

B. B. Warfield. "Calvin's Doctrine of Creation," *Princeton Theological Review* 13 (1915).

B. B. Warfield. "Charles Darwin's Religious Life: A Sketch in Spiritual Biography," *Presbyterian Review* 9 (1888): 569-601.

B. B. Warfield. "Creation versus Evolution," *Bible Student* 4 (1901): 1-8

B. B. Warfield. "Darwin's Arguments Against Christianity and Religion," *The Homiletic Review* 17 (1889): 9-16.

B. B. Warfield. "Introduction" to *Encyclopedia of Sacred Theology: Its Principles* by A. Kuyper. Translated by J. Hendrik de Vries. New York: Charles Scribner; London: Hodder & Stoughton, 1898.

B. B. Warfield. "Introduction" to *The Work of the Holy Spirit* by A. Kuyper, pp. xxv-xxxiv. New York: Funk & Wagnalls, 1900.

B. B. Warfield. *Het godsdienstige leven van den theologischen student.* Translated by C. M. E. Kuyper. Kampen: Kok, 1920. First published in *De Heraut,* 4-25 May 1913.

B. B. Warfield. "Introduction" to Francis R. Beattie's *Apologetics: Or the Rational Vindication of Christianity.* Richmond, Virginia: Presbyterian Committee of Publication, 1903.

B. B. Warfield. "Introduction" to *John Calvin, Institutes of the Christian Religion.* Translated from the Latin and collated with the author's last edition in French by John Allen. 7th American edition revised and corrected. Philadelphia: Presbyterian Board of Education, [1913?].

B. B. Warfield. "On the Antiquity and Unity of the Human Race" (1911), in B. B. Warfield, *Biblical and Theological Essays,* pp. 235-58. New York: Oxford University Press, 1932.

B. B. Warfield. *The Present-Day Conception of Evolution.* Emporia, Kansas [1895].

B. B. Warfield. Review of H. Bavinck's *De zekerheid des geloofs* (Kampen: Kok, 1901), *Princeton Theological Review* 1 (1903): 138-43.

B. B. Warfield. Review of H. P. Liddon's *Life of Edward Bouverie Pusey,* 4 vols. (London: Longmans, Green & Co., 1894), III, *The Presbyterian and Reformed Review* 7 (1896): 347-50.

B. B. Warfield. Review of James Orr's *God's Image in Man, and Its Defacement, in the Light of Modern Denials* (London: Hodder and Stoughton, 1905), *The Princeton Theological Review* 4 (1906): 555-58.

B. B. Warfield. "The Present-Day Attitude Toward Calvinism: Its Causes and Significance." Address given in 1909, published in appendix to B. B. Warfield,

Calvin and Augustine, edited by Samuel G. Craig. Philadelphia: The Presbyterian and Reformed Publishing Company, 1956.

B. B. Warfield. "The Religious Life of Theological Students," *Union Seminary Magazine* 24 (Dec. 1912/Jan. 1913): 208-22.

B. B. Warfield. *The Right of Systematic Theology.* With an Introduction by Professor J. Orr. Edinburgh: T. & T. Clark, 1897.

B. B. Warfield. *Selected Shorter Writings of Benjamin B. Warfield,* edited by John E. Meeter, 2 vols. Nutley, N.J.: Presbyterian and Reformed Publishing Company, 1973.

B. B. Warfield. *The Westminster Assembly and Its Work.* Oxford: Oxford University Press, 1931.

Claude Welch. *Protestant Thought in the Nineteenth Century,* 2 vols. New Haven: Yale University Press, 1985.

W. J. van Welderen Rengers. *Schets eener parlementaire geschiedenis van Nederland sedert 1848,* 4th edition, 4 vols. 's-Gravenhage, 1950-1955.

J. van Weringh. *Het maatschappijbeeld van Abraham Kuyper.* Assen: Van Gorcum, 1967.

W. J. Wieringa. 'De Vrije Universiteit als bijzondere instelling, 1880-1890', in *Wetenschap en rekenschap 1880-1890: een eeuw wetenshapsbeoefening en wetenshapsbeschouwing aan de Vrije Universiteit,* pp. 11-43. Kampen: Kok, 1980.

Nico Wilterdink. "The Netherlands Between the Greater Powers: Expressions of Resistance to Perceived or Feared Foreign Cultural Domination," in *Within the U.S. Orbit: Small National Cultures vis-à-vis the United States,* edited by Rob Kroes, pp. 13-31. Amsterdam: Free University Press, 1991.

W. F. A. Winckel. *Leven en arbeid van Dr. A. Kuyper.* Amsterdam: Ten Have, 1919.

Michael Wintle. *Pillars of Piety: Religion in the Netherlands in the Nineteenth Century, 1813-1901.* Hull: Hull University Press, 1987.

H. E. S. Woldring. *De Christen Democratie: Een critisch onderzoek naar haar politiekefilosofie.* Utrecht: Het Spectrum, 1996.

Albert M. Wolters. "On the Idea of Worldview and Its Relation to Philosophy," in *Stained Glass: Worldviews and Social Science,* edited by Paul A. Marshall, Sander Griffioen, and Richard J. Mouw, pp. 14-25. Lanham, Maryland: University Press of America, 1989.

Albert M. Wolters. *Creation Regained: A Transforming View of the World.* Leicester: InterVarsity Press, 1986.

Albert Wolters. "Dutch neo-Calvinism: Worldview, Philosophy and Rationality," in *Rationality in the Calvinian Tradition,* edited by Hendrik Hart, pp. 113-31. Lanham, Maryland: University Press of America, 1983.

Albert M. Wolters. "Weltanschauung in the History of Ideas: Preliminary Notes." Unpublished paper.

Nicholas Wolterstorff. "The Grace that Shaped My Life," in *Philosophers Who Believe: The Spiritual Journeys of Eleven Leading Thinkers,* edited by Kelly James Clark, pp. 259-75. Downers Grove, Illinois: IVP, 1993.

Nicholas Wolterstorff. *Until Justice and Peace Embrace: The Kuyper Lectures for 1981 Delivered at the Free University of Amsterdam.* Grand Rapids: Eerdmans, 1983.

Jan Woltjer. 'Ideëel en Reëel', in *Verzamelde redevoeringen en verhandelingen,* I, pp. 178-235. Amsterdam: N. V. Dagblad, De Standaard, 1931.

J. D. Woodbridge. *Biblical Authority: A Critique of the Rogers/McKim Proposal.* Grand Rapids: Zondervan, 1982.

N. T. Wright. *The New Testament and the People of God.* London: SPCK, 1992.

Gerrit Brillenburg Wurth. *J. H. Scholten als systematisch theoloog.* 's-Gravenhage: Van Haeringen, 1927.

Charlotte M. Yonge. *The Heir of Redclyffe,* 2 vols. London: John W. Parker, 1853.

S. U. Zuidema. "Common Grace and Christian Action in Abraham Kuyper," in *Communication and Confrontation* by S. U. Zuidema, pp. 52-105. Assen: Van Gorcum; Kampen: Kok, 1972.

S. U. Zuidema. *Communication and Confrontation.* Assen: Van Gorcum; Kampen: Kok, 1972.

H. Zwaanstra. "Abraham Kuyper's Conception of the Church," *Calvin Theological Journal* 9 (1974): 149-81.

R. S. Zwart. *'Gods wil in Nederland': Christelijke ideologieen en de vorming van het CDA (1880-1990).* Kampen: Kok, 1996.

Index